Building Computer Vision Projects with OpenCV 4 and C++

Implement complex computer vision algorithms and explore deep learning and face detection

David Millán Escrivá
Prateek Joshi
Vinícius G. Mendonça
Roy Shilkrot

BIRMINGHAM - MUMBAI

Building Computer Vision Projects with OpenCV 4 and C++

First published: March 2019

Production reference: 1220319

Published by Packt Publishing Ltd.
Livery Place
35 Livery Street
Birmingham
B3 2PB, UK.

ISBN 978-1-83864-467-3

www.packtpub.com

`mapt.io`

Mapt is an online digital library that gives you full access to over 5,000 books and videos, as well as industry-leading tools to help you plan your personal development and advance your career. For more information, please visit our website.

Why subscribe?

- Spend less time learning and more time coding with practical eBooks and Videos from over 4,000 industry professionals

- Improve your learning with Skill Plans built especially for you

- Get a free eBook or video every month

- Mapt is fully searchable

- Copy and paste, print, and bookmark content

Packt.com

Did you know that Packt offers eBook versions of every book published, with PDF and ePub files available? You can upgrade to the eBook version at `www.packt.com` and as a print book customer, you are entitled to a discount on the eBook copy. Get in touch with us at `customercare@packtpub.com` for more details.

At `www.packt.com`, you can also read a collection of free technical articles, sign up for a range of free newsletters, and receive exclusive discounts and offers on Packt books and eBooks.

Contributors

About the authors

David Millán Escrivá was eight years old when he wrote his first program on an 8086 PC using the BASIC language. He completed his studies in IT from the Universitat Politécnica de Valencia with honors in human-computer interaction supported by computer vision with OpenCV (v0.96). He has a master's degree in artificial intelligence, computer graphics, and pattern recognition, focusing on pattern recognition and computer vision. He also has more than nine years' experience in computer vision, computer graphics, and pattern recognition. He is the author of the Damiles Blog, where he publishes articles and tutorials on OpenCV, computer vision in general, and optical character recognition algorithms.

Prateek Joshi is an artificial intelligence researcher, an author of eight published books, and a TEDx speaker. He has been featured in Forbes 30 Under 30, CNBC, TechCrunch, Silicon Valley Business Journal, and many more publications. He is the founder of Pluto AI, a venture-funded Silicon Valley start-up building an intelligence platform for water facilities. He graduated from the University of Southern California with a Master's degree specializing in Artificial Intelligence. He has previously worked at NVIDIA and Microsoft Research.

Vinícius G. Mendonça is a computer graphics university professor at Pontifical Catholic University of Paraná (PUCPR). He started programming with C++ back in 1998, and ventured into the field of computer gaming and computer graphics back in 2006. He is currently a mentor at the Apple Developer Academy in Brazil, working with, and teaching, metal, machine learning and computer vision for mobile devices. He has served as a reviewer on other Pack books, including *OpenNI Cookbook*, and *Mastering OpenCV and Computer Vision with OpenCV 3 and Qt5*. In his research, he has used Kinect, OpenNI, and OpenCV to recognize Brazilian sign language gestures. His areas of interest include mobile, OpenGL, image processing, computer vision, and project management.

Roy Shilkrot is an assistant professor of computer science at Stony Brook University, where he leads the Human Interaction group. Dr. Shilkrot's research is in computer vision, human-computer interfaces, and the cross-over between these two domains, funded by US federal, New York State, and industry grants. Dr. Shilkrot graduated from the **Massachusetts Institute of Technology (MIT)** with a PhD, and has authored more than 25 peer-reviewed papers published at premier computer science conferences, such as CHI and SIGGRAPH, as well as in leading academic journals such as ACM **Transaction on Graphics (TOG)** and ACM **Transactions on Computer-Human Interaction (ToCHI)**.

Packt is searching for authors like you

If you're interested in becoming an author for Packt, please visit `authors.packtpub.com` and apply today. We have worked with thousands of developers and tech professionals, just like you, to help them share their insight with the global tech community. You can make a general application, apply for a specific hot topic that we are recruiting an author for, or submit your own idea.

Table of Contents

Preface

OpenCV is one of the best open source computer vision libraries available to developers. With OpenCV, developers can create complete projects for image processing, object detection, and motion detection. This learning path is for absolute beginners who wish to learn how to build OpenCV projects from scratch with working code samples. We will begin with the introduction on computer vision and its basic concepts such as filtering, histograms, Object segmentation, and object detection. As you progress through the course you will then dig deeper into image processing exploring various computer vision algorithms and understand how the latest advancement in machine learning and deep learning enhances the process of object detection. You will put this knowledge to practice by building real-world computer vision applications as you progress through the course.

Later you will get acquainted with the API functionality of OpenCV and gain insights into design choices in a complete computer vision project. You'll also go beyond the basics of computer vision to implement solutions for complex image processing projects such as skin color analysis, face landmark and pose estimation, Augmented reality applications, and Number plate recognition. Finally, towards the end of the learning path, you will learn about certain best practices and common pitfalls to avoid while building computer vision applications.

This learning path includes content from the following Packt products:

- Learn OpenCV 4 by Building Projects, Second Edition by David Millán Escrivá, Prateek Joshi and Vinícius G. Mendonça
- Mastering OpenCV 4, Third Edition by Roy Shilkrot, David Millán Escrivá

Who this book is for

If you are a software developer with a basic understanding of computer vision and image processing and want to develop interesting computer vision applications with OpenCV, then this course is for you. Prior knowledge of C++ will help you understand the concepts covered in this book.

What this book covers

Chapter 1, Getting Started with OpenCV, covers installation steps on various operating systems and provides an introduction to the human visual system, as well as various topics in computer vision.

Chapter 2, Introduction to OpenCV Basics, discusses how to read/write images and videos in OpenCV, and also explains how to build a project using CMake.

Chapter 3, Learning Graphical User Interface and Basic Filtering, covers how to build a graphical user interface and mouse event detector to build interactive applications.

Chapter 4, Delving into Histograms and Filters, explores histograms and filters and also shows how we can cartoonize an image.

Chapter 5, Automated Optical Inspection, Object Segmentation, and Detection, describes various image pre-processing techniques, such as noise removal, thresholding, and contour analysis.

Chapter 6, Learning Object Classification, deals with object recognition and machine learning, and how to use support vector machines to build an object classification system.

Chapter 7, Detecting Face Parts and Overlaying Masks, discusses face detection and Haar Cascades and then explains how these methods can be used to detect various parts of the human face.

Chapter 8, Video Surveillance, Background Modeling, and Morphological Operations, explores background subtraction, video surveillance, and morphological image processing, and describes how they are connected to one another.

Chapter 9, Learning Object Tracking, covers how to track objects in a live video using different techniques, such as color-based and feature-based tracking.

Chapter 10, Developing Segmentation Algorithms for Text Recognition, covers optical character recognition, text segmentation, and provides an introduction to the Tesseract OCR engine.

Chapter 11, Text Recognition with Tesseract, delves deeper into the Tesseract OCR engine to explain how it can be used for text detection, extraction, and recognition.

Chapter 12, Deep Learning with OpenCV, explores how to apply deep learning in OpenCV with two commonly used deep learning architectures: YOLO v3 for object detection, and Single Shot Detector for face detection.

Chapter 13, Cartoonifier and Skin Color Analysis on the RaspberryPi, demonstrates how to write some image processing filters for desktops and for small embedded systems such as Raspberry Pi.

Chapter 14, Explore Structure from Motion with the SfM Module, demonstrates how to use the SfM module to reconstruct a scene to a sparse point cloud, including camera poses, and also obtain a dense point cloud using multi-view stereo.

Chapter 15, Face Landmark and Pose with the Face Module, explains the process of face landmark (also known as facemark) detection using the face module.

Chapter 16, Number Plate Recognition with Deep Convolutional Networks, introduces image segmentation and feature extraction, pattern recognition basics, and two important pattern recognition algorithms, the Support Vector Machine (SVM) and deep neural network (DNN).

Chapter 17, Face Detection and Recognition with the DNN Module, demonstrates different techniques for detecting faces on the images, ranging from more classic algorithms using cascade classifiers with Haar features through to newer techniques employing deep learning.

Chapter 18, Android Camera Calibration and AR Using the ArUco Module, shows how to implement an augmented reality (AR) application in the Android ecosystem, using OpenCV's ArUco module, Android's Camera2 APIs, and the JMonkeyEngine 3D game engine.

Chapter 19, iOS Panoramas with the Stitching Module, shows how to build a panoramic image stitching application on the iPhone using OpenCV's precompiled library for iOS.

Chapter 20, Finding the Best OpenCV Algorithm for the Job, discusses a number of methods to follow when considering options within OpenCV.

Chapter 21, Avoiding Common Pitfalls in OpenCV, reviews the historical development of OpenCV, and the gradual increase in the framework and algorithmic offering, alongside the development of computer vision at large.

To get the most out of this book

To start using this course, you will need the following software installed on your local desktop:

- OpenCV 4.0
- CMake 3.3.x or newer
- Tesseract, Leptonica (a dependency of Tesseract)
- Qt (optional) and OpenGL (optional)
- Some chapters will require a Python, others an Android, installation

Download the example code files

You can download the example code files for this book from your account at www.packt.com. If you purchased this book elsewhere, you can visit www.packt.com/support and register to have the files emailed directly to you.

You can download the code files by following these steps:

1. Log in or register at www.packt.com.
2. Select the **SUPPORT** tab.
3. Click on **Code Downloads & Errata**.
4. Enter the name of the book in the **Search** box and follow the onscreen instructions.

Once the file is downloaded, please make sure that you unzip or extract the folder using the latest version of:

- WinRAR/7-Zip for Windows
- Zipeg/iZip/UnRarX for Mac
- 7-Zip/PeaZip for Linux

The code bundle for the book is also hosted on GitHub at https://github.com/PacktPublishing/Building-Computer-Vision-Projects-with-OpenCV4-and-CPlusPlus In case there's an update to the code, it will be updated on the existing GitHub repository.

We also have other code bundles from our rich catalog of books and videos available at https://github.com/PacktPublishing/. Check them out!

Conventions used

There are a number of text conventions used throughout this book.

CodeInText: Indicates code words in text, database table names, folder names, filenames, file extensions, pathnames, dummy URLs, user input, and Twitter handles. Here is an example: "The input() method is used to get an input from the user."

A block of code is set as follows:

```
Mat bigImg;
resize(smallImg, bigImg, size, 0,0, INTER_LINEAR);
dst.setTo(0);
bigImg.copyTo(dst, mask);
```

Any command-line input or output is written as follows:

```
sudo apt-get purge -y wolfram-engine
```

Bold: Indicates a new term, an important word, or words that you see onscreen. For example, words in menus or dialog boxes appear in the text like this. Here is an example: "If you need something different, click on the **DOWNLOADS** link in the header for all possible downloads: "

Warnings or important notes appear like this.

Tips and tricks appear like this.

Get in touch

Feedback from our readers is always welcome.

General feedback: If you have questions about any aspect of this book, mention the book title in the subject of your message and email us at `customercare@packtpub.com`.

Errata: Although we have taken every care to ensure the accuracy of our content, mistakes do happen. If you have found a mistake in this book, we would be grateful if you would report this to us. Please visit `www.packt.com/submit-errata`, selecting your book, clicking on the Errata Submission Form link, and entering the details.

Piracy: If you come across any illegal copies of our works in any form on the Internet, we would be grateful if you would provide us with the location address or website name. Please contact us at `copyright@packt.com` with a link to the material.

If you are interested in becoming an author: If there is a topic that you have expertise in and you are interested in either writing or contributing to a book, please visit `authors.packtpub.com`.

Reviews

Please leave a review. Once you have read and used this book, why not leave a review on the site that you purchased it from? Potential readers can then see and use your unbiased opinion to make purchase decisions, we at Packt can understand what you think about our products, and our authors can see your feedback on their book. Thank you!

For more information about Packt, please visit `packt.com`.

Getting Started with OpenCV 1

Computer vision applications are interesting and useful, but the underlying algorithms are computationally intensive. With the advent of cloud computing, we are getting more processing power to work with.

The OpenCV library enables us to run computer vision algorithms efficiently in real time. It has been around for many years and has become the standard library in this field. One of the main advantages of OpenCV is that it is highly optimized and available on almost all platforms.

This book will cover the various algorithms we will be using, why we are using them, and how to implement them in OpenCV.

In this chapter, we are going to learn how to install OpenCV on various operating systems. We will discuss what OpenCV offers out of the box, and the various things that we can do using the inbuilt functions.

By the end of this chapter, you will be able to answer the following questions:

- How do humans process visual data, and how do they understand image content?
- What can we do with OpenCV, and what are the various modules available in OpenCV that can be used to achieve those things?
- How do we install OpenCV on Windows, Linux, and Mac OS X?

Understanding the human visual system

Before we jump into OpenCV functionalities, we need to understand why those functions were built in the first place. It's important to understand how the human visual system works so that you can develop the right algorithms.

The goal of computer vision algorithms is to understand the content of images and videos. Humans seem to do it effortlessly! So, how do we get machines to do it with the same accuracy?

Let's consider the following diagram:

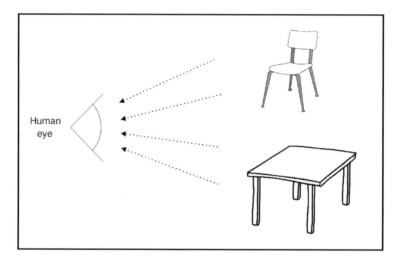

The human eye captures all the information that comes along the way, such as color, shape, brightness, and so on. In the preceding image, the human eye captures all the information about the two main objects and stores it in a certain way. Once we understand how our system works, we can take advantage of it to achieve what we want.

For example, here are a few things we need to know:

- Our visual system is more sensitive to low-frequency content than high-frequency content. Low-frequency content refers to planar regions where pixel values don't change rapidly, and high-frequency content refers to regions with corners and edges where pixel values fluctuate a lot. We can easily see if there are blotches on a planar surface, but it's difficult to spot something like that on a highly-textured surface.
- The human eye is more sensitive to changes in brightness than to changes in color.
- Our visual system is sensitive to motion. We can quickly recognize if something is moving in our field of vision, even though we are not directly looking at it.

- We tend to make a mental note of salient points in our field of vision. Let's say you look at a white table with four black legs and a red dot at one of the corners of the table surface. When you look at this table, you'll immediately make a mental note that the surface and legs have opposing colors and that there is a red dot on one of the corners. Our brain is really smart that way! We do this automatically so that we can immediately recognize an object if we encounter it again.

To get an idea of our field of view, let's look at the top view of a human, and the angles at which we see various things:

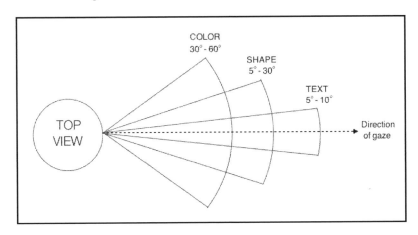

Our visual system is actually capable of a lot more, but this should be good enough to get us started. You can explore further by reading up on **Human Visual System (HVS)** models on the web.

How do humans understand image content?

If you look around, you will see a lot of objects. You encounter many different objects every day, and you recognize them almost instantaneously without any effort. When you see a chair, you don't wait for a few minutes before realizing that it is in fact a chair. You just know that it's a chair right away.

Computers, on the other hand, find it very difficult to do this task. Researchers have been working for many years to find out why computers are not as good as we are at this.

To get an answer to that question, we need to understand how humans do it. The visual data processing happens in the ventral visual stream. This ventral visual stream refers to the pathway in our visual system that is associated with object recognition. It is basically a hierarchy of areas in our brain that helps us recognize objects.

Humans can recognize different objects effortlessly, and can cluster similar objects together. We can do this because we have developed some sort of invariance toward objects of the same class. When we look at an object, our brain extracts the salient points in such a way that factors such as orientation, size, perspective, and illumination don't matter.

A chair that is double the normal size and rotated by 45 degrees is still a chair. We can recognize it easily because of the way we process it. Machines cannot do that so easily. Humans tend to remember an object based on its shape and important features. Regardless of how the object is placed, we can still recognize it.

In our visual system, we build up these hierarchical invariances with respect to position, scale, and viewpoint that help us to be very robust. If you look deeper into our system, you will see that humans have cells in their visual cortex that can respond to shapes such as curves and lines.

As we move further along our ventral stream, we will see more complex cells that are trained to respond to more complex objects such as trees, gates, and so on. The neurons along our ventral stream tend to show an increase in the size of the receptive field. This is coupled with the fact that the complexity of their preferred stimuli increases as well.

Why is it difficult for machines to understand image content?

We now understand how visual data enters the human visual system, and how our system processes it. The issue is that we still don't fully understand how our brain recognizes and organizes this visual data. In machine learning, we just extract some features from images, and ask the computers to learn them using algorithms. We still have these variations, such as shape, size, perspective, angle, illumination, occlusion, and so on.

For example, the same chair looks very different to a machine when you look at it from the profile view. Humans can easily recognize that it's a chair, regardless of how it's presented to us. So, how do we explain this to our machines?

One way to do this would be to store all the different variations of an object, including sizes, angles, perspectives, and so on. But this process is cumbersome and time-consuming. Also, it's actually not possible to gather data that can encompass every single variation. The machines would consume a huge amount of memory and a lot of time to build a model that can recognize these objects.

Even with all this, if an object is partially occluded, computers still won't recognize it. This is because they think this is a new object. So when we build a computer vision library, we need to build the underlying functional blocks that can be combined in many different ways to formulate complex algorithms.

OpenCV provides a lot of these functions, and they are highly optimized. So once we understand what OpenCV is capable of, we can use it effectively to build interesting applications.

Let's go ahead and explore that in the next section.

What can you do with OpenCV?

Using OpenCV, you can pretty much do every computer vision task you can think of. Real-life problems require you to use many computer vision algorithms and modules together to achieve the desired result. So, you just need to understand which OpenCV modules and functions to use, in order to get what you want.

Let's look at what OpenCV can do out of the box.

Inbuilt data structures and input/output

One of the best things about OpenCV is that it provides a lot of in-built primitives to handle operations related to image processing and computer vision. If you have to write something from scratch, you will have to define `Image`, `Point`, `Rectangle`, and so on. These are fundamental to almost any computer vision algorithm.

OpenCV comes with all these basic structures out of the box, contained in the core module. Another advantage is that these structures have already been optimized for speed and memory, and so you don't have to worry about the implementation details.

The `imgcodecs` module handles reading and writing of image files. When you operate on an input image and create an output image, you can save it as a `.jpg` or a `.png` file with a simple command.

You will be dealing with a lot of video files when you work with cameras. The videoio module handles everything related to the input and output of video files. You can easily capture a video from the webcam or read a video file in many different formats. You can even save a bunch of frames as a video file by setting properties such as frames per second, frame size, and so on.

Image processing operations

When you write a computer vision algorithm, there are a lot of basic image processing operations that you will use over and over again. Most of these functions are present in the imgproc module. You can do things such as image filtering, morphological operations, geometric transformations, color conversions, drawing on images, histograms, shape analysis, motion analysis, feature detection, and more.

Let's consider the following photo:

The right image is a rotated version of the one on the left. We can carry out this transformation with a single line in OpenCV.

There is another module, called ximgproc, which contains advanced image processing algorithms such as structured forests for edge detection, domain transform filter, adaptive manifold filter, and so on.

GUI

OpenCV provides a module called `highgui` that handles all the high-level user interface operations. Let's say you are working on a problem, and you want to check what the image looks like before you proceed to the next step. This module has functions that can be used to create windows to display images and/or videos.

There is a waiting function that will wait until you hit a key on your keyboard before it goes on to the next step. There is also a function that can detect mouse events. This is very useful in developing interactive applications.

Using this functionality, you can draw rectangles on those input windows, and then proceed based on the selected region. Consider the following screenshot:

As you can see, we drew a green rectangle on top of the window. Once we have the coordinates of that rectangle, we can operate only on that region.

Video analysis

Video analysis includes tasks such as analyzing the motion between successive frames in a video, tracking different objects in a video, creating models for video surveillance, and so on. OpenCV provides a module called `video` that can handle all of this.

There is also a module called `videostab` that deals with video stabilization. Video stabilization is important, as when you are capturing videos by holding the camera in your hands, there's usually a lot of shake that needs correcting. All modern devices use video stabilization to process the video before it's presented to the end user.

3D reconstruction

3D reconstruction is an important topic in computer vision. Given a set of 2D images, we can reconstruct the 3D scene using relevant algorithms. OpenCV provides algorithms that can find the relationship between various objects in those 2D images to compute their 3D positions in its `calib3d` module.

This module can also handle camera calibration, which is essential for estimating the parameters of the camera. These parameters define how the camera sees the scene in front of it. We need to know these parameters to design algorithms, or else we might get unexpected results.

Let's consider the following diagram:

As we can see here, the same object is captured from multiple positions. Our job is to reconstruct the original object using these 2D images.

Feature extraction

As we discussed earlier, the human visual system tends to extract the salient features from a given scene to remember it for retrieval later. To mimic this, people started designing various feature extractors that can extract these salient points from a given image. Popular algorithms include **Scale Invariant Feature Transform (SIFT)**, **Speeded Up Robust Features (SURF)**, and **Features From Accelerated Segment Test (FAST)**.

An OpenCV module called `features2d` provides functions to detect and extract all these features. Another module called `xfeatures2d` provides a few more feature extractors, some of which are still in the experimental phase. You can play around with these if you get the chance.

There is also a module called `bioinspired` that provides algorithms for biologically-inspired computer vision models.

Object detection

Object detection refers to detecting the location of an object in a given image. This process is not concerned with the type of object. If you design a chair detector, it will not tell you whether the chair in a given image is red with a high back, or blue with a low back—it will just tell you the location of the chair.

Detecting the location of objects is a critical step in many computer vision systems. Consider the following photo:

If you run a chair detector on this image, it will put a green box around all the chairs—but it won't tell you what kind of chair it is.

Object detection used to be a computationally-intensive task because of the number of calculations required to perform the detection at various scales. To solve this, Paul Viola and Michael Jones came up with a great algorithm in their seminal 2001 paper, which you can read at the following link: https://www.cs.cmu.edu/~efros/courses/LBMV07/Papers/viola-cvpr-01.pdf. They provided a fast way to design an object detector for any object.

OpenCV has modules called `objdetect` and `xobjdetect` that provide the framework to design an object detector. You can use it to develop detectors for random items such as sunglasses, boots, and so on.

Machine learning

Machine learning algorithms are used extensively to build computer vision systems for object recognition, image classification, face detection, visual search, and so on.

OpenCV provides a module called `ml`, which has many machine learning algorithms bundled into it, including a **Bayes classifier**, **k-nearest neighbors (KNN)**, **support vector machines (SVM)**, **decision trees**, **neural networks**, and more.

It also has a module called **Fast Approximate Nearest Neighbor Search Library (FLANN)**, which contains algorithms for fast nearest neighbor searches in large datasets.

Computational photography

Computational photography refers to using advanced image processing techniques to improve the images captured by cameras. Instead of focusing on optical processes and image capture methods, computational photography uses software to manipulate visual data. Applications include high dynamic range imaging, panoramic images, image relighting, and light field cameras.

Let's look at the following image:

Look at those vivid colors! This is an example of a high dynamic range image, and it wouldn't be possible to get this using conventional image capture techniques. To do this, we have to capture the same scene at multiple exposures, register those images with each other, and then blend them nicely to create this image.

The `photo` and `xphoto` modules contain various algorithms that provide algorithms pertaining to computational photography. There is also a module called `stitching` that provides algorithms to create panoramic images.

 The image shown can be found here: `https://pixabay.com/en/hdr-high-dynamic-range-landscape-806260/`.

Shape analysis

The notion of shape is crucial in computer vision. We analyze visual data by recognizing various different shapes in the image. This is actually an important step in many algorithms.

Let's say you are trying to identify a particular logo in an image. You know that it can appear in various shapes, orientations, and sizes. One good way to get started is to quantify the characteristics of the shape of the object.

The `shape` module provides all the algorithms required to extract different shapes, measure similarity between them, transform the shapes of objects, and more.

Optical flow algorithms

Optical flow algorithms are used in videos to track features across successive frames. Let's say you want to track a particular object in a video. Running a feature extractor on each frame would be computationally expensive; hence, the process would be slow. So, you just extract the features from the current frame, and then track those features in successive frames.

Optical flow algorithms are heavily used in video-based applications in computer vision. The `optflow` module contains all the algorithms required to perform optical flow. There is also a module called `tracking` that contains more algorithms that can be used to track features.

Face and object recognition

Face recognition refers to identifying the person in a given image. This is not the same as face detection, where you simply identify the location of a face in the given image.

If you want to build a practical biometric system that can recognize the person in front of the camera, you first need to run a face detector to identify the location of the face, and then run a separate face recognizer to identify who the person is. There is an OpenCV module called `face` that deals with face recognition.

As we discussed earlier, computer vision tries to model algorithms based on how humans perceive visual data. So, it would be helpful to find salient regions and objects in the images that can help with different applications such as object recognition, object detection and tracking, and so on. There is a module called `saliency` that's designed for this purpose. It provides algorithms that can detect salient regions in static images and videos.

Surface matching

We are increasingly interacting with devices that can capture the 3D structure of the objects around us. These devices essentially capture depth information, along with the regular 2D color images. So, it's important for us to build algorithms that can understand and process 3D objects.

Kinect is a good example of a device that captures depth information along with the visual data. The task at hand is to recognize the input 3D object, by matching it to one of the models in our database. If we have a system that can recognize and locate objects, then it can be used for many different applications.

There is a module called `surface_matching` that contains algorithms for 3D object recognition and a pose estimation algorithm using 3D features.

Text detection and recognition

Identifying text in a given scene and recognizing the content is becoming increasingly important. Applications include number plate recognition, recognizing road signs for self-driving cars, book scanning to digitize content, and more.

There is a module called `text` that contains various algorithms to handle text detection and recognition.

Deep learning

Deep learning has a big impact on computer vision and image recognition, and achieves a higher level of accuracy than other machine learning and artificially intelligent algorithms. Deep learning is not a new concept; it was introduced to the community around 1986, but it started a revolution around 2012 when new GPU hardware was optimized for parallel computing and **Convolutional Neural Network (CNN)** implementations and other techniques allowed the training of complex neural network architectures in reasonable times.

Deep learning can be applied to multiple use cases such as image recognition, object detection, voice recognition, and natural language processing. Since version 3.4, OpenCV has been implementing deep learning algorithms—in the latest version, multiple importers for important frameworks such as **TensorFlow** and **Caffe** have been added.

Installing OpenCV

Let's see how to get OpenCV up and running on various operating systems.

Windows

To keep things easy, let's install OpenCV using pre-built libraries. Go to `opencv.org` and download the latest version for Windows. The current version is 4.0.0, and you can get the download link from the OpenCV homepage. You should make sure you have admin rights before you proceed.

The downloaded file will be an executable file, so just double-click on it to start the installation. The installer expands the content into a folder. You will be able to choose the installation path, and check the installation by inspecting the files.

Once you are done with the previous step, we need to set the OpenCV environment variables and add them to the system path to complete the installation. We will set up an environment variable that will hold the build directory of the OpenCV library. We will be using this in our projects.

Open up the Terminal and type the following:

```
C:> setx -m OPENCV_DIR D:OpenCVBuildx64vc14
```

 We are assuming that you have a 64-bit machine with Visual Studio 2015 installed. If you have Visual Studio 2012, replace `vc14` with `vc11` in the command. The path specified is where we would have our OpenCV binaries, and you should see two folders inside that path called `lib` and `bin`. If you are using Visual Studio 2018, you should compile OpenCV from scratch.

Let's go ahead and add a path to the `bin` folder to our system path. The reason we need to do this is because we will be using the OpenCV library in the form of **dynamic link libraries** (**DLLs**). Essentially, all the OpenCV algorithms are stored here, and our operating system will only load them during runtime.

In order to do that, our operating system needs to know where they are located. The `PATH` system variable contains a list of all the folders where it can find DLLs. So, naturally, we need to add the path of the OpenCV library to this list.

Why do we need to do all this? Well, the other option is to copy the required DLLs in the same folder as the application's executable file (`.exe` file). This is an unnecessary overhead, especially when we are working with many different projects.

We need to edit the PATH variable to add this folder. You can use software such as Path Editor to do this, which you can download from here: https://patheditor2.codeplex.com. Once you install it, start it up and add the following new entry (you can right-click on the path to insert a new item):

```
%OPENCV_DIR%bin
```

Go ahead and save it to the registry. We are done!

Mac OS X

In this section, we will see how to install OpenCV on Mac OS X. Precompiled binaries are not available for Mac OS X, so we need to compile OpenCV from scratch.

Before we proceed, we need to install CMake. If you don't already have CMake installed, you can download it from here: https://cmake.org/files/v3.12/cmake-3.12.0-rc1-Darwin-x86_64.dmg. It's a .dmg file, so once you download it, just run the installer.

Download the latest version of OpenCV from opencv.org. The current version is 4.0.0, and you can download it from here: https://github.com/opencv/opencv/archive/4.0.0.zip. Unzip the contents into a folder of your choice.

OpenCV 4.0.0 also has a new package called opencv_contrib, containing user contributions that are not yet considered stable, and some algorithms that are not freely available for commercial use in all the latest computer vision algorithms, which is worth keeping in mind. Installing this package is optional—OpenCV will work just fine if you don't install opencv_contrib.

Since we are installing OpenCV anyway, it's good to install this package so that you can experiment with it later on (as opposed to going through the whole installation process again). It is a great way to learn and play around with new algorithms. You can download it from the following link:
https://github.com/opencv/opencv_contrib/archive/4.0.0.zip.

Unzip the contents of the zip file into a folder of your choice. For convenience, unzip it into the same folder as before, so that the opencv-4.0.0 and opencv_contrib-4.0.0 folders are in the same main folder.

We are now ready to build OpenCV. Open up your Terminal and navigate to the folder where you unzipped the contents of OpenCV 4.0.0. Run the following commands after substituting the right paths in the commands:

```
$ cd /full/path/to/opencv-4.0.0/
$ mkdir build
$ cd build
$ cmake -D CMAKE_BUILD_TYPE=RELEASE -D
CMAKE_INSTALL_PREFIX=/full/path/to/opencv-4.0.0/build -D
INSTALL_C_EXAMPLES=ON -D BUILD_EXAMPLES=ON -D
OPENCV_EXTRA_MODULES_PATH=/full/path/to/opencv_contrib-4.0.0/modules ../
```

It's time to install OpenCV 4.0.0. Go to the `/full/path/to/opencv-4.0.0/build` directory, and run the following commands on your Terminal:

```
$ make -j4
$ make install
```

In the preceding command, the `-j4` flag indicates that it should be using four cores to install it. It's faster this way! Now, let's set the library path. Open up your `~/.profile` file in your Terminal using the `vi ~/.profile` command, and add the following line:

```
export
DYLD_LIBRARY_PATH=/full/path/to/opencv-4.0.0/build/lib:$DYLD_LIBRARY_PATH
```

We need to copy the `pkgconfig` file in `opencv.pc` to `/usr/local/lib/pkgconfig` and name it `opencv4.pc`. This way, if you already have an existing OpenCV 3.x.x installation, there will be no conflict. Let's go ahead and do that:

```
$ cp /full/path/to/opencv-4.0.0/build/lib/pkgconfig/opencv.pc
/usr/local/lib/pkgconfig/opencv4.pc
```

We need to update our `PKG_CONFIG_PATH` variable as well. Open up your `~/.profile` file and add the following line:

```
export PKG_CONFIG_PATH=/usr/local/lib/pkgconfig/:$PKG_CONFIG_PATH
```

Reload your `~/.profile` file using the following command:

```
$ source ~/.profile
```

We're finished! Let's see if it's working:

```
$ cd /full/path/to/opencv-4.0.0/samples/cpp
$ g++ -ggdb `pkg-config --cflags --libs opencv4` opencv_version.cpp -o
/tmp/opencv_version && /tmp/opencv_version
```

If you see **Welcome to OpenCV 4.0.0** printed on your Terminal, you are good to go. We will be using CMake to build our OpenCV projects throughout this book. We will cover it in more detail in `Chapter 2`, *An Introduction to the Basics of OpenCV*.

Linux

Let's see how to install OpenCV on Ubuntu. We need to install some dependencies before we begin. Let's install them using the package manager by running the following command in your Terminal:

```
$ sudo apt-get -y install libopencv-dev build-essential cmake libdc1394-22
libdc1394-22-dev libjpeg-dev libpng12-dev libtiff5-dev libjasper-dev
libavcodec-dev libavformat-dev libswscale-dev libxine2-dev
libgstreamer0.10-dev libgstreamer-plugins-base0.10-dev libv4l-dev libtbb-
dev libqt4-dev libmp3lame-dev libopencore-amrnb-dev libopencore-amrwb-dev
libtheora-dev libvorbis-dev libxvidcore-dev x264 v4l-utils
```

Now that you have installed the dependencies, let's download, build, and install OpenCV:

```
$ wget "https://github.com/opencv/opencv/archive/4.0.0.tar.gz" -O
opencv.tar.gz
$ wget "https://github.com/opencv/opencv_contrib/archive/4.0.0.tar.gz" -O
opencv_contrib.tar.gz
$ tar -zxvf opencv.tar.gz
$ tar -zxvf opencv_contrib.tar.gz
$ cd opencv-4.0.0
$ mkdir build
$ cd build
$ cmake -D CMAKE_BUILD_TYPE=RELEASE -D
CMAKE_INSTALL_PREFIX=/full/path/to/opencv-4.0.0/build -D
INSTALL_C_EXAMPLES=ON -D BUILD_EXAMPLES=ON -D
OPENCV_EXTRA_MODULES_PATH=/full/path/to/opencv_contrib-4.0.0/modules ../
$ make -j4
$ sudo make install
```

Let's copy the `pkgconfig` file in `opencv.pc` to `/usr/local/lib/pkgconfig`, and name it `opencv4.pc`:

```
$ cp /full/path/to/opencv-4.0.0/build/lib/pkgconfig/opencv.pc
/usr/local/lib/pkgconfig/opencv4.pc
```

We're finished! We will now be able to use it to compile our OpenCV programs from the command line. Also, if you already have an existing OpenCV 3.x.x installation, there will be no conflict.

Let's check the installation is working properly:

```
$ cd /full/path/to/opencv-4.0.0/samples/cpp
$ g++ -ggdb `pkg-config --cflags --libs opencv4` opencv_version.cpp -o
/tmp/opencv_version && /tmp/opencv_version
```

If you see **Welcome to OpenCV 4.0.0** printed on your Terminal, you should be good to go. In the following chapters, we will learn how to use CMake to build our OpenCV projects.

Summary

In this chapter, we discussed the human visual system, and how humans process visual data. We explained why it's difficult for machines to do the same, and what we need to consider when designing a computer vision library.

We learned what could be done using OpenCV, and the various modules that can be used to complete those tasks. Finally, we learned how to install OpenCV in various operating systems.

In the next chapter, we will discuss how to operate on images and how we can manipulate them using various functions. We will also learn about building a project structure for our OpenCV applications.

2
An Introduction to the Basics of OpenCV

After covering OpenCV installation on different operating systems in Chapter 1, *Getting Started with OpenCV*, we are going to introduce the basics of OpenCV development in this chapter. It begins with showing how to create our project using CMake. We are going to introduce the basic image data structures and matrices, along with other structures that are required to work in our projects. We are going to introduce how to save our variables and data into files using the XML/YAML persistence OpenCV functions.

In this chapter, we will cover the following topics:

- Configuring projects with CMake
- Reading/writing images from/to disk
- Reading videos and accessing camera devices
- The main image structures (for example, matrices)
- Other important and basic structures (for example, vectors and scalars)
- An introduction to basic matrix operations
- File storage operations with XML/YAML persistence OpenCV API

Technical requirements

This chapter requires familiarity with the basic C++ programming language. All the code used in this chapter can be downloaded from the following GitHub link: https://github.com/PacktPublishing/Building-Computer-Vision-Projects-with-OpenCV4-and-CPlusPlus/tree/master/Chapter02. The code can be executed on any operating system, though it is only tested on Ubuntu.
Check out the following video to see the Code in Action:
http://bit.ly/2QxhNBa

Basic CMake configuration file

To configure and check all the requisite dependencies for our project, we are going to use CMake, but it is not the only way that this can be done; we can configure our project in any other tool or IDE, such as **Makefiles** or **Visual Studio**, but CMake is a more portable way to configure multiplatform **C++** projects.

CMake uses configuration files called `CMakeLists.txt`, where the compilation and dependencies process is defined. For a basic project based on an executable built from a single source code file, a `CMakeLists.txt` file comprising three lines is all that is required. The file looks as follows:

```
cmake_minimum_required (VERSION 3.0)
project (CMakeTest)
add_executable(${PROJECT_NAME} main.cpp)
```

The first line defines the minimum version of CMake required. This line is mandatory in our `CMakeLists.txt` file and allows us to use the functionality of CMake defined from a specific version; in our case, we require a minimum of CMake 3.0. The second line defines the project name. This name is saved in a variable called `PROJECT_NAME`.

The last line creates an executable command (`add_executable()`) from the `main.cpp` file, gives it the same name as our project (`${PROJECT_NAME}`), and compiles our source code into an executable called **CMakeTest** which is the name that we set up as a project name. The `${}` expression allows access to any variable defined in our environment. Then, we can use the `${PROJECT_NAME}` variable as an executable output name.

Creating a library

CMake allows us to create libraries used by the OpenCV build system. Factorizing shared code among multiple applications is a common and useful practice in software development. In big applications, or common code shared in multiple applications, this practice is very useful. In this case, we do not create a binary executable, but instead we create a compiled file that includes all the functions, classes, and so on. We can then share this library file with other applications without sharing our source code.

CMake includes the `add_library` function to this end:

```
# Create our hello library
   add_library(Hello hello.cpp hello.h)

# Create our application that uses our new library
```

```
add_executable(executable main.cpp)

# Link our executable with the new library
  target_link_libraries(executable Hello)
```

The lines starting with # add comments and are ignored by CMake. The
`add_library`(Hello hello.cpp hello.h) command defines the source files of our
library and its name, where `Hello` is the library name and `hello.cpp` and `hello.h` are the
source files. We add the header file too to allow IDEs such as Visual Studio to link to the
header files. This line is going to generate a shared (`.so` for Mac OS X, and Unix or `.dll` for
Windows) or static library (`.a` for Mac OS X, and Unix or `.lib` for Windows) file,
depending on whether we add a `SHARED` or `STATIC` word between library name and source
files. `target_link_libraries`(executable Hello) is the function that links our
executable to the desired library, in our case, the `Hello` library.

Managing dependencies

CMake has the ability to search our dependencies and external libraries, giving us the
ability to build complex projects, depending on the external components in our projects,
and add some requirements.

In this book, the most important dependency is, of course, OpenCV, and we will add it to
all of our projects:

```
cmake_minimum_required (VERSION 3.0)
PROJECT(Chapter2)
# Requires OpenCV
  FIND_PACKAGE( OpenCV 4.0.0 REQUIRED )
# Show a message with the opencv version detected
  MESSAGE("OpenCV version : ${OpenCV_VERSION}")
# Add the paths to the include directories/to the header files
  include_directories(${OpenCV_INCLUDE_DIRS})
# Add the paths to the compiled libraries/objects
  link_directories(${OpenCV_LIB_DIR})
# Create a variable called SRC
  SET(SRC main.cpp)
# Create our executable
  ADD_EXECUTABLE(${PROJECT_NAME} ${SRC})
# Link our library
  TARGET_LINK_LIBRARIES(${PROJECT_NAME} ${OpenCV_LIBS})
```

Now, let's understand the working of the script from the following:

```
cmake_minimum_required (VERSION 3.0)
cmake_policy(SET CMP0012 NEW)
PROJECT(Chapter2)
```

The first line defines the minimum CMake version, and the second line tells CMake to use the new behavior of CMake to facilitate recognition of the correct numbers and Boolean constants without dereferencing variables with such names; this policy was introduced in CMake 2.8.0, and CMake warns when the policy is not set from version 3.0.2. Finally, the last line defines the project title. After defining the project name, we have to define the requirements, libraries, and dependencies:

```
# Requires OpenCV
   FIND_PACKAGE( OpenCV 4.0.0 REQUIRED )
# Show a message with the opencv version detected
   MESSAGE("OpenCV version : ${OpenCV_VERSION}")
   include_directories(${OpenCV_INCLUDE_DIRS})
   link_directories(${OpenCV_LIB_DIR})
```

Here is where we search for our OpenCV dependency. `FIND_PACKAGE` is the function that allows us to find our dependencies, the minimum version required, and whether this dependency is required or optional. In this sample script, we look for OpenCV in version 4.0.0 or greater and state that it is a required package.

The `FIND_PACKAGE` command includes all OpenCV submodules, but you can specify the submodules that you want to include in the project by executing your application smaller and faster. For example, if we are only going to work with the basic OpenCV types and core functionality, we can use the following command: `FIND_PACKAGE(OpenCV 4.0.0 REQUIRED core)`.

If CMake does not find it, it returns an error and does not prevent us from compiling our application. The `MESSAGE` function shows a message in the terminal or CMake GUI. In our case, we are showing the OpenCV version as follows:

```
OpenCV version : 4.0.0
```

The `${OpenCV_VERSION}` is a variable where CMake stores the OpenCV package version. `include_directories()` and `link_directories()` add to our environment the headers and the directory of the specified library. OpenCV CMake's module saves this data in the `${OpenCV_INCLUDE_DIRS}` and `${OpenCV_LIB_DIR}` variables. These lines are not required in all platforms, such as Linux, because these paths normally are in the environment, but it's recommended to have more than one OpenCV version to choose the correct link and include directories. Now is the time to include our developed sources:

```
# Create a variable called SRC
    SET(SRC main.cpp)
# Create our executable
    ADD_EXECUTABLE(${PROJECT_NAME} ${SRC})
# Link our library
    TARGET_LINK_LIBRARIES(${PROJECT_NAME} ${OpenCV_LIBS})
```

This last line creates the executable and links the executable with the OpenCV library, as we saw in the previous section, *Creating a library*. There is a new function in this piece of code, `SET`; this function creates a new variable and adds to it any value that we need. In our case, we incorporate the `main.cpp` value in the `SRC` variable. We can add more and more values to the same variable, as can be seen in the following script:

```
SET(SRC main.cpp
        utils.cpp
        color.cpp
)
```

Making the script more complex

In this section, we are showing a more complex script that includes subfolders, libraries, and executables; all told, just two files and a few lines, as demonstrated in this script. It's not mandatory to create multiple `CMakeLists.txt` files, because we can specify everything in the main `CMakeLists.txt` file. However, it is more common to use different `CMakeLists.txt` files for each project subfolder, thereby making it more flexible and portable.

This example has a code structure folder, which contains one folder for a `utils` library and the root folder, which contains the main executable:

```
CMakeLists.txt
main.cpp
utils/
    CMakeLists.txt
    computeTime.cpp
```

```
computeTime.h
logger.cpp
logger.h
plotting.cpp
plotting.h
```

Then, we have to define two CMakeLists.txt files, one in the root folder and the other in the utils folder. The CMakeLists.txt root folder file has the following content:

```
cmake_minimum_required (VERSION 3.0)
project (Chapter2)

# Opencv Package required
FIND_PACKAGE( OpenCV 4.0.0 REQUIRED )

#Add opencv header files to project
include_directories(${OpenCV_INCLUDE_DIR})
link_directories(${OpenCV_LIB_DIR})

# Add a subdirectory to the build.
add_subdirectory(utils)

# Add optional log with a precompiler definition
option(WITH_LOG "Build with output logs and images in tmp" OFF)
if(WITH_LOG)
    add_definitions(-DLOG)
endif(WITH_LOG)

# generate our new executable
add_executable(${PROJECT_NAME} main.cpp)
# link the project with his dependencies
target_link_libraries(${PROJECT_NAME} ${OpenCV_LIBS} Utils)
```

Almost all lines are described in previous sections, except some functions which we will explain. add_subdirectory() tells CMake to analyze CMakeLists.txt of a desired subfolder. Before continuing with the main CMakeLists.txt file explanation, we are going to explain the CMakeLists.txt file in utils.

In the CMakeLists.txt file of the utils folders, we are going to write a new library to include in our main project folder:

```
# Add new variable for src utils lib
SET(UTILS_LIB_SRC
    computeTime.cpp
    logger.cpp
    plotting.cpp
)
```

```
# create our new utils lib
    add_library(Utils ${UTILS_LIB_SRC})
# make sure the compiler can find include files for our library
    target_include_directories(Utils PUBLIC ${CMAKE_CURRENT_SOURCE_DIR})
```

This CMake script file defines a variable, UTILS_LIB_SRC, where we add all source files included in our library, generate the library with the add_library function, and use the target_include_directories function to allow our main project to detect all header files. Leaving the utils subfolder and continuing with the root CMake script, the Option function creates a new variable, in our case WITH_LOG, with a small description attached. This variable could be changed through the ccmake command line or CMake GUI interface, where the description appears, and a check that allows users to enable or disable this option. This function is very useful for allowing the user to decide about compile-time features, such as whether we want enabling or disabling logs or not, compiling with Java or Python support, just as OpenCV does, and so on.

In our case, we use this option to enable a logger in our application. To enable the logger, we use a pre-compiler definition in our code, as follows:

```
#ifdef LOG
    logi("Number of iteration %d", i);
#endif
```

This LOG macro can be defined in our CMakeLists.txt through a call to the add_definitions function (-DLOG), which itself can be run or hidden by the CMake variable WITH_LOG with a simple condition:

```
if(WITH_LOG)
    add_definitions(-DLOG)
endif(WITH_LOG)
```

Now we are ready to create our CMake script files to compile our computer vision projects in any operating system. Then, we are going to continue with the OpenCV basics before starting with a sample project.

Images and matrices

The most important structure in computer vision is, without doubt, the images. The image in a computer vision is the representation of the physical world captured with a digital device. This picture is only a sequence of numbers stored in a matrix format (refer to the following diagram). Each number is a measurement of the light intensity for the considered wavelength (for example, red, green, or blue in color images) or for a wavelength range (for panchromatic devices). Every point in an image is called a **pixel** (for a picture element), and each pixel can store one or more values depending on whether it is a black and white image (also referred to as a binary image) that stores only one value, such as 0 or 1, a grayscale-level image that stores two values, or a color image that stores three values. These values are usually between 0 and 255 in an integer number, but you can use other ranges, for example 0 to 1 in floating point numbers, as in **high dynamic range imaging (HDRI)** or thermal images:

The image is stored in a matrix format, where each pixel has a position in it and can be referenced by the number of the column and row. OpenCV uses the Mat class for this purpose. In the case of a grayscale image, a single matrix is used, as demonstrated in the following diagram:

159	165	185	187	185	190	189	198	193	197	184	152	123
174	167	186	194	185	196	204	191	200	178	149	129	125
168	184	185	188	195	192	191	195	169	141	116	115	129
178	188	190	195	196	199	195	164	128	120	118	126	135
188	194	189	195	201	196	166	114	113	120	128	131	129
187	200	197	198	190	144	107	106	113	120	125	125	125
198	195	202	183	134	98	97	112	114	115	116	116	118
194	206	178	111	87	99	97	101	107	105	101	97	95
206	168	107	82	80	100	102	91	98	102	104	99	72
160	97	90	86	80	92	80	79	71	74	81	81	64
98	66	76	86	76	83	72	71	55	53	51	51	55
80	76	74	70	67	64	63	60	55	49	54	52	54

In the case of a color image, such as the following diagram, we use a matrix of width x height x the number of color channels:

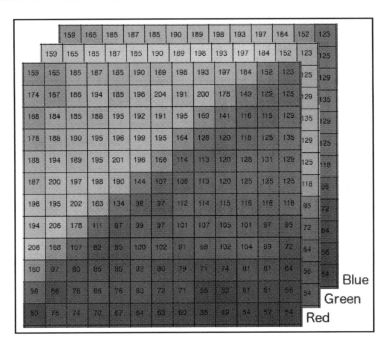

But the `Mat` class is not only for storing images; it also enables you to store any type of matrix and different sizes. You can use it as an algebraic matrix and perform operations with it. In the following sections, we are going to describe the most important matrix operations, such as addition, multiplication, diagonalization. But, before that, it's important to know how the matrix is stored internally in the computer memory, because it is always more efficient to access the memory slots instead of accessing each pixel with the OpenCV functions.

In memory, the matrix is saved as an array or sequence of values ordered by columns and rows. The following table shows the sequence of pixels in **BGR** image format:

Row 0			Row 1			Row 2		
Col 0	Col 1	Col 2	Col 0	Col 1	Col 2	Col 0	Col 1	Col 2
Pixel 1	Pixel 2	Pixel 3	Pixel 4	Pixel 5	Pixel 6	Pixel 7	Pixel 8	Pixel 9
B G R	B G R	B G R	B G R	B G R	B G R	B G R	B G R	B G R

With this order, we can access any pixel by observing the following formula:

```
Value= Row_i*num_cols*num_channels + Col_i + channel_i
```

OpenCV functions are quite optimized for random access, but sometimes, direct access to the memory (work with pointer arithmetic) is more efficient, for example, when we have to access all pixels in a loop.

Reading/writing images

Following the introduction to matrices, we are going to start with the OpenCV code basics. The first thing that we have to learn is how to read and write images:

```cpp
#include <iostream>
#include <string>
#include <sstream>
using namespace std;

// OpenCV includes
#include "opencv2/core.hpp"
#include "opencv2/highgui.hpp"
using namespace cv;

int main(int argc, const char** argv)
{
    // Read images
    Mat color= imread("../lena.jpg");
    Mat gray= imread("../lena.jpg",CV_LOAD_IMAGE_GRAYSCALE);

  if(! color.data ) // Check for invalid input
  {
 cout << "Could not open or find the image" << std::endl ;
 return -1;
 }
    // Write images
    imwrite("lenaGray.jpg", gray);
    // Get same pixel with opencv function
    int myRow=color.cols-1;
    int myCol=color.rows-1;
    Vec3b pixel= color.at<Vec3b>(myRow, myCol);
    cout << "Pixel value (B,G,R): (" << (int)pixel[0] << "," <<
(int)pixel[1] << "," << (int)pixel[2] << ")" << endl;
    // show images
    imshow("Lena BGR", color);
    imshow("Lena Gray", gray);
    // wait for any key press
    waitKey(0);
    return 0;
}
```

Let's now move on to understanding the code:

```
// OpenCV includes
#include "opencv2/core.hpp"
#include "opencv2/highgui.hpp"
using namespace cv;
```

First, we have to include the declarations of the functions that we need in our sample. These functions come from core (basic image data handling) and highgui (cross-platform I/O functions provided by OpenCV are core and highui;; the first includes the basic classes, such as matrices, while the second includes the functions to read, write, and show images with graphical interfaces). Now it is time to read images:

```
// Read images
Mat color= imread("../lena.jpg");
Mat gray= imread("../lena.jpg",CV_LOAD_IMAGE_GRAYSCALE);
```

imread is the main function for reading images. This function opens an image and stores it in a matrix format. imread accepts two parameters. The first parameter is a string containing the image's path, while the second is optional and, by default, loads the image as a color image. The second parameter allows the following options:

- cv::IMREAD_UNCHANGED: If set, this returns a 16-bit/32-bit image when the input has the corresponding depth, otherwise it converts it to 8-bit
- cv::IMREAD_COLOR: If set, this always converts an image to a color one (BGR, 8-bit unsigned)
- cv::IMREAD_GRAYSCALE: If set, this always converts an image to a grayscale one (8-bit unsigned)

To save images, we can use the imwrite function, which stores a matrix image in our computer:

```
// Write images
imwrite("lenaGray.jpg", gray);
```

The first parameter is the path where we want to save the image with the extension format that we desire. The second parameter is the matrix image that we want to save. In our code sample, we create and store a gray version of the image and then save it as a .jpg file. The gray image that we loaded will be stored in the gray variable:

```
// Get same pixel with opencv function
int myRow=color.cols-1;
int myCol=color.rows-1;
```

Using the .cols and .rows attributes of a matrix, we can get access to the number of columns and rows in an image, or, in other words, the width and height:

```
Vec3b pixel= color.at<Vec3b>(myRow, myCol);
cout << "Pixel value (B,G,R): (" << (int)pixel[0] << "," << (int)pixel[1]
<< "," << (int)pixel[2] << ")" << endl;
```

To access one pixel of the image, we use the template function cv::Mat::at<typename t>(row,col) from the Mat OpenCV class. The template parameter is the desired return type. A type name in an 8-bit color image is a Vec3b class that stores three unsigned char data (Vec = vector, 3 = number of components, and b = 1 byte). In the case of the gray image, we can directly use the unsigned character, or any other number format used in the image, such as uchar pixel= color.at<uchar>(myRow, myCol). Finally, in order to show the images, we can use the imshow function, which creates a window with a title as a first parameter and the image matrix as a second parameter:

```
// show images
imshow("Lena BGR", color);
imshow("Lena Gray", gray);
// wait for any key press
waitKey(0);
```

 If we want to stop the application from waiting, we can use the OpenCV function waitKey, with a parameter of the number of milliseconds we want to wait for a key press. If we set up the parameter to 0, then the function will wait until a key is pressed.

The result of the preceding code is demonstrated in the following image. The left-hand image is a color image, and the right-hand image is a grayscale image:

Finally, by way of an example for the following samples, we are going to create the CMakeLists.txt file and see how to compile the code using the file.

The following code describes the CMakeLists.txt file:

```
cmake_minimum_required (VERSION 3.0)
cmake_policy(SET CMP0012 NEW)
PROJECT(project)

# Requires OpenCV
FIND_PACKAGE( OpenCV 4.0.0 REQUIRED )
MESSAGE("OpenCV version : ${OpenCV_VERSION}")

include_directories(${OpenCV_INCLUDE_DIRS})
link_directories(${OpenCV_LIB_DIR})

ADD_EXECUTABLE(sample main.cpp)
TARGET_LINK_LIBRARIES(sample ${OpenCV_LIBS})
```

To compile our code using this `CMakeLists.txt` file, we have to carry out the following steps:

1. Create a `build` folder.
2. Inside the `build` folder, execute CMake or open CMake GUI app in Windows, choose the `source` and `build` folders, and press the **Configure** and **Generate** buttons.
3. If you are on Linux or macOS, generate a Makefile as usual, and then compile the project using the `make` command. If you are on Windows, open the project using the editor selected in step 2 and then compile.

Finally, after compiling our application, we will have an executable called `app` in the build folder that we can execute.

Reading videos and cameras

This section introduces you to video and camera reading using this simple example. Before explaining how to read videos or camera input, we want to introduce a new, very useful class that helps us to manage the input command-line parameters. This new class was introduced in OpenCV version 3.0, and is the `CommandLineParser` class:

```
// OpenCV command line parser functions
// Keys accepted by command line parser
const char* keys =
{
    "{help h usage ? | | print this message}"
     "{@video | | Video file, if not defined try to use webcamera}"
};
```

The first thing that we have to do for `CommandLineParser` is define what parameters we need or allow in a constant `char` vector; each line has the following pattern:

```
"{name_param | default_value | description}"
```

`name_param` can be preceded with `@`, which defines this parameter as a default input. We can use more than one `name_param`:

```
CommandLineParser parser(argc, argv, keys);
```

The constructor will get the inputs of the main function and the key constants defined previously:

```
//If requires help show
if (parser.has("help"))
{
        parser.printMessage();
        return 0;
}
```

The `.has` class method checks the existence of the parameter. In the sample, we check whether the user adds the parameter `help` or `?`, and then use the class function `printMessage` to show all the description parameters:

```
String videoFile= parser.get<String>(0);
```

With the `.get<typename>(parameterName)` function, we can access and read any of input parameters:

```
// Check if params are correctly parsed in his variables
if (!parser.check())
{
    parser.printErrors();
    return 0;
}
```

After obtaining all the requisite parameters, we can check whether these parameters are parsed correctly and show an error message if one of the parameters was not parsed, for example, add a string instead of a number:

```
VideoCapture cap; // open the default camera
if(videoFile != "")
    cap.open(videoFile);
else
    cap.open(0);
if(!cap.isOpened())  // check if we succeeded
    return -1;
```

The class for video reading and camera reading is the same: the `VideoCapture` class that belongs to the `videoio` submodule instead of the `highgui` submodule, as in the previous version of OpenCV. After creating the object, we check whether the input command-line parameter `videoFile` has a path filename. If it's empty, then we try to open a web camera; if it has a filename, then open the video file. To do this, we use the `open` function, giving as a parameter the video filename or the index camera that we want to open. If we have a single camera, we can use 0 as a parameter.

To check whether we can read the video filename or the camera, we use the `isOpened` function:

```
namedWindow("Video",1);
for(;;)
{
    Mat frame;
    cap >> frame; // get a new frame from camera
    if(frame)
        imshow("Video", frame);
    if(waitKey(30) >= 0) break;
}
// Release the camera or video cap
cap.release();
```

Finally, we create a window to show the frames with the `namedWindow` function and, with an infinite loop, we grab each frame using the >> operation and show the frame with the `imshow` function if we retrieve the frame correctly. In this case, we don't want to stop the application, but will wait 30 milliseconds to check whether any users want to stop the application execution with any key using `waitKey(30)`.

The time required to wait for the next frame using camera access is calculated from the camera speed and our spent algorithm time. For example, if a camera works at 20 fps, and our algorithm spent 10 milliseconds, a great waiting value is $30 = (1000/20) - 10$ milliseconds. This value is calculated considering a wait of a sufficient amount of time to ensure that the next frame is in the buffer. If our camera takes 40 milliseconds to take each image, and we use 10 milliseconds in our algorithm, then we only need to stop with waitKey 30 milliseconds, because 30 milliseconds of wait time, plus 10 milliseconds of our algorithm, is the same amount of time for which each frame of the camera is accessible.

When the user wants to finish the application, all they have to do is press any key and then we have to release all video resources using the release function.

It is very important to release all resources that we use in a computer vision application. If we do not, we can consume all RAM memory. We can release the matrices using the `release` function.

The result of the previous code is a new window showing a video or web camera in BGR format.

Other basic object types

We have learned about the `Mat` and `Vec3b` classes, but there are many more classes that we have to learn.

In this section, we will learn the most basic object types required in the majority of projects:

- `Vec`
- `Scalar`
- `Point`
- `Size`
- `Rect`
- `RotatedRect`

Vec object type

`Vec` is a template class mainly for numerical vectors. We can define any type of vector and the number of components:

```
Vec<double,19> myVector;
```

We can also use any of the predefined types:

```
typedef Vec<uchar, 2> Vec2b;
typedef Vec<uchar, 3> Vec3b;
typedef Vec<uchar, 4> Vec4b;

typedef Vec<short, 2> Vec2s;
typedef Vec<short, 3> Vec3s;
typedef Vec<short, 4> Vec4s;

typedef Vec<int, 2> Vec2i;
typedef Vec<int, 3> Vec3i;
typedef Vec<int, 4> Vec4i;

typedef Vec<float, 2> Vec2f;
typedef Vec<float, 3> Vec3f;
typedef Vec<float, 4> Vec4f;
typedef Vec<float, 6> Vec6f;

typedef Vec<double, 2> Vec2d;
typedef Vec<double, 3> Vec3d;
```

```
typedef Vec<double, 4> Vec4d;
typedef Vec<double, 6> Vec6d;
```

All the following vector operations are also implemented:

```
v1 = v2 + v3
v1 = v2 - v3
v1 = v2 * scale
v1 = scale * v2
v1 = -v2
v1 += v2
```

Other augmenting operations implemented are the following:

```
v1 == v2, v1 != v2
norm(v1) (euclidean norm).
```

Scalar object type

The `Scalar` object type is a template class derived from `Vec` with four elements. The `Scalar` type is widely used in OpenCV to pass and read pixel values.

To access `Vec` and `Scalar` values, we use the `[]` operator, which can be initialized from another scalar, vector, or value by value, as in the following sample:

```
Scalar s0(0);
Scalar s1(0.0, 1.0, 2.0, 3.0);
Scalar s2(s1);
```

Point object type

Another very common class template is `Point`. This class defines a 2D point specified by its coordinates x and y.

Like `Point`, there is a `Point3` template class for 3D point support.

Like the `Vec` class, OpenCV defines the following `Point` aliases for our convenience:

```
typedef Point_<int> Point2i;
typedef Point2i Point;
typedef Point_<float> Point2f;
```

```
typedef Point_<double> Point2d;
  The following operators are defined for points:
    pt1 = pt2 + pt3;
    pt1 = pt2 - pt3;
    pt1 = pt2 * a;
    pt1 = a * pt2;
    pt1 = pt2 / a;
    pt1 += pt2;
    pt1 -= pt2;
    pt1 *= a;
    pt1 /= a;
    double value = norm(pt); // L2 norm
    pt1 == pt2;
    pt1 != pt2;
```

Size object type

Another template class that is very important and widely used in OpenCV is the template class for specifying the size of an image or rectangle—Size. This class adds two members, width and height, and the useful area() function. In the following sample, we can see a number of ways of using size:

```
Size s(100,100);
Mat img=Mat::zeros(s, CV_8UC1); // 100 by 100 single channel matrix
s.width= 200;
int area= s.area(); returns 100x200
```

Rect object type

Rect is another important template class for defining 2D rectangles defined by the following parameters:

- The coordinates of the upper-left corner

- The width and height of a rectangle

The Rect template class can be used to define a **region of interest** (ROI) of an image, as follows:

```
Mat img=imread("lena.jpg");
Rect rect_roi(0,0,100,100);
Mat img_roi=img(r);
```

RotatedRect object type

The last useful class is a particular rectangle called `RotatedRect`. This class represents a rotated rectangle specified by a center point, the width and height of a rectangle, and the rotation angle in degrees:

```
RotatedRect(const Point2f& center, const Size2f& size, float angle);
```

An interesting function of this class is `boundingBox`. This function returns `Rect`, which contains the rotated rectangle:

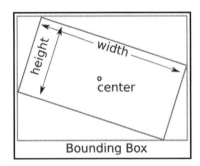

Basic matrix operations

In this section, we will learn a number of basic and important matrix operations that we can apply to images or any matrix data. We learned how to load an image and store it in a `Mat` variable, but we can create `Mat` manually. The most common constructor is giving the matrix a size and type, as follows:

```
Mat a= Mat(Size(5,5), CV_32F);
```

 You can create a new matrix linking with a stored buffer from third-party libraries without copying data using this constructor: `Mat(size, type, pointer_to_buffer)`.

The types supported depend on the type of number you want to store and the number of channels. The most common types are as follows:

```
CV_8UC1
CV_8UC3
CV_8UC4
CV_32FC1
```

```
CV_32FC3
CV_32FC4
```

 You can create any type of matrix using `CV_number_typeC(n)`, where the `number_type` is 8 bits unsigned (8U) to 64 float (64F), and where `(n)` is the number of channels; the number of channels permitted ranges from 1 to `CV_CN_MAX`.

The initialization does not set up the data values, and hence you can get undesirable values. To avoid undesirable values, you can initialize the matrix with 0 or 1 values with their respective functions:

```
Mat mz= Mat::zeros(5,5, CV_32F);
Mat mo= Mat::ones(5,5, CV_32F);
```

The results of the preceding matrix are as follows:

```
[0, 0, 0, 0, 0;     [1, 1, 1, 1, 1;
 0, 0, 0, 0, 0;      1, 1, 1, 1, 1;
 0, 0, 0, 0, 0;      1, 1, 1, 1, 1;
 0, 0, 0, 0, 0;      1, 1, 1, 1, 1;
 0, 0, 0, 0, 0]      1, 1, 1, 1, 1]
```

A special matrix initialization is the eye function that creates an identity matrix with the specified type and size:

```
Mat m= Mat::eye(5,5, CV_32F);
```

The output is as follows:

```
[1, 0, 0, 0, 0;
 0, 1, 0, 0, 0;
 0, 0, 1, 0, 0;
 0, 0, 0, 1, 0;
 0, 0, 0, 0, 1]
```

All matrix operations are allowed in OpenCV's `Mat` class. We can add or subtract two matrices of the same size using the + and – operators, as demonstrated in the following code block:

```
Mat a= Mat::eye(Size(3,2), CV_32F);
Mat b= Mat::ones(Size(3,2), CV_32F);
Mat c= a+b;
Mat d= a-b;
```

The results of the preceding operations are as follows:

$$\begin{matrix} [1, 0, 0; \\ 0, 1, 0] \end{matrix} + \begin{matrix} [1, 1, 1; \\ 1, 1, 1] \end{matrix} = \begin{matrix} [2, 1, 1; \\ 1, 2, 1] \end{matrix}$$

$$\begin{matrix} [1, 0, 0; \\ 0, 1, 0] \end{matrix} - \begin{matrix} [1, 1, 1; \\ 1, 1, 1] \end{matrix} = \begin{matrix} [0, -1, -1; \\ -1, 0, -1] \end{matrix}$$

We can multiply by a scalar using the $*$ operator or a matrix per element using the `mul` function, and we can perform matrix multiplication using the $*$ operator:

```
Mat m1= Mat::eye(2,3, CV_32F);
Mat m2= Mat::ones(3,2, CV_32F);
// Scalar by matrix
cout << "nm1.*2n" << m1*2 << endl;
// matrix per element multiplication
cout << "n(m1+2).*(m1+3)n" << (m1+1).mul(m1+3) << endl;
// Matrix multiplication
cout << "nm1*m2n" << m1*m2 << endl;
```

The results of the preceding operations are as follows:

$$\begin{matrix} [1, 0, 0; \\ 0, 1, 0] \end{matrix} * 2 = \begin{matrix} [2, 0, 0; \\ 0, 2, 0] \end{matrix}$$

$$\begin{matrix} [2, 1, 1; \\ 1, 2, 1] \end{matrix} * \begin{matrix} [4, 3, 3; \\ 3, 4, 3] \end{matrix} = \begin{matrix} [8, 3, 3; \\ 3, 8, 3] \end{matrix}$$

$$\begin{matrix} [1, 0, 0; \\ 0, 1, 0] \end{matrix} * \begin{matrix} [1, 1; \\ 1, 1; \\ 1, 1] \end{matrix} = \begin{matrix} [1, 1; \\ 1, 1] \end{matrix}$$

Other common mathematical matrix operations are **transposition** and **matrix inversion**, defined by the `t()` and `inv()` functions, respectively. Other interesting functions that OpenCV provides are array operations in matrix, for example, counting the nonzero elements. This is useful for counting the pixels or areas of objects:

```
int countNonZero(src);
```

OpenCV provides some statistical functions. Mean and standard deviation by channel can be calculated using the `meanStdDev` function:

```
meanStdDev(src, mean, stddev);
```

Another useful statistical function is `minMaxLoc`. This function finds the minimum and the maximum of a matrix or array, and returns the location and value:

```
minMaxLoc(src, minVal, maxVal, minLoc, maxLoc);
```

Here `src` is the input matrix, `minVal` and `maxVal` are double values detected, and `minLoc` and `maxLoc` are `Point` values detected.

> Other core and useful functions are described in detail
> at: `http://docs.opencv.org/modules/core/doc/core.html`.

Basic data persistence and storage

Before finishing this chapter, we will explore the OpenCV functions to store and read our data. In many applications, such as calibration or machine learning, when we finish performing a number of calculations, we need to save these results to retrieve them in subsequent operations. OpenCV provides an XML/YAML persistence layer to this end.

Writing to FileStorage

To write a file with some OpenCV or other numeric data, we can use the `FileStorage` class, using a streaming << operator such as STL streaming:

```
#include "opencv2/opencv.hpp"
using namespace cv;

int main(int, char** argv)
{
   // create our writer
    FileStorage fs("test.yml", FileStorage::WRITE);
    // Save an int
    int fps= 5;
    fs << "fps" << fps;
    // Create some mat sample
    Mat m1= Mat::eye(2,3, CV_32F);
    Mat m2= Mat::ones(3,2, CV_32F);
    Mat result= (m1+1).mul(m1+3);
    // write the result
    fs << "Result" << result;
    // release the file
    fs.release();

    FileStorage fs2("test.yml", FileStorage::READ);

    Mat r;
    fs2["Result"] >> r;
```

```
        std::cout << r << std::endl;

        fs2.release();

        return 0;
}
```

To create a file storage where we save the data, we only need to call the constructor, giving a path filename with the extension format desired (XML or YAML), and the second parameter set to write:

```
FileStorage fs("test.yml", FileStorage::WRITE);
```

If we want to save data, we only need to use the stream operator by giving an identifier in the first stage, and later the matrix or value that we want to save. For example, to save an `int` variable, we only have to write the following lines of code:

```
int fps= 5;
fs << "fps" << fps;
```

Otherwise, we can write/save `mat` as shown:

```
Mat m1= Mat::eye(2,3, CV_32F);
Mat m2= Mat::ones(3,2, CV_32F);
Mat result= (m1+1).mul(m1+3);
// write the result
fs << "Result" << result;
```

The result of the preceding code is a YAML format:

```
%YAML:1.0
fps: 5
Result: !!opencv-matrix
    rows: 2
    cols: 3
    dt: f
    data: [ 8., 3., 3., 3., 8., 3. ]
```

Reading from a file storage to read a file saved previously is very similar to the save functions:

```
#include "opencv2/opencv.hpp"
using namespace cv;

int main(int, char** argv)
{
    FileStorage fs2("test.yml", FileStorage::READ);
```

```
Mat r;
fs2["Result"] >> r;
std::cout << r << std::endl;

fs2.release();

return 0;
}
```

The first stage is to open a saved file with the `FileStorage` constructor using the appropriate parameters, path, and `FileStorage::READ`:

```
FileStorage fs2("test.yml", FileStorage::READ);
```

To read any stored variable, we only need to use the common stream operator `>>` using our `FileStorage` object and the identifier with the `[]` operator:

```
Mat r;
fs2["Result"] >> r;
```

Summary

In this chapter, we learned the basics and the most important types and operations of OpenCV, access to images and videos, and how they are stored in matrices. We learned the basic matrix operations and other basic OpenCV classes to store pixels, vectors, and so on. Finally, we learned how to save our data in files to allow them to be read in other applications or other executions.

In the next chapter, we are going to learn how to create our first application, learning the basics of graphical user interfaces that OpenCV provides. We will create buttons and sliders, and introduce some image processing basics.

3
Learning Graphical User Interfaces

In `Chapter 2`, *An Introduction to the Basics of OpenCV*, we learned the basic classes and structures of OpenCV and the most important class, called `Mat`. We learned how to read and save images and videos and the internal structure in the memory of images. We are now ready to work with OpenCV, but, in most cases, we need to show our image results and retrieve user interaction with our images using a number of user interfaces. OpenCV provides us with a few basic user interfaces to facilitate the creation of our applications and prototypes. To better understand how the user interface works, we are going to create a small application called **PhotoTool** at the end of this chapter. In this application, we will learn how to use filters and color conversions.

This chapter introduces the following topics:

- The OpenCV basic user interface
- The OpenCV Qt interface
- Sliders and buttons
- An advanced user interface – OpenGL
- Color conversion
- Basic filters

Technical requirements

This chapter requires familiarity with the basic C++ programming language. All the code used in this chapter can be downloaded from the following GitHub link: `https://github.com/PacktPublishing/Building-Computer-Vision-Projects-with-OpenCV4-and-CPlusPlus/tree/master/Chapter03`. The code can be executed on any operating system, although it has only been tested on Ubuntu.

Check out the following video to see the code in action:
`http://bit.ly/2KH2QXD`

Introducing the OpenCV user interface

OpenCV has its own cross-OS user interface that allows developers to create their own applications without the need to learn complex user interface libraries. The OpenCV user interface is basic, but it gives computer vision developers the basic functions to create and manage their software developments. All of them are native and optimized for real-time use.

OpenCV provides two user interface options:

- A basic interface based on native user interfaces, cocoa or carbon for Mac OS X, and GTK for Linux or Windows user interfaces, selected by default when compiling OpenCV.
- A slightly more advanced interface based on Qt library that is a cross-platform interface. You have to enable the Qt option manually in CMake before compiling OpenCV.

In the following screenshot, you can see the basic user interface window on the left, and the Qt user interface on the right:

Basic graphical user interface with OpenCV

We are going to create a basic user interface with OpenCV. The OpenCV user interface allows us to create windows, add images to it, and move, resize, and destroy it. The user interface is in OpenCV's `highui` module. In the following code, we are going to learn how to create and show two images by pressing a key to display multiple windows with the image moving in the window on our desktop.

Don't worry about reading the full code; we are going to explain it in small chunks:

```
#include <iostream>
#include <string>
#include <sstream>
using namespace std;

// OpenCV includes
#include <opencv2/core.hpp>
#include <opencv2/highgui.hpp>
using namespace cv;

int main(int argc, const char** argv)
{
   // Read images
   Mat lena= imread("../lena.jpg");
   # Checking if Lena image has been loaded
   if (!lena.data) {
 cout << "Lena image missing!" << enld;
 return -1;
   }
   Mat photo= imread("../photo.jpg");
   # Checking if Lena image has been loaded
   if (!photo.data) {
 cout << "Lena image missing!" << enld;
 return -1;
}
   // Create windows
   namedWindow("Lena", WINDOW_NORMAL);
   namedWindow("Photo", WINDOW_AUTOSIZE);

   // Move window
   moveWindow("Lena", 10, 10);
   moveWindow("Photo", 520, 10);
   // show images
   imshow("Lena", lena);
   imshow("Photo", photo);

   // Resize window, only non autosize
```

```
        resizeWindow("Lena", 512, 512);

        // wait for any key press
        waitKey(0);

        // Destroy the windows
        destroyWindow("Lena");
        destroyWindow("Photo");

        // Create 10 windows
        for(int i =0; i< 10; i++)
        {
                ostringstream ss;
                ss << "Photo" << i;
                namedWindow(ss.str());
                moveWindow(ss.str(), 20*i, 20*i);
                imshow(ss.str(), photo);
        }

        waitKey(0);
        // Destroy all windows
        destroyAllWindows();
        return 0;
}
```

Let's understand the code:

1. The first task we have to do in order to facilitate a graphical user interface is to import OpenCV's `highui` module:

   ```
   #include <opencv2/highgui.hpp>
   ```

2. Now that we are prepared to create our new windows, we have to load some images:

   ```
   // Read images
   Mat lena= imread("../lena.jpg");
   Mat photo= imread("../photo.jpg");
   ```

3. To create the windows, we use the `namedWindow` function. This function has two parameters; the first is a constant string with the window's name, and the second is the flags that we require. This second parameter is optional:

   ```
   namedWindow("Lena", WINDOW_NORMAL);
   namedWindow("Photo", WINDOW_AUTOSIZE);
   ```

4. In our case, we create two windows: the first is called `Lena`, and the second is called `Photo`.

   There are three flags by default for Qt and native:

   - `WINDOW_NORMAL`: This flag allows the user to resize the window
   - `WINDOW_AUTOSIZE`: If this flag is set, the window size is automatically adjusted to fit the display image and it is not possible to resize the window
   - `WINDOW_OPENGL`: This flag enables the OpenGL support

   Qt has a number of additional flags:

   - `WINDOW_FREERATIO` or `WINDOW_KEEPRATIO`: If `WINDOW_FREERATIO` is set, the image is adjusted with no respect for its ratio. If `WINDOW_FREERATIO` is set, the image is adjusted with respect to its ratio.
   - `WINDOW_GUI_NORMAL` or `WINDOW_GUI_EXPANDED`: The first flag facilitates a basic interface without the status bar and the toolbar. The second flag facilitates the most advanced graphical user interface, with the status bar and the toolbar.

   If we compile OpenCV with Qt, all the windows that we create are, by default, in the expanded interface, but we can use native interfaces and more basic ones adding the `CV_GUI_NORMAL` flag. By default, the flags are `WINDOW_AUTOSIZE`, `WINDOW_KEEPRATIO`, and `WINDOW_GUI_EXPANDED`.

5. When we create multiple windows, they are superimposed, but we can move the windows to any area of our desktop using the `moveWindow` function, as follows:

```
// Move window
moveWindow("Lena", 10, 10);
moveWindow("Photo", 520, 10);
```

6. In our code, we move the `Lena` window 10 pixels to the left, and 10 pixels up, and the `Photo` window 520 pixels to the left, and 10 pixels up:

```
// show images
imshow("Lena", lena);
imshow("Photo", photo);
// Resize window, only non autosize
resizeWindow("Lena", 512, 512);
```

7. After showing the images that we loaded previously using the imshow function, we resize the Lena window to 512 pixels, calling the resizeWindow function. This function has three parameters: the window name, width, and height.

 The specific window size is for the image area. Toolbars are not counted. Only windows without the WINDOW_AUTOSIZE flag enabled can be resized.

8. After waiting for a key press with the waitKey function, we are going to remove or delete our windows using the destroyWindow function, where the name of the window is the only parameter required:

```
waitKey(0);

// Destroy the windows
destroyWindow("Lena");
destroyWindow("Photo");
```

9. OpenCV has a function to remove all windows that we create in only one call. The function is called destroyAllWindows. To demonstrate how this works, we create 10 windows in our sample and await a key press. When the user presses any key, it destroys all the windows:

```
 // Create 10 windows
for(int i =0; i< 10; i++)
{
    ostringstream ss;
    ss << "Photo" << i;
    namedWindow(ss.str());
    moveWindow(ss.str(), 20*i, 20*i);
    imshow(ss.str(), photo);
}

waitKey(0);
// Destroy all windows
destroyAllWindows();
```

In any event, OpenCV handles the destruction of all windows automatically when the application is terminated, and it is not necessary to call this function at the end of our application.

The result of all this code can be seen in the following images across two steps. First, it shows two windows:

After pressing any key, the application continues and draws several windows changing their positions:

With a few lines of code, we are able to create and manipulate windows and show images. We are now ready to facilitate user interaction with images and add user interface controls.

Adding slider and mouse events to our interfaces

Mouse events and slider control are very useful in computer vision and OpenCV. Using these control users, we can interact directly with the interface and change the properties of the input images or variables. In this section, we are going to introduce the mouse events and slider controls for basic interactions. To facilitate proper understanding, we have created the following code, by means of which we are going to paint green circles in an image, using mouse events, and blur the image with the slider:

```
// Create a variable to save the position value in track
int blurAmount=15;

// Trackbar call back function
static void onChange(int pos, void* userInput);

//Mouse callback
static void onMouse(int event, int x, int y, int, void* userInput);

int main(int argc, const char** argv)
{
    // Read images
    Mat lena= imread("../lena.jpg");
    // Create windows
    namedWindow("Lena");
    // create a trackbar
    createTrackbar("Lena", "Lena", &blurAmount, 30, onChange, &lena);
    setMouseCallback("Lena", onMouse, &lena);

    // Call to onChange to init
    onChange(blurAmount, &lena);
    // wait app for a key to exit
    waitKey(0);
    // Destroy the windows
    destroyWindow("Lena");
    return 0;
}
```

Let's understand the code!

First, we create a variable to save the slider position. We need to save the slider position for access from other functions:

```
// Create a variable to save the position value in track
int blurAmount=15;
```

Now, we define our callbacks for our slider and mouse event, required for the OpenCV functions `setMouseCallback` **and** `createTrackbar`:

```
// Trackbar call back function
static void onChange(int pos, void* userInput);

//Mouse callback
static void onMouse(int event, int x, int y, int, void* userInput);
```

In the main function, we load an image and create a new window called `Lena`:

```
int main(int argc, const char** argv)
{
    // Read images
    Mat lena= imread("../lena.jpg");
    // Create windows
    namedWindow("Lena");
```

Now is the time to create the slider. OpenCV has the `createTrackbar` function to generate a slider with the following parameters in order:

1. Trackbar name.
2. Window name.
3. Integer pointer to use as a value; this parameter is optional. If it is set, the slider attains this position when created.
4. Maximum position on slider.
5. Callback function when the position of the slider changes.
6. User data to send to callback. It can be used to send data to callbacks without using global variables.

To this code, we add `trackbar` for the `Lena` window and call the `Lena` trackbar too in order to blur the image. The value of the trackbar is stored in the `blurAmount` integer that we pass as a pointer and set the maximum value of the bar to 30. We set up `onChange` as a callback function and send the lena mat image as user data:

```
// create a trackbar
createTrackbar("Lena", "Lena", &blurAmount, 30, onChange, &lena);
```

After creating the slider, we add the mouse events to paint circles when a user clicks the left button on the mouse. OpenCV has the `setMouseCallback` function. This function has three parameters:

- A window name where we get mouse events.

- A callback function to call when there is any mouse interaction.

- **User data**: this is any data that will be sent to the callback function when it's fired. In our example, we'll send the entire `Lena` image.

Using the following code, we can add a mouse callback to the `Lena` window and set up `onMouse` as a callback function, passing the lena mat image as user data:

```
setMouseCallback("Lena", onMouse, &lena);
```

To finalize the main function only, we need to initialize the image with the same parameter as the slider. To carry out the initialization, we only need to call the `onChange` callback function and wait for events before closing the windows with `destroyWindow`, as can be seen in the following code:

```
// Call to onChange to init
onChange(blurAmount, &lena);
// wait app for a key to exit
waitKey(0);
// Destroy the windows
destroyWindow("Lena");
```

The slider callback applies a basic blur filter to the image using the slider value as a blur quantity:

```
// Trackbar call back function
static void onChange(int pos, void* userData) {
    if(pos <= 0) return;
    // Aux variable for result
    Mat imgBlur;
    // Get the pointer input image
    Mat* img= (Mat*)userInput;
    // Apply a blur filter
    blur(*img, imgBlur, Size(pos, pos));
    // Show the result
    imshow("Lena", imgBlur);
}
```

This function checks whether the slider value is 0 using the variable pos. In this case, we do not apply the filter because it generates a bad execution. We cannot apply a 0 pixel blur either. After checking the slider value, we create an empty matrix called imgBlur to store the blur result. To retrieve the image sent through user data in the callback function, we have to cast void* userData to the correct image type pointer Mat*.

Now we have the correct variables to apply the blur filter. The blur function applies a basic median filter to an input image, *img in our case; to an output image, the last required parameter is the size of the blur kernel (a kernel is a small matrix used to calculate the means of convolution between the kernel and the image) that we want to apply. In our case, we are using a squared kernel of pos size. Finally, we only need to update the image interface using the imshow function.

The mouse events callback has five input parameters: the first parameter defines the event type; the second and third define the mouse position; the fourth parameter defines the wheel movement; and the fifth parameter defines the user input data.

The mouse event types are as follows:

Event type	Description
EVENT_MOUSEMOVE	When the user moves the mouse.
EVENT_LBUTTONDOWN	When the user clicks the left mouse button.
EVENT_RBUTTONDOWN	When the user clicks the right mouse button.
EVENT_MBUTTONDOWN	When the user clicks the middle mouse button.
EVENT_LBUTTONUP	When the user releases the left mouse button.
EVENT_RBUTTONUP	When the user releases the right mouse button.
EVENT_MBUTTONUP	When the user releases the middle mouse button.
EVENT_LBUTTONDBLCLK	When the user double-clicks the left mouse button.
EVENT_RBUTTONDBLCLK	When the user double-clicks the right mouse button.
EVENT_MBUTTONDBLCLK	When the user double-clicks the middle mouse button.
EVENTMOUSEWHEEL	When the user executes a vertical scroll with the mousewheel.
EVENT_MOUSEHWHEEL	When the user executes a horizontal scroll with the mousewheel.

In our sample, we only manage events that result from a left-click of the mouse, and any event other than EVENT_LBUTTONDOWN is discarded. After discarding other events, we obtain the input image like that with the slider callback, and with a circle in the image using the circle OpenCV function:

```
//Mouse callback
static void onMouse(int event, int x, int y, int, void* userInput)
{
    if(event != EVENT_LBUTTONDOWN)
            return;

    // Get the pointer input image
    Mat* img= (Mat*)userInput;
    // Draw circle
    circle(*img, Point(x, y), 10, Scalar(0,255,0), 3);

    // Call on change to get blurred image
    onChange(blurAmount, img);

}
```

Graphic user interface with Qt

The Qt user interface gives us more control and options to work with our images.

The interface is divided into the following three main areas:

- Toolbar
- Image area
- Status bar

We can see these three areas in the following picture. At the top of the image is the toolbar, the image is the main area, and the status bar can be seen at the bottom of the image:

The toolbar has the following buttons from left to right:

- Four buttons for panning
- Zoom x1
- Zoom x30, show labels
- Zoom in
- Zoom out
- Save current image
- Show properties

These options can be seen clearly in the following image:

The image area shows an image and a contextual menu when we push the right mouse button over the image. This area can show an overlay message at the top of the area using the `displayOverlay` function. This function accepts three parameters: the window name, the text that we want to show, and the period in milliseconds for which the overlay text is displayed. If this time is set to 0, the text never disappears:

```
// Display Overlay
displayOverlay("Lena", "Overlay 5secs", 5000);
```

We can see the result of the preceding code in the following image. You can see a small black box at the top of the image with the sentence **Overlay 5secs**:

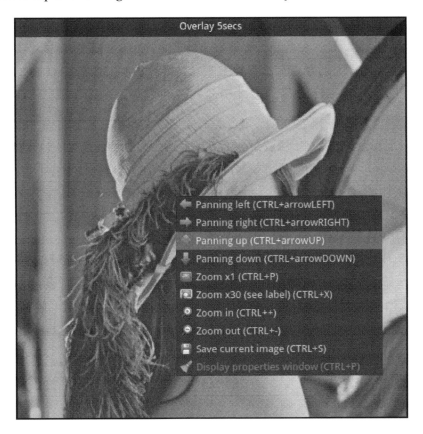

Finally, the status bar shows the bottom part of the window and shows the pixel value and position of the coordinates in the image:

We can use the status bar to show messages like an overlay. The function that can change the status bar message is `displayStatusBar`. This function has the same parameters as those of the overlay functions: the window name, the text to show, and the period of time for which to show it:

Adding buttons to the user interface

In the previous sections, we learned how to create normal or Qt interfaces and interact with them using the mouse and sliders, but we can create different types of buttons too.

Buttons are only supported in Qt windows.

The types of buttons supported by OpenCV Qt are as follows:

- Push button
- Checkbox
- RadioBox

The buttons only appear in the control panel. The control panel is an independent window per program where we can attach buttons and trackbars. To show the control panel, we can push the last toolbar button, right-click in any part of the Qt window and select the **Display properties** window, or use the *Ctrl + P* shortcut. Let's create a basic sample with buttons. The code is extensive, and we are going to explain the main function first and later each callback separately so as to understand everything better. The following code shows us the main code function that generates the user interface:

```
Mat img;
bool applyGray=false;
bool applyBlur=false;
bool applySobel=false;
...
int main(int argc, const char** argv)
{
    // Read images
    img= imread("../lena.jpg");
    // Create windows
    namedWindow("Lena");
    // create Buttons
    createButton("Blur", blurCallback, NULL, QT_CHECKBOX, 0);

    createButton("Gray",grayCallback,NULL,QT_RADIOBOX, 0);
    createButton("RGB",bgrCallback,NULL,QT_RADIOBOX, 1);

    createButton("Sobel",sobelCallback,NULL,QT_PUSH_BUTTON, 0);
    // wait app for a key to exit
    waitKey(0);
    // Destroy the windows
    destroyWindow("Lena");
    return 0;
}
```

We are going to apply thee types of filters: blur, a sobel filter, and a color conversion to gray. All these are optional and the user can choose each one using the buttons that we are going to create. Then, to get the status of each filter, we create three global Boolean variables:

```
bool applyGray=false;
bool applyBlur=false;
bool applySobel=false;
```

In the main function, after loading the image and creating the window, we have to use the `createButton` function to create each button.

There are three button types defined in OpenCV:

- QT_CHECKBOX
- QT_RADIOBOX
- QT_PUSH_BUTTON

Each button has five parameters with the following order:

1. The button name
2. A callback function
3. A pointer to user variable data passed to callback
4. The button type
5. The default initialized state used for the checkbox and RadioBox button types

Then, we create a blur checkbox button, two radio buttons for color conversion, and a push button for a sobel filter, as you can see in the following code:

```
// create Buttons
createButton("Blur", blurCallback, NULL, QT_CHECKBOX, 0);

createButton("Gray",grayCallback,NULL,QT_RADIOBOX, 0);
createButton("RGB",bgrCallback,NULL,QT_RADIOBOX, 1);

createButton("Sobel",sobelCallback,NULL,QT_PUSH_BUTTON, 0);
```

These are the most important parts of the main function. We are going to explore the `Callback` functions. Each `Callback` changes its status variable to call another function called `applyFilters` in order to add the filters activated to the input image:

```
void grayCallback(int state, void* userData)
{
    applyGray= true;
    applyFilters();
```

```
}
void bgrCallback(int state, void* userData)
{
    applyGray= false;
    applyFilters();
}

void blurCallback(int state, void* userData)
{
    applyBlur= (bool)state;
    applyFilters();
}

void sobelCallback(int state, void* userData)
{
    applySobel= !applySobel;
    applyFilters();
}
```

The `applyFilters` function checks the status variable for each filter:

```
void applyFilters(){
    Mat result;
    img.copyTo(result);
    if(applyGray){
        cvtColor(result, result, COLOR_BGR2GRAY);
    }
    if(applyBlur){
        blur(result, result, Size(5,5));
    }
    if(applySobel){
        Sobel(result, result, CV_8U, 1, 1);
    }
    imshow("Lena", result);
}
```

To change the color to gray, we use the `cvtColor` function which accepts three parameters: input image, output image, and the color conversion type.

The most useful color space conversions are as follows:

- RGB or BGR to gray (COLOR_RGB2GRAY, COLOR_BGR2GRAY)
- RGB or BGR to YcrCb (or YCC) (COLOR_RGB2YCrCb, COLOR_BGR2YCrCb)
- RGB or BGR to HSV (COLOR_RGB2HSV, COLOR_BGR2HSV)
- RGB or BGR to Luv (COLOR_RGB2Luv, COLOR_BGR2Luv)
- Gray to RGB or BGR (COLOR_GRAY2RGB, COLOR_GRAY2BGR)

We can see that the codes are easy to memorize.

 OpenCV works by default with the BGR format, and the color conversion is different for RGB and BGR, even when converted to gray. Some developers think that $R+G+B/3$ is true for gray, but the optimal gray value is called **luminosity** and has the formula $0,21*R + 0,72*G + 0,07*B$.

The blur filter was described in the previous section, and finally, if the `applySobel` variable is true, we apply the sobel filter. The sobel filter is an image derivate obtained using the sobel operator, commonly used to detect edges. OpenCV allows us to generate different derivates with kernel size, but the most common is a 3x3 kernel to calculate the x derivates or y derivate.

The most important sobel parameters are the following:

- Input image
- Output image
- Output image depth (`CV_8U`, `CV_16U`, `CV_32F`, `CV_64F`)
- Order of the derivate x
- Order of the derivate y
- Kernel size (a value of 3 by default)

To generate a 3 x 3 kernel and a first x order derivate, we have to use the following parameters:

```
Sobel(input, output, CV_8U, 1, 0);
```

The following parameters are used for y order derivates:

```
Sobel(input, output, CV_8U, 0, 1);
```

In our example, we use the x and y derivate simultaneously, overwriting the input. The following snippet shows how to generate the x and y derivates simultaneously, adding 1 in the fourth and fifth parameters:

```
Sobel(result, result, CV_8U, 1, 1);
```

The result of applying x and y derivatives simultaneously looks like following image applied to the **Lena** picture:

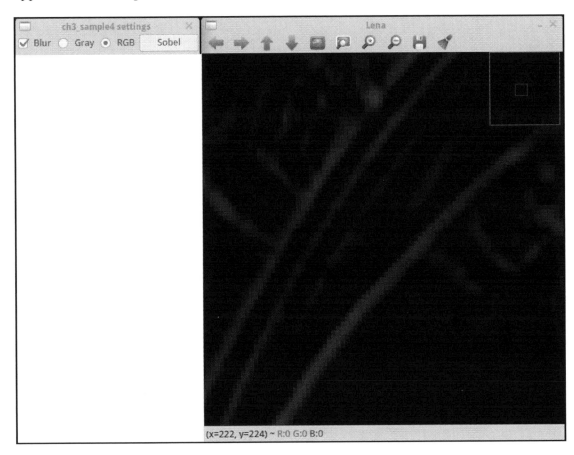

OpenGL support

OpenCV includes OpenGL support. OpenGL is a graphical library integrated in almost all graphical cards as a standard. OpenGL allows us to draw 2D up to complex 3D scenes. OpenCV includes OpenGL support due to the importance of representing 3D spaces in a number of tasks. To allow window support in OpenGL, we have to set up the WINDOW_OPENGL flag when we create the window using the namedWindow call.

The following code creates a window with OpenGL support and draws a rotate plane where we are going to show the web camera frames:

```
Mat frame;
GLfloat angle= 0.0;
GLuint texture;
VideoCapture camera;

int loadTexture() {

    if (frame.data==NULL) return -1;

    glBindTexture(GL_TEXTURE_2D, texture);
    glTexParameteri(GL_TEXTURE_2D,GL_TEXTURE_MAG_FILTER,GL_LINEAR);
    glTexParameteri(GL_TEXTURE_2D,GL_TEXTURE_MIN_FILTER,GL_LINEAR);
    glPixelStorei(GL_UNPACK_ALIGNMENT, 1);

    glTexImage2D(GL_TEXTURE_2D, 0, GL_RGB, frame.cols, frame.rows,0, GL_BGR,
GL_UNSIGNED_BYTE, frame.data);
    return 0;

}

void on_opengl(void* param)
{
    glLoadIdentity();
    // Load frame Texture
    glBindTexture(GL_TEXTURE_2D, texture);
    // Rotate plane before draw
    glRotatef(angle, 1.0f, 1.0f, 1.0f);
    // Create the plane and set the texture coordinates
    glBegin (GL_QUADS);
        // first point and coordinate texture
     glTexCoord2d(0.0,0.0);
     glVertex2d(-1.0,-1.0);
        // second point and coordinate texture
     glTexCoord2d(1.0,0.0);
     glVertex2d(+1.0,-1.0);
        // third point and coordinate texture
     glTexCoord2d(1.0,1.0);
     glVertex2d(+1.0,+1.0);
        // last point and coordinate texture
     glTexCoord2d(0.0,1.0);
     glVertex2d(-1.0,+1.0);
    glEnd();

}
```

```
int main(int argc, const char** argv)
{
    // Open WebCam
    camera.open(0);
    if(!camera.isOpened())
        return -1;

    // Create new windows
    namedWindow("OpenGL Camera", WINDOW_OPENGL);
    // Enable texture
    glEnable( GL_TEXTURE_2D );
    glGenTextures(1, &texture);
    setOpenGlDrawCallback("OpenGL Camera", on_opengl);
    while(waitKey(30)!='q'){
        camera >> frame;
        // Create first texture
        loadTexture();
        updateWindow("OpenGL Camera");
        angle =angle+4;
    }
    // Destroy the windows
    destroyWindow("OpenGL Camera");
    return 0;
}
```

Let's understand the code!

The first task is to create the required global variables, where we store the video capture, save the frames, and control the animation angle plane and the OpenGL texture:

```
Mat frame;
GLfloat angle= 0.0;
GLuint texture;
VideoCapture camera;
```

In our main function, we have to create the video camera capture to retrieve the camera frames:

```
camera.open(0);
    if(!camera.isOpened())
        return -1;
```

If the camera is opened correctly, we can create our window with OpenGL support using the WINDOW_OPENGL flag:

```
// Create new windows
namedWindow("OpenGL Camera", WINDOW_OPENGL);
```

In our example, we want to draw the images that come from the web camera in a plane; then, we need to enable the OpenGL textures:

```
// Enable texture
glEnable(GL_TEXTURE_2D);
```

Now we are ready to draw with OpenGL in our window, but we need to set up a draw OpenGL callback like a typical OpenGL application. OpenCV gives us the `setOpenGLDrawCallback` function which has two parameters – the window name and the callback function:

```
setOpenGlDrawCallback("OpenGL Camera", on_opengl);
```

With the OpenCV window and callback function defined, we need to create a loop to load the texture, update the window content calling the OpenGL draw callback, and finally update the angle position. To update the window content, we use the OpenCV function update window with the window name as a parameter:

```
while(waitKey(30)!='q'){
        camera >> frame;
        // Create first texture
        loadTexture();
        updateWindow("OpenGL Camera");
        angle =angle+4;
    }
```

We are in the loop when the user presses the *Q* key. Before compiling our application sample, we need to define the `loadTexture` function and our `on_opengl` callback draw function. The `loadTexture` function converts our `Mat` frame to an OpenGL texture image ready to load and use in each callback drawing. Before loading the image as a texture, we have to ensure that we have data in our frame matrix, checking that the data variable object is not empty:

```
if (frame.data==NULL) return -1;
```

If we have data in our matrix frame, then we can create the OpenGL texture binding and set the OpenGL texture parameter as a linear interpolation:

```
glGenTextures(1, &texture);

glBindTexture(GL_TEXTURE_2D, texture);
    glTexParameteri(GL_TEXTURE_2D,GL_TEXTURE_MAG_FILTER,GL_LINEAR);
    glTexParameteri(GL_TEXTURE_2D,GL_TEXTURE_MIN_FILTER,GL_LINEAR);
```

Now, we have to define how the pixels are stored in our matrix and generate the pixels with the OpenGL `glTexImage2D` function. It's very important to note that OpenGL uses the RGB format, and OpenCV the BGR format, by default, and we have to set up the correct format in this function:

```
glPixelStorei(GL_UNPACK_ALIGNMENT, 1);
glTexImage2D(GL_TEXTURE_2D, 0, GL_RGB, frame.cols, frame.rows,0, GL_BGR,
GL_UNSIGNED_BYTE, frame.data);
    return 0;
```

Now, we only need to finish drawing our plane on every callback when we call `updateWindow` in the main loop. We use the common OpenGL functions, and then we load the identity OpenGL matrix to reset all our previous changes:

```
glLoadIdentity();
```

We also have to bring the frame texture to memory:

```
    // Load Texture
    glBindTexture(GL_TEXTURE_2D, texture);
```

Before drawing our plane, we apply all transformations to our scene. In our case, we are going to rotate our plane in the 1, 1, 1 axis:

```
    // Rotate plane
    glRotatef(angle, 1.0f, 1.0f, 1.0f);
```

Now that we have the scene correctly set to draw our plane, we are going to draw quads faces (faces with four vertices) and use `glBegin (GL_QUADS)` for this purpose:

```
// Create the plane and set the texture coordinates
    glBegin (GL_QUADS);
```

Next, we will draw a plane centered in the 0, 0 position, which is 2 units in size. Then, we have to define the texture coordinate to use and the vertex position using the `glTextCoord2D` and `glVertex2D` functions:

```
    // first point and coordinate texture
glTexCoord2d(0.0,0.0);
glVertex2d(-1.0,-1.0);
    // seccond point and coordinate texture
glTexCoord2d(1.0,0.0);
glVertex2d(+1.0,-1.0);
    // third point and coordinate texture
glTexCoord2d(1.0,1.0);
glVertex2d(+1.0,+1.0);
    // last point and coordinate texture
```

```
glTexCoord2d(0.0,1.0);
glVertex2d(-1.0,+1.0);
   glEnd();
```

 This OpenGL code becomes obsolete, but it is appropriated to understand better the OpenCV and OpenGL integration without complex OpenGL code. By way of an introduction to modern OpenGL, read *Introduction to Modern OpenGL*, from *Packt Publishing*.

We can see the result in the following image:

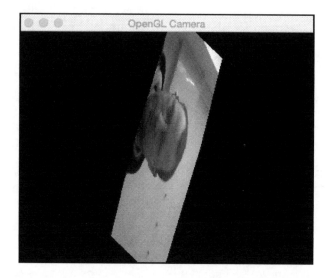

Summary

In this chapter, we learned how to create different types of user interfaces to show images or 3D interfaces using OpenGL. We learned how to create sliders and buttons or draw in 3D. We learned some basic image processing filters too with native OpenCV, but there are new open source alternatives that allow us to add more functionalities, such as cvui (https://dovyski.github.io/cvui/) or OpenCVGUI (https://damiles.github.io/OpenCVGUI/).

In the next chapter, we are going to construct a complete photo tool application where we will be applying all the knowledge that we have learned thus far. With the graphical user interface, we are going to learn how to apply multiple filters to an input image.

4
Delving into Histogram and Filters

In the last chapter, we learned the basics of user interfaces in OpenCV, using Qt libraries or native ones; we also learned how to use advanced OpenGL user interfaces. We learned about basic color conversions, and filters that allow us to create our first application. This chapter will introduce you to the following concepts:

- Histogram and histogram equalization
- Look-up tables
- Blur and median blur
- Canny filter
- Image-color equalization
- Understanding the conversion between image types

After we learn the basics of OpenCV and user interfaces, we are going to create our first complete application in this chapter, a basic photo tool, and cover the following topics:

- Generating a CMake script file
- Creating the graphical user interface
- Calculating and drawing a histogram
- Histogram equalization
- The lomography camera effect
- The cartoonize effect

This application will help us to understand how to create an entire project from scratch and understand the histogram concept. We will see how to equalize the histogram of the color image and create two effects, using a combination of filters and the use of look-up tables.

Technical requirements

This chapter requires familiarity with the basics of the C++ programming language. All the code used in this chapter can be downloaded from the following GitHub link: `https://github.com/PacktPublishing/Building-Computer-Vision-Projects-with-OpenCV4-and-CPlusPlus/tree/master/Chapter04`. The code can be executed on any operating system, though it is only tested on Ubuntu.

Check out the following video to see the Code in Action:
`http://bit.ly/2Sid17y`

Generating a CMake script file

Before we start creating our source file, we are going to generate the `CMakeLists.txt` file to allow us to compile our project, structure it, and execute it. The following CMake script is simple and basic but enough to compile and generate the executable:

```
cmake_minimum_required (VERSION 3.0)

PROJECT(Chapter4_Phototool)

set (CMAKE_CXX_STANDARD 11)

# Requires OpenCV
FIND_PACKAGE( OpenCV 4.0.0 REQUIRED )
MESSAGE("OpenCV version : ${OpenCV_VERSION}")

include_directories(${OpenCV_INCLUDE_DIRS})
link_directories(${OpenCV_LIB_DIR})

ADD_EXECUTABLE(${PROJECT_NAME} main.cpp)
TARGET_LINK_LIBRARIES(${PROJECT_NAME} ${OpenCV_LIBS})
```

The first line indicates the minimum CMake version required to generate our project, the second one sets the project name that we can use as the ${PROJECT_NAME} variable, and the third one sets the required C++ version; in our case, we require the **C++11** version, as we can see in the next snippet:

```
cmake_minimum_required (VERSION 3.0)

PROJECT(Chapter4_Phototool)

set (CMAKE_CXX_STANDARD 11)
```

Moreover, we require the OpenCV library. First, we need to find the library, and then we'll show a message on the OpenCV library version found with the MESSAGE function:

```
# Requires OpenCV
FIND_PACKAGE( OpenCV 4.0.0 REQUIRED )
MESSAGE("OpenCV version : ${OpenCV_VERSION}")
```

If the library, with a minimum version of 4.0, is found, then we include the headers and library files in our project:

```
include_directories(${OpenCV_INCLUDE_DIRS})
link_directories(${OpenCV_LIB_DIR})
```

Now, we only need to add the source files to compile and link with the OpenCV library. The project name variable is used as the executable name, and we use only a single source file, called main.cpp:

```
ADD_EXECUTABLE(${PROJECT_NAME} main.cpp)
TARGET_LINK_LIBRARIES(${PROJECT_NAME} ${OpenCV_LIBS})
```

Creating the graphical user interface

Before we start with the image processing algorithms, we create the main user interface for our application. We are going to use the Qt-based user interface to allow us to create single buttons. The application receives one input parameter to load the image to process, and we are going to create four buttons, as follows:

- **Show histogram**
- **Equalize histogram**
- **Lomography effect**
- **Cartoonize effect**

We can see the four results in the following screenshot:

Let's begin developing our project. First of all, we are going to include the OpenCV –
required headers, define an image matrix to store the input image, and create a constant
string to use the new command-line parser already available from OpenCV 3.0; in this
constant, we allow only two input parameters, `help` and the required image input:

```
// OpenCV includes
#include "opencv2/core/utility.hpp"
#include "opencv2/imgproc.hpp"
#include "opencv2/highgui.hpp"
using namespace cv;
// OpenCV command line parser functions
// Keys accepted by command line parser
const char* keys =
{
    "{help h usage ? | | print this message}"
     "{@image | | Image to process}"
};
```

The main function starts with the command-line parser variable; next, we set the about
instruction and print the help message. This line sets up the help instructions of our final
executable:

```
int main(int argc, const char** argv)
{
    CommandLineParser parser(argc, argv, keys);
     parser.about("Chapter 4. PhotoTool v1.0.0");
     //If requires help show
     if (parser.has("help"))
    {
        parser.printMessage();
        return 0;
    }
}
```

If the user doesn't require help, then we have to get the file path image in the `imgFile`
variable string and check that all required parameters are added with the `parser.check()`
function:

```
String imgFile= parser.get<String>(0);

// Check if params are correctly parsed in his variables
if (!parser.check())
{
    parser.printErrors();
    return 0;
}
```

Now, we can read the image file with the `imread` function, and then create the window in which the input image will be shown later with the `namedWindow` function:

```
// Load image to process
Mat img= imread(imgFile);

// Create window
namedWindow("Input");
```

With the image loaded and the window created, we only need to create the buttons for our interface and link them with the callback functions; each callback function is defined in the source code and we are going to explain these functions later in this chapter. We are going to create the buttons with the `createButton` function with the `QT_PUSH_BUTTON` constant to button style:

```
// Create UI buttons
createButton("Show histogram", showHistoCallback, NULL, QT_PUSH_BUTTON, 0);
createButton("Equalize histogram", equalizeCallback, NULL, QT_PUSH_BUTTON,
0);
createButton("Lomography effect", lomoCallback, NULL, QT_PUSH_BUTTON, 0);
createButton("Cartoonize effect", cartoonCallback, NULL, QT_PUSH_BUTTON,
0);
```

To finish our main function, we show the input image and wait for a key press to finish our application:

```
// Show image
imshow("Input", img);

waitKey(0);
return 0;
```

Now, we only have to define each callback function, and in the next sections, we are going to do just that.

Drawing a histogram

A histogram is a statistical graphic representation of variable distribution that allows us to understand the density estimation and probability distribution of data. A histogram is created by dividing the entire range of variable values into a small range of values, and then counting how many values fall into each interval.

If we apply this histogram concept to an image, it seems to be difficult to understand but, in fact, it is very simple. In a gray image, our variable values' ranges are each possible gray value (from 0 to 255), and the density is the number of pixels of the image that have this value. This means that we have to count the number of pixels of the image that have a value of 0, the number of pixels with a value of 1, and so on.

The callback function that shows the histogram of the input image is `showHistoCallback`; this function calculates the histogram of each channel image and shows the result of each histogram channel in a new image.

Now, check the following code:

```
void showHistoCallback(int state, void* userData)
{
    // Separate image in BRG
    vector<Mat> bgr;
    split(img, bgr);

    // Create the histogram for 256 bins
    // The number of possibles values [0..255]
    int numbins= 256;

    /// Set the ranges for B,G,R last is not included
    float range[] = { 0, 256 } ;
    const float* histRange = { range };

    Mat b_hist, g_hist, r_hist;

    calcHist(&bgr[0], 1, 0, Mat(), b_hist, 1, &numbins, &histRange);
    calcHist(&bgr[1], 1, 0, Mat(), g_hist, 1, &numbins, &histRange);
    calcHist(&bgr[2], 1, 0, Mat(), r_hist, 1, &numbins, &histRange);

    // Draw the histogram
    // We go to draw lines for each channel
    int width= 512;
    int height= 300;
    // Create image with gray base
    Mat histImage(height, width, CV_8UC3, Scalar(20,20,20));

    // Normalize the histograms to height of image
    normalize(b_hist, b_hist, 0, height, NORM_MINMAX);
    normalize(g_hist, g_hist, 0, height, NORM_MINMAX);
    normalize(r_hist, r_hist, 0, height, NORM_MINMAX);

    int binStep= cvRound((float)width/(float)numbins);
    for(int i=1; i< numbins; i++)
    {
```

```
        line(histImage,
                Point( binStep*(i-1), height-cvRound(b_hist.at<float>(i-1)
)),
                Point( binStep*(i), height-cvRound(b_hist.at<float>(i) )),
                Scalar(255,0,0)
            );
        line(histImage,
                Point(binStep*(i-1), height-
cvRound(g_hist.at<float>(i-1))),
                Point(binStep*(i), height-cvRound(g_hist.at<float>(i))),
                Scalar(0,255,0)
            );
        line(histImage,
                Point(binStep*(i-1), height-
cvRound(r_hist.at<float>(i-1))),
                Point(binStep*(i), height-cvRound(r_hist.at<float>(i))),
                Scalar(0,0,255)
            );
    }

    imshow("Histogram", histImage);

}
```

Let's understand how to extract each channel histogram and how to draw it. First, we need to create three matrices to process each input image channel. We use a vector-type variable to store each one and use the split OpenCV function to divide the input image among these three channels:

```
// Separate image in BRG
    vector<Mat> bgr;
    split(img, bgr);
```

Now, we are going to define the number of bins of our histogram, in our case, one per possible pixel value:

```
int numbins= 256;
```

Let's define our range of variables and create three matrices to store each histogram:

```
/// Set the ranges for B,G,R
float range[] = {0, 256} ;
const float* histRange = {range};

Mat b_hist, g_hist, r_hist;
```

We can calculate the histograms using the `calcHist` OpenCV function. This function has several parameters with this order:

- **The input image**: In our case, we use one image channel stored in the `bgr` vector
- **The number of images in the input to calculate the histogram**: In our case, we only use 1 image
- **The number channel dimensions used to compute the histogram**: We use 0 in our case
- The optional mask matrix.
- The variable to store the calculated histogram.
- **Histogram dimensionality**: This is the dimension of the space where the image (here, a gray plane) is taking its values, in our case 1
- **Number of bins to calculate**: In our case 256 bins, one per pixel value
- **Range of input variables**: In our case, from 0 to 255 possible pixels values

Our `calcHist` function for each channel looks as follows:

```
calcHist(&bgr[0], 1, 0, Mat(), b_hist, 1, &numbins, &histRange );
calcHist(&bgr[1], 1, 0, Mat(), g_hist, 1, &numbins, &histRange );
calcHist(&bgr[2], 1, 0, Mat(), r_hist, 1, &numbins, &histRange );
```

Now that we have calculated each channel histogram, we have to draw each one and show it to the user. To do this, we are going to create a color image that is 512 by 300 pixels in size:

```
// Draw the histogram
// We go to draw lines for each channel
int width= 512;
int height= 300;
// Create image with gray base
Mat histImage(height, width, CV_8UC3, Scalar(20,20,20));
```

Before we draw the histogram values into our image, we are going to normalize the histogram matrices between the minimum value, 0, and a maximum value; the maximum value is the same as the height of our output histogram image:

```
// Normalize the histograms to height of image
normalize(b_hist, b_hist, 0, height, NORM_MINMAX);
normalize(g_hist, g_hist, 0, height, NORM_MINMAX);
normalize(r_hist, r_hist, 0, height, NORM_MINMAX);
```

Now we have to draw a line from bin 0 to bin 1, and so on. Between each bin, we have to calculate how many pixels there are; then, a `binStep` variable is calculated by dividing the width by the number of bins. Each small line is drawn from horizontal position i-1 to i; the vertical position is the histogram value in the corresponding i, and it is drawn with the color channel representation:

```
int binStep= cvRound((float)width/(float)numbins);
    for(int i=1; i< numbins; i++)
    {
        line(histImage,
                Point(binStep*(i-1), height-
cvRound(b_hist.at<float>(i-1))),
                Point(binStep*(i), height-cvRound(b_hist.at<float>(i))),
                Scalar(255,0,0)
            );
        line(histImage,
                Point(binStep*(i-1), height-
cvRound(g_hist.at<float>(i-1))),
                Point( binStep*(i), height-cvRound(g_hist.at<float>(i))),
                Scalar(0,255,0)
            );
        line(histImage,
                Point(binStep*(i-1), height-
cvRound(r_hist.at<float>(i-1))),
                Point( binStep*(i), height-cvRound(r_hist.at<float>(i))),
                Scalar(0,0,255)
            );
    }
```

Finally, we show the histogram image with the `imshow` function:

```
imshow("Histogram", histImage);
```

This is the result for the `lena.png` image:

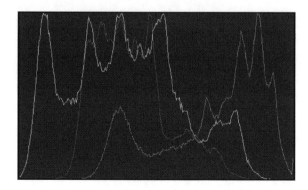

Image color equalization

In this section, we are going to learn how to equalize a color image. Image equalization, or histogram equalization, tries to obtain a histogram with a uniform distribution of values. The result of equalization is an increase in the contrast of an image. Equalization allows lower local contrast areas to gain high contrast, spreading out the most frequent intensities. This method is very useful when the image is extremely dark or bright and there is a very small difference between the background and foreground. Using histogram equalization, we increase the contrast and the details that are over- or under-exposed. This technique is very useful in medical images, such as X-rays.

However, there are two main disadvantages to this method: the increase in background noise and a consequent decrease in useful signals. We can see the effect of equalization in the following photograph, and the histogram changes and spreads when increasing the image contrast:

Let's implement our equalization histogram; we are going to implement it in the `Callback` function defined in the user interface's code:

```
void equalizeCallback(int state, void* userData)
{
    Mat result;
    // Convert BGR image to YCbCr
    Mat ycrcb;
```

```
            cvtColor(img, ycrcb, COLOR_BGR2YCrCb);

            // Split image into channels
            vector<Mat> channels;
            split(ycrcb, channels);
            // Equalize the Y channel only
            equalizeHist(channels[0], channels[0]);

            // Merge the result channels
            merge(channels, ycrcb);

            // Convert color ycrcb to BGR
            cvtColor(ycrcb, result, COLOR_YCrCb2BGR);

            // Show image
            imshow("Equalized", result);
    }
```

To equalize a color image, we only have to equalize the luminance channel. We can do this
with each color channel but the result is not usable. Alternatively, we can use any other
color image format, such as **HSV** or **YCrCb**, that separates the luminance component in an
individual channel. Thus, we choose **YCrCb** and use the Y channel (luminance) to equalize.
Then, we follow these steps:

1. Convert or input the **BGR** image into **YCrCb** using the `cvtColor` function:

```
        Mat result;
        // Convert BGR image to YCbCr
        Mat ycrcb;
        cvtColor(img, ycrcb, COLOR_BGR2YCrCb);
```

2. Split the **YCrCb** image into different channels matrix:

```
        // Split image into channels
        vector<Mat> channels;
        split(ycrcb, channels);
```

3. Equalize the histogram only in the Y channel, using the `equalizeHist` function
which has only two parameters, the input and output matrices:

```
        // Equalize the Y channel only
        equalizeHist(channels[0], channels[0]);
```

4. Merge the resulting channels and convert them into the **BGR** format to show the
user the result:

```
        // Merge the result channels
        merge(channels, ycrcb);
```

```
    // Convert color ycrcb to BGR
    cvtColor(ycrcb, result, COLOR_YCrCb2BGR);

    // Show image
    imshow("Equalized", result);
```

The process applied to a low-contrast `Lena` image will have the following result:

Lomography effect

In this section, we are going to create another image effect, which is a photograph effect that is very common in different mobile applications, such as Google Camera or Instagram. We are going to discover how to use a **look-up table** (LUT). We will go through LUTs later in this same section. We are going to learn how to add an over image, in this case a dark halo, to create our desired effect. The function that implements this effect is the `lomoCallback` callback and it has the following code:

```
    void lomoCallback(int state, void* userData)
    {
        Mat result;
```

```
        const double exponential_e = std::exp(1.0);
        // Create Look-up table for color curve effect
        Mat lut(1, 256, CV_8UC1);
        for (int i=0; i<256; i++)
        {
            float x= (float)i/256.0;
            lut.at<uchar>(i)= cvRound( 256 * (1/(1 + pow(exponential_e, -
((x-0.5)/0.1)) )) );
        }
        // Split the image channels and apply curve transform only to red
channel
        vector<Mat> bgr;
        split(img, bgr);
        LUT(bgr[2], lut, bgr[2]);
        // merge result
        merge(bgr, result);
        // Create image for halo dark
        Mat halo(img.rows, img.cols, CV_32FC3, Scalar(0.3,0.3,0.3) );
        // Create circle
        circle(halo, Point(img.cols/2, img.rows/2), img.cols/3, Scalar(1,1,1),
-1);
        blur(halo, halo, Size(img.cols/3, img.cols/3));
        // Convert the result to float to allow multiply by 1 factor
        Mat resultf;
        result.convertTo(resultf, CV_32FC3);
        // Multiply our result with halo
        multiply(resultf, halo, resultf);
        // convert to 8 bits
        resultf.convertTo(result, CV_8UC3);

        // show result
        imshow("Lomography", result);
}
```

Let's look at how the lomography effect works and how to implement it. The lomography effect is divided into different steps, but in our example, we did a very simple lomography effect with two steps:

1. A color manipulation effect by using a look-up table to apply a curve to the red channel
2. A vintage effect by applying a dark halo to the image

The first step was to manipulate the red color with a curve transform by applying the following function:

$$\frac{1}{1 + e^{-\frac{x - 0.5}{s}}}$$

This formula generates a curve that makes the dark values darker and the light values lighter, where **x** is the possible pixels value (0 to 255) and **s** is a constant that we set to 0.1 in our example. A lower constant value that generates pixels with values lower than 128 is very dark, and over 128 is very bright. Values near to 1 convert the curve into a line and do not generate our desired effect:

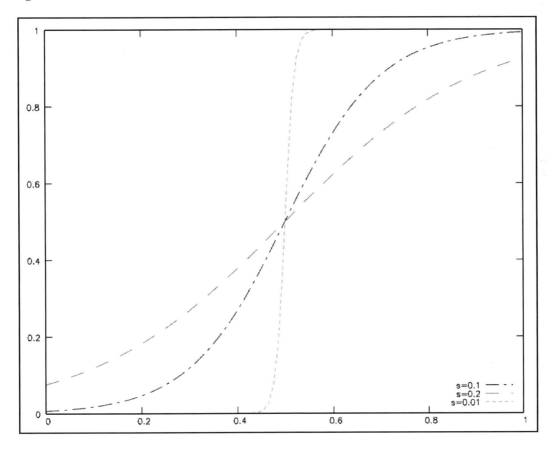

This function is very easy to implement by applying an LUT. An LUT is a vector or table that returns a preprocessed value for a given value to perform computation in the memory. An LUT is a common technique used to spare CPU cycles by avoiding performing costly computations repeatedly. Instead of calling the `exponential/divide` function for each pixel, we perform it only once for each possible pixel value (`256` times) and store the result in a table. Thus, we have saved CPU time at the cost of a bit of memory. While this may not make a great difference on a standard PC with small image sizes, this makes a huge one for CPU-limited hardware, such as Raspberry Pi.

For example, in our case, if we want to apply a function for every pixel in our image, then we have to make *width* x *height* operations; for example, in 100 x 100 pixels, there will be 10,000 calculations. If we can pre-calculate all possible results for all possible inputs, we can create the LUT table. In an image, there are only **256** possible values as a pixel value. If we want to change the color by applying a function, we can pre-calculate the 256 values and save them in an LUT vector. In our sample code, we define the E variable and create an `lut` matrix of `1` row and `256` columns. Then, we do a loop over all possible pixel values by applying our formula and saving it into an `lut` variable:

```
const double exponential_e = std::exp(1.0);
// Create look-up table for color curve effect
Mat lut(1, 256, CV_8UC1);
Uchar* plut= lut.data;
for (int i=0; i<256; i++)
{
    double x= (double)i/256.0;
    plut[i]= cvRound( 256.0 * (1.0/(1.0 + pow(exponential_e, -
((x-0.5)/0.1)) )) );
}
```

As we mentioned earlier in this section, we don't apply the function to all channels; thus, we need to split our input image by channels using the `split` function:

```
// Split the image channels and apply curve transform only to red channel
vector<Mat> bgr;
split(img, bgr);
```

We then apply our `lut` table variable to the red channel. OpenCV gives us the LUT function, which has three parameters:

- Input image
- Matrix of look-up table
- Output image

Then, our call to the LUT function and red channel looks like this:

```
LUT(bgr[2], lut, bgr[2]);
```

Now, we only have to merge our computed channels:

```
// merge result
merge(bgr, result);
```

The first step is done and we only have to create the dark halo to finish our effect. Then, we create a gray image with a white circle inside, with the same input image size:

```
// Create image for halo dark
Mat halo(img.rows, img.cols, CV_32FC3, Scalar(0.3,0.3,0.3));
// Create circle
circle(halo, Point(img.cols/2, img.rows/2), img.cols/3, Scalar(1,1,1),
-1);
```

Check out the following screenshot:

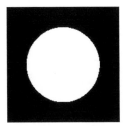

If we apply this image to our input image, we will get a strong change from dark to white; thus, we can apply a big blur using the `blur` filter function to our circle halo image to get a smooth effect:

```
blur(halo, halo, Size(img.cols/3, img.cols/3));
```

The image will be altered to give us the following result:

Now, if we have to apply this halo to our image from step 1, an easy way to do this is to multiply both images. However, we will have to convert our input image from an 8-bit image to a 32-bit float, because we need to multiply our blurred image, which has values in the 0 to 1 range, with our input image, which has integer values. The following code will do it for us:

```
// Convert the result to float to allow multiply by 1 factor
Mat resultf;
result.convertTo(resultf, CV_32FC3);
```

After converting our image, we only need to multiply each matrix per element:

```
// Multiply our result with halo
multiply(resultf, halo, resultf);
```

Finally, we will convert the float image matrix result to an 8-bit image matrix:

```
// convert to 8 bits
resultf.convertTo(result, CV_8UC3);

// show result
imshow("Lomograpy", result);
```

This will be the result:

Cartoonize effect

The last section of this chapter is dedicated to creating another effect, called **cartoonize**; the purpose of this effect is to create an image that looks like a cartoon. To do this, we divide the algorithm into two steps: **edge detection** and **color filtering**.

The `cartoonCallback` function defines this effect, which has the following code:

```
void cartoonCallback(int state, void* userData)
{
    /** EDGES **/
    // Apply median filter to remove possible noise
    Mat imgMedian;
    medianBlur(img, imgMedian, 7);

    // Detect edges with canny
    Mat imgCanny;
    Canny(imgMedian, imgCanny, 50, 150);
    // Dilate the edges
    Mat kernel= getStructuringElement(MORPH_RECT, Size(2,2));
    dilate(imgCanny, imgCanny, kernel);

    // Scale edges values to 1 and invert values
    imgCanny= imgCanny/255;
    imgCanny= 1-imgCanny;
    // Use float values to allow multiply between 0 and 1
    Mat imgCannyf;
    imgCanny.convertTo(imgCannyf, CV_32FC3);

    // Blur the edgest to do smooth effect
    blur(imgCannyf, imgCannyf, Size(5,5));

    /** COLOR **/
    // Apply bilateral filter to homogenizes color
    Mat imgBF;
    bilateralFilter(img, imgBF, 9, 150.0, 150.0);

    // truncate colors
    Mat result= imgBF/25;
    result= result*25;

    /** MERGES COLOR + EDGES **/
    // Create a 3 channles for edges
    Mat imgCanny3c;
    Mat cannyChannels[]={ imgCannyf, imgCannyf, imgCannyf};
    merge(cannyChannels, 3, imgCanny3c);
```

```
// Convert color result to float
Mat resultf;
result.convertTo(resultf, CV_32FC3);

// Multiply color and edges matrices
multiply(resultf, imgCanny3c, resultf);

// convert to 8 bits color
resultf.convertTo(result, CV_8UC3);

// Show image
imshow("Result", result);

}
```

The first step is to detect the most important *edges* of the image. We need to remove noise from the input image before detecting the edges. There are several ways to do it. We are going to use a median filter to remove all possible small noise, but we can use other methods, such as Gaussian blur. The OpenCV function is medianBlur, which accepts three parameters: input image, output image, and the kernel size (a kernel is a small matrix used to apply some mathematical operation, such as convolutional means, to an image):

```
Mat imgMedian;
medianBlur(img, imgMedian, 7);
```

After removing any possible noise, we detect the strong edges with the Canny filter:

```
// Detect edges with canny
Mat imgCanny;
Canny(imgMedian, imgCanny, 50, 150);
```

The Canny filter accepts the following parameters:

- Input image
- Output image
- First threshold
- Second threshold
- Sobel size aperture
- Boolean value to indicate whether we need to use a more accurate image gradient magnitude

The smallest value between the first threshold and the second threshold is used for edge linking. The largest value is used to find initial segments of strong edges. The sobel size aperture is the kernel size for the sobel filter that will be used in the algorithm. After detecting edges, we are going to apply a small dilation to join broken edges:

```
// Dilate the edges
Mat kernel= getStructuringElement(MORPH_RECT, Size(2,2));
dilate(imgCanny, imgCanny, kernel);
```

Similar to what we did in the lomography effect, if we need to multiply our edges' result image with the color image, then we require the pixel values to be in the 0 and 1 range. For this, we will divide the canny result by 256 and invert the edges to black:

```
// Scale edges values to 1 and invert values
imgCanny= imgCanny/255;
imgCanny= 1-imgCanny;
```

We will also transform the canny 8 unsigned bit pixel format to a float matrix:

```
// Use float values to allow multiply between 0 and 1
Mat imgCannyf;
imgCanny.convertTo(imgCannyf, CV_32FC3);
```

To give a cool result, we can blur the edges, and to give smooth result lines, we can apply a `blur` filter:

```
// Blur the edgest to do smooth effect
blur(imgCannyf, imgCannyf, Size(5,5));
```

The first step of the algorithm is finished, and now we are going to work with the color. To get a cartoon look, we are going to use the `bilateral` filter:

```
// Apply bilateral filter to homogenizes color
Mat imgBF;
bilateralFilter(img, imgBF, 9, 150.0, 150.0);
```

The `bilateral` filter is a filter that reduces the noise of an image while keeping the edges. With appropriate parameters, which we will explore later, we can get a cartoonish effect.

The `bilateral` filter's parameters are as follows:

- Input image
- Output image
- Diameter of pixel neighborhood; if it's set to negative, it is computed from a sigma space value

- Sigma color value
- Sigma coordinate space

 With a diameter greater than five, the `bilateral` filter starts to become slow. With sigma values greater than 150, a cartoonish effect appears.

To create a stronger cartoonish effect, we truncate the possible color values to 10 by multiplying and dividing the pixels values:

```
// truncate colors
Mat result= imgBF/25;
result= result*25;
```

Finally, we have to merge the color and edges results. Then, we have to create a three-channel image as follows:

```
// Create a 3 channles for edges
Mat imgCanny3c;
Mat cannyChannels[]={ imgCannyf, imgCannyf, imgCannyf};
merge(cannyChannels, 3, imgCanny3c);
```

We can convert our color result image to a 32-bit float image and then multiply both images per element:

```
// Convert color result to float
Mat resultf;
result.convertTo(resultf, CV_32FC3);

// Multiply color and edges matrices
multiply(resultf, imgCanny3c, resultf);
```

Finally, we only need to convert our image to 8 bits and then show the resulting image to the user:

```
// convert to 8 bits color
resultf.convertTo(result, CV_8UC3);

// Show image
imshow("Result", result);
```

In the next screenshot, we can see the input image (left image) and the result of applying the cartoonize effect (right image):

Summary

In this chapter, we saw how to create a complete project that manipulates images by applying different effects. We also split a color image into multiple matrices to apply effects to only one channel. We saw how to create look-up tables, merge multiple matrices into one, use the `Canny` and `bilateral` filters, draw circles, and multiply images to get halo effects.

In the next chapter, we will learn how to do object inspection, and how to segment an image into different parts and detect those parts.

5
Automated Optical Inspection, Object Segmentation, and Detection

In Chapter 4, *Delving into Histogram and Filters*, we learned about histograms and filters, which allow us to understand image manipulation and create a photo application.

In this chapter, we are going to introduce the basic concepts of object segmentation and detection. This means isolating the objects that appear in an image for future processing and analysis.

This chapter introduces the following topics:

- Noise removal
- Light/background removal basics
- Thresholding
- Connected components for object segmentation
- Finding contours for object segmentation

Many industries use complex computer vision systems and hardware. Computer vision tries to detect problems and minimize errors produced in the production process, improving the quality of final products.

In this sector, the name for this computer vision task is **Automated Optical Inspection (AOI)**. This name appears in the inspection of printed circuit board manufacturers, where one or more cameras scan each circuit to detect critical failures and quality defects. This nomenclature was used in other manufacturing industries so that they could use optical camera systems and computer vision algorithms to increase product quality. Nowadays, optical inspection using different camera types (infrared or 3D cameras), depending on the requirements, and complex algorithms are used in thousands of industries for different purposes such as defect detection, classification, and so on.

Technical requirements

This chapter requires familiarity with the basic C++ programming language. All of the code that's used in this chapter can be downloaded from the following GitHub link: `https://github.com/PacktPublishing/Building-Computer-Vision-Projects-with-OpenCV4-and-CPlusPlus/tree/master/Chapter05`. The code can be executed on any operating system, though it is only tested on Ubuntu.

Check out the following video to see the Code in Action:
`http://bit.ly/2DRbMbz`

Isolating objects in a scene

In this chapter, we are going to introduce the first step in an AOI algorithm and try to isolate different parts or objects in a scene. We are going to take the example of the object detection and classification of three object types (screw, packing ring, and nut) and develop them in this chapter and `Chapter` 6, *Learning Object Classification*.

Imagine that we are in a company that produces these three objects. All of them are in the same carrier tape. Our objective is to detect each object in the carrier tape and classify each one to allow a robot to put each object on the correct shelf:

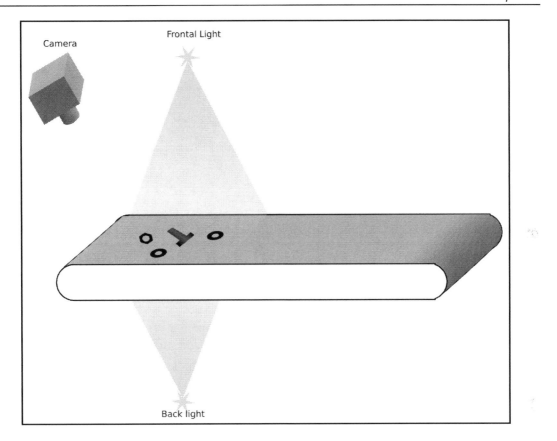

In this chapter, we are going to learn how to isolate each object and detect its position in the image in pixels. In the next chapter, we are going to learn how to classify each isolated object to recognize if it is a nut, screw, or a packing ring.

In the following screenshot, we show our desired result, where there are a few objects in the left image. In the right image, we have drawn each one in a different color, showing different features such as area, height, width, and contour size:

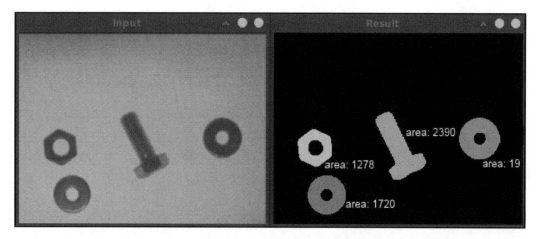

To reach this result, we are going to follow different steps that allow us to understand and organize our algorithms better. We can see these steps in the following diagram:

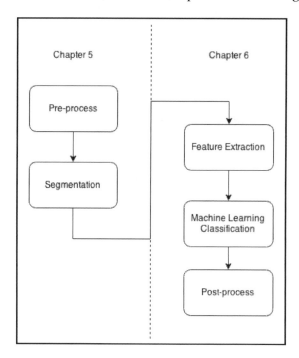

Our application will be divided into two chapters. In this chapter, we are going to develop and understand the preprocessing and segmentation steps. In Chapter 6, *Learning Object Classification*, we are going to extract the characteristics of each segmented object and train our machine learning system/algorithm on how to recognize each object class.

Our preprocessing steps will be divided into three more subsets:

- **Noise Removal**
- **Light Removal**
- **Binarization**

In the segmentation step, we are going to use two different algorithms:

- Contour detection
- **Connected components** extraction (labeling)

We can see these steps and the application flow in the following diagram:

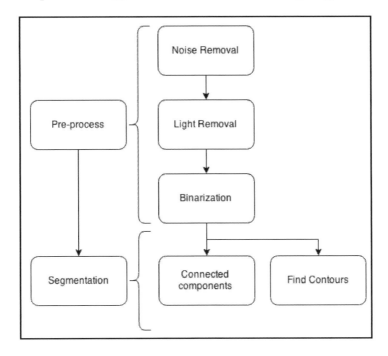

Now, it's time to start the preprocessing step so that we can get the best **Binarization** image by removing the noise and lighting effects. This minimizes any possible detection errors.

Creating an application for AOI

To create our new application, we require a few input parameters. When a user executes the application, all of them are optional, excluding the input image to process. The input parameters are as follows:

- Input image to process
- Light image pattern
- Light operation, where a user can choose between difference or divide operations
- If the user sets 0 as a value, the difference operation is applied
- If the user set 1 as a value, the division operation is applied
- Segmentation, where the user can choose between connected components with or without statistics and find contour methods
- If the user sets 1 as the input value, the connected components method for segment is applied
- If the user sets 2 as the input value, the connected components method with the statistics area is applied
- If the user sets 3 as the input value, the find contours method is applied for Segmentation

To enable this user selection, we are going to use the command line parser class with the following keys:

```
// OpenCV command line parser functions
// Keys accepted by command line parser
const char* keys =
{
   "{help h usage ? | | print this message}"
   "{@image || Image to process}"
   "{@lightPattern || Image light pattern to apply to image input}"
   "{lightMethod | 1 | Method to remove background light, 0 difference, 1 div }"
   "{segMethod | 1 | Method to segment: 1 connected Components, 2 connected components with stats, 3 find Contours }"
};
```

We are going to use the command line parser class in the main function by checking the parameters. The CommandLineParser is explained in Chapter 2, *An Introduction to the Basics of OpenCV*, in the *Reading videos and cameras* section:

```
int main(int argc, const char** argv)
{
   CommandLineParser parser(argc, argv, keys);
```

```
parser.about("Chapter 5. PhotoTool v1.0.0");
//If requires help show
if (parser.has("help"))
{
    parser.printMessage();
    return 0;
}

String img_file= parser.get<String>(0);
String light_pattern_file= parser.get<String>(1);
auto method_light= parser.get<int>("lightMethod");
auto method_seg= parser.get<int>("segMethod");
// Check if params are correctly parsed in his variables
if (!parser.check())
{
    parser.printErrors();
    return 0;
}
```

After parsing our command-line user data, we need to check the input image has been loaded correctly. We then load the image and check it has data:

```
// Load image to process
  Mat img= imread(img_file, 0);
  if(img.data==NULL){
    cout << "Error loading image "<< img_file << endl;
    return 0;
  }
```

Now, we are ready to create our AOI process of segmentation. We are going to start with the preprocessing task.

Preprocessing the input image

This section introduces some of the most common techniques that we can apply for preprocessing images in the context of object segmentation/detection. The preprocessing is the first change we make to a new image before we start working and extracting the information we require from it. Normally, in the preprocessing step, we try to minimize the image noise, light conditions, or image deformation due to a camera lens. These steps minimize errors while detecting objects or segments in our image.

Noise removal

If we don't remove the noise, we can detect more objects than we expect because noise is normally represented as small points in the image and can be segmented as an object. The sensor and scanner circuit normally produces this noise. This variation of brightness or color can be represented in different types, such as Gaussian noise, spike noise, and shot noise.

There are different techniques that can be used to remove the noise. Here, we are going to use a smooth operation, but depending on the type of noise, some are better than others. A median filter is normally used for removing salt-and-pepper noise; for example, consider the following image:

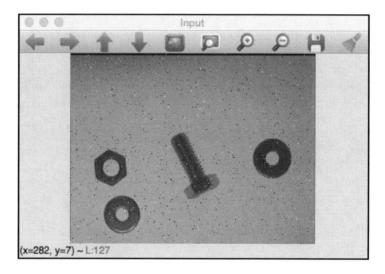

The preceding image is the original input with salt-and-pepper noise. If we apply a median blur, we get an awesome result in which we lose small details. For example, we lose the borders of the screw, but we maintain perfect edges. See the result in the following image:

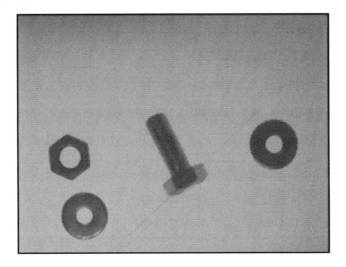

If we apply a box filter or Gaussian filter, the noise is not removed but made smooth, and the details of the objects are lost and smoothened too. See the following image for the result:

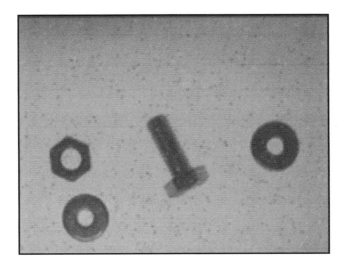

OpenCV brings us the `medianBlur` function, which requires three parameters:

- An input image with the 1, 3, or 4 channel's image. When the kernel size is bigger than 5, the image depth can only be `CV_8U`.
- An output image, which is the resulting image on applying median blur with the same type and depth as the input.

- Kernel size, which is an aperture size greater than 1 and odd, for example, 3, 5, 7, and so on.

The following code is used to remove noise:

```
Mat img_noise;
medianBlur(img, img_noise, 3);
```

Removing the background using the light pattern for segmentation

In this section, we are going to develop a basic algorithm that will enable us to remove the background using a light pattern. This preprocessing gives us better segmentation. The input image without noise is as follows:

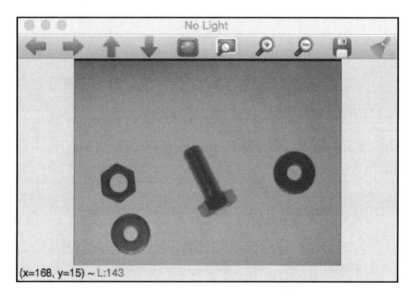

If we apply a basic threshold, we will obtain an image result like this:

We can see that the top image artifact has a lot of white noise. If we apply a light pattern and background removal technique, we can obtain an awesome result in which we can see that there are no artifacts in the top of image, like the previous threshold operation, and we will obtain better results when we have to segment. We can see the result of background removal and thresholding in the following image:

Now, how can we remove the light from our image? This is very simple: we only need a picture of our scenario without any objects, taken from exactly the same position and under the same lighting conditions that the other images were taken under; this is a very common technique in AOI because the external conditions are supervised and well-known. The image result for our case is similar to the following image:

Now, using a simple mathematical operation, we can remove this light pattern. There are two options for removing it:

- Difference
- Division

The difference option is the simplest approach. If we have the light pattern L and the image picture I, the resulting removal R is the difference between them:

```
R= L-I
```

This division is a bit more complex, but simple at the same time. If we have the light pattern matrix L and the image picture matrix I, the result removal R is as follows:

```
R= 255*(1-(I/L))
```

In this case, we divide the image by the light pattern, and we have the assumption that if our light pattern is white and the objects are darker than the background carrier tape, then the image pixel values are always the same or lower than the light pixel values. The result we obtain from I/L is between 0 and 1. Finally, we invert the result of this division to get the same color direction range and multiply it by 255 to get values within the range of 0-255.

In our code, we are going to create a new function called `removeLight` with the following parameters:

- An input image to remove the light/background
- A light pattern, `Mat`
- A method, with a `0` value for difference and `1` for division

The result is a new image matrix without light/background. The following code implements the removal of the background through the use of the light pattern:

```
Mat removeLight(Mat img, Mat pattern, int method)
{
  Mat aux;
  // if method is normalization
  if(method==1)
  {
    // Require change our image to 32 float for division
    Mat img32, pattern32;
    img.convertTo(img32, CV_32F);
    pattern.convertTo(pattern32, CV_32F);
    // Divide the image by the pattern
    aux= 1-(img32/pattern32);
    // Convert 8 bits format and scale
    aux.convertTo(aux, CV_8U, 255);
  }else{
    aux= pattern-img;
  }
  return aux;
}
```

Let's explore this. After creating the `aux` variable to save the result, we select the method chosen by the user and pass the parameter to the function. If the method that was selected is `1`, we apply the division method.

The division method requires a 32-bit float of images to allow us to divide the images and not truncate the numbers into integers. The first step is to convert the image and light pattern mat to floats of 32 bits. To convert images of this format, we can use the `convertTo` function of the `Mat` class. This function accepts four parameters; the output converted image and the format you wish to convert to the required parameters, but you can define alpha and beta parameters, which allow you to scale and shift the values following the next function, where *O* is the output image and *I* the input image:

$O(x,y)=cast<Type>(\alpha * I(x,y)+\beta)$

The following code changes the image to 32-bit float:

```
// Required to change our image to 32 float for division
Mat img32, pattern32;
img.convertTo(img32, CV_32F);
pattern.convertTo(pattern32, CV_32F);
```

Now, we can carry out the mathematical operations on our matrix as we described, by dividing the image by the pattern and inverting the result:

```
// Divide the image by the pattern
aux= 1-(img32/pattern32);
```

Now, we have the result but it is required to return it to an 8-bit depth image, and then use the convert function as we did previously to convert the image's mat and scale from 0 to 255 using the alpha parameter:

```
// Convert 8 bits format
aux.convertTo(aux, CV_8U, 255);
```

Now, we can return the aux variable with the result. For the difference method, the development is very easy because we don't have to convert our images; we only need to apply the difference between the pattern and image and return it. If we don't assume that the pattern is equal to or greater than an image, then we will require a few checks and truncate values that can be less than 0 or greater than 255:

```
aux= pattern-img;
```

The following images are the results of applying the image light pattern to our input image:

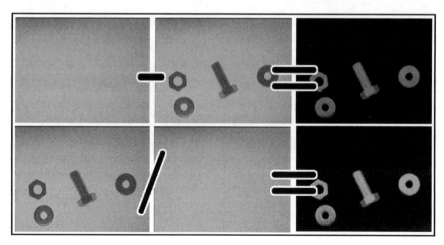

In the results that we obtain, we can check how the light gradient and the possible artifacts are removed. But what happens when we don't have a light/background pattern? There are a few different techniques to obtain this; we are going to present the most basic one here. Using a filter, we can create one that can be used, but there are better algorithms to learn about the background of images where the pieces appear in different areas. This technique sometimes requires a background estimation image initialization, where our basic approach can play very well. These advanced techniques will be explored in Chapter 8, *Video Surveillance, Background Modeling, and Morphological Operations*. To estimate the background image, we are going to use a blur with a large kernel size applied to our input image. This is a common technique used in **optical character recognition (OCR)**, where the letters are thin and small relative to the whole document, allowing us to do an approximation of the light patterns in the image. We can see the light/background pattern reconstruction in the left-hand image and the ground truth in the right-hand:

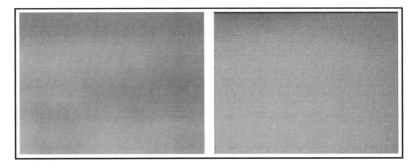

We can see that there are minor differences in the light patterns, but this result is enough to remove the background. We can also see the result in the following image when using different images. In the following image, the result of applying the image difference between the original input image and the estimated background image computed with the previous approach is depicted:

The `calculateLightPattern` function creates this light pattern or background approximation:

```
Mat calculateLightPattern(Mat img)
{
  Mat pattern;
  // Basic and effective way to calculate the light pattern from one image
  blur(img, pattern, Size(img.cols/3,img.cols/3));
  return pattern;
}
```

This basic function applies a blur to an input image by using a big kernel size relative to the image size. From the code, it is **one-third** of the original width and height.

Thresholding

After removing the background, we only have to binarize the image for future segmentation. We are going to do this with threshold. `Threshold` is a simple function that sets each pixel's values to a maximum value (255, for example). If the pixel's value is greater than the **threshold** value or if the pixel's value is lower than the **threshold** value, it will be set to a minimum (0):

$$I(x,y) = \begin{cases} 0, & \text{if } I(x,y) < \text{threshold} \\ 1, & \text{if } I(x,y) > \text{threshold} \end{cases}$$

Now, we are going to apply the `threshold` function using two different `threshold` values: we will use a 30 `threshold` value when we remove the light/background because all non-interesting regions are black. This is because we apply background removal. We will also a medium value `threshold` (140) when we do not use a light removal method, because we have a white background. This last option is used to allow us to check the results with and without background removal:

```
// Binarize image for segment
Mat img_thr;
if(method_light!=2){
  threshold(img_no_light, img_thr, 30, 255, THRESH_BINARY);
}else{
  threshold(img_no_light, img_thr, 140, 255, THRESH_BINARY_INV);
}
```

Now, we are going to continue with the most important part of our application: the segmentation. We are going to use two different approaches or algorithms here: connected components and find contours.

Segmenting our input image

Now, we are going to introduce two techniques to segment our threshold image:

- Connected components
- Find contours

With these two techniques, we are allowed to extract each **region of interest (ROI)** of our image where our targets objects appear. In our case, these are the nut, screw, and ring.

The connected components algorithm

The connected component algorithm is a very common algorithm that's used to segment and identify parts in binary images. The connected component is an iterative algorithm with the purpose of labeling an image using eight or four connectivity pixels. Two pixels are connected if they have the same value and are neighbors. In an image, each pixel has eight neighbor pixels:

Four-connectivity means that only the **2, 4, 5,** and **7** neighbors can be connected to the center if they have the same value as the center pixel. With eight-connectivity, the **1, 2, 3, 4, 5, 6, 7,** and **8** neighbors can be connected if they have the same value as the center pixel. We can see the differences in the following example from a four- and eight-connectivity algorithm. We are going to apply each algorithm to the next binarized image. We have used a small **9 x 9** image and zoomed in to show how connected components work and the differences between four- and eight-connectivity:

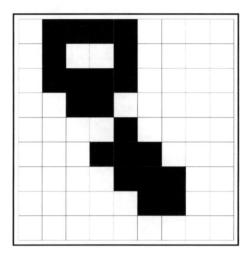

The four-connectivity algorithm detects two objects; we can see this in the left image. The eight-connectivity algorithm detects only one object (the right image) because two diagonal pixels are connected. Eight-connectivity takes care of diagonal connectivity, which is the main difference compared with four-connectivity, since this where only vertical and horizontal pixels are considered. We can see the result in the following image, where each object has a different gray color value:

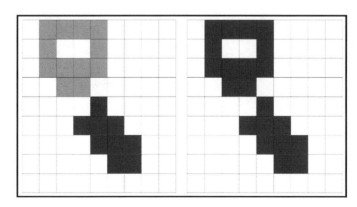

OpenCV brings us the connected components algorithm with two different functions:

- `connectedComponents` (image, labels, connectivity= 8, type= CV_32S)
- `connectedComponentsWithStats` (image, labels, stats, centroids, connectivity= 8, type= CV_32S)

Both functions return an integer with the number of detected labels, where label 0 represents the background. The difference between these two functions is basically the information that is returned. Let's check the parameters of each one. The `connectedComponents` function gives us the following parameters:

- **Image**: The input image to be labeled.
- **Labels**: An output mat that's the same size as the input image, where each pixel has the value of its label, where all OS represents the background, pixels with 1 value represent the first connected component object, and so on.
- **Connectivity**: Two possible values, 8 or 4, that represent the connectivity we want to use.
- **Type**: The type of label image we want to use. Only two types are allowed: CV32_S and CV16_U. By default, this is CV32_S.
- The `connectedComponentsWithStats` function has two more parameters defined. These are stats and centroids:
    - **Stats**: This is an output parameter that gives us the following statistical values for each label (background inclusive):
        - CC_STAT_LEFT: The leftmost x coordinate of the connected component object
        - CC_STAT_TOP: The topmost y coordinate of the connected component object
        - CC_STAT_WIDTH: The width of the connected component object defined by its bounding box
        - CC_STAT_HEIGHT: The height of the connected component object defined by its bounding box
        - CC_STAT_AREA: The number of pixels (area) of the connected component object
    - **Centroids**: The centroid points to the float type for each label, inclusive of the background that's considered for another connected component.

In our example application, we are going to create two functions so that we can apply these two OpenCV algorithms. We will then show the user the obtained result in a new image with colored objects in the basic connected component algorithm. If we select the connected component with the stats method, we are going to draw the respective calculated area that returns this function over each object.

Let's define the basic drawing for the connected component function:

```
void ConnectedComponents(Mat img)
{
  // Use connected components to divide our image in multiple connected
component objects
    Mat labels;
    auto num_objects= connectedComponents(img, labels);
  // Check the number of objects detected
    if(num_objects < 2 ){
       cout << "No objects detected" << endl;
       return;
     }else{
      cout << "Number of objects detected: " << num_objects - 1 << endl;
     }
  // Create output image coloring the objects
    Mat output= Mat::zeros(img.rows,img.cols, CV_8UC3);
    RNG rng(0xFFFFFFFF);
    for(auto i=1; i<num_objects; i++){
       Mat mask= labels==i;
       output.setTo(randomColor(rng), mask);
     }
    imshow("Result", output);
}
```

First of all, we call the OpenCV `connectedComponents` function, which returns the number of objects detected. If the number of objects is less than two, this means that only the background object is detected, and then we don't need to draw anything and we can finish. If the algorithm detects more than one object, we show the number of objects that have been detected on the console:

```
Mat labels;
auto num_objects= connectedComponents(img, labels);
// Check the number of objects detected
if(num_objects < 2){
  cout << "No objects detected" << endl;
  return;
}else{
  cout << "Number of objects detected: " << num_objects - 1 << endl;
```

Now, we are going to draw all detected objects in a new image with different colors. After this, we need to create a new black image with the same input size and three channels:

```
Mat output= Mat::zeros(img.rows,img.cols, CV_8UC3);
```

We will loop over each label, except for the 0 value, because this is the background:

```
for(int i=1; i<num_objects; i++){
```

To extract each object from the label image, we can create a mask for each i label using a comparison and save this in a new image:

```
Mat mask= labels==i;
```

Finally, we set a pseudo-random color to the output image using the mask:

```
output.setTo(randomColor(rng), mask);
}
```

After looping all of the images, we have all of the detected objects with different colors in our output and we only have to show the output image in a window:

```
imshow("Result", output);
```

This is the result in which each object is painted with different colors or a gray value:

Now, we are going to explain how to use the connected components with the `stats` OpenCV algorithm and show some more information in the resultant image. The following function implements this functionality:

```
void ConnectedComponentsStats(Mat img)
{
  // Use connected components with stats
  Mat labels, stats, centroids;
```

```
  auto num_objects= connectedComponentsWithStats(img, labels, stats,
centroids);
  // Check the number of objects detected
  if(num_objects < 2 ){
    cout << "No objects detected" << endl;
    return;
  }else{
    cout << "Number of objects detected: " << num_objects - 1 << endl;
  }
  // Create output image coloring the objects and show area
  Mat output= Mat::zeros(img.rows,img.cols, CV_8UC3);
  RNG rng( 0xFFFFFFFF );
  for(auto i=1; i<num_objects; i++){
    cout << "Object "<< i << " with pos: " << centroids.at<Point2d>(i) << "
with area " << stats.at<int>(i, CC_STAT_AREA) << endl;
    Mat mask= labels==i;
    output.setTo(randomColor(rng), mask);
    // draw text with area
    stringstream ss;
    ss << "area: " << stats.at<int>(i, CC_STAT_AREA);

    putText(output,
      ss.str(),
      centroids.at<Point2d>(i),
      FONT_HERSHEY_SIMPLEX,
      0.4,
      Scalar(255,255,255));
  }
  imshow("Result", output);
}
```

Let's understand this code. As we did in the non-stats function, we call the connected components algorithm, but here, we do this using the `stats` function, checking whether we detected more than one object:

```
Mat labels, stats, centroids;
  auto num_objects= connectedComponentsWithStats(img, labels, stats,
centroids);
  // Check the number of objects detected
  if(num_objects < 2){
    cout << "No objects detected" << endl;
    return;
  }else{
    cout << "Number of objects detected: " << num_objects - 1 << endl;
  }
```

Now, we have two more output results: the stats and centroid variables. Then, for each detected label, we are going to show the centroid and area through the command line:

```
for(auto i=1; i<num_objects; i++){
    cout << "Object "<< i << " with pos: " << centroids.at<Point2d>(i) << "
with area " << stats.at<int>(i, CC_STAT_AREA) << endl;
```

You can check the call to the stats variable to extract the area using the column constant `stats.at<int>(I, CC_STAT_AREA)`. Now, like before, we paint the object labeled with `i` over the output image:

```
Mat mask= labels==i;
output.setTo(randomColor(rng), mask);
```

Finally, in the centroid position of each segmented object, we want to draw some information (such as the area) on the resultant image. To do this, we use the stats and centroid variables using the `putText` function. First, we have to create a `stringstream` so that we can add the stats area information:

```
// draw text with area
stringstream ss;
ss << "area: " << stats.at<int>(i, CC_STAT_AREA);
```

Then, we need to use `putText`, using the centroid as the text position:

```
putText(output,
    ss.str(),
    centroids.at<Point2d>(i),
    FONT_HERSHEY_SIMPLEX,
    0.4,
    Scalar(255,255,255));
```

The result for this function is as follows:

The findContours algorithm

The `findContours` algorithm is one of the most used OpenCV algorithms in regards to segment objects. This is because this algorithm was included in OpenCV from version 1.0 and gives developers more information and descriptors, including shapes, topological organizations, and so on:

```
void findContours(InputOutputArray image, OutputArrayOfArrays contours,
OutputArray hierarchy, int mode, int method, Point offset=Point())
```

Let's explain each parameter:

- **Image**: Input binary image.
- **Contours**: A contour's output where each detected contour is a vector of points.
- **Hierarchy**: This is the optional output vector where the hierarchy of contours is saved. This is the topology of the image where we can get the relations between each contour. The hierarchy is represented as a vector of four indices, which are (next contour, previous contour, first child, parent contour). Negative indices are given where the given contour has no relationship with other contours. A more detailed explanation can be found at `https://docs.opencv.org/3.4/d9/d8b/tutorial_py_contours_hierarchy.html`.
- **Mode**: This method is used to retrieve the contours:
    - `RETR_EXTERNAL` retrieves only the external contours.
    - `RETR_LIST` retrieves all contours without establishing the hierarchy.
    - `RETR_CCOMP` retrieves all contours with two levels of hierarchy, external and holes. If another object is inside one hole, this is put at the top of the hierarchy.
    - `RETR_TREE` retrieves all contours, creating a full hierarchy between contours.
- **Method**: This allows us to use the approximation method for retrieving the contour's shapes:
    - If `CV_CHAIN_APPROX_NONE` is set, then this does not apply any approximation to the contours and stores the contour's points.
    - `CV_CHAIN_APPROX_SIMPLE` compresses all horizontal, vertical, and diagonal segments, storing only the start and end points.
    - `CV_CHAIN_APPROX_TC89_L1` and `CV_CHAIN_APPROX_TC89_KCOS` apply the **Telchin chain approximation** algorithm.
- **Offset**: This is an optional point value to shift all contours. This is very useful when we are working in an ROI and need to retrieve global positions.

Note: The input image is modified by the `findContours` function. Create a copy of your image before sending it to this function if you need it.

Now that we know the parameters of the `findContours` function, let's apply this to our example:

```
void FindContoursBasic(Mat img)
{
  vector<vector<Point> > contours;
  findContours(img, contours, RETR_EXTERNAL, CHAIN_APPROX_SIMPLE);
  Mat output= Mat::zeros(img.rows,img.cols, CV_8UC3);
  // Check the number of objects detected
  if(contours.size() == 0 ){
    cout << "No objects detected" << endl;
    return;
  }else{
    cout << "Number of objects detected: " << contours.size() << endl;
  }
  RNG rng(0xFFFFFFFF);
  for(auto i=0; i<contours.size(); i++){
    drawContours(output, contours, i, randomColor(rng));
    imshow("Result", output);
  }
}
```

Let's explain our implementation, line by line.

In our case, we don't need any hierarchy, so we are only going to retrieve the external contours of all possible objects. To do this, we can use the RETR_EXTERNAL mode and basic contour encoding by using the CHAIN_APPROX_SIMPLE method:

```
vector<vector<Point> > contours;
vector<Vec4i> hierarchy;
findContours(img, contours, RETR_EXTERNAL, CHAIN_APPROX_SIMPLE);
```

Like the connected component examples we looked at before, first we check how many contours we have retrieved. If there are none, then we exit our function:

```
// Check the number of objects detected
  if(contours.size() == 0){
    cout << "No objects detected" << endl;
    return;
  }else{
    cout << "Number of objects detected: " << contours.size() << endl;
  }
```

Finally, we draw the contour for each detected object. We draw this in our output image with different colors. To do this, OpenCV gives us a function to draw the result of the find contours image:

```
for(auto i=0; i<contours.size(); i++)
    drawContours(output, contours, i, randomColor(rng));
  imshow("Result", output);
}
```

The `drawContours` function allows the following parameters:

- **Image**: The output image to draw the contours.
- **Contours**: The vector of contours.
- **Contour index**: A number indicating the contour to draw. If this is negative, all contours are drawn.
- **Color**: The color to draw the contour.
- **Thickness**: If it is negative, the contour is filled with the chosen color.
- **Line type**: This specifies whether we want to draw with anti-aliasing or another drawing method.
- **Hierarchy**: This is an optional parameter that is only needed if you want to draw some of the contours.
- **Max Level**: This is an optional parameter that is only taken into account when the hierarchy parameter is available. If it is set to 0, only the specified contour is drawn. If it is 1, the function draws the current contour and the nested contours too. If it is set to 2, then the algorithm draws all of the specified contour hierarchy.
- **Offset**: This is an optional parameter for shifting the contours.

The result of our example can be seen in the following image:

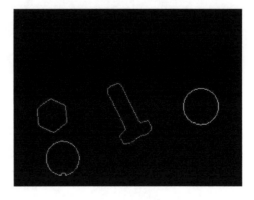

Summary

In this chapter, we explored the basics of object segmentation in a controlled situation where a camera takes pictures of different objects. Here, we learned how to remove background and light to allow us to binarize our image better, thus minimizing the noise. After binarizing the image, we learned about three different algorithms that we can use to divide and separate each object of one image, allowing us to isolate each object to manipulate or extract features.

We can see this whole process in the following image:

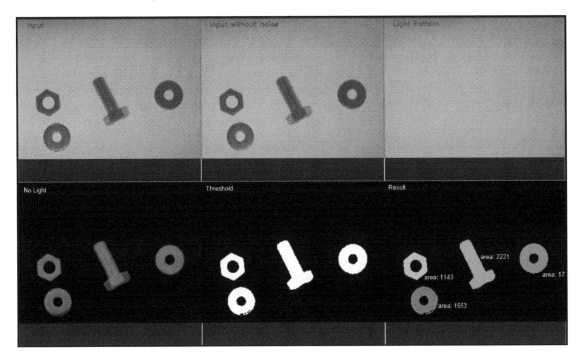

Finally, we extracted all of the objects on an image. You will need to do this to continue with the next chapter, where we are going to extract characteristics of each of these objects to train a machine learning system.

In the next chapter, we are going to predict the class of any objects in an image and then call a robot or any other system to pick any of them, or detect an object that is not in the correct carrier tape. We will then look at notifying a person to pick it up.

6
Learning Object Classification

In Chapter 5, *Automated Optical Inspection, Object Segmentation, and Detection*, we introduced the basic concepts of object segmentation and detection. This refers to isolating the objects that appear in an image for future processing and analysis. This chapter explains how to classify each of these isolated objects. To allow us to classify each object, we have to train our system to be capable of learning the required parameters so that it decides which specific label will be assigned to the detected object (depending on the different categories taken into account during the training phase).

This chapter introduces the basics concepts of machine learning to classify images with different labels. To do this, we are going to create a basic application based on the segmentation algorithm of Chapter 5, *Automated Optical Inspection, Object Segmentation, and Detection*. This segmentation algorithm extracts parts of images that contain unknown objects. For each detected object, we are going to extract different features that are going to be classified using a machine learning algorithm. Finally, we are going to show the obtained results using our user interface, together with the labels of each object detected in the input image.

This chapter involves different topics and algorithms, including the following:

- Introduction to machine learning concepts
- Common machine learning algorithms and processes
- Feature extraction
- support vector machines (SVM)
- Training and prediction

Technical requirements

This chapter requires familiarity with the basic C++ programming language. All of the code that's used in this chapter can be downloaded from the following GitHub link: `https://github.com/PacktPublishing/Building-Computer-Vision-Projects-with-OpenCV4-and-CPlusPlus/tree/master/Chapter06`. This code can be executed on any operating system, though it is only tested on Ubuntu.

Check out the following video to see the Code in Action:
`http://bit.ly/2KGD4CO`

Introducing machine learning concepts

Machine learning is a concept that was defined by *Arthur Samuel* in 1959 as a field of study that gives computers the ability to learn without being explicitly programmed. *Tom M. Mitchel* provided a more formal definition for machine learning, in which he links the concept of samples with experience data, labels, and performance measurement of algorithms.

> The **machine learning** definition by *Arthur Samuel* is referenced in *Some Studies in Machine Learning Using the Game of Checkers* in *IBM Journal of Research and Development* (*Volume: 3, Issue: 3*), *p. 210*. It was also referenced in *The New Yorker* and *Office Management* in the same year.
> The more formal definition from *Tom M. Mitchel* is referenced in *Machine Learning Book, McGray Hill*
> *1997:* (`http://www.cs.cmu.edu/afs/cs.cmu.edu/user/mitchell/ftp/mlbook.html`).

Machine learning involves pattern recognition and learning theory in artificial intelligence, and is related with computational statistics. It is used in hundreds of applications, such as **optical character recognition** (**OCR**), spam filtering, search engines, and thousands of computer vision applications, such as the example that we will develop in this chapter, where a machine learning algorithm tries to classify objects that appear in the input image.

Depending on how machine learning algorithms learn from the input data, we can divide them into three categories:

- **Supervised learning**: The computer learns from a set of labeled data. The goal here is to learn the parameters of the model and rules that allow computers to map the relationship between data and output label results.

- **Unsupervised learning**: No labels are given and the computer tries to discover the input structure of the given data.
- **Reinforcement learning**: The computer interacts with a dynamic environment, reaching their goal and learning from their mistakes.

Depending on the results we wish to gain from our machine learning algorithm, we can categorize the results as follows:

- **Classification**: The space of the inputs can be divided into **N** classes, and the prediction results for a given sample are one of these training classes. This is one of the most used categories. A typical example can be email spam filtering, where there are only two classes: spam and non-spam. Alternatively, we can use OCR, where only N characters are available and each character is one class.
- **Regression**: The output is a continuous value instead of a discrete value like a classification result. One example of regression could be the prediction of a house price given the house's size, number of years since it was built, and location.
- **Clustering**: The input is to be divided into N groups, which is typically done using unsupervised training.
- **Density estimation**: Finds the (probability) distribution of inputs.

In our example, we are going to use a supervised learning and classification algorithm where a training dataset with labels is used to train the model and the result of the model's prediction is one of the possible labels. In machine learning, there are several approaches and methods for this. Some of the more popular ones include the following: **support vector machines (SVM)**, **artificial neural networks (ANN)**, clustering, k-nearest neighbors, decision trees, and deep learning. Almost all of these methods and approaches are supported, implemented, and well documented in OpenCV. In this chapter, we are going to explain support vector machines.

OpenCV machine learning algorithms

OpenCV implements eight of these machine learning algorithms. All of them are inherited from the StatModel class:

- Artificial neural networks
- Random trees
- Expectation maximization
- k-nearest neighbors
- Logistic regression
- Normal Bayes classifiers

- support vector machine
- Stochastic gradient descent SVMs

Version 3 supports deep learning at a basic level, but version 4 is stable and more supported. We will delve into deep learning in detail in further chapters.

 To get more information about each algorithm, read the OpenCV document page for machine learning at http://docs.opencv.org/trunk/dc/dd6/ml_intro.html.

The following diagram shows the machine learning class hierarchy:

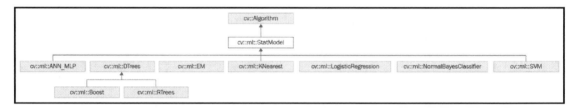

The StatModel class is the base class for all machine learning algorithms. This provides the prediction and all the read and write functions that are very important for saving and reading our machine learning parameters and training data.

In machine learning, the most time-consuming and computing resource-consuming part is the training method. Training can take from seconds to weeks or months for large datasets and complex machine learning structures. For example, in deep learning, big neural network structures with more than 100,000 image datasets can take a long time to train. With deep learning algorithms, it is common to use parallel hardware processing such as GPUs with CUDA technology to decrease the computing time during training, or most new chip devices such as Intel Movidius. This means that we cannot train our algorithm each time we run our application, and therefore it's recommended to save our trained model with all of the parameters that have been learned. In future executions, we only have to load/read from our saved model without training, except if we need to update our model with more sample data.

StatModel is the base class of all machine learning classes, such as SVM or ANN, except deep learning methods. StatModel is basically a virtual class that defines the two most important functions—train and predict. The train method is the main method that's responsible for learning model parameters using a training dataset. This has the following three possible calls:

```
bool train(const Ptr<TrainData>& trainData, int flags=0 );
bool train(InputArray samples, int layout, InputArray responses);
Ptr<_Tp> train(const Ptr<TrainData>& data, int flags=0 );
```

The train function has the following parameters:

- TrainData: Training data that can be loaded or created from the TrainData class. This class is new in OpenCV 3 and helps developers create training data and abstract from the machine learning algorithm. This is done because different algorithms require different types of structures of arrays for training and prediction, such as the ANN algorithm.
- samples: An array of training array samples such as training data in the format required by the machine learning algorithm.
- layout: ROW_SAMPLE (training samples are the matrix rows) or COL_SAMPLE (training samples are the matrix columns).
- responses: Vector of responses associated with the sample data.
- flags: Optional flags defined by each method.

The last train method creates and trains a model of the _TP class type. The only classes accepted are the classes that implement a static create method with no parameters or with all default parameter values.

The predict method is much simpler and has only one possible call:

```
float StatModel::predict(InputArray samples, OutputArray results=noArray(),
int flags=0)
```

The predict function has the following parameters:

- samples: The input samples to predict results from the model can consist of any amount of data, whether single or multiple.
- results: The results of each input row sample (computed by the algorithm from the previously trained model).
- flags: These optional flags are model-dependent. Some models, such as Boost, are recognized by the SVM StatModel::RAW_OUTPUT flag, which makes the method return the raw results (the sum), and not the class label.

The `StatModel` class provides an interface for other very useful methods:

- `isTrained()` returns true if the model is trained
- `isClassifier()` returns true if the model is a classifier, or false in the case of regression
- `getVarCount()` returns the number of variables in training samples
- `save(const string& filename)` saves the model in the filename
- `Ptr<_Tp> load(const string& filename)` loads the `<indexentry content="StatModel class:Ptr load(const string& filename)">` model from a filename, for example—`Ptr<SVM> svm = StatModel::load<SVM>("my_svm_model.xml")`
- `calcError(const Ptr<TrainData>& data, bool test, OutputArray resp)` calculates the error from test data, where the data is the training data. If the test parameter is true, the method calculates the error from a test subset of data; if its false, the method calculates the error from all training data. `resp` is the optional output result.

Now, we are going to introduce how a basic application that uses machine learning in a computer vision application is constructed.

Computer vision and the machine learning workflow

Computer vision applications with machine learning have a common basic structure. This structure is divided into different steps:

1. **Pre-process**
2. **Segmentation**
3. **Feature extraction**
4. **Classification result**
5. **Post-process**

These are common in almost all computer vision applications, while others are omitted. In the following diagram, you can see the different steps that are involved:

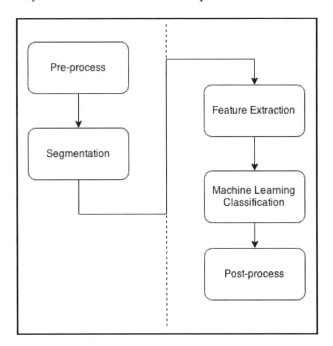

Almost all computer vision applications start with a **Pre-process** applied to the input image, which consists of the removal of light and noise, filtering, blurring, and so on. After applying all pre-processing required to the input image, the second step is **Segmentation**. In this step, we have to extract the regions of interest in the image and isolate each one as a unique object of interest. For example, in a face detection system, we have to separate the faces from the rest of the parts in the scene. After detecting the objects inside the image, we continue to the next step. Here, we have to extract the features of each one; the features are normally a vector of characteristics of objects. A characteristic describes our objects and can be the area of an object, contour, texture pattern, pixels, and so on.

Now, we have the descriptor, also known as a feature vector or feature set, of our object. Descriptors are the features that describe an object, and we use these to train or predict a model. To do this, we have to create a large dataset of features where thousands of images are pre-processed. We then use the extracted features (image/object characteristics) such as area, size, and aspect ration, in the **Train** model function we choose. In the following diagram, we can see how a dataset is fed into a **Machine Learning Algorithm** to train and **generate** a **Model**:

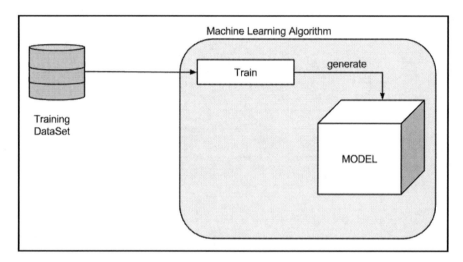

When we **Train** with a dataset, the **Model** learns all the parameters required to be able to predict when a new vector of features with an unknown label is given as input to our algorithm. In the following diagram, we can see how an unknown vector of features is used to **Predict** using the generated **Model**, thus returning the **Classification result** or regression:

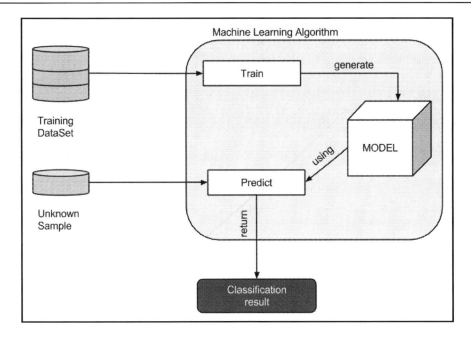

After predicting the result, the post-processing of output data is sometimes required, for example, merging multiple classifications to decrease the prediction error or merging multiple labels. A sample case in Optical Character recognition is where the **Classification result** is according to each predicted character, and by combining the results of character recognition, we construct a word. This means that we can create a post-processing method to correct errors in detected words. With this small introduction to machine learning for computer vision, we are going to implement our own application that uses machine learning to classify objects in a slide tape. We are going to use support vector machines as our classification method and explain how to use them. The other machine learning algorithms are used in a very similar way. The OpenCV documentation has detailed information about all of the machine learning algorithms at the following link: `https://docs.opencv.org/master/dd/ded/group__ml.html`.

Automatic object inspection classification example

In Chapter 5, *Automated Optical Inspection, Object Segmentation, and Detection*, we looked at an example of automatic object inspection segmentation where a carrier tape contained three different types of object: nuts, screws, and rings. With computer vision, we will be able to recognize each one of these so that we can send notifications to a robot or put each one in a different box. The following is a basic diagram of the carrier tape:

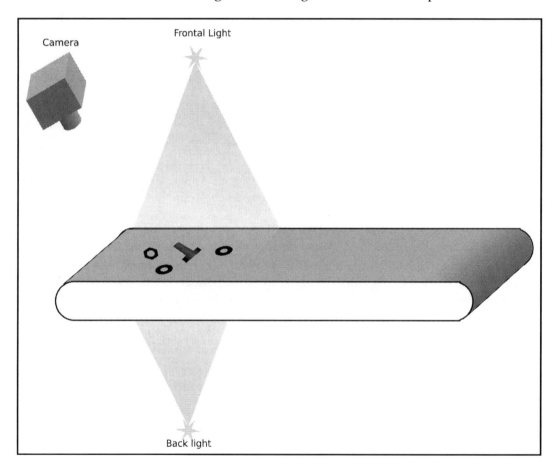

In `Chapter 5`, *Automated Optical Inspection, Object Segmentation, and Detection*, we pre-processed the input images and extracted the regions of interest, isolating each object using different techniques. Now, we are going to apply all the concepts we explained in the previous sections in this example to extract features and classify each object, allowing the robot to put each one in a different box. In our application, we are only going to show the labels of each image, but we could send the positions in the image and the label to other devices, such as a robot. At this point, our goal is to give an input image with different objects, allowing the computer to detect the objects and show the objects' names over each image, as demonstrated in the following images. However, to learn the steps of the whole process, we are going to train our system by creating a plot to show the feature distribution that we are going to use, and visualize it with different colors. We will also show the pre-processed input image, and the output classification result obtained. The final result looks as follows:

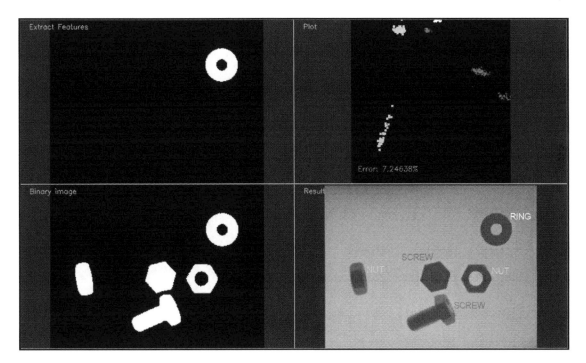

We are going to follow these steps for our example application:

1. For each input image:

   • Preprocess the image
   • Segment the image

2. For each object in an image:
   - Extract the features
   - Add the features to the training feature vector with a corresponding label (nut, screw, ring)
3. Create an SVM model.
4. Train our SVM model with the training feature vector.
5. Preprocess the input image to classify each segmented object.
6. Segment the input image.
7. For each object detected:
   - Extract the features
   - Predict it with the SVM
   - model
   - Paint the result in the output image

For pre-processing and segmentation, we are going to use the code found in Chapter 5, *Automated Optical Inspection, Object Segmentation, and Detection*. We are then going to explain how to extract the features and create the vectors required to **train** and **predict** our model.

Feature extraction

The next thing we need to do is extract the features for each object. To understand the feature vector concept, we are going to extract very simple features in our example, as this is enough to get good results. In other solutions, we can get more complex features such as texture descriptors, contour descriptors, and so on. In our example, we only have nuts, rings, and screws in different positions and orientations in the image. The same object can be in any position of image and orientation, for example, the screw or the nut. We can see different orientations in the following image:

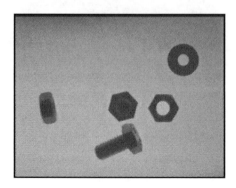

We are going to explore some features or characteristics that could improve the accuracy of our machine learning algorithm. These possible characteristics of our different objects (nuts, screws, and rings) are as follows:

- The area of the object
- The aspect ratio, that is, the width divided by the height of the bounding rectangle
- The number of holes
- The number of contour sides

These characteristics can describe our objects very well, and if we use all of them, the classification error will be very small. However, in our implemented example, we are only going to use the first two characteristics, area and aspect ratio, for learning purposes, because we can plot these characteristics in a 2D graphic and show that these values correctly describe our objects. We can also show that we can visually differentiate between one kind of object and another in the graphic plot. To extract these features, we are going to use the black/white ROI image as input, where only one object appears in white with a black background. This input is the segmentation result of Chapter 5, *Automated Optical Inspection, Object Segmentation, and Detection*. We are going to use the findCountours algorithm for segmenting objects and create the ExtractFeatures function for this purpose, as we can see in the following code:

```
vector< vector<float> > ExtractFeatures(Mat img, vector<int>* left=NULL,
vector<int>* top=NULL)
{
  vector< vector<float> > output;
  vector<vector<Point> > contours;
  Mat input= img.clone();
  vector<Vec4i> hierarchy;
  findContours(input, contours, hierarchy, RETR_CCOMP,
CHAIN_APPROX_SIMPLE);
  // Check the number of objects detected
  if(contours.size() == 0){
    return output;
  }
  RNG rng(0xFFFFFFFF);
  for(auto i=0; i<contours.size(); i++){
    Mat mask= Mat::zeros(img.rows, img.cols, CV_8UC1);
    drawContours(mask, contours, i, Scalar(1), FILLED, LINE_8, hierarchy,
1);
    Scalar area_s= sum(mask);
    float area= area_s[0];

    if(area>500){ //if the area is greater than min.
      RotatedRect r= minAreaRect(contours[i]);
```

```
        float width= r.size.width;
        float height= r.size.height;
        float ar=(width<height) ?height/width:width/height;

        vector<float> row;
        row.push_back(area);
        row.push_back(ar);
        output.push_back(row);
        if(left!=NULL){
            left->push_back((int)r.center.x);
        }
        if(top!=NULL){
            top->push_back((int)r.center.y);
        }
        // Add image to the multiple image window class, See the class on
    full github code
        miw->addImage("Extract Features", mask*255);
        miw->render();
        waitKey(10);
        }
    }
    return output;
}
```

Let's explain the code that we use to extract features. We are going to create a function that has one image as input and return two vectors of the left and top position for each object detected in the image as a parameter. This data will be used for drawing the corresponding label over each object. The output of a function is a vector of vectors of floats. In other words, it is a matrix where each row contains the features of each object that's detected.

First, we have to create the output vector variable and the contours variable that are going to be used in our find contours algorithm segmentation. We also have to create a copy of our input image, because the findCoutours OpenCV functions modify the input image:

```
    vector< vector<float> > output;
    vector<vector<Point> > contours;
    Mat input= img.clone();
    vector<Vec4i> hierarchy;
    findContours(input, contours, hierarchy, RETR_CCOMP,
CHAIN_APPROX_SIMPLE);
```

Now, we can use the `findContours` function to retrieve each object in an image. If we don't detect any contour, we return an empty output matrix, as we can see in the following snippet:

```
if(contours.size() == 0){
    return output;
}
```

If objects are detected, for each contour we are going to draw the object in white on a black image (zero values). This will be done using 1 values, like a mask image. The following piece of code generates the mask image:

```
for(auto i=0; i<contours.size(); i++){
    Mat mask= Mat::zeros(img.rows, img.cols, CV_8UC1);
    drawContours(mask, contours, i, Scalar(1), FILLED, LINE_8, hierarchy,
1);
```

It's important to use the value of 1 to draw inside the shape because we can calculate the area by summing all of the values inside the contour, as shown in the following code:

```
        Scalar area_s= sum(mask);
        float area= area_s[0];
```

This area is our first feature. We are going to use this value as a filter to remove all possible small objects that we have to avoid. All objects with an area less than the minimum threshold area that we considered will be discarded. After passing the filter, we create the second feature and the aspect ratio of the object. This refers to the maximum of the width or height, divided by the minimum of the width or height. This feature can tell the difference between the screw and other objects easily. The following code describes how to calculate the aspect ratio:

```
if(area>MIN_AREA){ //if the area is greater than min.
        RotatedRect r= minAreaRect(contours[i]);
        float width= r.size.width;
        float height= r.size.height;
        float ar=(width<height)?height/width:width/height;
```

Now we have the features, we only have to add them to the output vector. To do this, we will create a row vector of floats and add the values, followed by adding this row to the output vector, as shown in the following code:

```
vector<float> row;
row.push_back(area);
row.push_back(ar);
output.push_back(row);
```

If the left and top parameters are passed, then add the top-left values to output the parameters:

```
if(left!=NULL){
    left->push_back((int)r.center.x);
}
if(top!=NULL){
    top->push_back((int)r.center.y);
}
```

Finally, we are going to show the detected objects in a window for user feedback. When we finish processing all of the objects in the image, we are going to return the output feature vector, as described in the following code snippet:

```
        miw->addImage("Extract Features", mask*255);
        miw->render();
        waitKey(10);
    }
}
return output;
```

Now that we have extracted the features of each input image, we can continue with the next step.

Training an SVM model

We are now going to use supervised learning and then obtain a set of images for each object and its corresponding label. There is no minimum number of images in the dataset; if we provide more images for the training process, we will get a better classification model (in most cases). However, for simple classifiers, it could be enough to train simple models. To do this, we created three folders (`screw`, `nut`, and `ring`), where all of the images of each type are placed together. For each image in the folder, we have to extract the features, add them to the `train` feature matrix and, at the same time, create a new vector with the labels for each row corresponding to each training matrix. To evaluate our system, we will split each folder into a number of images according to testing and training. We will leave around 20 images for testing and the others for training. We are then going to create two vectors of labels and two matrices for training and testing.

Let's go inside of our code. First, we have to create our model. We are going to declare the model out of all functions to be able to gain access to it as a global variable. OpenCV uses the `Ptr` template class for pointer management:

```
Ptr<SVM> svm;
```

After declaring the pointer to the new SVM model, we are going to create it and train it. We created the `trainAndTest` function for this purpose. The complete function code is as follows:

```
void trainAndTest()
{
  vector< float > trainingData;
  vector< int > responsesData;
  vector< float > testData;
  vector< float > testResponsesData;

  int num_for_test= 20;

  // Get the nut images
  readFolderAndExtractFeatures("../data/nut/nut_%04d.pgm", 0, num_for_test,
trainingData, responsesData, testData, testResponsesData);
  // Get and process the ring images
  readFolderAndExtractFeatures("../data/ring/ring_%04d.pgm", 1,
num_for_test, trainingData, responsesData, testData, testResponsesData);
  // get and process the screw images
  readFolderAndExtractFeatures("../data/screw/screw_%04d.pgm", 2,
num_for_test, trainingData, responsesData, testData, testResponsesData);
  cout << "Num of train samples: " << responsesData.size() << endl;

  cout << "Num of test samples: " << testResponsesData.size() << endl;
  // Merge all data
  Mat trainingDataMat(trainingData.size()/2, 2, CV_32FC1,
&trainingData[0]);
  Mat responses(responsesData.size(), 1, CV_32SC1, &responsesData[0]);

  Mat testDataMat(testData.size()/2, 2, CV_32FC1, &testData[0]);
  Mat testResponses(testResponsesData.size(), 1, CV_32FC1,
&testResponsesData[0]);
  Ptr<TrainData> tdata= TrainData::create(trainingDataMat, ROW_SAMPLE,
responses);

  svm = cv::ml::SVM::create();
  svm->setType(cv::ml::SVM::C_SVC);
  svm->setNu(0.05);
  svm->setKernel(cv::ml::SVM::CHI2);
  svm->setDegree(1.0);
  svm->setGamma(2.0);
  svm->setTermCriteria(TermCriteria(TermCriteria::MAX_ITER, 100, 1e-6));
  svm->train(tdata);

  if(testResponsesData.size()>0){
    cout << "Evaluation" << endl;
    cout << "==========" << endl;
```

```
    // Test the ML Model
    Mat testPredict;
    svm->predict(testDataMat, testPredict);
    cout << "Prediction Done" << endl;
    // Error calculation
    Mat errorMat= testPredict!=testResponses;
    float error= 100.0f * countNonZero(errorMat) /
testResponsesData.size();
    cout << "Error: " << error << "%" << endl;
    // Plot training data with error label
    plotTrainData(trainingDataMat, responses, &error);

  }else{
    plotTrainData(trainingDataMat, responses);
  }
}
```

Now, let's explain the code. First of all, we have to create the required variables to store the training and testing data:

```
vector< float > trainingData;
vector< int > responsesData;
vector< float > testData;
vector< float > testResponsesData;
```

As we mentioned previously, we have to read all of the images from each folder, extract the features, and save them in our training and testing data. To do this, we are going to use the readFolderAndExtractFeatures function, as follows:

```
int num_for_test= 20;
// Get the nut images
readFolderAndExtractFeatures("../data/nut/tuerca_%04d.pgm", 0,
num_for_test, trainingData, responsesData, testData, testResponsesData);
// Get and process the ring images
readFolderAndExtractFeatures("../data/ring/arandela_%04d.pgm", 1,
num_for_test, trainingData, responsesData, testData, testResponsesData);
// get and process the screw images
readFolderAndExtractFeatures("../data/screw/tornillo_%04d.pgm", 2,
num_for_test, trainingData, responsesData, testData, testResponsesData);
```

The readFolderAndExtractFeatures function uses the VideoCapture OpenCV function to read all of the images in a folder, including videos and camera frames. For each image that's read, we extract the features and add them to the corresponding output vector:

```
bool readFolderAndExtractFeatures(string folder, int label, int
num_for_test,
  vector<float> &trainingData, vector<int> &responsesData,
  vector<float> &testData, vector<float> &testResponsesData)
```

```
{
  VideoCapture images;
  if(images.open(folder)==false){
    cout << "Can not open the folder images" << endl;
    return false;
  }
  Mat frame;
  int img_index=0;
  while(images.read(frame)){
    //// Preprocess image
    Mat pre= preprocessImage(frame);
    // Extract features
    vector< vector<float> > features= ExtractFeatures(pre);
    for(int i=0; i< features.size(); i++){
      if(img_index >= num_for_test){
        trainingData.push_back(features[i][0]);
        trainingData.push_back(features[i][1]);
        responsesData.push_back(label);
      }else{
        testData.push_back(features[i][0]);
        testData.push_back(features[i][1]);
        testResponsesData.push_back((float)label);
      }
    }
    img_index++;
  }
  return true;
}
```

After filling all of the vectors with features and labels, we have to convert from vectors to an OpenCV `Mat` format so that we can send it to the training function:

```
// Merge all data
Mat trainingDataMat(trainingData.size()/2, 2, CV_32FC1, &trainingData[0]);
Mat responses(responsesData.size(), 1, CV_32SC1, &responsesData[0]);
Mat testDataMat(testData.size()/2, 2, CV_32FC1, &testData[0]);
Mat testResponses(testResponsesData.size(), 1, CV_32FC1,
&testResponsesData[0]);
```

Now, we are ready to create and train our machine learning model. As we stated previously, we are going to use the support vector machine for this. First, we are going to set up the basic model parameters, as follows:

```
// Set up SVM's parameters
svm = cv::ml::SVM::create();
svm->setType(cv::ml::SVM::C_SVC);
svm->setNu(0.05);
svm->setKernel(cv::ml::SVM::CHI2);
```

```
svm->setDegree(1.0);
svm->setGamma(2.0);
svm->setTermCriteria(TermCriteria(TermCriteria::MAX_ITER, 100, 1e-6));
```

We are now going to define the SVM type and kernel to use, as well as the criteria to stop the learning process. In our case, we are going to use a number of maximum iterations, stopping at 100 iterations. For more information about each parameter and what it does, check the OpenCV documentation at the following link: `https://docs.opencv.org/master/d1/d2d/classcv_1_1ml_1_1SVM.html`. After creating the setup parameters, we are going to create the model by calling the `train` method and using `trainingDataMat` and response matrices as a `TrainData` object:

```
// Train the SVM
svm->train(tdata);
```

We use the test vector (setting the `num_for_test` variable to greater than 0) to obtain an approximation error of our model. To get the error estimation, we are going to predict all test vector features to obtain the SVM prediction results and compare these results to the original labels:

```
if(testResponsesData.size()>0){
    cout << "Evaluation" << endl;
    cout << "==========" << endl;
    // Test the ML Model
    Mat testPredict;
    svm->predict(testDataMat, testPredict);
    cout << "Prediction Done" << endl;
    // Error calculation
    Mat errorMat= testPredict!=testResponses;
    float error= 100.0f * countNonZero(errorMat) /
testResponsesData.size();
    cout << "Error: " << error << "%" << endl;
    // Plot training data with error label
    plotTrainData(trainingDataMat, responses, &error);

}else{
    plotTrainData(trainingDataMat, responses);
}
```

We use the `predict` function by using the `testDataMat` features and a new `Mat` for prediction results. The `predict` function makes it possible to make multiple predictions at the same time, giving a matrix as the result instead of only one row or vector. After prediction, we only have to compute the differences of `testPredict` with our `testResponses` (the original labels). If there are differences, we only have to count how many there are and divide this by the total number of tests in order to calculate the error.

We can use the new `TrainData` class to generate the feature vectors, samples, and split our train data between test and train vectors.

Finally, we are going to show the training data in a 2D plot, where the *y*-axis is the aspect ratio feature and the *x*-axis is the area of objects. Each point has different colors and shapes (cross, square, and circle) that show each different kind of object, and we can clearly see the groups of objects in the following image:

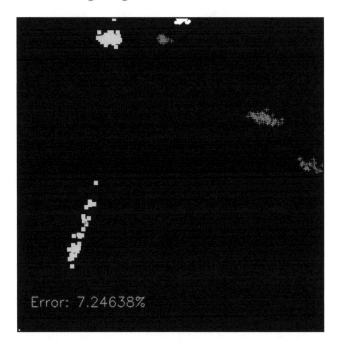

We are now very close to finishing our application sample. At this point, we have trained the SVM model; we can now use it for classification to detect the type of a new incoming and unknown feature vector. The next step is to predict an input image with unknown objects.

Input image prediction

We are now ready to explain the main function, which loads the input image and predicts the objects that appear inside it. We are going to use something like the following picture as the input image. Here, multiple different objects appear in the image. We did not have the labels or names of these, but the computer must be able to identify them:

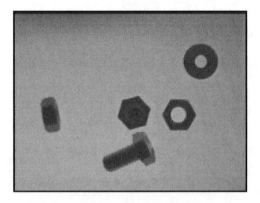

As with all training images, we have to load and pre-process the input image, as follows:

1. First, we load and convert the image into gray color values.
2. Then, we apply the pre-processing tasks (as we learned in Chapter 5, *Automated Optical Inspection, Object Segmentation, and Detection*) using the preprocessImage function:

```
Mat pre= preprocessImage(img);
```

3. Now, we are going to extract the feature of vectors for all objects that appear in the image and the top-left positions of each one by using the ExtractFeatures that we previously described:

```
// Extract features
vector<int> pos_top, pos_left;
vector< vector<float> >
features=ExtractFeatures(pre, &pos_left,        &pos_top);
```

4. We store each object we detect as a feature row and then convert each row as a Mat of one row and two features:

```
for(int i=0; i< features.size(); i++){
    Mat trainingDataMat(1, 2, CV_32FC1, &features[i][0]);
```

5. After this, we can predict the single object using the `predict` function of our `StatModel` SVM. The float result of the prediction is the label of the object detected. Then, to finish the application, we have to draw the label of each object that's detected and classified over the output image:

```
float result= svm->predict(trainingDataMat);
```

6. We are going to use a `stringstream` to store the text and a `Scalar` to store the color for each different label:

```
stringstream ss;
Scalar color;
if(result==0){
  color= green; // NUT
  ss << "NUT";
}else if(result==1){
  color= blue; // RING
  ss << "RING" ;
}else if(result==2){
  color= red; // SCREW
  ss << "SCREW";
}
```

7. We are also going to draw the label text over each object using its detected position in the `ExtractFeatures` function:

```
putText(img_output,
        ss.str(),
        Point2d(pos_left[i], pos_top[i]),
        FONT_HERSHEY_SIMPLEX,
        0.4,
        color);
```

8. Finally, we are going to draw our results in the output window:

```
miw->addImage("Binary image", pre);
miw->addImage("Result", img_output);
miw->render();
waitKey(0);
```

The final result of our application shows a window tiled with four screens. Here, the top-left image is the input training image, the top-right is the plot training image, the bottom left is the input image to analyze pre-processed images, and the bottom-right is the final result of the prediction:

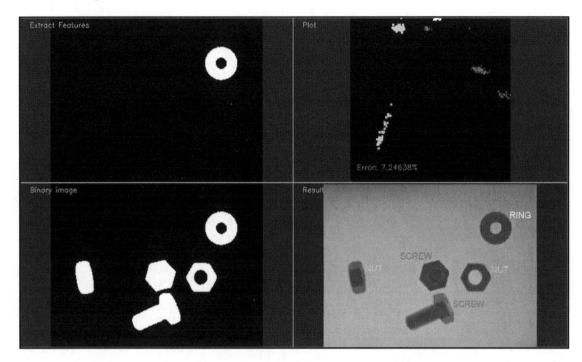

Summary

In this chapter, we learned about the basics of machine learning and applied them to a small sample application. This allowed us to understand the basic techniques that we can use to create our own machine learning application. Machine learning is complex and involves different techniques for each use case (supervised learning, unsupervised, clustering, and so on). We also learned how to create the most typical machine learning application, the supervised learning application, with SVM. The most important concepts in supervised machine learning are as follows: you must have an appropriate number of samples or a dataset, you must accurately choose the features that describe our objects (for more information on image features, go to Chapter 8, *Video Surveillance, Background Modeling, and Morphological Operations*), and you must choose a model that gives the best predictions.

If we don't get the correct predictions, we have to check each one of these concepts to find the issue.

In the next chapter, we are going to introduce background subtraction methods, which are very useful for video surveillance applications where the background doesn't give us any interesting information and must be discarded so that we can segment the image to detect and analyze the image objects.

7
Detecting Face Parts and Overlaying Masks

In `Chapter 6`, *Learning Object Classification*, we learned about object classification and how machine learning can be used to achieve it. In this chapter, we are going to learn how to detect and track different face parts. We will start the discussion by understanding the face detection pipeline and how it's built. We will then use this framework to detect face parts, such as the eyes, ears, mouth, and nose. Finally, we will learn how to overlay funny masks on these face parts in a live video.

By the end of this chapter, we should be familiar with the following topics:

- Understanding Haar cascades
- Integral images and why we need them
- Building a generic face detection pipeline
- Detecting and tracking faces, eyes, ears, noses, and mouths in a live video stream from the webcam
- Automatically overlaying a face mask, sunglasses, and a funny nose on a person's face in a video

Technical requirements

This chapter requires basic familiarity with the C++ programming language. All the code used in this chapter can be downloaded from the following GitHub link: `https://github.com/PacktPublishing/Building-Computer-Vision-Projects-with-OpenCV4-and-CPlusPlus/tree/master/Chapter07`. The code can be executed on any operating system, though it is only tested on Ubuntu.

Check out the following video to see the Code in Action:
`http://bit.ly/2SlpTK6`

Understanding Haar cascades

Haar cascades are cascade classifiers that are based on Haar features. What is a cascade classifier? It is simply a concatenation of a set of weak classifiers that can be used to create a strong classifier. What do we mean by **weak** and **strong** classifiers? Weak classifiers are classifiers whose performance is limited. They don't have the ability to classify everything correctly. If you keep the problem really simple, they might perform at an acceptable level. Strong classifiers, on the other hand, are really good at classifying our data correctly. We will see how it all comes together in the next couple of paragraphs. Another important part of Haar cascades is **Haar features**. These features are simple summations of rectangles and differences of those areas across the image. Let's consider the following diagram:

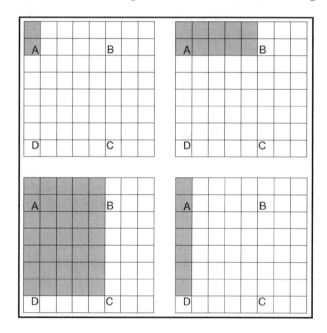

If we want to compute the Haar features for region ABCD, we just need to compute the difference between the white pixels and the blue pixels in that region. As we can see from the four diagrams, we use different patterns to build Haar features. There are a lot of other patterns that are used as well. We do this at multiple scales to make the system scale-invariant. When we say multiple scales, we just scale the image down to compute the same features again. This way, we can make it robust against size variations of a given object.

As it turns out, this concatenation system is a very good method for detecting objects in an image. In 2001, Paul Viola and Michael Jones published a seminal paper where they described a fast and effective method for object detection. If you are interested in learning more about it, you can check out their paper
at `http://www.cs.ubc.ca/~lowe/425/slides/13-ViolaJones.pdf`.

Let's dive deeper into it to understand what they actually did. They basically described an algorithm that uses a boosted cascade of simple classifiers. This system is used to build a strong classifier that can perform really well. Why did they use these simple classifiers instead of complex classifiers, which can be more accurate? Well, using this technique they were able to avoid the problem of having to build a single classifier that can perform with high precision. These single-step classifiers tend to be complex and computationally intensive. The reason their technique works so well is because the simple classifiers can be weak learners, which means they don't need to be complex. Consider the problem of building a table detector. We want to build a system that will automatically learn what a table looks like. Based on that knowledge, it should be able to identify whether there is a table in any given image. To build this system, the first step is to collect images that can be used to train our system. There are a lot of techniques available in the machine learning world that can be used to train a system such as this. Bear in mind that we need to collect a lot of table and non-table images if we want our system to perform well. In machine learning lingo, table images are called **positive** samples and the non-table images are called **negative** samples. Our system will ingest this data and then learn to differentiate between these two classes. In order to build a real-time system, we need to keep our classifier nice and simple. The only concern is that simple classifiers are not very accurate. If we try to make them more accurate, then the process will end up being computationally intensive, and hence slow. This trade-off between accuracy and speed is very common in machine learning. So, we overcome this problem by concatenating a bunch of weak classifiers to create a strong and unified classifier. We don't need the weak classifiers to be very accurate. To ensure the quality of the overall classifier, Viola and Jones have described a nifty technique in the cascading step. You can go through the paper to understand the full system.

Now that we understand the general pipeline, let's see how to build a system that can detect faces in a live video. The first step is to extract features from all the images. In this case, the algorithms need these features to learn and understand what faces look like. They used Haar features in their paper to build the feature vectors. Once we extract these features, we pass them through a cascade of classifiers. We just check all the different rectangular sub-regions and keep discarding the ones that don't have faces in them. This way, we arrive at the final answer quickly to see whether a given rectangle contains a face or not.

What are integral images?

In order to extract these Haar features, we will have to calculate the sum of the pixel values enclosed in many rectangular regions of the image. To make it scale-invariant, we are required to compute these areas at multiple scales (for various rectangle sizes). Implemented naively, this would be a very computationally-intensive process; we would have to iterate over all the pixels of each rectangle, including reading the same pixels multiple times if they are contained in different overlapping rectangles. If you want to build a system that can run in real-time, you cannot spend so much time in computation. We need to find a way to avoid this huge redundancy during the area computation because we iterate over the same pixels multiple times. To avoid it, we can use something called integral images. These images can be initialized at a linear time (by iterating only twice over the image) and then provide the sum of the pixels inside any rectangle of any size by reading only four values. To understand it better, let's look at the following diagram:

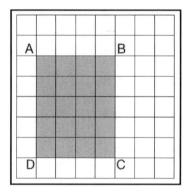

If we want to calculate the area of any rectangle in our diagram, we don't have to iterate through all the pixels in that region. Let's consider a rectangle formed by the top-left point in the image and any point, P, as the opposite corner. Let A_P denote the area of this rectangle. For example, in the previous image, A_B denotes the area of the 5 x 2 rectangle formed by taking the top-left point and **B** as opposite corners. Let's look at the following diagram for clarity:

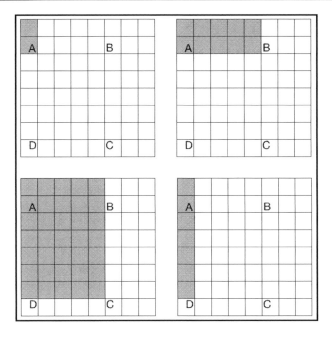

Let's consider the top-left square in the previous image. The blue pixels indicate the area between the top-left pixel and point **A**. This is denoted by A_A. The remaining diagrams are denoted by their respective names: A_B, A_C, and A_D. Now, if we want to calculate the area of the ABCD rectangle, as shown in the preceding diagram, we would use the following formula:

Area of the rectangle: $ABCD = A_C - (A_B + A_D - A_A)$

What's so special about this particular formula? As we know, extracting Haar features from the image includes computing these summations and we would have to do it for a lot of rectangles at multiple scales in the image. A lot of those calculations are repetitive because we would be iterating over the same pixels over and over again. It is so slow that building a real-time system wouldn't be feasible. Hence, we need this formula. As you can see, we don't have to iterate over the same pixels multiple times. If we want to compute the area of any rectangle, all the values on the right-hand side of the preceding equation are readily available in our integral image. We just pick up the right values, substitute them in the preceding equation, and extract the features.

Overlaying a face mask in a live video

OpenCV provides a nice face detection framework. We just need to load the cascade file and use it to detect the faces in an image. When we capture a video stream from the webcam, we can overlay funny masks on our faces. It will look something like this:

Let's look at the main parts of the code to see how to overlay this mask on the face in the input video stream. The full code is available in the downloadable code bundle provided along with this book:

```
#include "opencv2/core/utility.hpp"
#include "opencv2/objdetect/objdetect.hpp"
#include "opencv2/imgproc.hpp"
#include "opencv2/highgui.hpp"

using namespace cv;
using namespace std;

...

int main(int argc, char* argv[])
{
```

```
    string faceCascadeName = argv[1];
    // Variable declaration and initialization
    ...
    // Iterate until the user presses the Esc key
    while(true)
    {
        // Capture the current frame
        cap >> frame;
        // Resize the frame
        resize(frame, frame, Size(), scalingFactor, scalingFactor,
INTER_AREA);
        // Convert to grayscale
        cvtColor(frame, frameGray, COLOR_BGR2GRAY);
        // Equalize the histogram
        equalizeHist(frameGray, frameGray);
        // Detect faces
        faceCascade.detectMultiScale(frameGray, faces, 1.1, 2,
0|HAAR_SCALE_IMAGE, Size(30, 30) );
```

Let's take a quick stop to see what happened here. We start reading input frames from the webcam and resize it to our size of choice. The captured frame is a color image and face detection works on grayscale images. So, we convert it to grayscale and equalize the histogram. Why do we need to equalize the histogram? We need to do this to compensate for any issues, such as lighting or saturation. If the image is too bright or too dark, the detection will be poor. So, we need to equalize the histogram to ensure that our image has a healthy range of pixel values:

```
        // Draw green rectangle around the face
        for(auto& face:faces)
        {
            Rect faceRect(face.x, face.y, face.width, face.height);
            // Custom parameters to make the mask fit your face. You may
have to play around with them to make sure it works.
            int x = face.x - int(0.1*face.width);
            int y = face.y - int(0.0*face.height);
            int w = int(1.1 * face.width);
            int h = int(1.3 * face.height);
            // Extract region of interest (ROI) covering your face
            frameROI = frame(Rect(x,y,w,h));
```

At this point, we know where the face is. So we extract the region of interest to overlay the mask in the right position:

```
        // Resize the face mask image based on the dimensions of the
above ROI
        resize(faceMask, faceMaskSmall, Size(w,h));
        // Convert the previous image to grayscale
        cvtColor(faceMaskSmall, grayMaskSmall, COLOR_BGR2GRAY);
        // Threshold the previous image to isolate the pixels
associated only with the face mask
        threshold(grayMaskSmall, grayMaskSmallThresh, 230, 255,
THRESH_BINARY_INV);
```

We isolate the pixels associated with the face mask. We want to overlay the mask in such a way that it doesn't look like a rectangle. We want the exact boundaries of the overlaid object so that it looks natural. Let's go ahead and overlay the mask now:

```
        // Create mask by inverting the previous image (because we
don't want the background to affect the overlay)
        bitwise_not(grayMaskSmallThresh, grayMaskSmallThreshInv);
        // Use bitwise "AND" operator to extract precise boundary of
face mask
        bitwise_and(faceMaskSmall, faceMaskSmall, maskedFace,
grayMaskSmallThresh);
        // Use bitwise "AND" operator to overlay face mask
        bitwise_and(frameROI, frameROI, maskedFrame,
grayMaskSmallThreshInv);
        // Add the previously masked images and place it in the
original frame ROI to create the final image
        add(maskedFace, maskedFrame, frame(Rect(x,y,w,h)));
    }
  // code dealing with memory release and GUI

  return 1;
}
```

What happened in the code?

The first thing to note is that this code takes two input arguments—the **face cascade XML** file and the **mask image**. You can use the `haarcascade_frontalface_alt.xml` and `facemask.jpg` files that are provided under the `resources` folder. We need a classifier model that can be used to detect faces in an image and OpenCV provides a prebuilt XML file that can be used for this purpose. We use the `faceCascade.load()` function to load the XML file and also check whether the file is loaded correctly. We initiate the video-capture object to capture the input frames from the webcam. We then convert it to grayscale to run the detector. The `detectMultiScale` function is used to extract the boundaries of all the faces in the input image. We may have to scale down the image according to our needs, so the second argument in this function takes care of this. This scaling factor is the jump we take at each scale; since we need to look for faces at multiple scales, the next size will be 1.1 times bigger than the current size. The last parameter is a threshold that specifies the number of adjacent rectangles needed to keep the current rectangle. It can be used to increase the robustness of the face detector. We start the `while` loop and keep detecting the face in every frame until the user presses the *Esc* key. Once we detect a face, we need to overlay a mask on it. We may have to modify the dimensions slightly to ensure that the mask fits nicely. This customization is slightly subjective and it depends on the mask that's being used. Now that we have extracted the region of interest, we need to place our mask on top of this region. If we overlay the mask with its white background, it will look weird. We have to extract the exact curvy boundaries of the mask and then overlay it. We want the skull mask pixels to be visible and the remaining area should be transparent.

As we can see, the input mask has a white background. So, we create a mask by applying a threshold to the mask image. Using trial and error, we can see that a threshold of 240 works well. In the image, all the pixels with an intensity value greater than 240 will become 0, and all others will become 255. As far as the region of interest is concerned, we have to black out all the pixels in this region. To do that, we simply use the inverse of the mask that was just created. In the last step, we just add the masked versions to produce the final output image.

Get your sunglasses on

Now that we understand how to detect faces, we can generalize that concept to detect different parts of the face. We will be using an eye detector to overlay sunglasses in a live video. It's important to understand that the Viola-Jones framework can be applied to any object. The accuracy and robustness will depend on the uniqueness of the object. For example, the human face has very unique characteristics, so it's easy to train our system to be robust. On the other hand, an object such as a towel is too generic, and it has no distinguishing characteristics as such, so it's more difficult to build a robust towel detector. Once you build the eye detector and overlay the glasses, it will look something like this:

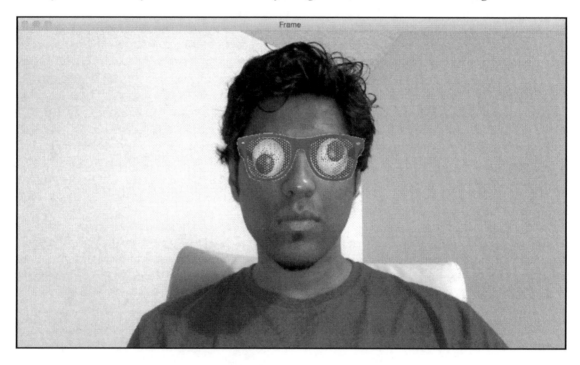

Let's look at the main parts of the code:

```
...
int main(int argc, char* argv[])
{
    string faceCascadeName = argv[1];
    string eyeCascadeName = argv[2];

    // Variable declaration and initialization
    ....
    // Face detection code
```

```
    ....
    vector<Point> centers;
    ....
    // Draw green circles around the eyes
    for( auto& face:faces )
    {
        Mat faceROI = frameGray(face[i]);
        vector<Rect> eyes;
        // In each face, detect eyes eyeCascade.detectMultiScale(faceROI,
  eyes, 1.1, 2, 0 |CV_HAAR_SCALE_IMAGE, Size(30, 30));
```

As we can see here, we run the eye detector only in the face region. We don't need to search the entire image for eyes because we know eyes will always be on a face:

```
        // For each eye detected, compute the center
        for(auto& eyes:eyes)
        {
            Point center( face.x + eye.x + int(eye.width*0.5), face.y +
  eye.y + int(eye.height*0.5) );
            centers.push_back(center);
        }
    }
    // Overlay sunglasses only if both eyes are detected
    if(centers.size() == 2)
    {
        Point leftPoint, rightPoint;
        // Identify the left and right eyes
        if(centers[0].x < centers[1].x)
        {
            leftPoint = centers[0];
            rightPoint = centers[1];
        }
        else
        {
            leftPoint = centers[1];
            rightPoint = centers[0];
        }
```

We detect the eyes and store them only when we find both of them. We then use their coordinates to determine which one is the left eye and which one is the right eye:

```
        // Custom parameters to make the sunglasses fit your face. You
  may have to play around with them to make sure it works.
        int w = 2.3 * (rightPoint.x - leftPoint.x);
        int h = int(0.4 * w);
        int x = leftPoint.x - 0.25*w;
        int y = leftPoint.y - 0.5*h;
        // Extract region of interest (ROI) covering both the eyes
```

```
                frameROI = frame(Rect(x,y,w,h));
                // Resize the sunglasses image based on the dimensions of the
above ROI
                resize(eyeMask, eyeMaskSmall, Size(w,h));
```

In the preceding code, we adjusted the size of the sunglasses to fit the scale of our faces on the webcam. Let's check the remaining code:

```
                // Convert the previous image to grayscale
                cvtColor(eyeMaskSmall, grayMaskSmall, COLOR_BGR2GRAY);
                // Threshold the previous image to isolate the foreground
object
                threshold(grayMaskSmall, grayMaskSmallThresh, 245, 255,
THRESH_BINARY_INV);
                // Create mask by inverting the previous image (because we
don't want the background to affect the overlay)
                bitwise_not(grayMaskSmallThresh, grayMaskSmallThreshInv);
                // Use bitwise "AND" operator to extract precise boundary of
sunglasses
                bitwise_and(eyeMaskSmall, eyeMaskSmall, maskedEye,
grayMaskSmallThresh);
                // Use bitwise "AND" operator to overlay sunglasses
                bitwise_and(frameROI, frameROI, maskedFrame,
grayMaskSmallThreshInv);
                // Add the previously masked images and place it in the
original frame ROI to create the final image
                add(maskedEye, maskedFrame, frame(Rect(x,y,w,h)));
            }

        // code for memory release and GUI

    return 1;
}
```

Looking inside the code

You may have noticed that the flow of the code looks similar to the face detection code that we discussed in the *Overlaying a face mask in a live video* section. We load a face detection cascade classifier as well as the eye detection cascade classifier. Now, why do we need to load the face cascade classifier when we are detecting eyes? Well, we don't really need to use the face detector, but it helps us in limiting our search for the eyes' location. We know that the eyes are always located on somebody's face, so we can limit eye detection to the face region. The first step would be to detect the face and then run our eye detector code on this region. Since we would be operating on a smaller region, it would be faster and way more efficient.

For each frame, we start by detecting the face. We then go ahead and detect the location of the eyes by operating on this region. After this step, we need to overlay the sunglasses. To do that, we need to resize the sunglasses image to make sure it fits our face. To get the proper scale, we can consider the distance between the two eyes that are being detected. We overlay the sunglasses only when we detect both eyes. That's why we run the eye detector first, collect all the centers, and then overlay the sunglasses. Once we have this, we just need to overlay the sunglasses mask. The principle used for masking is very similar to the principle we used to overlay the face mask. You may have to customize the sizing and position of the sunglasses, depending on what you want. You can play around with different types of sunglasses to see what they look like.

Tracking the nose, mouth, and ears

Now that you know how to track different things using the framework, you can try tracking your nose, mouth, and ears too. Let's use a nose detector to overlay a funny nose:

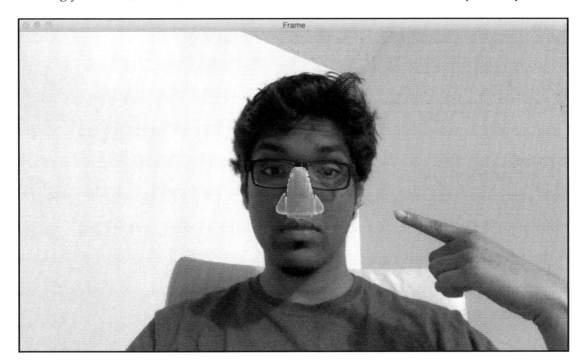

You can refer to the code files for a full implementation of this detector. The `haarcascade_mcs_nose.xml`, `haarcascade_mcs_mouth.xml`, `haarcascade_mcs_leftear.xml`, and `haarcascade_mcs_rightear.xml` cascade files can be used to track the different face parts. Play around with them and try to overlay a mustache or Dracula ears on yourself.

Summary

In this chapter, we discussed Haar cascades and integral images. We looked at how the face detection pipeline is built. We learned how to detect and track faces in a live video stream. We discussed using the face detection framework to detect various face parts, such as eyes, ears, nose, and mouth. Finally, we learned how to overlay masks on the input image using the results of face part detection.

In the next chapter, we are going to learn about video surveillance, background removal, and morphological image processing.

8
Video Surveillance, Background Modeling, and Morphological Operations

In this chapter, we are going to learn how to detect a moving object in a video taken from a static camera. This is used extensively in video surveillance systems. We will discuss the different characteristics that can be used to build this system. We will learn about background modeling and see how we can use it to build a model of the background in a live video. Once we do this, we will combine all the blocks to detect the object of interest in the video.

By the end of this chapter, you should be able to answer the following questions:

- What is naive background subtraction?
- What is frame differencing?
- How do we build a background model?
- How do we identify a new object in a static video?
- What is morphological image processing and how is it related to background modeling?
- How do we achieve different effects using morphological operators?

Technical requirements

This chapter requires familiarity with the basics of the C++ programming language. All the code used in this chapter can be downloaded from the following GitHub link: `https://github.com/PacktPublishing/Building-Computer-Vision-Projects-with-OpenCV4-and-CPlusPlus/tree/master/Chapter08`. The code can be executed on any operating system, though it is only tested on Ubuntu.

Check out the following video to see the Code in Action:

`http://bit.ly/2SfqzRo`

Understanding background subtraction

Background subtraction is very useful in video surveillance. Basically, the background subtraction technique performs really well in cases where we have to detect moving objects in a static scene. How is this useful for video surveillance? The process of video surveillance involves dealing with constant data flow. The data stream keeps coming in and we need to analyze it to recognize any suspicious activity. Let's consider the example of a hotel lobby. All the walls and furniture have a fixed location. If we build a background model, we can use it to identify suspicious activity in the lobby. We are taking advantage of the fact that the background scene remains static (which happens to be true in this case). This helps us avoid any unnecessary computational overhead. As the name indicates, this algorithm works by detecting and assigning each pixel of an image to two classes, either the background (assumed static and stable) or the foreground, and subtracting it from the current frame to obtain the foreground image part, which includes moving objects such as persons, cars, and so on. With the static assumption, the foreground objects will naturally correspond to objects or people moving in front of the background.

In order to detect moving objects, we need to build a model of the background. This is not the same as direct frame differencing, because we are actually modeling the background and using this model to detect moving objects. When we say that we are modeling the background, we are basically building a mathematical formula that can be used to represent the background. This is much better than the simple frame-differencing technique. This technique tries to detect static parts of the scene and then include small updates in the build statistic formula of the background model. This background model is then used to detect background pixels. So, it's an adaptive technique that can adjust according to the scene.

Naive background subtraction

Let's start the discussion from the beginning. What does a background subtraction process look like? Consider the following image:

The previous image represents the background scene. Now, let's introduce a new object into this scene:

As we can see, there is a new object in the scene. So, if we compute the difference between this image and our background model, you should be able to identify the location of the TV remote:

The overall process looks like this:

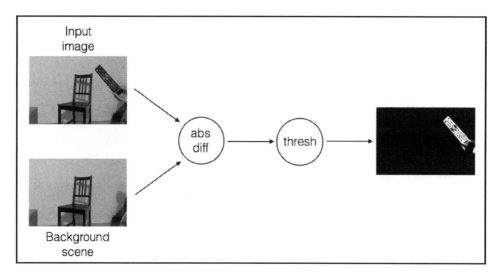

Does it work well?

There's a reason we call it the **naive** approach! It works under ideal conditions and, as we know, nothing is ideal in the real world. It does a reasonably good job of computing the shape of the given object, but it does so under some constraints. One of the main requirements of this approach is that the color and intensity of the object should be sufficiently different from that of the background. Some of the factors that affect this kind of algorithm are image noise, lighting conditions, and autofocus in cameras.

Once a new object enters our scene and stays there, it will be difficult to detect new objects that are in front of it. This is because we are not updating our background model, and the new object is now a part of our background. Consider the following image:

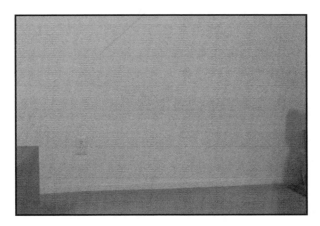

Now, let's say a new object enters our scene:

We detect this to be a new object, which is fine! Let's say another object comes into the scene:

It will be difficult to identify the location of these two different objects because their locations are overlapping. Here's what we get after subtracting the background and applying the threshold:

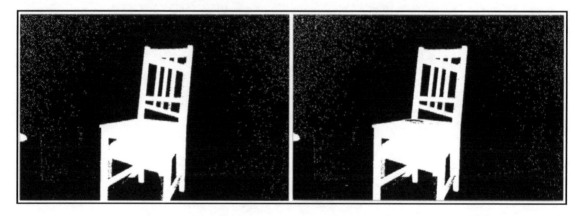

In this approach, we assume that the background is static. If some parts of our background start moving, those parts will start getting detected as new objects. So, even movements that are minor, say a waving flag, will cause problems in our detection algorithm. This approach is also sensitive to changes in illumination and it cannot handle any camera movement. Needless to say, it's a delicate approach! We need something that can handle all these things in the real world.

Frame differencing

We know that we cannot keep a static background image pattern that can be used to detect objects. One of the ways to fix this would be by using frame differencing. It is one of the simplest techniques we can use to see what parts of the video are moving. When we consider a live video stream, the difference between successive frames gives a lot of information. The concept is fairly straightforward! We just take the difference between successive frames and display the differences between them.

If I move my laptop rapidly, we can see something like this:

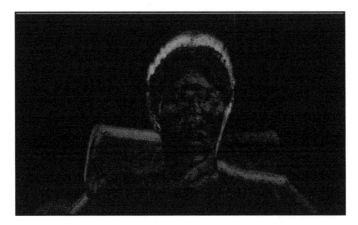

Instead of the laptop, let's move the object and see what happens. If I rapidly shake my head, it will look something like this:

As you can see from the previous images, only the moving parts of the video get highlighted. This gives us a good starting point to see what areas are moving in the video. Let's look at the function to compute the frame differences:

```
Mat frameDiff(Mat prevFrame, Mat curFrame, Mat nextFrame)
{
    Mat diffFrames1, diffFrames2, output;
    // Compute absolute difference between current frame and the next
    absdiff(nextFrame, curFrame, diffFrames1);
    // Compute absolute difference between current frame and the previous
    absdiff(curFrame, prevFrame, diffFrames2);
    // Bitwise "AND" operation between the previous two diff images
    bitwise_and(diffFrames1, diffFrames2, output);
    return output;
}
```

Frame differencing is fairly straightforward! You compute the absolute differences between the current frame and the previous frame, and between the current frame and the next frame. We then take these frame differences and apply a bitwise **AND** operator. This will highlight the moving parts in the image. If you just compute the difference between the current frame and the previous frame, it tends to be noisy. Hence, we need to use the bitwise AND operator between successive frame differences to get some stability when we see the moving objects.

Let's look at the function that can extract and return a frame from the webcam:

```
Mat getFrame(VideoCapture cap, float scalingFactor)
{
    Mat frame, output;

    // Capture the current frame
    cap >> frame;

    // Resize the frame
    resize(frame, frame, Size(), scalingFactor, scalingFactor, INTER_AREA);

    // Convert to grayscale
    cvtColor(frame, output, COLOR_BGR2GRAY);

    return output;
}
```

As we can see, it's pretty straightforward. We just need to resize the frame and convert it to grayscale. Now that we have the helper functions ready, let's look at the main function and see how it all comes together:

```
int main(int argc, char* argv[])
{
    Mat frame, prevFrame, curFrame, nextFrame;
    char ch;

    // Create the capture object
    // 0 -> input arg that specifies it should take the input from the
webcam
    VideoCapture cap(0);

    // If you cannot open the webcam, stop the execution!
    if(!cap.isOpened())
        return -1;

    //create GUI windows
    namedWindow("Frame");


    // Scaling factor to resize the input frames from the webcam
    float scalingFactor = 0.75;

    prevFrame = getFrame(cap, scalingFactor);
    curFrame = getFrame(cap, scalingFactor);
    nextFrame = getFrame(cap, scalingFactor);

    // Iterate until the user presses the Esc key
    while(true)
    {
        // Show the object movement
        imshow("Object Movement", frameDiff(prevFrame, curFrame,
nextFrame));

        // Update the variables and grab the next frame
        prevFrame = curFrame;
        curFrame = nextFrame;
        nextFrame = getFrame(cap, scalingFactor);

        // Get the keyboard input and check if it's 'Esc'
        // 27 -> ASCII value of 'Esc' key
        ch = waitKey( 30 );
        if (ch == 27) {
            break;
        }
    }
}
```

```
    // Release the video capture object
    cap.release();

    // Close all windows
    destroyAllWindows();

    return 1;
}
```

How well does it work?

As we can see, frame differencing addresses a couple of important problems we faced earlier. It can quickly adapt to lighting changes or camera movement. If an object comes in to the frame and stays there, it will not be detected in future frames. One of the main concerns of this approach is about detecting uniformly colored objects. It can only detect the edges of a uniformly colored object. The reason is that a large portion of this object will result in very low pixel differences:

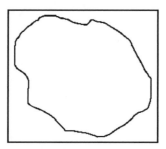

Let's say this object moved slightly. If we compare this with the previous frame, it will look like this:

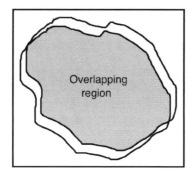

Hence, we have very few pixels that are labeled on that object. Another concern is that it is difficult to detect whether an object moving toward the camera or away from it.

The Mixture of Gaussians approach

Before we talk about **Mixture of Gaussians** (MOG), let's see what a **mixture model** is. A mixture model is just a statistical model that can be used to represent the presence of subpopulations within our data. We don't really care about what category each data point belongs to. All we need to do is identify that the data has multiple groups inside it. If we represent each subpopulation using the Gaussian function, then it's called Mixture of Gaussians. Let's consider the following photograph:

Now, as we gather more frames in this scene, every part of the image will gradually become a part of the background model. This is what we discussed earlier in the *Frame differencing* section as well. If a scene is static, the model adapts itself to make sure the background model is updated. The foreground mask, which is supposed to represent the foreground object, looks like a black image at this point because every pixel is part of the background model.

OpenCV has multiple algorithms implemented for the Mixture of Gaussians approach. One of them is called **MOG** and the other is called **MOG2**: refer to this link for a detailed explanation: `http://docs.opencv.org/master/db/d5c/tutorial_py_bg_subtraction. html#gsc.tab=0`. You will also be able check out the original research papers that were used to implement these algorithms.

Let's wait for some time and then introduce a new object into the scene. Let's look at what the new foreground mask looks like, using the MOG2 approach:

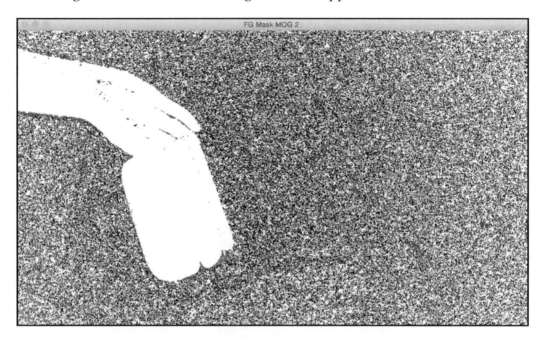

As you can see, the new objects are being identified correctly. Let's look at the interesting part of the code (you can get the full code in the .cpp files):

```cpp
int main(int argc, char* argv[])
{

    // Variable declaration and initialization
    ....
    // Iterate until the user presses the Esc key
    while(true)
    {
        // Capture the current frame
        cap >> frame;

        // Resize the frame
        resize(frame, frame, Size(), scalingFactor, scalingFactor,
INTER_AREA);

        // Update the MOG2 background model based on the current frame
        pMOG2->apply(frame, fgMaskMOG2);

        // Show the MOG2 foreground mask
```

```
        imshow("FG Mask MOG 2", fgMaskMOG2);

        // Get the keyboard input and check if it's 'Esc'
        // 27 -> ASCII value of 'Esc' key
        ch = waitKey( 30 );
        if (ch == 27) {
            break;
        }
    }

    // Release the video capture object
    cap.release();

    // Close all windows
    destroyAllWindows();

    return 1;
}
```

What happened in the code?

Let's quickly go through the code and see what's happening there. We use the Mixture of Gaussians model to create a background subtractor object. This object represents the model that will be updated as and when we encounter new frames from the webcam. We initialized two background subtraction models—BackgroundSubtractorMOG and BackgroundSubtractorMOG2. They represent two different algorithms that are used for background subtraction. The first one refers to the paper by *P. KadewTraKuPong* and *R. Bowden,* titled *An Improved Adaptive Background Mixture Model for Real-time Tracking with Shadow Detection.* You can check it out at
http://personal.ee.surrey.ac.uk/Personal/R.Bowden/publications/avbs01/avbs01.pd
f. The second one refers to the paper by *Z. Zivkovic,* titled *Improved Adaptive Gaussian Mixture Model for Background Subtraction.* You can check it out here:
http://www.zoranz.net/Publications/zivkovic2004ICPR.pdf.
We start an infinite while loop and continuously read the input frames from the webcam. With each frame, we update the background model, as indicated in the following lines:

```
    pMOG2->apply(frame, fgMaskMOG2);
```

The background model gets updated in these steps. Now, if a new object enters the scene and stays there, it will become part of the background model. This helps us overcome one of the biggest shortcomings of the **naive** background subtraction model.

Morphological image processing

As we discussed earlier, background subtraction methods are affected by many factors. Their accuracy depends on how we capture the data and how it's processed. One of the biggest factors that affects these algorithms is the noise level. When we say **noise**, we are talking about things such as graininess in an image and isolated black/white pixels. These issues tend to affect the quality of our algorithms. This is where morphological image processing comes into play. Morphological image processing is used extensively in a lot of real-time systems to ensure the quality of the output. Morphological image processing refers to processing the shapes of features in the image; for example, you can make a shape thicker or thinner. Morphological operators rely not on how the pixels are ordered in an image, but on their values. This is why they are really well suited to manipulating shapes in binary images. Morphological image processing can be applied to grayscale images as well, but the pixel values will not matter much.

What's the underlying principle?

Morphological operators use a structuring element to modify an image. What is a structuring element? A structuring element is basically a small shape that can be used to inspect a small region in the image. It is positioned at all the pixel locations in the image so that it can inspect that neighborhood. We basically take a small window and overlay it on a pixel. Depending on the response, we take appropriate action at that pixel location.

Let's consider the following input image:

We are going to apply a bunch of morphological operations to this image to see how the shape changes.

Slimming the shapes

We achieve this effect using an operation called **erosion**. This is the operation that makes a shape thinner by peeling the boundary layers of all the shapes in the image:

Let's look at the function that performs morphological erosion:

```cpp
Mat performErosion(Mat inputImage, int erosionElement, int erosionSize)
{
    Mat outputImage;
    int erosionType;

    if(erosionElement == 0)
        erosionType = MORPH_RECT;
    else if(erosionElement == 1)
        erosionType = MORPH_CROSS;
    else if(erosionElement == 2)
        erosionType = MORPH_ELLIPSE;

    // Create the structuring element for erosion
    Mat element = getStructuringElement(erosionType, Size(2*erosionSize +
1, 2*erosionSize + 1), Point(erosionSize, erosionSize));

    // Erode the image using the structuring element
    erode(inputImage, outputImage, element);

    // Return the output image
    return outputImage;
}
```

You can check out the full code in the `.cpp` files to understand how to use this function. We basically build a structuring element using a built-in OpenCV function. This object is used as a probe to modify each pixel based on certain conditions. These conditions refer to what's happening around that particular pixel in the image. For example, is it surrounded by white pixels? Or is it surround by black pixels? Once we have an answer, we take the appropriate action.

Thickening the shapes

We use an operation called **dilation** to achieve thickening. This is the operation that makes a shape thicker by adding boundary layers to all the shapes in the image:

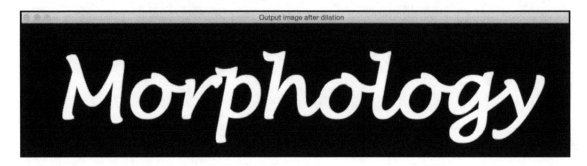

Here is the code to do it:

```
Mat performDilation(Mat inputImage, int dilationElement, int dilationSize)
{
    Mat outputImage;
    int dilationType;

    if(dilationElement == 0)
        dilationType = MORPH_RECT;
    else if(dilationElement == 1)
        dilationType = MORPH_CROSS;
    else if(dilationElement == 2)
        dilationType = MORPH_ELLIPSE;

    // Create the structuring element for dilation
    Mat element = getStructuringElement(dilationType, Size(2*dilationSize +
1, 2*dilationSize + 1), Point(dilationSize, dilationSize));

    // Dilate the image using the structuring element
    dilate(inputImage, outputImage, element);

    // Return the output image
    return outputImage;
}
```

Other morphological operators

Here are some other interesting morphological operators. Let's look at the output image first. We can look at the code at the end of this section.

Morphological opening

This is the operation that **opens** a shape. This operator is frequently used for noise removal in images. It's basically erosion followed by dilation. Morphological opening removes small objects from the foreground in the image by placing them in the background:

Here is the function to perform morphological opening:

```
Mat performOpening(Mat inputImage, int morphologyElement, int
morphologySize)
{

    Mat outputImage, tempImage;
    int morphologyType;

    if(morphologyElement == 0)
        morphologyType = MORPH_RECT;
    else if(morphologyElement == 1)
        morphologyType = MORPH_CROSS;
    else if(morphologyElement == 2)
        morphologyType = MORPH_ELLIPSE;

    // Create the structuring element for erosion
    Mat element = getStructuringElement(morphologyType,
Size(2*morphologySize + 1, 2*morphologySize + 1), Point(morphologySize,
morphologySize));

    // Apply morphological opening to the image using the structuring
```

```
element
    erode(inputImage, tempImage, element);
    dilate(tempImage, outputImage, element);

    // Return the output image
    return outputImage;
}
```

As we can see here, we apply **erosion** and **dilation** on the image to perform morphological opening.

Morphological closing

This is the operation that **closes** a shape by filling the gaps, as shown in the following screenshot. This operation is also used for noise removal. It's basically dilation followed by erosion. This operation removes tiny holes in the foreground by changing small objects in the background into the foreground:

Let's quickly look at the function to perform morphological closing:

```
Mat performClosing(Mat inputImage, int morphologyElement, int
morphologySize)
{

    Mat outputImage, tempImage;
    int morphologyType;

    if(morphologyElement == 0)
        morphologyType = MORPH_RECT;
    else if(morphologyElement == 1)
        morphologyType = MORPH_CROSS;
    else if(morphologyElement == 2)
        morphologyType = MORPH_ELLIPSE;
```

```
    // Create the structuring element for erosion
    Mat element = getStructuringElement(morphologyType,
Size(2*morphologySize + 1, 2*morphologySize + 1), Point(morphologySize,
morphologySize));

    // Apply morphological opening to the image using the structuring
element
    dilate(inputImage, tempImage, element);
    erode(tempImage, outputImage, element);
    // Return the output image
    return outputImage;
}
```

Drawing the boundary

We achieve this using a morphological gradient. This is the operation that draws the boundary around a shape by taking the difference between the dilation and erosion of an image:

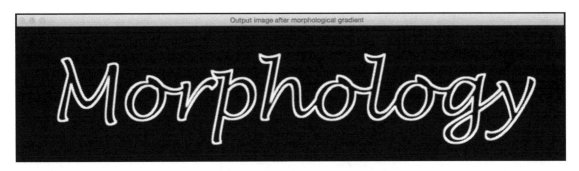

Let's look at the function to perform morphological gradient:

```
Mat performMorphologicalGradient(Mat inputImage, int morphologyElement, int
morphologySize)
{
    Mat outputImage, tempImage1, tempImage2;
    int morphologyType;

    if(morphologyElement == 0)
        morphologyType = MORPH_RECT;
    else if(morphologyElement == 1)
        morphologyType = MORPH_CROSS;
    else if(morphologyElement == 2)
        morphologyType = MORPH_ELLIPSE;
```

```
    // Create the structuring element for erosion
    Mat element = getStructuringElement(morphologyType,
Size(2*morphologySize + 1, 2*morphologySize + 1), Point(morphologySize,
morphologySize));
    // Apply morphological gradient to the image using the structuring
element
    dilate(inputImage, tempImage1, element);
    erode(inputImage, tempImage2, element);

    // Return the output image
    return tempImage1 - tempImage2;
}
```

Top Hat transform

This transform extracts finer details from the images. This is the difference between the input image and its morphological opening. This gives us the objects in the image that are smaller than the structuring element and brighter than the surroundings. Depending on the size of the structuring element, we can extract various objects in the given image:

If you look at the output image carefully, you can see those black rectangles. It means that the structuring element was able to fit in there, and so those regions are blackened out. Here is the function:

```
Mat performTopHat(Mat inputImage, int morphologyElement, int
morphologySize)
{

    Mat outputImage;
    int morphologyType;

    if(morphologyElement == 0)
        morphologyType = MORPH_RECT;
    else if(morphologyElement == 1)
```

```
        morphologyType = MORPH_CROSS;
    else if(morphologyElement == 2)
        morphologyType = MORPH_ELLIPSE;

    // Create the structuring element for erosion
    Mat element = getStructuringElement(morphologyType,
Size(2*morphologySize + 1, 2*morphologySize + 1), Point(morphologySize,
morphologySize));

    // Apply top hat operation to the image using the structuring element
    outputImage = inputImage - performOpening(inputImage,
morphologyElement, morphologySize);

    // Return the output image
    return outputImage;
}
```

Black Hat transform

This transform extract finer details from the image as well. This is the difference between the morphological closing of an image and the image itself. This gives us the objects in the image that are smaller than the structuring element and darker than its surroundings:

Let's look at the function to perform a Black Hat transform:

```
Mat performBlackHat(Mat inputImage, int morphologyElement, int
morphologySize)
{
    Mat outputImage;
    int morphologyType;

    if(morphologyElement == 0)
        morphologyType = MORPH_RECT;
    else if(morphologyElement == 1)
        morphologyType = MORPH_CROSS;
```

```
    else if(morphologyElement == 2)
        morphologyType = MORPH_ELLIPSE;

    // Create the structuring element for erosion
    Mat element = getStructuringElement(morphologyType,
Size(2*morphologySize + 1, 2*morphologySize + 1), Point(morphologySize,
morphologySize));

    // Apply black hat operation to the image using the structuring element
    outputImage = performClosing(inputImage, morphologyElement,
morphologySize) - inputImage;

    // Return the output image
    return outputImage;
}
```

Summary

In this chapter, we learned about the algorithms that are used for background modeling and morphological image processing. We discussed naive background subtraction and its limitations. We looked at how to get motion information using frame differencing and how it can be limiting when we want to track different types of objects. This led to our discussion about the Mixture of Gaussians. We discussed the formula and how we can implement it. We then discussed morphological image processing, which can be used for various purposes, and different operations were covered to show the use cases.

In the next chapter, we are going to discuss object tracking and the various techniques that can be used to do it.

Learning Object Tracking

9

In the previous chapter, we learned about video surveillance, background modeling, and morphological image processing. We discussed how we can use different morphological operators to apply cool visual effects to input images. In this chapter, we are going to learn how to track an object in a live video. We will discuss the different characteristics of an object that can be used to track it. We will also learn about different methods and techniques for object tracking. Object tracking is used extensively in robotics, self-driving cars, vehicle tracking, player tracking in sports, and video compression.

By the end of this chapter, you will know the following:

- How to track objects of a specific color
- How to build an interactive object tracker
- What a corner detector is
- How to detect good features to track
- How to build an optical flow-based feature tracker

Technical requirements

This chapter requires familiarity with the basics of the C++ programming language. All the code used in this chapter can be downloaded from the following GitHub link: `https://github.com/PacktPublishing/Building-Computer-Vision-Projects-with-OpenCV4-and-CPlusPlus/tree/master/Chapter09`. The code can be executed on any operating system, though it is only tested on Ubuntu.

Check out the following video to see the Code in Action:
`http://bit.ly/2SidbMc`

Tracking objects of a specific color

In order to build a good object tracker, we need to understand what characteristics can be used to make our tracking robust and accurate. So, let's take a baby step in that direction and see whether we can use colorspace information to come up with a good visual tracker. One thing to keep in mind is that color information is sensitive to lighting conditions. In real-world applications, you will have to do some preprocessing to take care of that. But for now, let's assume that somebody else is doing that and we are getting clean color images.

There are many different colorspaces, and picking a good one will depend on the different applications that a user is using. While RGB is the native representation on a computer screen, it's not necessarily ideal for humans. When it comes to humans, we give names to colors more naturally based on their hue, which is why **hue saturation value (HSV)** is probably one of the most informative colorspaces. It closely aligns with how we perceive colors. Hue refers to the color spectrum, saturation refers to the intensity of a particular color, and value refers to the brightness of that pixel. This is actually represented in a cylindrical format. You can find a simple explanation at http://infohost.nmt.edu/tcc/help/pubs/colortheory/web/hsv.html. We can take the pixels of an image to the HSV colorspace and then use this colorspace to measure distances in this colorspace and threshold in this space thresholding to track a given object.

Consider the following frame in the video:

If you run it through the colorspace filter and track the object, you will see something like this:

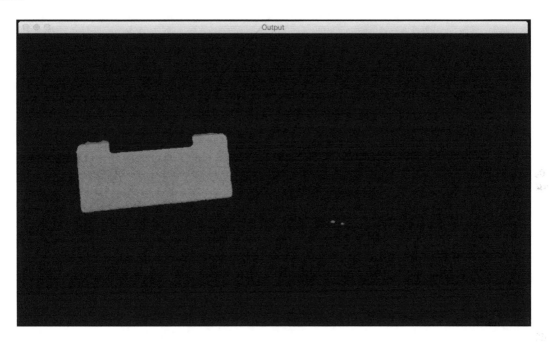

As we can see here, our tracker recognizes a particular object in the video based on the color characteristics. In order to use this tracker, we need to know the color distribution of our target object. Here is the code to track a colored object, which selects only pixels that have a certain given hue. The code is well-commented, so read the explanation about each term to see what's happening:

```
int main(int argc, char* argv[])
{
    // Variable declarations and initializations
    // Iterate until the user presses the Esc key
    while(true)
    {
        // Initialize the output image before each iteration
        outputImage = Scalar(0,0,0);
        // Capture the current frame
        cap >> frame;
        // Check if 'frame' is empty
        if(frame.empty())
            break;
        // Resize the frame
        resize(frame, frame, Size(), scalingFactor, scalingFactor,
```

```
INTER_AREA);
        // Convert to HSV colorspace
        cvtColor(frame, hsvImage, COLOR_BGR2HSV);
        // Define the range of "blue" color in HSV colorspace
        Scalar lowerLimit = Scalar(60,100,100);
        Scalar upperLimit = Scalar(180,255,255);
        // Threshold the HSV image to get only blue color
        inRange(hsvImage, lowerLimit, upperLimit, mask);
        // Compute bitwise-AND of input image and mask
        bitwise_and(frame, frame, outputImage, mask=mask);
        // Run median filter on the output to smoothen it
        medianBlur(outputImage, outputImage, 5);
        // Display the input and output image
        imshow("Input", frame);
        imshow("Output", outputImage);
        // Get the keyboard input and check if it's 'Esc'
        // 30 -> wait for 30 ms
        // 27 -> ASCII value of 'ESC' key
        ch = waitKey(30);
        if (ch == 27) {
            break;
        }
    }
    return 1;
}
```

Building an interactive object tracker

A colorspace-based tracker gives us the freedom to track a colored object, but we are also constrained to a predefined color. What if we just want to pick an object at random? How do we build an object tracker that can learn the characteristics of the selected object and just track it automatically? This is where the **continuously-adaptive meanshift (CAMShift)** algorithm comes into picture. It's basically an improved version of the meanshift algorithm.

The concept of meanshift is actually nice and simple. Let's say we select a region of interest and we want our object tracker to track that object. In this region, we select a bunch of points based on the color histogram and we compute the centroid of spatial points. If the centroid lies at the center of this region, we know that the object hasn't moved. But if the centroid is not at the center of this region, then we know that the object is moving in some direction. The movement of the centroid controls the direction in which the object is moving. So, we move the bounding box of the object to a new location so that the new centroid becomes the center of this bounding box. Hence, this algorithm is called meanshift, because the mean (the centroid) is shifting. This way, we keep ourselves updated with the current location of the object.

But the problem with meanshift is that the size of the bounding box is not allowed to change. When you move the object away from the camera, the object will appear smaller to the human eye, but meanshift will not take that into account. The size of the bounding box will remain the same throughout the tracking session. Hence, we need to use CAMShift. The advantage of CAMShift is that it can adapt the size of the bounding box to the size of the object. Along with that, it can also keep track of the orientation of the object.

Let's consider the following frame, in which the object is highlighted:

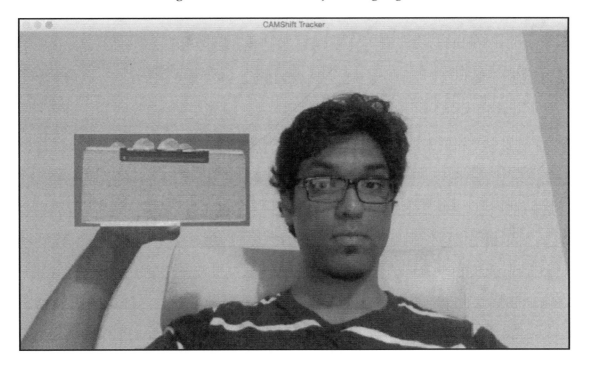

Now that we have selected the object, the algorithm computes the histogram backprojection and extracts all the information. What is histogram backprojection? It's just a way of identifying how well the image fits into our histogram model. We compute the histogram model of a particular thing and then use this model to find that thing in an image. Let's move the object and see how it's getting tracked:

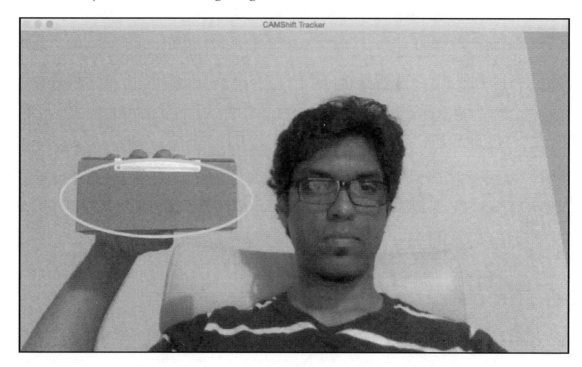

It looks like the object is getting tracked fairly well. Let's change the orientation and see whether the tracking is maintained:

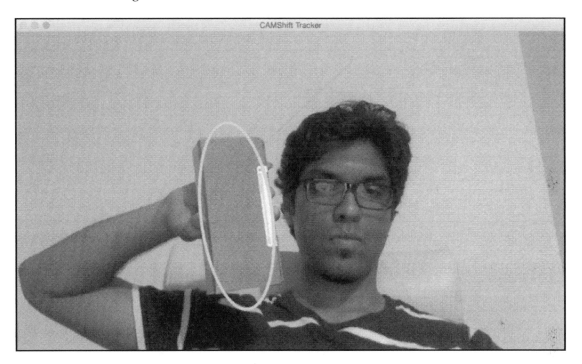

As we can see, the bounding ellipse has changed its location as well as orientation. Let's change the perspective of the object and see whether it's still able to track it:

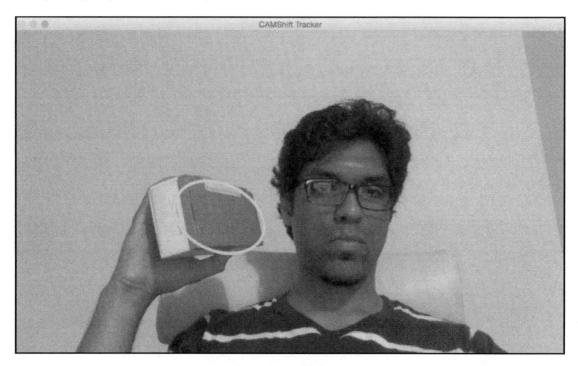

We're still good! The bounding ellipse has changed the aspect ratio to reflect the fact that the object looks skewed now (because of the perspective transformation). Let's look at the user interface functionality in the code:

```
Mat image;
Point originPoint;
Rect selectedRect;
bool selectRegion = false;
int trackingFlag = 0;

// Function to track the mouse events
void onMouse(int event, int x, int y, int, void*)
{
    if(selectRegion)
    {
        selectedRect.x = MIN(x, originPoint.x);
        selectedRect.y = MIN(y, originPoint.y);
        selectedRect.width = std::abs(x - originPoint.x);
        selectedRect.height = std::abs(y - originPoint.y);
```

```
            selectedRect &= Rect(0, 0, image.cols, image.rows);
    }
    switch(event)
    {
        case EVENT_LBUTTONDOWN:
            originPoint = Point(x,y);
            selectedRect = Rect(x,y,0,0);
            selectRegion = true;
            break;
        case EVENT_LBUTTONUP:
            selectRegion = false;
            if( selectedRect.width > 0 && selectedRect.height > 0 )
            {
                trackingFlag = -1;
            }
            break;
    }
}
```

This function basically captures the coordinates of the rectangle that was selected in the window. The user just needs to click and drag with the mouse. There are a set of built-in functions in OpenCV that help us to detect these different mouse events.

Here is the code for performing object tracking based on CAMShift:

```
int main(int argc, char* argv[])
{
    // Variable declaration and initialization
    ....
    // Iterate until the user presses the Esc key
    while(true)
    {
        // Capture the current frame
        cap >> frame;
        // Check if 'frame' is empty
        if(frame.empty())
            break;
        // Resize the frame
        resize(frame, frame, Size(), scalingFactor, scalingFactor,
INTER_AREA);
        // Clone the input frame
        frame.copyTo(image);
        // Convert to HSV colorspace
        cvtColor(image, hsvImage, COLOR_BGR2HSV);
```

We now have the HSV image waiting to be processed. Let's go ahead and see how we can use our thresholds to process this image:

```
if(trackingFlag)
{
    // Check for all the values in 'hsvimage' that are within the
specified range
    // and put the result in 'mask'
    inRange(hsvImage, Scalar(0, minSaturation, minValue),
Scalar(180, 256, maxValue), mask);
    // Mix the specified channels
    int channels[] = {0, 0};
    hueImage.create(hsvImage.size(), hsvImage.depth());
    mixChannels(&hsvImage, 1, &hueImage, 1, channels, 1);
    if(trackingFlag < 0)
    {
        // Create images based on selected regions of interest
        Mat roi(hueImage, selectedRect), maskroi(mask,
selectedRect);
        // Compute the histogram and normalize it
        calcHist(&roi, 1, 0, maskroi, hist, 1, &histSize,
&histRanges);
        normalize(hist, hist, 0, 255, NORM_MINMAX);
        trackingRect = selectedRect;
        trackingFlag = 1;
    }
```

As we can see here, we use the HSV image to compute the histogram of the region. We use our thresholds to locate the required color in the HSV spectrum and then filter out the image based on that. Let's go ahead and see how we can compute the histogram backprojection:

```
    // Compute the histogram backprojection
    calcBackProject(&hueImage, 1, 0, hist, backproj, &histRanges);
    backproj &= mask;
    RotatedRect rotatedTrackingRect = CamShift(backproj,
trackingRect, TermCriteria(TermCriteria::EPS | TermCriteria::COUNT, 10,
1));
    // Check if the area of trackingRect is too small
    if(trackingRect.area() <= 1)
    {
        // Use an offset value to make sure the trackingRect has a
minimum size
        int cols = backproj.cols, rows = backproj.rows;
        int offset = MIN(rows, cols) + 1;
        trackingRect = Rect(trackingRect.x - offset, trackingRect.y
- offset, trackingRect.x + offset, trackingRect.y + offset) & Rect(0, 0,
cols, rows);
```

```
          }
```

We are now ready to display the results. Using the rotated rectangle, let's draw an ellipse around our region of interest:

```
            // Draw the ellipse on top of the image
            ellipse(image, rotatedTrackingRect, Scalar(0,255,0), 3,
    LINE_AA);
        }
        // Apply the 'negative' effect on the selected region of interest
        if(selectRegion && selectedRect.width > 0 && selectedRect.height >
    0)
        {
            Mat roi(image, selectedRect);
            bitwise_not(roi, roi);
        }
        // Display the output image
        imshow(windowName, image);
        // Get the keyboard input and check if it's 'Esc'
        // 27 -> ASCII value of 'Esc' key
        ch = waitKey(30);
        if (ch == 27) {
            break;
        }
    }
    return 1;
}
```

Detecting points using the Harris corner detector

Corner detection is a technique used to detect points of interest in an image. These interest points are also called feature points, or simply features, in computer vision terminology. A corner is basically an intersection of two edges. An interest point is basically something that can be uniquely detected in an image. A corner is a particular case of an interest point. These interest points help us characterize an image. These points are used extensively in applications such as object tracking, image classification, and visual search. Since we know that the corners are interesting, let's see how can detect them.

In computer vision, there is a popular corner detection technique called the Harris corner detector. We basically construct a 2 x 2 matrix based on partial derivatives of the grayscale image, and then analyze the eigenvalues. What does that even mean? Well, let's dissect it so that we can understand it better. Let's consider a small patch in the image. Our goal is to identify whether this patch has a corner in it. So, we consider all the neighboring patches and compute the intensity difference between our patch and all those neighboring patches. If the difference is high in all directions, then we know that our patch has a corner in it. This is an oversimplification of the actual algorithm, but it covers the gist. If you want to understand the underlying mathematical details, you can check out the original paper by *Harris* and *Stephens* at http://www.bmva.org/bmvc/1988/avc-88-023.pdf. A corner is a point with strong intensity differences along two directions.

If we run the Harris corner detector, it will look like this:

As we can see, the green circles on the TV remote are the detected corners. This will change based on the parameters you choose for the detector. If you modify the parameters, you can see that more points might get detected. If you make it strict, you might not be able to detect soft corners. Let's look at the code to detect Harris corners:

```
int main(int argc, char* argv[])
{
// Variable declaration and initialization

// Iterate until the user presses the Esc key
while(true)
{
    // Capture the current frame
    cap >> frame;

    // Resize the frame
    resize(frame, frame, Size(), scalingFactor, scalingFactor, INTER_AREA);

    dst = Mat::zeros(frame.size(), CV_32FC1);

    // Convert to grayscale
    cvtColor(frame, frameGray, COLOR_BGR2GRAY );

    // Detecting corners
    cornerHarris(frameGray, dst, blockSize, apertureSize, k,
BORDER_DEFAULT);

    // Normalizing
    normalize(dst, dst_norm, 0, 255, NORM_MINMAX, CV_32FC1, Mat());
    convertScaleAbs(dst_norm, dst_norm_scaled);
```

We converted the image to grayscale and detected corners using our parameters. You can find the full code in the .cpp files. These parameters play an important role in the number of points that will be detected. You can check out the OpenCV documentation of cornerHarris() at https://docs.opencv.org/master/dd/d1a/group__imgproc__feature.html#gac1fc3598018010880e370e2f709b4345.

We now have all the information we need. Let's go ahead and draw circles around our corners to display the results:

```
// Drawing a circle around each corner
for(int j = 0; j < dst_norm.rows ; j++)
{
    for(int i = 0; i < dst_norm.cols; i++)
    {
        if((int)dst_norm.at<float>(j,i) > thresh)
        {
```

```
                              circle(frame, Point(i, j), 8, Scalar(0,255,0), 2, 8,
        0);
                    }
                }
            }

            // Showing the result
            imshow(windowName, frame);

            // Get the keyboard input and check if it's 'Esc'
            // 27 -> ASCII value of 'Esc' key
            ch = waitKey(10);
            if (ch == 27) {
                break;
            }
        }

        // Release the video capture object
        cap.release();

        // Close all windows
        destroyAllWindows();

        return 1;
    }
```

As we can see, this code takes an input argument: `blockSize`. Depending on the size you choose, the performance will vary. Start with a value of four and play around with it to see what happens.

Good features to track

Harris corner detector performs well in many cases, but it can still be improved. Around six years after the original paper by *Harris* and *Stephens*, *Shi* and *Tomasi* came up with something better and they called it *Good Features to Track*. You can read the original paper here: http://www.ai.mit.edu/courses/6.891/handouts/shi94good.pdf. They used a different scoring function to improve the overall quality. Using this method, we can find the N strongest corners in the given image. This is very useful when we don't want to use every single corner to extract information from the image. As we discussed, a good interest point detector is very useful in applications such as object tracking, object recognition, and image search.

If you apply the Shi-Tomasi corner detector to an image, you will see something like this:

As we can see here, all the important points in the frame are captured. Let's look at the code to track these features:

```
int main(int argc, char* argv[])
{
    // Variable declaration and initialization
    // Iterate until the user presses the Esc key
    while(true)
    {
        // Capture the current frame
        cap >> frame;
        // Resize the frame
        resize(frame, frame, Size(), scalingFactor, scalingFactor,
INTER_AREA);
        // Convert to grayscale
        cvtColor(frame, frameGray, COLOR_BGR2GRAY );
        // Initialize the parameters for Shi-Tomasi algorithm
        vector<Point2f> corners;
        double qualityThreshold = 0.02;
        double minDist = 15;
        int blockSize = 5;
```

```
        bool useHarrisDetector = false;
        double k = 0.07;
        // Clone the input frame
        Mat frameCopy;
        frameCopy = frame.clone();
        // Apply corner detection
        goodFeaturesToTrack(frameGray, corners, numCorners,
    qualityThreshold, minDist, Mat(), blockSize, useHarrisDetector, k);
```

As we can see, we extracted the frame and used `goodFeaturesToTrack` to detect the corners. It's important to understand that the number of corners detected will depend on our choice of parameters. You can find a detailed explanation at `http://docs.opencv.org/2.4/modules/imgproc/doc/feature_detection.html?highlight=goodfeaturestotrack#goodfeaturestotrack`. Let's go ahead and draw circles on these points to display the output image:

```
        // Parameters for the circles to display the corners
        int radius = 8;       // radius of the circles
        int thickness = 2;    // thickness of the circles
        int lineType = 8;
        // Draw the detected corners using circles
        for(size_t i = 0; i < corners.size(); i++)
        {
            Scalar color = Scalar(rng.uniform(0,255), rng.uniform(0,255),
    rng.uniform(0,255));
            circle(frameCopy, corners[i], radius, color, thickness,
    lineType, 0);
        }
        /// Show what you got
        imshow(windowName, frameCopy);
        // Get the keyboard input and check if it's 'Esc'
        // 27 -> ASCII value of 'Esc' key
        ch = waitKey(30);
        if (ch == 27) {
            break;
        }
    }
    // Release the video capture object
    cap.release();
    // Close all windows
    destroyAllWindows();
    return 1;
}
```

This program takes an input argument: `numCorners`. This value indicates the maximum number of corners you want to track. Start with a value of `100` and play around with it to see what happens. If you increase this value, you will see more feature points getting detected.

Feature-based tracking

Feature-based tracking refers to tracking individual feature points across successive frames in the video. The advantage here is that we don't have to detect feature points in every single frame. We can just detect them once and keep tracking them after that. This is more efficient than running the detector on every frame. We use a technique called optical flow to track these features. Optical flow is one of the most popular techniques in computer vision. We choose a bunch of feature points and track them through the video stream. When we detect the feature points, we compute the displacement vectors and show the motion of those keypoints between consecutive frames. These vectors are called motion vectors. A motion vector for a particular point is basically just a directional line indicating where that point has moved, as compared to the previous frame. Different methods are used to detect these motion vectors. The two most popular algorithms are the **Lucas-Kanade** method and the **Farneback** algorithm.

Lucas-Kanade method

The Lucas-Kanade method is used for sparse optical flow tracking. By sparse, we mean that the number of feature points is relatively low. You can refer to their original paper here: `http://cseweb.ucsd.edu/classes/sp02/cse252/lucaskanade81.pdf`. We start the process by extracting the feature points. For each feature point, we create 3 x 3 patches with the feature point at the center. The assumption here is that all the points within each patch will have a similar motion. We can adjust the size of this window depending on the problem at hand.

For each feature point in the current frame, we take the surrounding 3 x 3 patch as our reference point. For this patch, we look in its neighborhood in the previous frame to get the best match. This neighborhood is usually bigger than 3 x 3 because we want to get the patch that's closest to the patch under consideration. Now, the path from the center pixel of the matched patch in the previous frame to the center pixel of the patch under consideration in the current frame will become the motion vector. We do that for all the feature points and extract all the motion vectors.

Let's consider the following frame:

We need to add some points that we want to track. Just go ahead and click on a bunch of points on this window with your mouse:

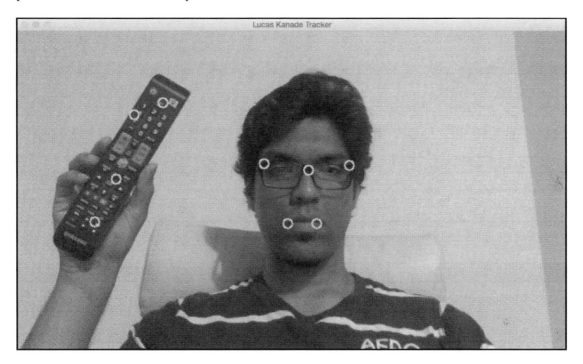

If I move into a different position, you will see that the points are still being tracked correctly within a small margin of error:

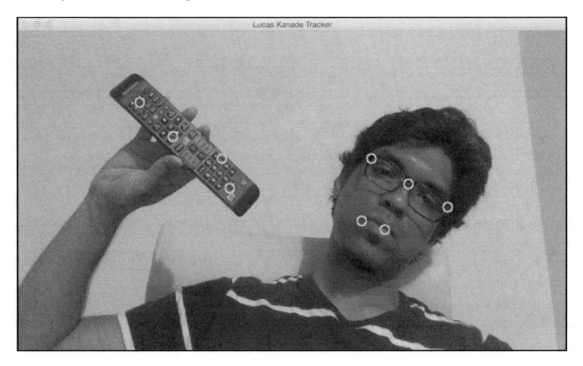

Let's add a lot of points and see what happens:

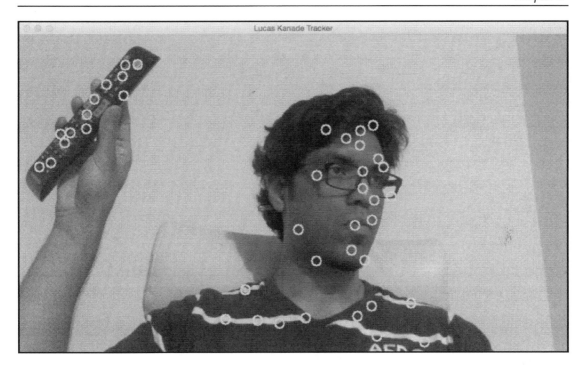

As we can see, it will keep tracking those points. But, you will notice that some of the points will be dropped because of factors such as prominence or speed of movement. If you want to play around with it, you can just keep adding more points to it. You can also let the user select a region of interest in the input video. You can then extract feature points from this region of interest and track the object by drawing a bounding box. It will be a fun exercise!

Here is the code to do Lucas-Kanade-based tracking:

```
int main(int argc, char* argv[])
{
    // Variable declaration and initialization
    // Iterate until the user hits the Esc key
    while(true)
    {
        // Capture the current frame
        cap >> frame;
        // Check if the frame is empty
        if(frame.empty())
            break;
        // Resize the frame
        resize(frame, frame, Size(), scalingFactor, scalingFactor,
INTER_AREA);
        // Copy the input frame
```

```
      frame.copyTo(image);
      // Convert the image to grayscale
      cvtColor(image, curGrayImage, COLOR_BGR2GRAY);
      // Check if there are points to track
      if(!trackingPoints[0].empty())
      {
            // Status vector to indicate whether the flow for the
corresponding features has been found
            vector<uchar> statusVector;
            // Error vector to indicate the error for the corresponding
feature
            vector<float> errorVector;
            // Check if previous image is empty
            if(prevGrayImage.empty())
            {
                  curGrayImage.copyTo(prevGrayImage);
            }
            // Calculate the optical flow using Lucas-Kanade algorithm
            calcOpticalFlowPyrLK(prevGrayImage, curGrayImage,
trackingPoints[0], trackingPoints[1], statusVector, errorVector,
windowSize, 3, terminationCriteria, 0, 0.001);
```

We use the current image and the previous image to compute the optical flow information. Needless to say, the quality of the output will depend on the parameters chosen. You can find more details about the parameters at http://docs.opencv.org/2.4/modules/video/ doc/motion_analysis_and_object_tracking.html#calcopticalflowpyrlk. To increase quality and robustness, we need to filter out the points that are very close to each other because they're not adding new information. Let's go ahead and do that:

```
      int count = 0;
      // Minimum distance between any two tracking points
      int minDist = 7;
      for(int i=0; i < trackingPoints[1].size(); i++)
      {
            if(pointTrackingFlag)
            {
                  // If the new point is within 'minDist' distance from
an existing point, it will not be tracked
                  if(norm(currentPoint - trackingPoints[1][i]) <=
minDist)
                  {
                        pointTrackingFlag = false;
                        continue;
                  }
            }
            // Check if the status vector is good
```

```
                        if(!statusVector[i])
                            continue;
                        trackingPoints[1][count++] = trackingPoints[1][i];

                        // Draw a filled circle for each of the tracking points
                        int radius = 8;
                        int thickness = 2;
                        int lineType = 8;
                        circle(image, trackingPoints[1][i], radius,
    Scalar(0,255,0), thickness, lineType);
                    }
                    trackingPoints[1].resize(count);
                }
```

We now have the tracking points. The next step is to refine the location of those points. What exactly does **refine** mean in this context? To increase the speed of computation, there is some level of quantization involved. In layman's terms, you can think of it as rounding off. Now that we have the approximate region, we can refine the location of the point within that region to get a more accurate outcome. Let's go ahead and do that:

```
                // Refining the location of the feature points
                if(pointTrackingFlag && trackingPoints[1].size() < maxNumPoints)
                {
                    vector<Point2f> tempPoints;
                    tempPoints.push_back(currentPoint);
                    // Function to refine the location of the corners to subpixel
    accuracy.
                    // Here, 'pixel' refers to the image patch of size 'windowSize'
    and not the actual image pixel
                    cornerSubPix(curGrayImage, tempPoints, windowSize, Size(-1,-1),
    terminationCriteria);
                    trackingPoints[1].push_back(tempPoints[0]);
                    pointTrackingFlag = false;
                }
                // Display the image with the tracking points
                imshow(windowName, image);
                // Check if the user pressed the Esc key
                char ch = waitKey(10);
                if(ch == 27)
                    break;
                // Swap the 'points' vectors to update 'previous' to 'current'
                std::swap(trackingPoints[1], trackingPoints[0]);
                // Swap the images to update previous image to current image
                cv::swap(prevGrayImage, curGrayImage);
            }
        return 1;
    }
```

Farneback algorithm

Gunnar Farneback proposed this optical flow algorithm and it's used for dense tracking. Dense tracking is used extensively in robotics, augmented reality, and 3D mapping. You can check out the original paper here: `http://www.diva-portal.org/smash/get/diva2:273847/FULLTEXT01.pdf`. The Lucas-Kanade method is a sparse technique, which means that we only need to process some pixels in the entire image. The Farneback algorithm, on the other hand, is a dense technique that requires us to process all the pixels in the given image. So, obviously, there is a trade-off here. Dense techniques are more accurate, but they are slower. Sparse techniques are less accurate, but they are faster. For real-time applications, people tend to prefer sparse techniques. For applications where time and complexity are not a factor, people tend to prefer dense techniques to extract finer details.

In his paper, Farneback describes a method for dense optical-flow estimation based on polynomial expansion for two frames. Our goal is to estimate the motion between these two frames, which is basically a three-step process. In the first step, each neighborhood in both frames is approximated by polynomials. In this case, we are only interested in quadratic polynomials. The next step is to construct a new signal by global displacement. Now that each neighborhood is approximated by a polynomial, we need to see what happens if this polynomial undergoes an ideal translation. The last step is to compute the global displacement by equating the coefficients in the yields of these quadratic polynomials.

Now, how this is feasible? If you think about it, we are assuming that an entire signal is a single polynomial and there is a global translation relating the two signals. This is not a realistic scenario! So, what are we looking for? Well, our goal is to find out whether these errors are small enough so that we can build a useful algorithm that can track the features.

Let's look at a static image:

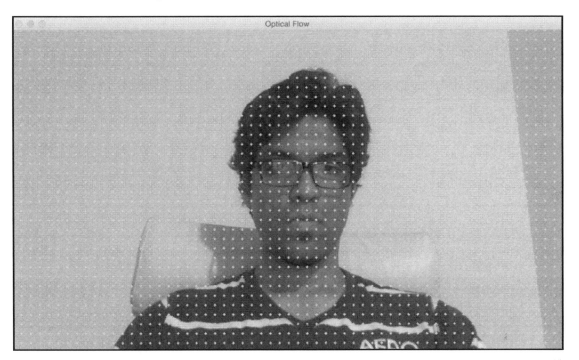

If I move sideways, we can see that the motion vectors are pointing in a horizontal direction. It is simply tracking the movement of my head:

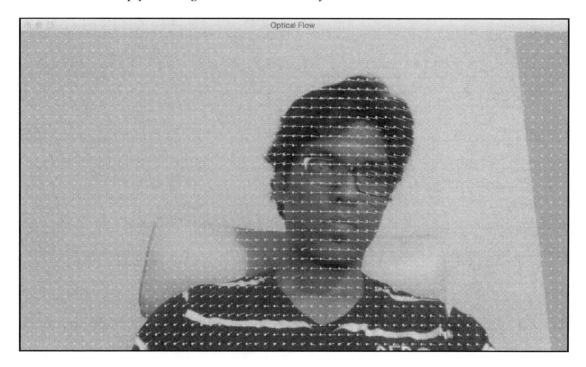

If I move away from the webcam, you can see that the motion vectors are pointing in a direction perpendicular to the image plane:

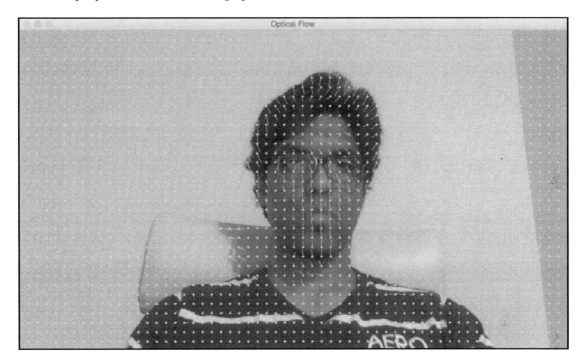

Here is the code to do optical-flow-based tracking using the Farneback algorithm:

```cpp
int main(int, char** argv)
{
    // Variable declaration and initialization
    // Iterate until the user presses the Esc key
    while(true)
    {
        // Capture the current frame
        cap >> frame;
        if(frame.empty())
            break;
        // Resize the frame
        resize(frame, frame, Size(), scalingFactor, scalingFactor,
INTER_AREA);
        // Convert to grayscale
        cvtColor(frame, curGray, COLOR_BGR2GRAY);
        // Check if the image is valid
        if(prevGray.data)
        {
```

```
                    // Initialize parameters for the optical flow algorithm
                    float pyrScale = 0.5;
                    int numLevels = 3;
                    int windowSize = 15;
                    int numIterations = 3;
                    int neighborhoodSize = 5;
                    float stdDeviation = 1.2;
                    // Calculate optical flow map using Farneback algorithm
                    calcOpticalFlowFarneback(prevGray, curGray, flowImage,
            pyrScale, numLevels, windowSize, numIterations, neighborhoodSize,
            stdDeviation, OPTFLOW_USE_INITIAL_FLOW);
```

As we can see, we use the Farneback algorithm to compute the optical flow vectors. The input parameters to `calcOpticalFlowFarneback` are important when it comes to the quality of tracking. You can find details about those parameters at `http://docs.opencv.org/3.0-beta/modules/video/doc/motion_analysis_and_object_tracking.html`. Let's go ahead and draw those vectors on the output image:

```
                    // Convert to 3-channel RGB
                    cvtColor(prevGray, flowImageGray, COLOR_GRAY2BGR);
                    // Draw the optical flow map
                    drawOpticalFlow(flowImage, flowImageGray);
                    // Display the output image
                    imshow(windowName, flowImageGray);
            }
            // Break out of the loop if the user presses the Esc key
            ch = waitKey(10);
            if(ch == 27)
                break;
            // Swap previous image with the current image
            std::swap(prevGray, curGray);
        }
        return 1;
    }
```

We used a function called `drawOpticalFlow` to draw those optical flow vectors. These vectors indicate the direction of motion. Let's look at the function to see how we draw those vectors:

```
    // Function to compute the optical flow map
    void drawOpticalFlow(const Mat& flowImage, Mat& flowImageGray)
    {
        int stepSize = 16;
        Scalar color = Scalar(0, 255, 0);
        // Draw the uniform grid of points on the input image along with the
    motion vectors
        for(int y = 0; y < flowImageGray.rows; y += stepSize)
```

```
    {
        for(int x = 0; x < flowImageGray.cols; x += stepSize)
        {
            // Circles to indicate the uniform grid of points
            int radius = 2;
            int thickness = -1;
            circle(flowImageGray, Point(x,y), radius, color, thickness);
            // Lines to indicate the motion vectors
            Point2f pt = flowImage.at<Point2f>(y, x);
            line(flowImageGray, Point(x,y), Point(cvRound(x+pt.x),
    cvRound(y+pt.y)), color);
        }
    }
}
```

Summary

In this chapter, we learned about object tracking. We learned how to use HSV colorspace to track objects of a specific color. We discussed clustering techniques for object tracking and how we can build an interactive object tracker using the CAMShift algorithm. We looked at corner detectors and how we can track corners in a live video. We discussed how to track features in a video using optical flow. Finally, we understood the concepts behind the Lucas-Kanade and Farneback algorithms and then implemented them.

In the next chapter, we are going to discuss segmentation algorithms and how we can use them for text recognition.

10
Developing Segmentation Algorithms for Text Recognition

In the previous chapters, we learned about a wide range of image processing techniques such as thresholding, contours descriptors, and mathematical morphology. In this chapter, we will discuss common problems that you may face while dealing with scanned documents, such as identifying where the text is or adjusting its rotation. We will also learn how to combine techniques presented in the previous chapters to solve those problems. By the end of this chapter, we will have segmented regions of text that can be sent to an **optical character recognition (OCR)** library.

By the end of this chapter, you should be able to answer the following questions:

- What kind of OCR applications exists?
- What are the common problems while writing an OCR application?
- How do I identify regions of documents?
- How do I deal with problems like skewing and other elements in the middle of the text?
- How do I use Tesseract OCR to identify my text?

Technical requirements

This chapter requires familiarity with the basic C++ programming language. All of the code that's used in this chapter can be downloaded from the following GitHub link: `https://github.com/PacktPublishing/Building-Computer-Vision-Projects-with-OpenCV4-and-CPlusPlus/tree/master/Chapter10`. The code can be executed on any operating system, though it has only been tested on Ubuntu.

Check out the following video to see the Code in Action:
`http://bit.ly/2KIoJFX`

Introducing optical character recognition

Identifying text in an image is a very popular application for computer vision. This process is commonly called **optical character recognition**, and is divided as follows:

- **Text preprocessing and segmentation**: During this step, the computer must deal with image noise, and rotation (skewing), and identify what areas are candidate text.
- **Text identification**: This is the process of identifying each letter in text which will be covered in the later chapters.

The preprocessing and segmentation phase can vary greatly depending on the source of the text. Let's take a look at common situations where preprocessing is done:

- **Production OCR applications with a scanner**: This is a very reliable source of text. In this scenario, the background of the image is usually white and the document is almost aligned with the scanner margins. The content that's being scanned contains basically text, with almost no noise. This kind of application relies on simple preprocessing techniques that can adjust text quickly and maintain a fast scanning pace. When writing production OCR software, it is common to delegate the identification of important text regions to the user, and create a quality pipeline for text verification and indexing.

- **Scanning text in a casually taken picture or in a video**: This is a much more complex scenario, since there's no indication of where the text can be. This scenario is called **scene text recognition**, and OpenCV 4.0 contains a contrib library to deal with it. We will cover this in `Chapter 11`, *Text Recognition with Tesseract*. Usually, the preprocessor will use texture analysis techniques to identify the text patterns.
- **Creating a production quality OCR for historical texts**: Historical texts are also scanned, but they have several additional problems, such as noise that's created by the old paper color and the use of ink. Other common problems are decorated letters and specific text fonts, and low contrast content that's created by ink that is erased over time. It's not uncommon to write specific OCR software for the documents at hand.
- **Scanning maps, diagrams, and charts**: Maps, diagrams, and charts pose an especially difficult scenario since the text is usually in any orientation and in the middle of image content. For example, city names are often clustered, and ocean names often follow country shore contour lines. Some charts are heavily colored, with text appearing in both clear and dark tones.

OCR application strategies also vary according to the objective of the identification. Will it be used for a full text search? Or should the text be separated into logical fields to index a database with information for a structured search?

In this chapter, we will focus on preprocessing scanned text, or text that's been photographed by a camera. We'll consider that the text is the main purpose of the image, such as in a photographed piece of paper or card, for example, in this parking ticket:

We'll try to remove common noise, deal with text rotation (if any), and crop the possible text regions. While most OCR APIs already do these things automatically – and probably with state-of-the-art algorithms—it is still worth knowing how things happen under the hood. This will allow you to better understand most OCR APIs parameters and will give you better knowledge about the potential OCR problems you may face.

Preprocessing stage

Software that identifies letters does so by comparing text with previously recorded data. Classification results can be improved greatly if the input text is clear, if the letters are in a vertical position, and if there's no other elements, such as images sent to the classification software. In this section, we'll learn how to adjust text by using **preprocessing**.

Thresholding the image

We usually start preprocessing by thresholding the image. This eliminates all color information. Most OpenCV functions consider information to be written in white, and the background to be black. So, let's start by creating a threshold function to match this criteria:

```
#include opencv2/opencv.hpp;
#include vector;

using namespace std;
using namespace cv;

Mat binarize(Mat input)
{
    //Uses otsu to threshold the input image
    Mat binaryImage;
    cvtColor(input, input, COLOR_BGR2GRAY);
    threshold(input, binaryImage, 0, 255, THRESH_OTSU);

    //Count the number of black and white pixels
    int white = countNonZero(binaryImage);
    int black = binaryImage.size().area() - white;

    //If the image is mostly white (white background), invert it
    return white black ? binaryImage : ~binaryImage;
}
```

The `binarize` function applies a threshold, similar to what we did in `Chapter 4`, *Delving into Histogram and Filters*. But here, we will use the Otsu method by passing `THRESH_OTSU` in the fourth parameter of the function. The Otsu method maximizes inter-class variance. Since a threshold creates only two classes (the black and white pixels), this is the same as minimizing the intraclass variance. This method works using the image histogram. Then, it iterates through all the possible threshold values and calculates the spread for the pixel values for each side of the threshold, that is, the pixels that are either in the background or in the foreground of the image. The purpose of this process is to find the threshold value where the sum of both spreads are at their minimum.

After the thresholding is done, the function counts how many white pixels are in the image. The black pixels are simply the total number of pixels in the image, given by the image area, minus the white pixel count. Since text is usually written over a plain background, we will verify whether there are more white pixels than there are black pixels. In this case, we are dealing with black text over a white background, so we will invert the image for further processing.

The result of the thresholding process with the parking ticket image is as follows:

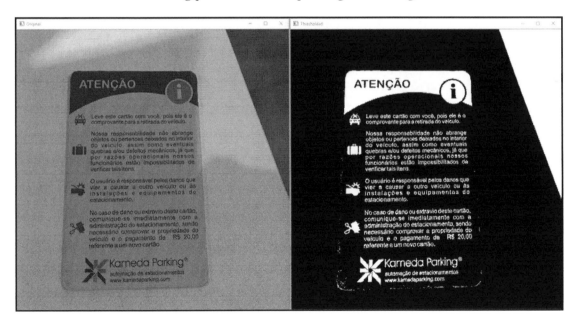

Text segmentation

The next step is to find where the text is located and extract it. There are two common strategies for this:

- **Using connected component analysis**: Searching groups of connected pixels in the image. This will be the technique that will be used in this chapter.
- **Use classifiers to search for a previously trained letter texture pattern**: with texture features such as **Haralick** features, wavelet transforms are often used. Anther option is to identify **maximally stable extremal regions (MSERs)** in this task. This approach is more robust for text in a complex background and will be studied in Chapter 11, *Text Recognition with Tesseract*. You can read about Haralick features at his own website, which can be found at http://haralick.org/journals/TexturalFeatures.pdf.

Creating connected areas

If you take a closer look at the image, you'll notice that the letters are always together in blocks, formed by text paragraphs. That leaves us with the question, how do we detect and remove these blocks?

The first step is to make these blocks even more evident. We can do this by using the dilation morphological operator. Recall from Chapter 8, *Video Surveillance, Background Modeling, and Morphological Operations,* that dilation makes the image elements thicker. Let's look at a small code snippet that does the trick:

```
auto kernel = getStructuringElement(MORPH_CROSS, Size(3,3));
Mat dilated;
dilate(input, dilated, kernel, cv::Point(-1, -1), 5);
imshow("Dilated", dilated);
```

In the preceding code, we start by creating a 3 x 3 cross kernel that will be used in the morphological operation. Then, we apply dilation five times, centered on this kernel. The exact kernel size and number of times vary according to the situation. Just make sure that the values glue all of the letters in the same line together.

The result of this operation is presented in the following screenshot:

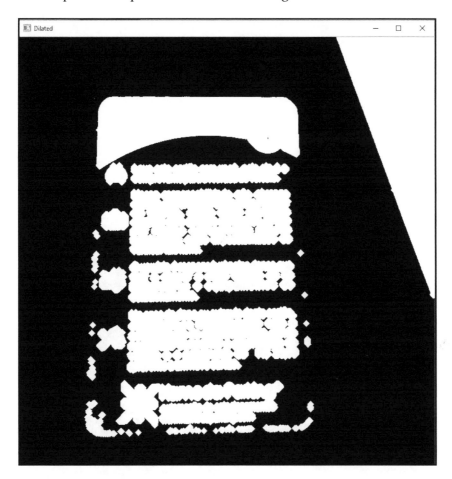

Notice that we now have huge white blocks. They match exactly with each paragraph of text, and also match with other non-textual elements, like images or the border noise.

 The ticket image that comes with the code is a low resolution image. OCR engines usually work with high resolution images (200 or 300 DPI), so it may be necessary to apply dilation more than five times.

Identifying paragraph blocks

The next step is to perform connect component analysis to find blocks that correspond with paragraphs. OpenCV has a function for this, which we previously used in Chapter 5, *Automated Optical Inspection, Object Segmentation, and Detection*. This is the findContours function:

```
vector;vector;Point;contours;
findContours(dilated, contours, RETR_EXTERNAL, CHAIN_APPROX_SIMPLE);
```

In the first parameter, we pass our dilated image. The second parameter is the vector of detected contours. Then, we use the option to retrieve only external contours and to use simple approximation. The image contours are presented as follows. Each tone of gray represents a different contour:

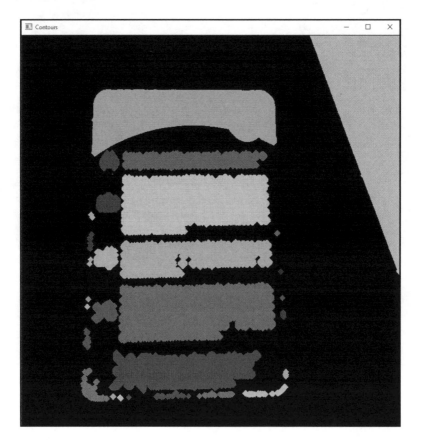

The last step is to identify the minimum rotated bounding rectangle of each contour. OpenCV provides a handy function for this operation called `minAreaRect`. This function receives a vector of arbitrary points and returns a `RoundedRect` containing the bounding box. This is also a good opportunity to discard unwanted rectangles, that is, rectangles that are obviously not text. Since we are making software for OCR, we'll assume that the text contains a group of letters. With this assumption, we'll discard text in the following situations:

- The rectangle width or size is too small, that is, smaller than 20 pixels. This will help discard border noises and other small artifacts.
- The rectangle of the image has a width/height proportion smaller than two. That is, rectangles that resemble a square, such as the image icons, or are much taller, will also be discarded.

There's a little caveat in the second condition. Since we are dealing with rotated bounding boxes, we must test whether the bounding box angle is smaller than -45 degrees. If it is, the text is vertically rotated, so the proportion that we must take into account is height/width.

Let's check this out by looking at the following code:

```
//For each contour

vector;RotatedRect; areas;
for (const auto& contour : contours)
{
    //Find it's rotated rect
    auto box = minAreaRect(contour);

    //Discard very small boxes
    if (box.size.width 20 || box.size.height 20)
        continue;

    //Discard squares shaped boxes and boxes
    //higher than larger
    double proportion = box.angle -45.0 ?
        box.size.height / box.size.width :
        box.size.width / box.size.height;

    if (proportion 2)
        continue;

    //Add the box
    areas.push_back(box);
}
```

Let's see which boxes this algorithm selected:

That's certainly a good result!

We should notice that the algorithm described in step 2, in the preceding code, will also discard single letters. This is not a big issue since we are creating an OCR preprocessor, and single symbols are usually meaningless with context information; one example of such a case is the page numbers. The page numbers will be discarded with this process since they usually appear alone at the bottom of the page, and the size and proportion of the text will also be disturbed. But this will not be a problem, since after the text passes through the OCR, you will end up with a huge amount of text files with no page division at all.

We'll place all of this code in a function with the following signature:

```
vector RotatedRect; findTextAreas(Mat input)
```

Text extraction and skewing adjustment

Now, all we must do is extract the text and adjust the text skew. This is done by the deskewAndCrop function, as follows:

```
Mat deskewAndCrop(Mat input, const RotatedRect& box)
{
    double angle = box.angle;
    auto size = box.size;

    //Adjust the box angle
    if (angle -45.0)
    {
        angle += 90.0;
         std::swap(size.width, size.height);
    }
    //Rotate the text according to the angle
    auto transform = getRotationMatrix2D(box.center, angle, 1.0);
    Mat rotated;
    warpAffine(input, rotated, transform, input.size(), INTER_CUBIC);

    //Crop the result
    Mat cropped;
    getRectSubPix(rotated, size, box.center, cropped);
    copyMakeBorder(cropped,cropped,10,10,10,10,BORDER_CONSTANT,Scalar(0));
    return cropped;
}
```

First, we start by reading the desired region angle and size. As we saw earlier, the angle may be less than -45 degrees. This means that the text is vertically aligned, so we must add 90 degrees to the rotation angle and switch the width and height properties. Next, we need to rotate the text. First, we start by creating a 2D affine transformation matrix that describes the rotation. We do so by using the `getRotationMatrix2D` OpenCV function. This function takes three parameters:

- **CENTER**: The central position of the rotation. The rotation will pivot around this center. In our case, we use the box center.
- **ANGLE**: The rotation angle. If the angle is negative, the rotation will occur in a clockwise direction.
- **SCALE**: The isotropic scale factor. We will use `1.0` since we want to keep the box's original scale untouched.

The rotation itself is made by using the `warpAffine` function. This function takes four mandatory arguments:

- **SRC**: The input `mat` array to be transformed.
- **DST**: The destination `mat` array.
- **M**: A transformation matrix. This matrix is a 2 x 3 affine transformation matrix. This may be a translation, scale, or rotation matrix. In our case, we will just use the matrix we recently created.
- **SIZE**: The size of the output image. We will generate an image that's the same size as our input image.

The following are another three optional arguments:

- **FLAGS**: These indicate how the image should be interpolated. We use `BICUBIC_INTERPOLATION` for better quality. The default is `LINEAR_INTERPOLATION`.
- **BORDER**: Border mode. We use the default, `BORDER_CONSTANT`.
- **BORDER VALUE**: The color of the border. We use the default, which is black. Then, we use the `getRectSubPix` function. After we rotate our image, we need to crop the rectangle area of our bounding box. This function takes four mandatory arguments and one optional argument, and returns the cropped image:
  - **IMAGE**: The image to crop.
  - **SIZE**: A `cv::Size` object describing the width and height of the box to be cropped.

- **CENTER**: The central pixel of the area to be cropped. Notice that since we rotated around the center, this point is conveniently the same.
- **PATCH**: The destination image.
- **PATCH_TYPE**: The depth of the destination image. We use the default value, representing the same depth of the source image.

The final step is done by the `copyMakeBorder` function. This function adds a border around the image. This is important, since the classification stage usually expects a margin around the text. The function parameters are very simple: the input and output images, the border thickness at the top, bottom, left, and right, the border type, and the color of the new border.

For the card image, the following images will be generated:

Now, it's time to put every function together. Let's present the main method that does the following:

- Loads the ticket image
- Calls our binarization function
- Find all text regions
- Shows each region in a window

We will present the main method as follows:

```cpp
int main(int argc, char* argv[])
{
    //Loads the ticket image and binarize it
    auto ticket = binarize(imread("ticket.png"));
    auto regions = findTextAreas(ticket);
    //For each region
    for (const auto& region : regions) {
        //Crop
        auto cropped = deskewAndCrop(ticket, region);

        //Show
        imshow("Cropped text", cropped);
        waitKey(0);
        destroyWindow("Border Skew");
    }
}
```

 For the complete source code, take a look at the segment.cpp file that comes with this book.

Installing Tesseract OCR on your operating system

Tesseract is an open source OCR engine that was originally developed by Hewlett-Packard Laboratories Bristol and Hewlett-Packard Co. All of its code is licensed under the Apache License and hosted on GitHub at `https://github.com/tesseract-ocr`. It is considered one of the most accurate OCR engines available: it can read a wide variety of image formats and can convert text written in more than 60 languages. In this session, we will teach you how to install Tesseract on Windows or Mac. Since there's lots of Linux distributions, we will not teach you how to install it on this operating system. Normally, Tesseract offers installation packages in your package repository, so, before compiling Tesseract yourself, just search for it there.

Installing Tesseract on Windows

Tesseract uses the **C++ Archive Network (CPPAN)** as its dependency manager. To install Tesseract, follow these steps.

Building the latest library

1. Download the latest CPPAN client from `https://cppan.org/client/`.
2. In the command line, run
   `cppan --build pvt.cppan.demo.google.tesseract.tesseract-master`.

Setting up Tesseract in Visual Studio

1. Set up `vcpkg`, the Visual C++ Package Manager, at `https://github.com/Microsoft/vcpkg`.
2. For a 64-bit compilation, use `vcpkg install tesseract:x64-windows`. You may also add `--head` for the master branch.

Static linking

It's also possible to static link (`https://github.com/tesseract-ocr/tesseract/wiki/Compiling#static-linking`) Tesseract in your project. This will avoid `dlls` to be packaged with your executable files. To do this, use `vcpkg`, like we did previously, with the following command for a 32-bit installation:

```
vcpkg install tesseract:x86-windows-static
```

Alternatively, you can use the following command for a 64-bit installation:

```
vckpg install tesseract:x64-windows-static
```

Installing Tesseract on Mac

The easiest way to install Tesseract OCR on Mac is using **Homebrew**. If you don't have Homebrew installed, just go to Homebrew's site (`http://brew.sh/`), open your console, and run the **Ruby script** that is on the front page. You may be required to type in your administrator password.

After Homebrew is installed, just type in the following:

```
brew install tesseract
```

The English language is already included in this installation. If you want to install other language packs, just run the following command:

```
brew install tesseract --all-languages
```

This will install all of the language packs. Then, just go to the Tesseract installation directory and delete any unwanted languages. Homebrew usually installs stuff in the `/usr/local/` directory.

Using the Tesseract OCR library

While Tesseract OCR is already integrated with OpenCV 3.0, it's still worth studying its API since it allows for finer grained control over Tesseract parameters. This integration will be studied in `Chapter 11`, *Text Recognition with Tesseract*.

Creating an OCR function

We'll change the previous example to work with Tesseract. Start by adding
`tesseract/baseapi.h` and `fstream` to the `include` list:

```
#include opencv2/opencv.hpp;
#include tesseract/baseapi.h;

#include vector;
#include fstream;
```

Then, we'll create a global `TessBaseAPI` object that represents our Tesseract OCR engine:

```
tesseract::TessBaseAPI ocr;
```

The `ocr` engine is completely self-contained. If you want to create a multithreaded piece of OCR software, just add a different `TessBaseAPI` object
in each thread, and the execution will be fairly thread-safe. You just need
to guarantee that file writing is not done over the same file, otherwise
you'll need to guarantee safety for this operation.

Next, we will create a function called **identify text** (`identifyText`) that will run the `ocr`:

```
const char* identifyText(Mat input, const char* language = "eng")
{
    ocr.Init(NULL, language, tesseract::OEM_TESSERACT_ONLY);
    ocr.SetPageSegMode(tesseract::PSM_SINGLE_BLOCK);
    ocr.SetImage(input.data, input.cols, input.rows, 1, input.step);
    const char* text = ocr.GetUTF8Text();
    cout   "Text:"   endl;
    cout   text   endl;
    cout   "Confidence: "   ocr.MeanTextConf() endl;
     // Get the text
    return text;
}
```

Let's explain this function line-by-line. In the first line, we start by initializing `tesseract`.
This is done by calling the `Init` function. This function has the following signature:

```
int Init(const char* datapath, const char* language,
  OcrEngineMode oem)
```

Let's explain each parameter:

- `datapath`: This is the path to the root directory of `tessdata` files. The path must end with a backslash / character. The `tessdata` directory contains the language files that you installed. Passing NULL to this parameter will make `tesseract` search its installation directory, which is the location that this folder is normally present in. It's common to change this value to `args[0]` when deploying an application, and include the `tessdata` folder in your application path.
- `language`: This is a three letter word for the language code (for example, eng for English, por for Portuguese, or hin for Hindi). Tesseract supports loading multiple language codes by using the + sign. Therefore, passing eng+por will load both the English and Portuguese languages. Of course, you can only use languages you have previously installed, otherwise the loading process will fail. A language config file may specify that two or more languages must be loaded together. To prevent that, you may use a tilde ~. For example, you can use hin+~eng to guarantee that English is not loaded with Hindi, even if it is configured to do so.
- `OcrEngineMode`: These are the OCR algorithms that will be used. It can have one of the following values:
  - OEM_TESSERACT_ONLY: Uses just `tesseract`. It's the fastest method, but it also has less precision.
  - OEM_CUBE_ONLY: Uses the Cube engine. It's slower, but more precise. This will only work if your language was trained to support this engine mode. To check if that's the case, look for .cube files for your language in the `tessdata` folder. The support for English language is guaranteed.
  - OEM_TESSERACT_CUBE_COMBINED: This combines both Tesseract and Cube to achieve the best possible OCR classification. This engine has the best accuracy and the slowest execution time.
  - OEM_DEFAULT: This infers the strategy based on the language config file, command-line config file or, in the absence of both, uses OEM_TESSERACT_ONLY.

It's important to emphasize that the `Init` function can be executed many times. If a different language or engine mode is provided, Tesseract will clear the previous configuration and start again. If the same parameters are provided, Tesseract is smart enough to simply ignore the command. The `init` function returns 0 in case of success and −1 in case of failure.

Our program will then proceed by setting the page segmentation mode:

```
ocr.SetPageSegMode(tesseract::PSM_SINGLE_BLOCK);
```

There are several segmentation modes available:

- PSM_OSD_ONLY: Using this mode, Tesseract will just run its preprocessing algorithms to detect orientation and script detection.
- PSM_AUTO_OSD: This tells Tesseract to do automatic page segmentation with orientation and script detection.
- PSM_AUTO_ONLY: This does page segmentation, but avoids doing orientation, script detection, or OCR.
- PSM_AUTO: This does page segmentation and OCR, but avoids doing orientation or script detection.
- PSM_SINGLE_COLUMN: This assumes that the text of variable sizes is displayed in a single column.
- PSM_SINGLE_BLOCK_VERT_TEXT: This treats the image as a single uniform block of vertically aligned text.
- PSM_SINGLE_BLOCK: This assumes a single block of text, and is the default configuration. We will use this flag since our preprocessing phase guarantees this condition.
- PSM_SINGLE_LINE: Indicates that the image contains only one line of text.
- PSM_SINGLE_WORD: Indicates that the image contains just one word.
- PSM_SINGLE_WORD_CIRCLE: Informs us that the image is a just one word disposed in a circle.
- PSM_SINGLE_CHAR: Indicates that the image contains a single character.

Notice that Tesseract already has **deskewing** and text segmentation algorithms implemented, just like most OCR libraries do. But it's interesting to know of such algorithms since you may provide your own preprocessing phase for specific needs. This allows you to improve text detection in many cases. For example, if you are creating an OCR application for old documents, the default threshold used by Tesseract may create a dark background. Tesseract may also be confused by borders or severe text skewing.

Next, we call the SetImage method with the following signature:

```
void SetImage(const unsigned char* imagedata, int width,
  int height, int bytes_per_pixel, int bytes_per_line);
```

The parameters are almost self-explanatory, and most of them can be read directly from our `Mat` object:

- `data`: A raw byte array containing image data. OpenCV contains a function called `data()` in the `Mat` class that provides a direct pointer to the data.
- `width`: Image width.
- `height`: Image height.
- `bytes_per_pixel`: Number of bytes per pixel. We are using 1, since we are dealing with a binary image. If you want the code to be more generic, you could also use the `Mat::elemSize()` function, which provides the same information.
- `bytes_per_line`: Number of bytes in a single line. We are using the `Mat::step` property since some images add trailing bytes.

Then, we call `GetUTF8Text` to run the recognition itself. The recognized text is returned, encoded with UTF8 and without BOM. Before returning it, we also print some debug information.

`MeanTextConf` returns a confidence index, which may by a number from 0 to 100:

```
auto text = ocr.GetUTF8Text();
cout  "Text:"  endl;
cout  text  endl;
cout  "Confidence: "  ocr.MeanTextConf()  endl;
```

Sending the output to a file

Let's change our main method to send the recognized output to a file. We do this by using a standard `ofstream`:

```
int main(int argc, char* argv[])
{
    //Loads the ticket image and binarize it
    Mat ticket = binarize(imread("ticket.png"));
    auto regions = findTextAreas(ticket);

    std::ofstream file;
    file.open("ticket.txt", std::ios::out | std::ios::binary);

    //For each region
    for (const auto& region : regions) {
        //Crop
        auto cropped = deskewAndCrop(ticket, region);
        auto text = identifyText(cropped, "por");
```

```
            file.write(text,  strlen(text));
            file endl;
    }
    file.close();
}
```

The following line opens the file in binary mode:

```
file.open("ticket.txt", std::ios::out | std::ios::binary);
```

This is important since Tesseract returns text encoded in UTF-8, taking into account special characters that are available in Unicode. We also write the output directly using the following command:

```
file.write(text,  strlen(text));
```

In this sample, we called the `identify` function using Portuguese as an input language (this is the language the ticket was written in). You may use another photo, if you like.

> The complete source file is provided in the `segmentOcr.cpp` file, which comes with this book.

> `ticket.png` is a low resolution image, since we imagined you would want to display a window with the image while studying this code. For this image, the Tesseract results are rather poor. If you want to test with a higher resolution image, the code for this book provides you with a `ticketHigh.png` image. To test with this image, change the dilation repetitions to `12` and the minimum box size from `20` to `60`. You'll get a much higher confidence rate (about 87%), and the resulting text will be almost fully readable. The `segmentOcrHigh.cpp` file contains these modifications.

Summary

In this chapter, we presented a brief introduction to OCR applications. We saw that the preprocessing phase of such systems must be adjusted according to the type of document we are planning to identify. We have learned about common operations while preprocessing text files, such as thresholding, cropping, skewing, and text region segmentation. Finally, we learned how to install and use Tesseract OCR to convert our image into text.

In the next chapter, we'll use a more sophisticated OCR technique to identify text in a casually taken picture or video –a situation known as scene text recognition. This is a much more complex scenario, since the text can be anywhere, in any font, and with different illuminations and orientations. There can even be no text at all! We'll also learn how to use the OpenCV 3.0 text contribution module, which is fully integrated with Tesseract.

11
Text Recognition with Tesseract

In Chapter 10, *Developing Segmentation Algorithms for Text Recognition*, we covered the very basic OCR processing functions. Although they are quite useful for scanned or photographed documents, they are almost useless when dealing with text that casually appears in a picture.

In this chapter, we'll explore the OpenCV 4.0 text module, which deals specifically with scene text detection. Using this API, it is possible to detect the text that appears in a webcam video, or to analyze photographed images (like the ones in Street View or taken by a surveillance camera) to extract text information in real time. This allows for a wide range of applications to be created, from accessibility, to marketing, and even robotics fields.

By the end of this chapter, you will be able to do the following:

- Understand what scene text recognition is
- Understand how the text API works
- Use the OpenCV 4.0 text API to detect text
- Extract the detected text into an image
- Use the text API and Tesseract integration to identify letters

Technical requirements

This chapter requires familiarity with the basic C++ programming language. All of the code used in this chapter can be downloaded from the following GitHub link: https://github. com/PacktPublishing/Building-Computer-Vision-Projects-with-OpenCV4-and-CPlusPlus/tree/master/Chapter11. The code can be executed on any operating system, though it is only tested on Ubuntu.

Check out the following video to see the Code in Action:
http://bit.ly/2Slht5A

How the text API works

The text API implements the algorithm that was proposed by *Lukás Neumann* and *Jiri Matas* in the article *Real-Time Scene Text Localization and Recognition* during the **computer vision and pattern recognition (CVPR)** conference in 2012. This algorithm represented a significant increase in scene text detection, performing state-of-the art detection both in the CVPR database, as well as in the Google Street View database. Before using the API, let's take a look at how this algorithm works under to hood, and how it addresses the scene text detection problem.

Remember: The OpenCV 4.0 text API does not come with the standard OpenCV modules. It's an additional module that's present in the OpenCV contrib package. If you installed OpenCV using the Windows Installer, you should take a look back at Chapter 1, *Getting Started with OpenCV*; this will guide you on how to install these modules.

The scene detection problem

Detecting text that randomly appears in a scene is a problem that's harder than it looks. There are several new variables that you need to take into account when you're comparing to identified scanned text, such as the following:

- **Tridimensionality**: The text may be in any scale, orientation, or perspective. Also, the text may be partially occluded or interrupted. There are literally thousands of possible regions where it may appear in the image.
- **Variety**: Text can be in several different fonts and colors. The font may have outline borders. The background can be dark, light, or a complex image.
- **Illumination and shadows**: The sunlight's position and apparent color changes over time. Different weather conditions like fog or rain can generate noise. Illumination may be a problem even in closed spaces, since light reflects over colored objects and hits the text.

- **Blurring**: Text may appear in a region that's not prioritized by lens auto-focus. Blurring is also common in moving cameras, in perspective text, or in the presence of fog.

The following picture, taken from Google Street View, illustrates these problems. Note how several of these situations occur simultaneously in just a single image:

Performing text detection to deal with such situations may prove computationally expensive, since there are 2^n subsets of pixels, n being the number of pixels in the image.

To reduce complexity, two strategies are commonly applied:

- **Use a sliding window to search just a subset of image rectangles**: This strategy just reduces the number of subsets to a smaller amount. The amount of regions varies according to the complexity of text being considered. Algorithms that deal just with text rotation may use small values, compared to the ones that also deal with rotation, skewing, perspective, and so on. The advantage of this approach is its simplicity, but they are usually limited to a narrow range of fonts and often to a lexicon of specific words.

- **Use of connected component analysis**: This approach assumes that pixels can be grouped into regions, where pixels have similar properties. These regions are supposed to have higher chances to be identified as characters. The advantage of this approach is that it does not depend on several text properties (orientation, scale, fonts, and so on), and they also provide a segmentation region that can be used to crop text to the OCR. This was the approach that we used in `Chapter 10`, *Developing Segmentation Algorithms for Text Recognition*. Lighting could also affect the result, for example, if a shadow is cast over the letters, creating two distinct regions. However, since scene detection is commonly used in moving vehicles (for example, drones or cars) and with videos, the text will end up being detected eventually, since these lighting conditions will differ from frame to frame.

The OpenCV 4.0 algorithm uses the second strategy by performing connected component analysis and searching for extremal regions.

Extremal regions

Extremal regions are connected areas that are characterized by almost uniform intensity, which is surrounded by a contrasted background. The stability of a region can be measured by calculating how resistant to thresholding variance the region is. This variance can be measured with a simple algorithm:

1. Apply the threshold, generating an image, A. Detect its connected pixels regions (extremal regions).
2. Increase the threshold by a delta amount, generating an image, B. Detect its connected pixels regions (extremal regions).
3. Compare image B with A. If a region in image A is similar to the same region in image B, add it to the same branch in the tree. The criteria of similarity may vary from implementation to implementation, but it's usually related to the image area or general shape. If a region in image A appears to be split in image B, create two new branches in the tree for the new regions and associate it with the previous branch.
4. Set $A = B$ and go back to step 2, until the maximum threshold is applied.

This will assemble a tree of regions, as follows:

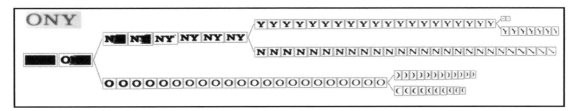

The resistance to variance is determined by counting how many nodes are in the same level. By analyzing this tree, it's also possible to determine the **maximally stable extremal regions** (**MSER**s), that is, the regions where the area remains stable in a wide variety of thresholds. In the previous diagram, it is clear that these areas would contain the letters *O*, *N*, and *Y*. The main disadvantage of maximally extremal regions is that they are weak in the presence of blur. OpenCV provides a MSER feature detector in the **feature2d** module. Extremal regions are interesting because they are strongly invariant to illumination, scale, and orientation. They are good candidates for text as well, since they are also invariant, with regards to the type of font used, even when the font is styled. Each region can also be analyzed to determine its boundary ellipsis, and can have properties like affine transformation and area numerically determined. Finally, it's worth mentioning that this entire process is fast, which makes it a very good candidate for real-time applications.

Extremal region filtering

Although MSERs are a common approach to define which extremal regions are worth working with, the *Neumann* and *Matas* algorithm uses a different approach, by submitting all extremal regions to a sequential classifier that's been trained for character detection. This classifier works in two different stages:

1. The first stage incrementally computes descriptors (bounding box, perimeter, area, and Euler number) for each region. These descriptors are submitted to a classifier that estimates how probable the region is to be a character in the alphabet. Then, only the regions of high probability are selected for stage 2.
2. In this stage, the features of the whole area ratio, convex hull ratio, and the number of outer boundary inflexion points are calculated. This provides more detailed information that allows the classifier to discard non-text characters, but they are also much slower to calculate.

Under OpenCV, this process is implemented in a class called `ERFilter`. It is also possible to use different image single channel projections, such as *R, G, B*, Luminance, or gray scale conversion to increase the character recognition rates. Finally, all of the characters must be grouped into text blocks (such as words or paragraphs). OpenCV 3.0 provides two algorithms for this purpose:

- **Prune exhaustive search**: Also proposed by *Mattas* in 2011, this algorithm does not need any previous training or classification, but is limited to horizontally aligned text
- **Hierarchical method for oriented text**: This deals with text in any orientation, but needs a trained classifier

 Note that since these operations require classifiers, it is also necessary to provide a trained set as input. OpenCV 4.0 provides some of these trained sets in the following sample package: `https://github.com/opencv/opencv_contrib/tree/master/modules/text/samples`. This also means that this algorithm is sensitive to the fonts used in classifier training.

A demonstration of this algorithm can be seen in the following video, which is provided by Neumann himself: `https://www.youtube.com/watch?v=ejd5gGea2Fofeature=youtu.be`. Once the text is segmented, it just needs to be sent to an OCR like Tesseract, similarly to what we did in `Chapter 10`, *Developing Segmentation Algorithms for Text Recognition*. The only difference is that now we will use OpenCV text module classes to interface with Tesseract, since they provide a way to encapsulate the specific OCR engine we are using.

Using the text API

Enough theory. It's time to see how the text module works in practice. Let's study how we can use it to perform text detection, extraction, and identification.

Text detection

Let's start by creating a simple program so that we can perform text segmentation using **ERFilters**. In this program, we will use the trained classifiers from text API samples. You may download this from the OpenCV repository, but they are also available in this book's companion code.

First, we start by including all of the necessary `libs` and `usings`:

```
#include  "opencv2/highgui.hpp"
#include  "opencv2/imgproc.hpp"
#include  "opencv2/text.hpp"

#include  <vector>
#include  <iostream>

using namespace std;
using namespace cv;
using namespace cv::text;
```

Recall from the *Extremal region filtering* section that the `ERFilter` works separately in each image channel. Therefore, we must provide a way to separate each desired channel in a different single channel, `cv::Mat`. This is done by the `separateChannels` function:

```
vector<Mat> separateChannels(const Mat& src)
{
    vector<Mat> channels;
    //Grayscale images
    if (src.type() == CV_8U || src.type() == CV_8UC1) {
        channels.push_back(src);
        channels.push_back(255-src);
        return channels;
    }

    //Colored images
    if (src.type() == CV_8UC3) {
        computeNMChannels(src, channels);
        int size = static_cast<int>(channels.size())-1;
        for (int c = 0; c < size; c++)
            channels.push_back(255-channels[c]);
        return channels;
    }

    //Other types
    cout << "Invalid image format!" << endl;
    exit(-1);
}
```

First, we verify whether the image is already a single channel image (grayscale image). If that's the case, we just add this image – it does not need to be processed. Otherwise, we check if it's an **RGB** image. For colored images, we call the computeNMChannels function to split the image into several channels. This function is defined as follows:

```
void computeNMChannels(InputArray src, OutputArrayOfArrays channels, int
mode = ERFILTER_NM_RGBLGrad);
```

The following are its parameters:

- src: The source input array. It must be a colored image of type 8UC3.
- channels: A vector of Mats that will be filled with the resulting channels.
- mode: Defines which channels will be computed. Two possible values can be used:
    - ERFILTER_NM_RGBLGrad: Indicates whether the algorithm will use RGB color, lightness, and gradient magnitude as channels (default)
    - ERFILTER_NM_IHSGrad: Indicates whether the image will be split by its intensity, hue, saturation, and gradient magnitude

We also append the negative of all color components in the vector. Since the image will have three distinct channels (*R*, *G*, and *B*), this is usually enough. It's also possible to add the non-flipped channels, just like we did with the de-grayscaled image, but we'll end up with six channels, and this could be computer-intensive. Of course, you're free to test with your images if this leads to a better result. Finally, if another kind of image is provided, the function will terminate the program with an error message.

 Negatives are appended, so the algorithms will cover both bright text in a dark background and dark text in a bright background. There is no sense in adding a negative for the gradient magnitude.

Let's proceed to the main method. We'll use this program to segment the easel.png image, which is provided with the source code:

This picture was taken by a mobile phone camera while I was walking on the street. Let's code this so that you may also use a different image easily by providing its name in the first program argument:

```
int main(int argc, const char * argv[])
{
    const char* image = argc < 2 ? "easel.png" : argv[1];
    auto input = imread(image);
```

Next, we'll convert the image to grayscale and separate its channels by calling the separateChannels function:

```
    Mat processed;
    cvtColor(input, processed, COLOR_RGB2GRAY);

    auto channels = separateChannels(processed);
```

If you want to work with all of the channels in a colored image, just replace the two first lines of this code extract to the following:

```
Mat processed = input;
```

We will need to analyze six channels (RGB and inverted) instead of two (gray and inverted). Actually, the processing times will increase much more than the improvements that we can get. With the channels in hand, we need to create `ERFilters` for both stages of the algorithm. Luckily, the OpenCV text contribution module provides functions for this:

```
// Create ERFilter objects with the 1st and 2nd stage classifiers
auto filter1 = createERFilterNM1(
    loadClassifierNM1("trained_classifierNM1.xml"),  15, 0.00015f,
    0.13f, 0.2f,true,0.1f);

auto filter2 = createERFilterNM2(
    loadClassifierNM2("trained_classifierNM2.xml"),0.5);
```

For the first stage, we call the `loadClassifierNM1` function to load a previously trained classification model. The .xml containing the training data is its only argument. Then, we call `createERFilterNM1` to create an instance of the `ERFilter` class that will perform the classification. The function has the following signature:

```
Ptr<ERFilter> createERFilterNM1(const Ptr<ERFilter::Callback>& cb, int
thresholdDelta = 1, float minArea = 0.00025, float maxArea = 0.13, float
minProbability = 0.4, bool nonMaxSuppression = true, float
minProbabilityDiff = 0.1);
```

The parameters for this function are as follows:

- `cb`: The classification model. This is the same model we loaded with the `loadCassifierNM1` function.
- `thresholdDelta`: The amount to be summed to the threshold in each algorithm iteration. The default value is 1, but we'll use 15 in our example.
- `minArea`: The minimum area of the **extremal region** (ER), where text may be found. This is measured by the percentage of the image's size. ERs with areas smaller than this are immediately discarded.
- `maxArea`: The maximum area of the ER where text may be found. This is also measured by the percentage of the image's size. ERs with areas greater than this are immediately discarded.
- `minProbability`: The minimum probability that a region must have to be a character in order to remain for the next stage.
- `nonMaxSupression`: This is used to indicate if non-maximum suppression will be done in each branch probability.
- `minProbabilityDiff`: The minimum probability difference between the minimum and maximum extreme region.

The process for the second stage is similar. We call `loadClassifierNM2` to load the classifier model for the second stage and `createERFilterNM2` to create the second stage classifier. This function only takes the input parameters of the loaded classification model and a minimum probability that a region must achieve to be considered as a character. So, let's call these algorithms in each channel to identify all possible text regions:

```
//Extract text regions using Newmann & Matas algorithm
cout << "Processing " << channels.size() << " channels...";
cout << endl;
vector<vector<ERStat> > regions(channels.size());
for (int c=0; c < channels.size(); c++)
{
    cout << "    Channel " << (c+1) << endl;
    filter1->run(channels[c], regions[c]);
    filter2->run(channels[c], regions[c]);
}
filter1.release();
filter2.release();
```

In the previous code, we used the `run` function of the `ERFilter` class. This function takes two arguments:

- **The input channel**: This includes the image to be processed.
- **The regions**: In the first stage algorithm, this argument will be filled with the detected regions. In the second stage (performed by `filter2`), this argument must contain the regions selected in stage 1. These will be processed and filtered by stage 2.

Finally, we release both filters, since they will not be needed in the program anymore. The final segmentation step is grouping all ERRegions into possible words and defining their bounding boxes. This is done by calling the `erGrouping` function:

```
//Separate character groups from regions
vector< vector<Vec2i> > groups;
vector<Rect> groupRects;
erGrouping(input, channels, regions, groups, groupRects,
ERGROUPING_ORIENTATION_HORIZ);
```

This function has the following signature:

```
void erGrouping(InputArray img, InputArrayOfArrays channels,
std::vector<std::vector<ERStat> > &regions, std::vector<std::vector<Vec2i>
> &groups, std::vector<Rect> &groups_rects, int method =
ERGROUPING_ORIENTATION_HORIZ, const std::string& filename = std::string(),
float minProbablity = 0.5);
```

Let's take a look at the meaning of each parameter:

- `img`: Input image, also called the original image.
- `regions`: Vector of single channel images where regions were extracted.
- `groups`: An output vector of indexes of grouped regions. Each group region contains all extremal regions of a single word.
- `groupRects`: A list of rectangles with the detected text regions.
- `method`: This is the method of grouping. It can be any of the following:
  - `ERGROUPING_ORIENTATION_HORIZ`: The default value. This only generates groups with horizontally oriented text by doing an exhaustive search, as proposed originally by *Neumann* and *Matas*.
  - `ERGROUPING_ORIENTATION_ANY`: This generates groups with text in any orientation, using single linkage clustering and classifiers. If you use this method, the filename of the classifier model must be provided in the next parameter.
  - `Filename`: The name of the classifier model. This is only needed if `ERGROUPING_ORIENTATION_ANY` is selected.
  - `minProbability`: The minimum detected probability of accepting a group. This is also only needed if `ERGROUPING_ORIENTATION_ANY` is selected.

The code also provides a call to the second method, but it's commented out. You may switch between the two to test this out. Just comment the previous call and uncomment this one:

```
erGrouping(input, channels, regions,
    groups, groupRects, ERGROUPING_ORIENTATION_ANY,
    "trained_classifier_erGrouping.xml", 0.5);
```

For this call, we also used the default trained classifier that's provided in the text module sample package. Finally, we draw the region boxes and show the results:

```
// draw groups boxes
for (const auto& rect : groupRects)
    rectangle(input, rect, Scalar(0, 255, 0), 3);

imshow("grouping",input);
waitKey(0);
```

This program outputs the following result:

You may check the entire source code in the detection.cpp file.

While most OpenCV text module functions are written to support both grayscale and colored images as its input parameter, at the time of writing this book, there were bugs preventing us from using grayscale images in functions such as erGrouping. For more information, take a look at the following GitHub link: https://github.com/Itseez/opencv_contrib/issues/309.
Always remember that the OpenCV contrib modules package is not as stable as the default OpenCV packages.

Text extraction

Now that we have detected the regions, we must crop the text before submitting it to the OCR. We could simply use a function like getRectSubpix or Mat::copy, using each region rectangle as a **region of interest (ROI)** but, since the letters are skewed, some undesired text may be cropped as well. For example, this is what one of the regions would look like if we just extract the ROI based on its given rectangle:

Fortunately, ERFilter provides us with an object called ERStat, which contains pixels inside each extremal region. With these pixels, we could use OpenCV's floodFill function to reconstruct each letter. This function is capable of painting similar colored pixels based on a seed point, just like the **bucket** tool of most drawing applications. This is what the function signature looks like:

```
int floodFill(InputOutputArray image, InputOutputArray mask,  Point
seedPoint, Scalar newVal,
 CV_OUT Rect* rect=0, Scalar loDiff = Scalar(), Scalar upDiff = Scalar(),
int flags = 4 );
```

Let's understand these parameters and how they will be used:

- image: The input image. We'll use the channel image where the extremal region was taken. This is where the function normally does the flood fill, unless FLOODFILL_MASK_ONLY is supplied. In this case, the image remains untouched and the drawing occurs in the mask. That's exactly what we will do.
- mask: The mask must be an image with two rows and two columns greater than the input image. When the flood fill draws a pixel, it verifies if the corresponding pixel in the mask is zero. In that case, it will draw and mark this pixel as one (or another value that's passed into the flags). If the pixel is not zero, the flood fill does not paint the pixel. In our case, we'll provide a blank mask so that every letter will get painted in the mask.
- seedPoint: The starting point. It's similar to the place you click when you want to use the **bucket** tool of a graphic application.
- newVal: The new value of the repainted pixels.

- `loDiff` and `upDiff`: These parameters represent the lower and upper differences between the pixel being processed and its neighbors. The neighbor will be painted if it falls into this range. If the FLOODFILL_FIXED_RANGE flag is used, the difference between the seed point and the pixels being processed will be used instead.
- `rect`: This is an optional parameter that limits the region where the flood fill will be applied.
- `flags`: This value is represented by a bit mask:
  - The least significant 8 bits of the flag contains a connectivity value. A value of 4 indicates that all four edge pixels will be used, and a value of 8 will indicate that the diagonal pixels must also be taken into account. We'll use 4 for this parameter.
  - The next 8 to 16 bits contains a value from 1 to 255, which is used to fill the mask. Since we want to fill the mask with white, we'll use 255 << 8 for this value.
  - There are two more bits that can be set by adding the FLOODFILL_FIXED_RANGE and FLOODFILL_MASK_ONLY flags, as we already described.

We'll create a function called drawER. This function will receive four parameters:

- A vector with all of the processed channels
- The ERStat region
- The group that must be drawn
- The group rectangle

This function will return an image with the word represented by this group. Let's start this function by creating the mask image and defining the flags:

```
Mat out = Mat::zeros(channels[0].rows+2, channels[0].cols+2, CV_8UC1);

int flags = 4                    //4 neighbors
    + (255 << 8)                        //paint mask in white (255)
    + FLOODFILL_FIXED_RANGE      //fixed range
    + FLOODFILL_MASK_ONLY;       //Paint just the mask
```

Then, we'll loop through each group. It's necessary to find the region index and its status. There's a chance of this extreme region being the root, which does not contain any points. In this case, we'll just ignore it:

```
for (int g=0; g < group.size(); g++)
{
    int idx = group[g][0];
    auto er = regions[idx][group[g][1]];

//Ignore root region
    if (er.parent == NULL)
            continue;
```

Now, we can read the pixel coordinate from the ERStat object. It's represented by the pixel number, counting from top to bottom, left to right. This linear index must be converted to a row (*y*) and column (*z*) notation, using a formula similar to the one we saw in Chapter 2, *An Introduction to the Basics of OpenCV*:

```
int px = er.pixel % channels[idx].cols;
int py = er.pixel / channels[idx].cols;
Point p(px, py);
```

Then, we can call the floodFill function. The ERStat object gives us the value to use in the loDiff parameter:

```
floodFill(
    channels[idx], out,         //Image and mask
    p, Scalar(255),             //Seed and color
    nullptr,                    //No rect
    Scalar(er.level),Scalar(0), //LoDiff and upDiff
    flags                       //Flags
```

After we do this for all of the regions in the group, we'll end with an image that's a little bigger than the original one, with a black background and the word in white letters. Now, let's crop just the area of the letters. Since the region rectangle was given, we start by defining it as our region of interest:

```
out = out(rect);
```

Then, we'll find all non-zero pixels. This is the value we'll use in the `minAreaRect` function to get the rotated rectangle around the letters. Finally, we will borrow the previous chapter's `deskewAndCrop` function to crop and rotate the image for us:

```
vector<Point> points;
findNonZero(out, points);
//Use deskew and crop to crop it perfectly
return deskewAndCrop(out, minAreaRect(points));
}
```

This is the result of the process for the easel image:

Text recognition

In `Chapter 10`, *Developing Segmentation Algorithms for Text Recognition*, we used the Tesseract API directly to recognize the text regions. This time, we'll use OpenCV classes to accomplish the same goal.

In OpenCV, all OCR-specific classes derive from the **BaseOCR** virtual class. This class provides a common interface for the OCR execution method itself. Specific implementations must inherit from this class. By default, the text module provides three different implementations: **OCRTesseract**, **OCRHMMDecoder**, and **OCRBeamSearchDecoder**.

This hierarchy is depicted in the following class diagram:

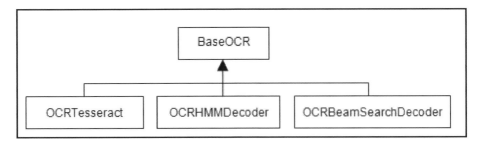

With this approach, we can separate the part of the code where the OCR mechanism is created from the execution itself. This makes it easier to change the OCR implementation in the future.

So, let's start by creating a method that decides which implementation we'll use based on a string. We currently support just Tesseract, but you may take a look in this chapter's code, where a demonstration with **HMMDecoder** is also provided. Also, we are accepting the OCR engine name in a string parameter, but we could improve our application's flexibility by reading it from an external JSON or XML configuration file:

```
cv::Ptr<BaseOCR> initOCR2(const string& ocr) { if (ocr == "tesseract") {
return OCRTesseract::create(nullptr, "eng+por"); } throw string("Invalid
OCR engine: ") + ocr; }
```

As you may have noticed, the function returns `Ptr<BaseOCR>`. Now, take a look at the highlighted code. It calls the `create` method to initialize a Tesseract OCR instance. Let's take a look at its official signature, since it allows several specific parameters:

```
Ptr<OCRTesseract> create(const char* datapath=NULL,
  const char* language=NULL,
  const char* char_whitelist=NULL,
  int oem=3, int psmode=3);
```

Let's dissect each of these parameters:

- `datapath`: This is the path to the root directory's `tessdata` files. The path must end with a backslash / character. The `tessdata` directory contains the language files you installed. Passing `nullptr` to this parameter will make Tesseract search in its installation directory, which is the location where this folder is normally present. It's common to change this value to `args[0]` when deploying an application and include the `tessdata` folder in your application path.
- `language`: This is a three letter word with the language code (for example, eng for English, por for Portuguese, or hin for Hindi). Tesseract supports the loading of multiple language codes by using the + sign. Therefore, passing eng+por will load both English and Portuguese languages. Of course, you can only use languages that you have previously installed, otherwise the loading will fail. A language `config` file may specify that two or more languages must be loaded together. To prevent that, you may use a tilde ~. For example, you can use hin+~eng to guarantee that English is not loaded with Hindi, even if it is configured to do so.

- `whitelist`: This is the character that's set to be considered for recognition. In the case that `nullptr` is passed, the characters will be
  `0123456789abcdefghijklmnopqrstuvwxyzABCDEFGHIJKLMNOPQRSTUVWXYZ`.
- `oem`: These are the OCR algorithms that will be used. It can have one of the following values:
    - `OEM_TESSERACT_ONLY`: Uses just Tesseract. It's the fastest method, but it also has less precision.
    - `OEM_CUBE_ONLY`: Uses Cube engine. It's slower, but more precise. This will only work if your language was trained to support this engine mode. To check if that's the case, look for `.cube` files for your language in the `tessdata` folder. The support for English language is guaranteed.
    - `OEM_TESSERACT_CUBE_COMBINED`: Combines both Tesseract and Cube to achieve the best possible OCR classification. This engine has the best accuracy and the slowest execution time.
    - `OEM_DEFAULT`: Infers the strategy based in the language config file, command-line config file or, in the absence of both, use `OEM_TESSERACT_ONLY`.
- `psmode`: This is the segmentation mode. It can be any of the following:
    - `PSM_OSD_ONLY`: Using this mode, Tesseract will just run its preprocessing algorithms to detect orientation and script detection.
    - `PSM_AUTO_OSD`: This tells Tesseract to do automatic page segmentation with orientation and script detection.
    - `PSM_AUTO_ONLY`: Does page segmentation, but avoids doing orientation, script detection, or OCR. This is the default value.
    - `PSM_AUTO`: Does page segmentation and OCR, but avoids doing orientation or script detection.
    - `PSM_SINGLE_COLUMN`: Assumes that the text of variable sizes is displayed in a single column.
    - `PSM_SINGLE_BLOCK_VERT_TEXT`: Treats the image as a single uniform block of vertically aligned text.
    - `PSM_SINGLE_BLOCK`: Assumes a single block of text. This is the default configuration. We will use this flag since our preprocessing phase guarantees this condition.

- `PSM_SINGLE_LINE`: Indicates that the image contains only one line of text.
- `PSM_SINGLE_WORD`: Indicates that the image contains just one word.
- `PSM_SINGLE_WORD_CIRCLE`: Indicates that the image is a just one word disposed in a circle.
- `PSM_SINGLE_CHAR`: Indicates that the image contains a single character.

For the last two parameters, it's recommended that you use the `#include` Tesseract directory to use the constant names instead of directly inserting their values. The last step is to add text detection in our main function. To do this, just add the following code to the end of the main method:

```
auto ocr = initOCR("tesseract");
for (int i = 0; i < groups.size(); i++)
{
    auto wordImage = drawER(channels, regions, groups[i],
    groupRects[i]);

    string word;
    ocr->run(wordImage, word);
    cout << word << endl;
}
```

In this code, we started by calling our `initOCR` method to create a Tesseract instance. Note that the remaining code will not change if we chose a different OCR engine, since the run method signature is guaranteed by the `BaseOCR` class. Next, we iterate over each detected `ERFilter` group. Since each group represents a different word, we will do the following:

1. Call the previously created `drawER` function to create an image with the word.
2. Create a text string called `word`, and call the `run` function to recognize the word image. The recognized word will be stored in the string.
3. Print the text string in the screen.

Let's take a look at the run method signature. This method is defined in the `BaseOCR` class, and will be equal for all specific OCR implementations – even the ones that might be implemented in the future:

```
virtual void run(Mat& image, std::string& output_text,
  std::vector<Rect>* component_rects=NULL,
  std::vector<std::string>* component_texts=NULL,
  std::vector<float>* component_confidences=NULL, int component_level=0) =
0;
```

Of course, this is a pure virtual function that must be implemented by each specific class (such as the `OCRTesseract` class we just used):

- `image`: The input image. It must be a RGB or a grayscale image.
- `component_rects`: We can provide a vector to be filled with the bounding box of each component (words or text lines) that's detected by the OCR engine.
- `component_texts`: If given, this vector will be filled with the text strings of each component detected by the OCR.
- `component_confidences`: If given, the vector will be filled with floats, with the confidence values of each component.
- `component_level`: Defines what a component is. It may have the values `OCR_LEVEL_WORD` (by default), or `OCR_LEVEL_TEXT_LINE`.

If necessary, you may prefer changing the component level to a word or line in the `run()` method instead of doing the same thing in the `psmode` parameter of the `create()` function. This is preferable since the `run` method will be supported by any OCR engine that decides to implement the `BaseOCR` class. Always remember that the `create()` method is where vendor-specific configurations are set.

This is the program's final output:

Despite a minor confusion with the & symbol, every word was perfectly recognized. You may check the entire source code in the `ocr.cpp` file, in this chapter's code file.

Summary

In this chapter, we saw that scene text recognition is a far more difficult OCR situation than working with scanned texts. We studied how the text module addresses this problem with extremal region identification using the *Newmann* and *Matas* algorithm. We also saw how to use this API with the `floodFill` function to extract the text into an image and submit it to Tesseract OCR. Finally, we studied how the OpenCV text module integrates with Tesseract and other OCR engines, and how can we use its classes to identify what's written in an image.

In the next chapter, you will be introduced to deep learning in OpenCV. You will learn about object detection and classification by using the **you only look once** (**YOLO**) algorithm.

Deep Learning with OpenCV

12

Deep learning is a state-of-the-art form of machine learning that is reaching its best accuracy in image classification and speech recognition. Deep learning is also used in other fields, such as robotics and artificial intelligence with reinforcement learning. This is the main reason OpenCV is making significant efforts to include deep learning at its core. We are going to learn the basic use of OpenCV deep learning interfaces and look at using them in two use cases: object detection and face detection.

In this chapter, we are going to learn the basics of deep learning and see how to use it in OpenCV. To reach our objective, we are going to learn object detection and classification using the **you only look once (YOLO)** algorithm.

The following topics will be covered in this chapter:

- What is deep learning?
- How OpenCV works with deep learning and implementing deep learning **neural networks(NN**s)
- YOLO – a very fast deep learning object detection algorithm
- Face detection using Single Shot Detector

Technical requirements

To follow the chapter with ease, it is required that you install OpenCV with the deep learning module compiled. If you do not have this module, you will not be able to compile and run the sample codes.

It's very useful to have an NVIDIA GPU with CUDA support. You can enable CUDA on OpenCV to improve the speed of training and detection.

Finally, you can download the code used in this chapter from `https://github.com/ PacktPublishing/Building-Computer-Vision-Projects-with-OpenCV4-and-CPlusPlus/ tree/master/Chapter12`.

Check out the following video to see the Code in Action:
`http://bit.ly/2SmbWf7`

Introduction to deep learning

Deep learning is most commonly written about in scientific papers nowadays with regards to image classification and speech recognition. This is a subfield of machine learning, based on traditional neural networks and inspired by the structure of the brain. To understand this technology, it is very important to understand what a neural network is and how it works.

What is a neural network and how can we learn from data?

The neural network is inspired by the structure of the brain, in which multiple neurons are interconnected, creating a network. Each neuron has multiple inputs and multiple outputs, like a biological neuron.

This network is distributed in layers, and each layer contains a number of neurons that are connected to all the previous layer's neurons. This always has an input layer, which normally consists of the features that describe the input image or data, and an output layer, which normally consists of the result of our classification. The other middle layers are called **hidden layers**. The following diagram shows a basic three-layer neural network in which the input layer contains three neurons, the output layer contains two neurons, and a hidden layer contains four neurons:

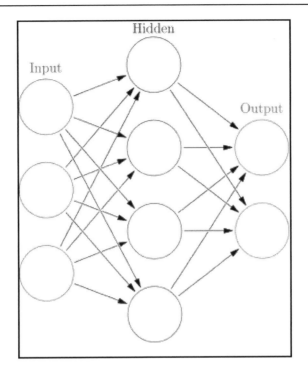

The neuron is the basic element of a neural network and it uses a simple mathematical formula that we can see in the following diagram:

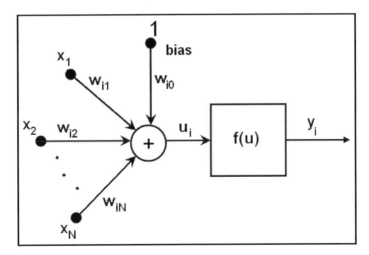

As we can see, for each neuron, **i**, we mathematically add all the previous neuron's output, which is the input of neuron i (**x1, x2**...), by a weight (**wi1, wi2**...) plus a bias value, and the result is the argument of an activation function, **f**. The final result is the output of **i** neuron:

$$yi = f(bias * W_{i0} + X_1 * W_{i1} + X_2 * W_{i2} + \ldots + X_n * W_{in})$$

The most common activation functions (**f**) on classical neural networks are the sigmoid function or linear functions. The sigmoid function is used most often, and it looks as follows:

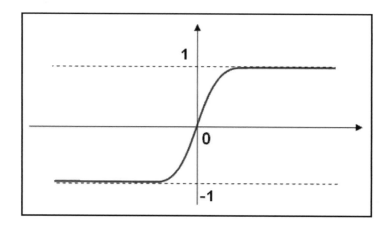

But how can we learn a neural network with this formula and these connections? How do we classify input data? The learn algorithm of neural networks can be called **supervised** if we know the desired output; while learning, the input pattern is given to the net's input layer. Initially, we set up all weights as random numbers and send the input features into the network, checking the output result. If this is wrong, we have to adjust all the weights of the network to get the correct output. This algorithm is called **backpropagation**. If you want to read more about how a neural network learns, check out `http://neuralnetworksanddeeplearning.com/chap2.html` and `https://youtu.be/IHZwWFHWa-w`.

Now that we have a brief introduction to what a neural network is and the internal architecture of NN, we are going to explore the differences between NN and deep learning.

Convolutional neural networks

Deep learning neural networks have the same background as the classical neural network. However, in the case of image analysis, the main difference is the input layer. In a classical machine learning algorithm, the researcher has to identify the best features that define the image target to classify. For example, if we want to classify numbers, we could extract the borders and lines of numbers in each image, measure the area of an object in an image, and all of these features are the input of the neural network, or any other machine learning algorithm. However, in deep learning, you don't have to explore what the features are; instead, you use whole image as an input of the neural network directly. Deep learning can learn what the most important features are and **deep neural networks** (**DNN**) are able to detect an image or input and recognize it.

To learn what these features are, we use one of the most important layers in deep learning and neural networks: the **convolutional layer**. A convolutional layer works like a convolutional operator, where a kernel filter is applied to the whole previous layer, giving us a new filtered image, like a sobel operator:

However, in a convolutional layer we can define different parameters, and one of them is the number of filters and the sizes we want to apply to the previous layer or image. These filters are calculated in the learning step, just like the weights on a classical neural network. This is the magic of deep learning: it can extract the most significant features from labeled images.

However, these convolutional layers are the main reason behind the name **deep**, and we are going to see why in the following basic example. Imagine we have a 100 x 100 image. In a classical neural network, we will extract the most relevant features we can imagine from the input image. This will normally approximately 1,000 features, and with each hidden layer we can increase or decrease this number, but the number of neurons to calculate its weights is reasonable to compute in a normal computer. However, in deep learning, we normally start applying a convolutional layer – with a 64 filter kernels of 3 x 3 size. This will generate a new layer of 100 x 100 x 64 neurons with 3 x 3 x 64 weights to calculate. If we continue adding more and more layers, these numbers quickly increase and require huge computing power to learn the good weights and parameters of our deep learning architecture.

Convolutional layers are one of the most important aspects of the deep learning architecture, but there are also other important layers, such as **Pooling, Dropout, Flatten,** and **Softmax**. In the following diagram, we can see a basic deep learning architecture in which some convolutional and pooling layers are stacked:

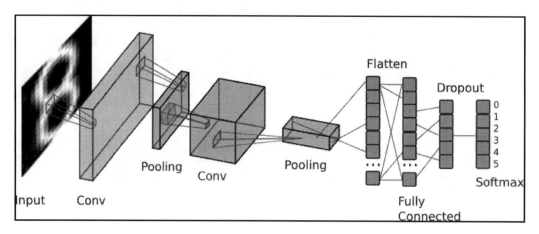

However, there is one more very important thing that makes deep learning get the best results: the amount of labeled data. If you have a small dataset, a deep learning algorithm will not help you in your classification because there is not enough data to learn the features (the weights and parameters of your deep learning architecture). However, if you have tons of data, you will get very good results. But take care, you will need a lot of time to compute and learn the weights and parameters of your architecture. This is why deep learning was not used early in the process, because computing requires a lot of time. However, thanks to new parallel architectures, such as NVIDIA GPUs, we can optimize the learning backpropagation and speed up the learning tasks.

Deep learning in OpenCV

The deep learning module was introduced to OpenCV in version 3.1 as a contribute module. This was moved to part of OpenCV in 3.3, but it was not widely adopted by developers until versions 3.4.3 and 4.

OpenCV implements deep learning only for inference, which means that you cannot create your own deep learning architecture and train in OpenCV; you can only import a pre-trained model, execute it under OpenCV library, and use it as **feedforward** (inference) to obtain the results.

The most important reason to implement the feedforward method is to optimize OpenCV to speed up computing time and performance in inference. Another reason to not implement backward methods is to avoid wasting time developing something that other libraries, such as TensorFlow or Caffe, are specialized in. OpenCV then created importers for the most important deep learning libraries and frameworks to make it possible to import pre-trained models.

Then if you wish to create a new deep learning model to use in OpenCV, you first have to create and train it using the TensorFlow, Caffe, Torch, or DarkNet frameworks or a framework that you can use to export your model in an **Open Neural Network Exchange (ONNX)** format. Creating a model with this framework can be easy or complex depending on the framework you use, but essentially you have to stack multiple layers like we did in the previous diagram, setting the parameters and the function required by the DNN. Nowadays there are other tools to help you to create your models without coding, such as `https://www.tensoreditor.com` or `lobe.ai`. TensorEditor allows you to download the TensorFlow code generated from a visual design architecture to train in your computer or in the cloud. In the following screenshot, we can see TensorEditor:

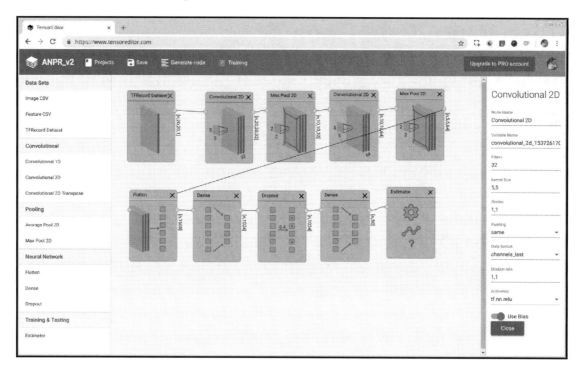

When you have your model trained and you are comfortable with the results, you can import it to OpenCV directly to predict new input images. In the next section, you will see how to import and use deep learning models in OpenCV.

YOLO – real-time object detection

To learn how to use deep learning in OpenCV, we are going to present an example of object detection and classification based on the YOLO algorithm. This is one of the fastest object detection and recognition algorithms, which can run at around 30 fps in an NVIDIA Titan X.

YOLO v3 deep learning model architecture

Common object detection in classical computer vision uses a sliding window to detect objects, scanning a whole image with different window sizes and scales. The main problem here is the huge time consumption in scanning the image several times to find objects.

YOLO uses a different approach by dividing the diagram into an S x S grid. For each grid, YOLO checks for B bounding boxes, and then the deep learning model extracts the bounding boxes for each patch, the confidence to contain a possible object, and the confidence of each category in the training dataset per each box. The following screenshot shows the S x S grid:

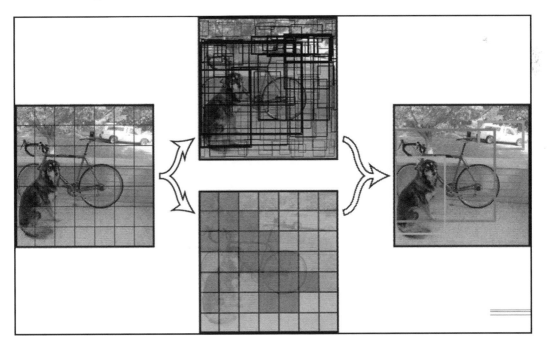

YOLO is trained with a grid of 19 and 5 bounding boxes per grid using 80 categories. Then, the output result is **19 x 19 x 425**, where 425 comes from the data of bounding box (x, y, width, height), the object confidence, and the 80 classes, confidence multiplied by the number of boxes per grid; *5_bounding boxes*(x,y,w,h,object_confidence, classify_confidence[80])=5*(4 + 1 + 80)*:

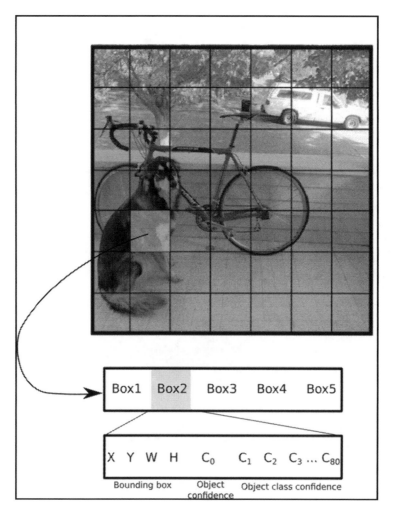

The YOLO v3 architecture is based on DarkNet, which contains 53 layer networks, and YOLO adds 53 more layers for a total of 106 network layers. If you want a faster architecture, you can check version 2 or TinyYOLO versions, which use fewer layers.

The YOLO dataset, vocabulary, and model

Before we start to import the model into our OpenCV code, we have to obtain it through the YOLO website: `https://pjreddie.com/darknet/yolo/`. This provides pre-trained model files based on the **COCO** dataset, which contains 80 object categories, such as person, umbrella, bike, motorcycle, car, apple, banana, computer, and chair.

To get all the names of categories and uses for visualization, check out `https://github.com/pjreddie/darknet/blob/master/data/coco.names?raw=true`.

The names are in the same order as the results of deep learning model confidences. If you want to see some images of the COCO dataset by category, you can explore the dataset at `http://cocodataset.org/#explore`, and download some of them to test our sample application.

To get the model configuration and pre-trained weights, you have to download the following files:

- `https://pjreddie.com/media/files/yolov3.weights`
- `https://github.com/pjreddie/darknet/blob/master/cfg/yolov3.cfg?raw=true`

Now we are ready to start to import the models into OpenCV.

Importing YOLO into OpenCV

The deep learning OpenCV module is found under the `opencv2/dnn.hpp` header, which we have to include in our source header and in `cv::dnn namespace`.

Then our header for OpenCV must look like this:

```
...
#include <opencv2/core.hpp>
#include <opencv2/dnn.hpp>
#include <opencv2/imgproc.hpp>
#include <opencv2/highgui.hpp>
using namespace cv;
using namespace dnn;
...
```

The first thing we have to do is import the COCO name's vocabulary, which is in the `coco.names` file. This file is a plaintext file that contains one class category per line, and is ordered in the same way as the confidence results. Then we are going to read each line of this file and store it in a vector of strings, called classes:

```
...
int main(int argc, char** argv)
{
    // Load names of classes
    string classesFile = "coco.names";
    ifstream ifs(classesFile.c_str());
    string line;
    while (getline(ifs, line)) classes.push_back(line);
    ...
```

Now we are going to import the deep learning model into OpenCV. OpenCV implements the most common readers/importers for deep learning frameworks, such as TensorFlow and DarkNet, and all of them have a similar syntax. In our case, we are going to import a DarkNet model using the weights, and the model using the `readNetFromDarknet` OpenCV function:

```
...
// Give the configuration and weight files for the model
String modelConfiguration = "yolov3.cfg";
String modelWeights = "yolov3.weights";
// Load the network
Net net = readNetFromDarknet(modelConfiguration, modelWeights);
...
```

Now we are in a position to read an image and send the deep neural network to inference. First we have to read an image with the `imread` function and convert it into a tensor/blob data that can read the **DotNetNuke (DNN)**. To create the blob from an image, we are going to use the `blobFromImage` function by passing the image. This function accepts the following parameters:

- **image**: Input image (with 1, 3, or 4 channels).
- **blob**: Output `mat`.
- **scalefactor**: Multiplier for image values.
- **size**: Spatial size for output blob required as input of DNN.
- **mean**: Scalar with mean values that are subtracted from channels. Values are intended to be in (mean-R, mean-G, and mean-B) order if the image has BGR ordering and `swapRB` is true.

- **swapRB**: A flag that indicates to swap the first and last channels in a 3-channel image is necessary.
- **crop**: A flag that indicates whether the image will be cropped after resize.

You can read the full code on how to read and convert an image into a blob in the following snippet:

```
...
input= imread(argv[1]);
// Stop the program if reached end of video
if (input.empty()) {
    cout << "No input image" << endl;
    return 0;
}
// Create a 4D blob from a frame.
blobFromImage(input, blob, 1/255.0, Size(inpWidth, inpHeight),
Scalar(0,0,0), true, false);
...
```

Finally, we have to feed the blob into Deep Net and call the inference with the `forward` function, which requires two parameters: the out `mat` results, and the names of the layers that the output needs to retrieve:

```
...
//Sets the input to the network
net.setInput(blob);

// Runs the forward pass to get output of the output layers
vector<Mat> outs;
net.forward(outs, getOutputsNames(net));
// Remove the bounding boxes with low confidence
postprocess(input, outs);
...
```

In the `mat` output vector, we have all bounding boxes detected by the neural network and we have to post-process the output to get only the results that have a confidence greater than a threshold, normally 0.5, and finally apply non-maximum suppression to eliminate redundant overlapping boxes. You can get the full post-process code on GitHub.

The final result of our example is multiple-object detection and classification in deep learning that shows a window similar to the following:

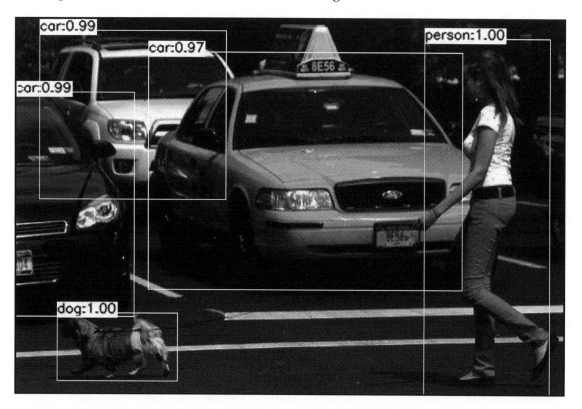

Now we are going to learn another commonly-used object detection function customized for face detection.

Face detection with SSD

Single Shot Detection (SSD) is another fast and accurate deep learning object-detection method with a similar concept to YOLO, in which the object and bounding box are predicted in the same architecture.

SSD model architecture

The SSD algorithm is called single shot because it predicts the bounding box and the class simultaneously as it processes the image in the same deep learning model. Basically, the architecture is summarized in the following steps:

1. A 300 x 300 image is input into the architecture.
2. The input image is passed through multiple convolutional layers, obtaining different features at different scales.
3. For each feature map obtained in 2, we use a 3 x 3 convolutional filter to evaluate small set of default bounding boxes.
4. For each default box evaluated, the bounding box offsets and class probabilities are predicted.

The model architecture looks like this:

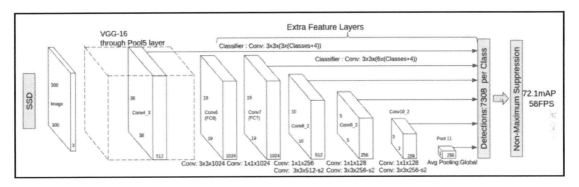

SSD is used for predicting multiple classes similar to that in YOLO, but it can be modified to detect a single object, changing the last layer and training for only one class – this is what we used in our example, a re-trained model for face detection, where only one class is predicted.

Importing SSD face detection into OpenCV

To work with deep learning in our code, we have to import the corresponding headers:

```
#include <opencv2/dnn.hpp>
#include <opencv2/imgproc.hpp>
#include <opencv2/highgui.hpp>
```

After that, we will import the required namespaces:

```
using namespace cv;
using namespace std;
using namespace cv::dnn;
```

Now we are going to define the input image size and constant that we are going to use in our code:

```
const size_t inWidth = 300;
const size_t inHeight = 300;
const double inScaleFactor = 1.0;
const Scalar meanVal(104.0, 177.0, 123.0);
```

In this example, we need a few parameters as input, such as the model configuration and pre-trained model, if we are going to process camera or video input. We also need the minimum confidence to accept a prediction as correct or not:

```
const char* params
= "{ help | false | print usage }"
"{ proto | | model configuration (deploy.prototxt) }"
"{ model | | model weights (res10_300x300_ssd_iter_140000.caffemodel) }"
"{ camera_device | 0 | camera device number }"
"{ video | | video or image for detection }"
"{ opencl | false | enable OpenCL }"
"{ min_confidence | 0.5 | min confidence }";
```

Now, we are going to start with the `main` function, where we are going to parse the arguments with the `CommandLineParser` function:

```
int main(int argc, char** argv)
{
 CommandLineParser parser(argc, argv, params);

 if (parser.get<bool>("help"))
 {
 cout << about << endl;
 parser.printMessage();
 return 0;
 }
```

We are also going to load the model architecture and pre-trained model files, and load the model in a deep learning network:

```
String modelConfiguration = parser.get<string>("proto");
String modelBinary = parser.get<string>("model");

//! [Initialize network]
```

```
dnn::Net net = readNetFromCaffe(modelConfiguration, modelBinary);
//! [Initialize network]
```

It's very important to check that we have imported the network correctly. We must also check whether the model is imported, using the `empty` function, as follows:

```
if (net.empty())
{
cerr << "Can't load network by using the following files" << endl;
exit(-1);
}
```

After loading our network, we are going to initialize our input source, a camera or video file, and load into `VideoCapture`, as follows:

```
VideoCapture cap;
if (parser.get<String>("video").empty())
{
int cameraDevice = parser.get<int>("camera_device");
cap = VideoCapture(cameraDevice);
if(!cap.isOpened())
{
cout << "Couldn't find camera: " << cameraDevice << endl;
return -1;
}
}
else
{
cap.open(parser.get<String>("video"));
if(!cap.isOpened())
{
cout << "Couldn't open image or video: " << parser.get<String>("video") <<
endl;
return -1;
}
}
```

Now we are prepared to start capturing frames and processing each one into the deep neural network to find faces.

First of all, we have to capture each frame in a loop:

```
for(;;)
{
Mat frame;
cap >> frame; // get a new frame from camera/video or read image

if (frame.empty())
```

```
{
waitKey();
break;
}
```

Next, we will put the input frame into a `Mat` blob structure that can manage the deep neural network. We have to send the image with the proper size of SSD, which is 300 x 300 (we will have initialized the `inWidth` and `inHeight` constant variables already) and we subtract from the input image a mean value, which is required in the SSD using the defined `meanVal` constant variable:

```
Mat inputBlob = blobFromImage(frame, inScaleFactor, Size(inWidth,
inHeight), meanVal, false, false);
```

Now we are ready to set the data into the network and get the predictions/detections using the `net.setInput` and `net.forward` functions, respectively. This converts the detection results into a detection `mat` that we can read, where `detection.size[2]` is the number of detected objects and `detection.size[3]` is the number of results per detection (bounding box data and confidence):

```
net.setInput(inputBlob, "data"); //set the network input
Mat detection = net.forward("detection_out"); //compute output
Mat detectionMat(detection.size[2], detection.size[3], CV_32F,
detection.ptr<float>());
```

The `Mat` detection contains the following per each row:

- **Column 0**: Confidence of object being present

- **Column 1**: Confidence of bounding box

- **Column 2**: Confidence of face detected

- **Column 3**: X bottom-left bounding box

- **Column 4**: Y bottom-left bounding box

- **Column 5**: X top-right bounding box

- **Column 6**: Y top-right bounding box

The bounding box is relative (zero to one) to the image size.

Now we have to apply the threshold to get only the desired detections based on the defined input threshold:

```
float confidenceThreshold = parser.get<float>("min_confidence");
 for(int i = 0; i < detectionMat.rows; i++)
 {
 float confidence = detectionMat.at<float>(i, 2);

 if(confidence > confidenceThreshold)
 {
```

Now we are going to extract the bounding box, draw a rectangle over each detected face, and show it as follows:

```
 int xLeftBottom = static_cast<int>(detectionMat.at<float>(i, 3) *
frame.cols);
 int yLeftBottom = static_cast<int>(detectionMat.at<float>(i, 4) *
frame.rows);
 int xRightTop = static_cast<int>(detectionMat.at<float>(i, 5) *
frame.cols);
 int yRightTop = static_cast<int>(detectionMat.at<float>(i, 6) *
frame.rows);

 Rect object((int)xLeftBottom, (int)yLeftBottom, (int)(xRightTop -
xLeftBottom), (int)(yRightTop - yLeftBottom));

 rectangle(frame, object, Scalar(0, 255, 0));
 }
 }
 imshow("detections", frame);
 if (waitKey(1) >= 0) break;
 }
```

The final result looks like this:

In this section, you learned a new deep learning architecture, SSD, and how to use it for face detection.

Summary

In this chapter, we learned what deep learning is and how to use it on OpenCV with object detection and classification. This chapter is a foundation for working with other models and deep neural networks for any purpose.

Till now we learned how to obtain and compile OpenCV, how to use the basic image and `mat` operations, and how to create your own graphical user interfaces. You used basic filters and applied all of them in an industrial inspection example. We looked at how to use OpenCV for face detection and how to manipulate it to add masks. Finally, we introduced you to very complex use cases of object tracking, text segmentation, and recognition. Now you are ready to create your own applications in OpenCV, thanks to these use cases, which show you how to apply each technique or algorithm. In the next chapter, we learn to write some image processing filters for desktops and for small embedded systems such as Raspberry Pi.

13
Cartoonifier and Skin Color Analysis on the RaspberryPi

This chapter will show how to write some image processing filters for desktops and for small embedded systems such as Raspberry Pi. First, we develop for the desktop (in C/C++) and then port the project to Raspberry Pi, since this is the recommended scenario when developing for embedded devices. This chapter will cover the following topics:

- How to convert a real-life image to a sketch drawing
- How to convert to a painting and overlay the sketch to produce a cartoon
- A scary evil mode to create bad characters instead of good characters
- A basic skin detector and skin color changer, to give someone green alien skin
- Finally, how to create an embedded system based on our desktop application

Note that an **embedded system** is basically a computer motherboard placed inside a product or device, designed to perform specific tasks, and **Raspberry Pi** is a very low-cost and popular motherboard for building an embedded system:

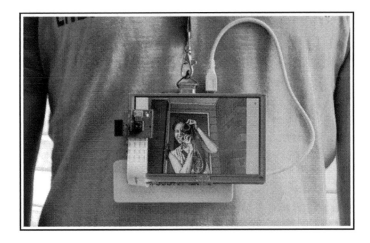

The preceding picture shows what you could make after this chapter: a battery-powered Raspberry Pi plus screen you could wear to Comic Con, turning everyone into a cartoon!

We want to make the real-world camera frames automatically look like they are from a cartoon. The basic idea is to fill the flat parts with some color and then draw thick lines on the strong edges. In other words, the flat areas should become much more flat and the edges should become much more distinct. We will detect edges, smooth the flat areas, and draw enhanced edges back on top, to produce a cartoon or comic book effect.

When developing an embedded computer vision system, it is a good idea to build a fully working desktop version first before porting it to an embedded system, since it is much easier to develop and debug a desktop program than an embedded system! So, this chapter will begin with a complete Cartoonifier desktop program that you can create using your favorite IDE (for example, Visual Studio, XCode, Eclipse, or QtCreator). After it is working properly on your desktop, the last section shows how to create an embedded system based on the desktop version. Many embedded projects require some custom code for the embedded system, such as to use different inputs and outputs, or use some platform-specific code optimizations. However, for this chapter, we will actually be running identical code on the embedded system and the desktop, so we only need to create one project.

The application uses an **OpenCV** GUI window, initializes the camera, and with each camera frame it calls the `cartoonifyImage()` function, containing most of the code in this chapter. It then displays the processed image in the GUI window. This chapter will explain how to create the desktop application from scratch using a USB webcam and the embedded system based on the desktop application, using the Raspberry Pi Camera Module. So, first you will create a desktop project in your favorite IDE, with a `main.cpp` file to hold the GUI code given in the following sections, such as the main loop, webcam functionality, and keyboard input, and you will create a `cartoon.cpp` file with the image processing operations with most of this chapter's code in a function called `cartoonifyImage()`.

Accessing the webcam

To access a computer's webcam or camera device, you can simply call the `open()` function on a `cv::VideoCapture` object (OpenCV's method of accessing your camera device), and pass 0 as the default camera ID number. Some computers have multiple cameras attached, or they do not work with a default camera of 0, so it is common practice to allow the user to pass the desired camera number as a command-line argument, in case they want to try camera 1, 2, or −1, for example. We will also try to set the camera resolution to 640 x 480 using `cv::VideoCapture::set()` to run faster on high-resolution cameras.

Depending on your camera model, driver, or system, OpenCV might not change the properties of your camera. It is not important for this project, so don't worry if it does not work with your webcam.

You can put this code in the main() function of your main.cpp file:

```
auto cameraNumber = 0;
if (argc> 1)
cameraNumber = atoi(argv[1]);

// Get access to the camera.
cv::VideoCapture camera;
camera.open(cameraNumber);
if (!camera.isOpened()) {
   std::cerr<<"ERROR: Could not access the camera or video!"<< std::endl;
   exit(1);
}

// Try to set the camera resolution.
camera.set(cv::CV_CAP_PROP_FRAME_WIDTH, 640);
camera.set(cv::CV_CAP_PROP_FRAME_HEIGHT, 480);
```

After the webcam has been initialized, you can grab the current camera image as a cv::Mat object (OpenCV's image container). You can grab each camera frame by using the C++ streaming operator from your cv::VideoCapture object in a cv::Mat object, just like if you were getting input from a console.

OpenCV makes it very easy to capture frames from a video file (such as an AVI or MP4 file) or network stream instead of a webcam. Instead of passing an integer such as camera.open(0), pass a string such as camera.open("my_video.avi") and then grab frames just like it was a webcam. The source code provided with this book has an initCamera() function that opens a webcam, video file, or network stream.

Main camera processing loop for a desktop app

If you want to display a GUI window on the screen using OpenCV, you call the `cv::namedWindow()` function and then the `cv::imshow()` function for each image, but you must also call `cv::waitKey()` once per frame, otherwise your windows will not update at all! Calling `cv::waitKey(0)` waits forever until the user hits a key in the window, but a positive number such as `waitKey(20)` or higher will wait for at least that many milliseconds.

Put this main loop in the `main.cpp` file, as the basis of your real-time camera app:

```
while (true) {
    // Grab the next camera frame.
    cv::Mat cameraFrame;
    camera >> cameraFrame;
    if (cameraFrame.empty()) {
        std::cerr<<"ERROR: Couldn't grab a camera frame."<<
        std::endl;
        exit(1);
    }
    // Create a blank output image, that we will draw onto.
    cv::Mat displayedFrame(cameraFrame.size(), cv::CV_8UC3);

    // Run the cartoonifier filter on the camera frame.
    cartoonifyImage(cameraFrame, displayedFrame);

    // Display the processed image onto the screen.
    imshow("Cartoonifier", displayedFrame);

    // IMPORTANT: Wait for atleast 20 milliseconds,
    // so that the image can be displayed on the screen!
    // Also checks if a key was pressed in the GUI window.
    // Note that it should be a "char" to support Linux.
    auto keypress = cv::waitKey(20); // Needed to see anything!
    if (keypress == 27) { // Escape Key
        // Quit the program!
        break;
    }
}//end while
```

Generating a black and white sketch

To obtain a sketch (black and white drawing) of the camera frame, we will use an edge detection filter, whereas to obtain a color painting, we will use an edge preserving filter (bilateral filter) to further smooth the flat regions while keeping edges intact. By overlaying the sketch drawing on top of the color painting, we obtain a cartoon effect, as shown earlier in the screenshot of the final app.

There are many different edge detection filters, such as Sobel, Scharr, and Laplacian filters, or a Canny edge detector. We will use a Laplacian edge filter since it produces edges that look most similar to hand sketches compared to Sobel or Scharr, and is quite consistent compared to a Canny edge detector, which produces very clean line drawings but is affected more by random noise in the camera frames, and therefore the line drawings would often change drastically between frames.

Nevertheless, we still need to reduce the noise in the image before we use a Laplacian edge filter. We will use a median filter because it is good at removing noise while keeping edges sharp, but is not as slow as a bilateral filter. Since Laplacian filters use grayscale images, we must convert from OpenCV's default BGR format to grayscale. In your empty `cartoon.cpp` file, put this code at the top so you can access OpenCV and STD C++ templates without typing `cv::` and `std::` everywhere:

```
// Include OpenCV's C++ Interface
 #include <opencv2/opencv.hpp>

 using namespace cv;
 using namespace std;
```

Put this and all remaining code in a `cartoonifyImage()` function in your `cartoon.cpp` file:

```
Mat gray;
 cvtColor(srcColor, gray, CV_BGR2GRAY);
 const int MEDIAN_BLUR_FILTER_SIZE = 7;
 medianBlur(gray, gray, MEDIAN_BLUR_FILTER_SIZE);
 Mat edges;
 const int LAPLACIAN_FILTER_SIZE = 5;
 Laplacian(gray, edges, CV_8U, LAPLACIAN_FILTER_SIZE);
```

The Laplacian filter produces edges with varying brightness, so to make the edges look more like a sketch, we apply a binary threshold to make the edges either white or black:

```
Mat mask;
 const int EDGES_THRESHOLD = 80;
 threshold(edges, mask, EDGES_THRESHOLD, 255, THRESH_BINARY_INV);
```

In the following diagram, you see the original image (to the left) and the generated edge mask (to the right), which looks similar to a sketch drawing. After we generate a color painting (explained later), we also put this edge mask on top to have black line drawings:

Generating a color painting and a cartoon

A strong bilateral filter smooths flat regions while keeping edges sharp, and therefore is great as an automatic cartoonifier or painting filter, except that it is extremely slow (that is, measured in seconds or even minutes, rather than milliseconds!). Therefore, we will use some tricks to obtain a nice cartoonifier, while still running at an acceptable speed. The most important trick we can use is that we can perform bilateral filtering at a lower resolution and it will still have a similar effect as a full resolution, but run much faster. Let's reduce the total number of pixels by four (for example, half width and half height):

```
Size size = srcColor.size();
Size smallSize;
smallSize.width = size.width/2;
smallSize.height = size.height/2;
Mat smallImg = Mat(smallSize, CV_8UC3);
resize(srcColor, smallImg, smallSize, 0,0, INTER_LINEAR);
```

Rather than applying a large bilateral filter, we will apply many small bilateral filters, to produce a strong cartoon effect in less time. We will truncate the filter (refer to the following diagram) so that instead of performing a whole filter (for example, a filter size of 21 x 21, when the bell curve is 21 pixels wide), it just uses the minimum filter size needed for a convincing result (for example, with a filter size of just 9 x 9 even if the bell curve is 21 pixels wide). This truncated filter will apply the major part of the filter (gray area) without wasting time on the minor part of the filter (white area under the curve), so it will run several times faster:

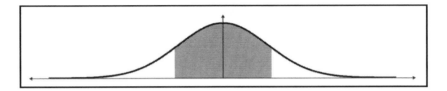

Therefore, we have four parameters that control the bilateral filter: color strength, positional strength, size, and repetition count. We need a temp `Mat` since the `bilateralFilter()` function can't overwrite its input (referred to as **in-place processing**), but we can apply one filter storing a temp `Mat` and another filter storing back the input:

```
Mat tmp = Mat(smallSize, CV_8UC3);
auto repetitions = 7; // Repetitions for strong cartoon effect.
for (auto i=0; i<repetitions; i++) {
    auto ksize = 9; // Filter size. Has large effect on speed.
    double sigmaColor = 9; // Filter color strength.
    double sigmaSpace = 7; // Spatial strength. Affects speed.
    bilateralFilter(smallImg, tmp, ksize, sigmaColor, sigmaSpace);
    bilateralFilter(tmp, smallImg, ksize, sigmaColor, sigmaSpace);
}
```

Remember that this was applied to the shrunken image, so we need to expand the image back to the original size. Then, we can overlay the edge mask that we found earlier. To overlay the edge mask sketch onto the bilateral filter painting (left-hand side of the following image), we can start with a black background and copy the painting pixels that aren't edges in the sketch mask:

```
Mat bigImg;
 resize(smallImg, bigImg, size, 0,0, INTER_LINEAR);
 dst.setTo(0);
 bigImg.copyTo(dst, mask);
```

The result is a cartoon version of the original photo, as shown on the right-hand side of the following image, where the *sketch* mask is overlaid on the painting:

Generating an evil mode using edge filters

Cartoons and comics always have both good and bad characters. With the right combination of edge filters, a scary image can be generated from the most innocent looking people! The trick is to use a small edge filter that will find many edges all over the image, then merge the edges using a small median filter.

We will perform this on a grayscale image with some noise reduction, so the preceding code for converting the original image to grayscale and applying a 7 x 7 median filter should still be used (the first image in the following diagram shows the output of the grayscale median blur). Instead of following it with a Laplacian filter and Binary threshold, we can get a scarier look if we apply a 3 x 3 Scharr gradient filter along *x* and *y* (second image in the diagram), then a binary threshold with a very low cutoff (third image in the diagram), and a 3 x 3 median blur, producing the final *evil* mask (fourth image in the diagram):

```
Mat gray;
 cvtColor(srcColor, gray, CV_BGR2GRAY);
 const int MEDIAN_BLUR_FILTER_SIZE = 7;
 medianBlur(gray, gray, MEDIAN_BLUR_FILTER_SIZE);
 Mat edges, edges2;
 Scharr(srcGray, edges, CV_8U, 1, 0);
 Scharr(srcGray, edges2, CV_8U, 1, 0, -1);
 edges += edges2;
 // Combine the x & y edges together.
 const int EVIL_EDGE_THRESHOLD = 12
 threshold(edges, mask, EVIL_EDGE_THRESHOLD, 255,
 THRESH_BINARY_INV);
 medianBlur(mask, mask, 3)
```

The following diagram shows the evil effect applied in the fourth image:

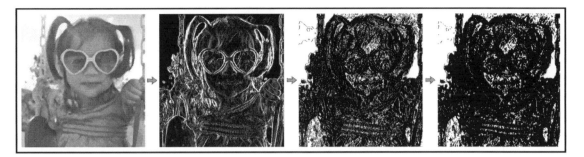

Now that we have an *evil* mask, we can overlay this mask onto the *cartoonified* painting image as we did with the regular *sketch* edge mask. The final result is shown on the right-hand side of the following diagram:

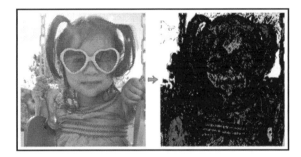

Generating an alien mode using skin detection

Now that we have a *sketch* mode, a *cartoon* mode (*painting + sketch* mask), and an *evil* mode (*painting + evil* mask), for fun, let's try something more complex: an *alien* mode, by detecting the skin regions of the face and then changing the skin color to green.

Skin detection algorithm

There are many different techniques used for detecting skin regions, from simple color thresholds using **RGB** (short for **Red-Green-Blue**) or **HSV** (short for **Hue-Saturation-Brightness**) values, or color histogram calculation and re-projection, to complex machine learning algorithms of mixture models that need camera calibration in the **CIELab** color space, offline training with many sample faces, and so on. But even the complex methods don't necessarily work robustly across various camera and lighting conditions and skin types. Since we want our skin detection to run on an embedded device, without any calibration or training, and we are just using skin detection for a fun image filter; it is sufficient for us to use a simple skin detection method. However, the color responses from the tiny camera sensor in the Raspberry Pi Camera Module tend to vary significantly, and we want to support skin detection for people of any skin color but without any calibration, so we need something more robust than simple color thresholds.

For example, a simple HSV skin detector can treat any pixel as skin if its hue color is fairly red, saturation is fairly high but not extremely high, and its brightness is not too dark or extremely bright. But cameras in mobile phones or Raspberry Pi Camera Modules often have bad white balancing; therefore, a person's skin might look slightly blue instead of red, for instance, and this would be a major problem for simple HSV thresholding.

A more robust solution is to perform face detection with a Haar or LBP cascade classifier (shown in `Chapter 17`, *Face Detection and Recognition with the DNN Module*), then look at the range of colors for the pixels in the middle of the detected face, since you know that those pixels should be skin pixels of the actual person. You could then scan the whole image or nearby region for pixels of a similar color as the center of the face. This has the advantage that it is very likely to find at least some of the true skin region of any detected person, no matter what their skin color is or even if their skin appears somewhat blueish or reddish in the camera image.

Unfortunately, face detection using cascade classifiers is quite slow on current embedded devices, so that method might be less ideal for some real-time embedded applications. On the other hand, we can take advantage of the fact that for mobile apps and some embedded systems, it can be expected that the user will be facing the camera directly from a very close distance, so it can be reasonable to ask the user to place their face at a specific location and distance, rather than try to detect the location and size of their face. This is the basis of many mobile phone apps, where the app asks the user to place their face at a certain position or perhaps to manually drag points on the screen to show where the corners of their face are in a photo. So, let's simply draw the outline of a face in the center of the screen, and ask the user to move their face to the position and size shown.

Showing the user where to put their face

When the *alien* mode is first started, we will draw the face outline on top of the camera frame so the user knows where to put their face. We will draw a big ellipse covering 70% of the image height, with a fixed aspect ratio of 0.72, so that the face will not become too skinny or fat depending on the aspect ratio of the camera:

```
// Draw the color face onto a black background.
Mat faceOutline = Mat::zeros(size, CV_8UC3);
Scalar color = CV_RGB(255,255,0); // Yellow.
auto thickness = 4;

// Use 70% of the screen height as the face height.
auto sw = size.width;
auto sh = size.height;
int faceH = sh/2 * 70/100; // "faceH" is radius of the ellipse.

// Scale the width to be the same nice shape for any screen width.
int faceW = faceH * 72/100;
// Draw the face outline.
ellipse(faceOutline, Point(sw/2, sh/2), Size(faceW, faceH),
0, 0, 360, color, thickness, CV_AA);
```

To make it more obvious that it is a face, let's also draw two eye outlines. Rather than drawing an eye as an ellipse, we can give it a bit more realism (refer to the following image) by drawing a truncated ellipse for the top of the eye and a truncated ellipse for the bottom of the eye, because we can specify the start and end angles when drawing with the ellipse() function:

```
// Draw the eye outlines, as 2 arcs per eye.
int eyeW = faceW * 23/100;
int eyeH = faceH * 11/100;
int eyeX = faceW * 48/100;
int eyeY = faceH * 13/100;
Size eyeSize = Size(eyeW, eyeH);

// Set the angle and shift for the eye half ellipses.
auto eyeA = 15; // angle in degrees.
auto eyeYshift = 11;

// Draw the top of the right eye.
ellipse(faceOutline, Point(sw/2 - eyeX, sh/2 -eyeY),
eyeSize, 0, 180+eyeA, 360-eyeA, color, thickness, CV_AA);

// Draw the bottom of the right eye.
ellipse(faceOutline, Point(sw/2 - eyeX, sh/2 - eyeY-eyeYshift),
eyeSize, 0, 0+eyeA, 180-eyeA, color, thickness, CV_AA);
```

```
// Draw the top of the left eye.
ellipse(faceOutline, Point(sw/2 + eyeX, sh/2 - eyeY),
eyeSize, 0, 180+eyeA, 360-eyeA, color, thickness, CV_AA);

// Draw the bottom of the left eye.
ellipse(faceOutline, Point(sw/2 + eyeX, sh/2 - eyeY-eyeYshift),
eyeSize, 0, 0+eyeA, 180-eyeA, color, thickness, CV_AA);
```

We can do the same to draw the bottom lip of the mouth:

```
// Draw the bottom lip of the mouth.
int mouthY = faceH * 48/100;
int mouthW = faceW * 45/100;
int mouthH = faceH * 6/100;
ellipse(faceOutline, Point(sw/2, sh/2 + mouthY), Size(mouthW,
mouthH), 0, 0, 180, color, thickness, CV_AA);
```

To make it even more obvious that the user should put their face where shown, let's write a message on the screen!

```
// Draw anti-aliased text.
int fontFace = FONT_HERSHEY_COMPLEX;
float fontScale = 1.0f;
int fontThickness = 2;
char *szMsg = "Put your face here";
putText(faceOutline, szMsg, Point(sw * 23/100, sh * 10/100),
fontFace, fontScale, color, fontThickness, CV_AA);
```

Now that we have the face outline drawn, we can overlay it onto the displayed image by using alpha blending to combine the cartoonified image with this drawn outline:

```
addWeighted(dst, 1.0, faceOutline, 0.7, 0, dst, CV_8UC3);
```

This results in the outline in the following image, showing the user where to put their face, so we don't have to detect the face location:

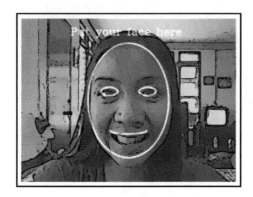

Implementation of the skin color changer

Rather than detecting the skin color and then the region with that skin color, we can use OpenCV's `floodFill()` function, which is similar to the bucket fill tool in most image editing software. We know that the regions in the middle of the screen should be skin pixels (since we asked the user to put their face in the middle), so to change the whole face to have green skin, we can just apply a green flood fill on the center pixel, which will always color some parts of the face green. In reality, the color, saturation, and brightness are likely to be different in different parts of the face, so a flood fill will rarely cover all the skin pixels of a face unless the threshold is so low that it also covers unwanted pixels outside of the face. So instead of applying a single flood fill in the center of the image, let's apply a flood fill on six different points around the face that should be skin pixels.

A nice feature of OpenCV's `floodFill()` is that it can draw the flood fill in an external image rather than modify the input image. So, this feature can give us a mask image for adjusting the color of the skin pixels without necessarily changing the brightness or saturation, producing a more realistic image than if all the skin pixels became an identical green pixel (losing significant face detail).

Skin color changing does not work so well in the RGB color space, because you want to allow brightness to vary in the face but not allow skin color to vary much, and RGB does not separate brightness from the color. One solution is to use the HSV color space since it separates the brightness from the color (hue) as well as the colorfulness (Saturation). Unfortunately, HSV wraps the hue value around red, and since the skin is mostly red, it means that you need to work both with *hue < 10%* and *hue > 90%* since these are both red. So, instead we will use the **Y'CrCb** color space (the variant of YUV that is in OpenCV), since it separates brightness from color and only has a single range of values for typical skin color rather than two. Note that most cameras, images, and videos actually use some type of YUV as their color space before conversion to RGB, so in many cases you can get a YUV image free without converting it yourself.

Since we want our alien mode to look like a cartoon, we will apply the alien filter after the image has already been cartoonified. In other words, we have access to the shrunken color image produced by the bilateral filter, and access to the full-sized edge mask. Skin detection often works better at low resolutions, since it is the equivalent of analyzing the average value of each high-resolution pixel's neighbors (or the low-frequency signal instead of the high-frequency noisy signal). So, let's work at the same shrunken scale as the bilateral filter (half-width and half-height). Let's convert the painting image to YUV:

```
Mat yuv = Mat(smallSize, CV_8UC3);
  cvtColor(smallImg, yuv, CV_BGR2YCrCb);
```

We also need to shrink the edge mask so it is on the same scale as the painting image. There is a complication with OpenCV's `floodFill()` function, when storing to a separate mask image, in that the mask should have a one-pixel border around the whole image, so if the input image is *W x H* pixels in size, then the separate mask image should be *(W+2) x (H+2)* pixels in size. But the `floodFill()` function also allows us to initialize the mask with edges that the flood fill algorithm will ensure it does not cross. Let's use this feature, in the hope that it helps prevent the flood fill from extending outside of the face. So, we need to provide two mask images: one is the edge mask of *W x H* in size, and the other image is the exact same edge mask but *(W+2) x (H+2)* in size because it should include a border around the image. It is possible to have multiple `cv::Mat` objects (or headers) referencing the same data, or even to have a `cv::Mat` object that references a sub-region of another `cv::Mat` image. So, instead of allocating two separate images and copying the edge mask pixels across, let's allocate a single mask image including the border, and create an extra `cv::Mat` header of *W x H* (which just references the region of interest in the flood fill mask without the border). In other words, there is just one array of pixels of size *(W+2) x (H+2)* but two `cv::Mat` objects, where one is referencing the whole *(W+2) x (H+2)* image and the other is referencing the *W x H* region in the middle of that image:

```
auto sw = smallSize.width;
auto sh = smallSize.height;
Mat mask, maskPlusBorder;
maskPlusBorder = Mat::zeros(sh+2, sw+2, CV_8UC1);
mask = maskPlusBorder(Rect(1,1,sw,sh));
// mask is now in maskPlusBorder.
resize(edges, mask, smallSize); // Put edges in both of them.
```

The edge mask (shown on the left of the following diagram) is full of both strong and weak edges, but we only want strong edges, so we will apply a binary threshold (resulting in the middle image in the following diagram). To join some gaps between edges, we will then combine the morphological operators `dilate()` and `erode()` to remove some gaps (also referred to as the close operator), resulting in the image on the right:

```
const int EDGES_THRESHOLD = 80;
 threshold(mask, mask, EDGES_THRESHOLD, 255, THRESH_BINARY);
 dilate(mask, mask, Mat());
 erode(mask, mask, Mat());
```

We can see the result of applying thresholding and morphological operation in the following image, first image is the input edge map, second the thresholding filter, and last image is the dilate and erode morphological filters:

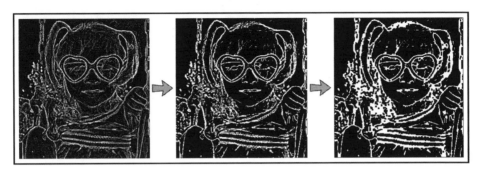

As mentioned earlier, we want to apply flood fills in numerous points around the face, to make sure we include the various colors and shades of the whole face. Let's choose six points around the nose, cheeks, and forehead, as shown on the left-hand side of the following screenshot. Note that these values are dependent on the face outline being drawn earlier:

```
auto const NUM_SKIN_POINTS = 6;
Point skinPts[NUM_SKIN_POINTS];
skinPts[0] = Point(sw/2, sh/2 - sh/6);
skinPts[1] = Point(sw/2 - sw/11, sh/2 - sh/6);
skinPts[2] = Point(sw/2 + sw/11, sh/2 - sh/6);
skinPts[3] = Point(sw/2, sh/2 + sh/16);
skinPts[4] = Point(sw/2 - sw/9, sh/2 + sh/16);
skinPts[5] = Point(sw/2 + sw/9, sh/2 + sh/16);
```

Now, we just need to find some good lower and upper bounds for the flood fill. Remember that this is being performed in the Y'CrCb color space, so we basically decide how much the brightness can vary, how much the red component can vary, and how much the blue component can vary. We want to allow the brightness to vary a lot, to include shadows as well as highlights and reflections, but we don't want the colors to vary much at all:

```
const int LOWER_Y = 60;
 const int UPPER_Y = 80;
 const int LOWER_Cr = 25;
 const int UPPER_Cr = 15;
 const int LOWER_Cb = 20;
 const int UPPER_Cb = 15;
 Scalar lowerDiff = Scalar(LOWER_Y, LOWER_Cr, LOWER_Cb);
 Scalar upperDiff = Scalar(UPPER_Y, UPPER_Cr, UPPER_Cb);
```

We will use the `floodFill()` function with its default flags, except that we want to store to an external mask, so we must specify `FLOODFILL_MASK_ONLY`:

```
const int CONNECTED_COMPONENTS = 4; // To fill diagonally, use 8.
const int flags = CONNECTED_COMPONENTS | FLOODFILL_FIXED_RANGE
| FLOODFILL_MASK_ONLY;
Mat edgeMask = mask.clone(); // Keep a copy of the edge mask.
// "maskPlusBorder" is initialized with edges to block floodFill().
for (int i = 0; i < NUM_SKIN_POINTS; i++) {
  floodFill(yuv, maskPlusBorder, skinPts[i], Scalar(), NULL,
  lowerDiff, upperDiff, flags);
}
```

The following image on the left-hand side shows the six flood fill locations (shown as circles), and the right-hand side of the image shows the external mask that is generated, where the skin is shown as gray and edges are shown as white. Note that the right-hand image was modified for this book so that skin pixels (of value 1) are clearly visible:

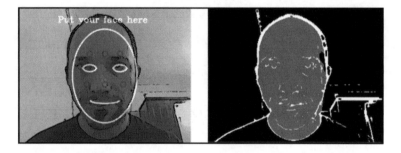

The `mask` image (shown on the right-hand side of the preceding image) now contains the following:

- Pixels of value 255 for the edge pixels
- Pixels of value 1 for the skin regions
- Pixels of value 0 for the rest

Meanwhile, `edgeMask` just contains edge pixels (as value 255). So to get just the skin pixels, we can remove the edges from it:

```
mask -= edgeMask;
```

The `mask` variable now just contains 1s for skin pixels and 0s for non-skin pixels. To change the skin color and brightness of the original image, we can use the `cv::add()` function with the skin mask to increase the green component in the original BGR image:

```
auto Red = 0;
```

```
auto Green = 70;
auto Blue = 0;
add(smallImgBGR, CV_RGB(Red, Green, Blue), smallImgBGR, mask);
```

The following diagram shows the original image on the left and the final alien cartoon image on the right, where at least six parts of the face will now be green!

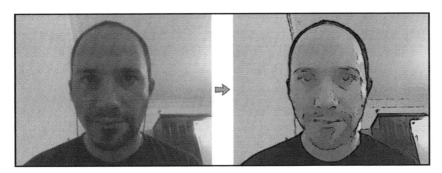

Notice that we have made the skin look green but also brighter (to look like an alien that glows in the dark). If you want to just change the skin color without making it brighter, you can use other color changing methods, such as adding 70 to green while subtracting 70 from red and blue, or convert to the HSV color space using cvtColor(src, dst, "CV_BGR2HSV_FULL") and adjust the hue and saturation.

Reducing the random pepper noise from the sketch image

Most of the tiny cameras in smartphones, Raspberry Pi Camera Modules, and some webcams have significant image noise. This is normally acceptable, but it has a big effect on our 5 x 5 Laplacian edge filter. The edge mask (shown as the sketch mode) will often have thousands of small blobs of black pixels called **pepper noise**, made of several black pixels next to each other on a white background. We are already using a median filter, which is usually strong enough to remove pepper noise, but in our case it may not be strong enough. Our edge mask is mostly a pure white background (value of 255) with some black edges (value of 0) and the dots of noise (also value of 0). We could use a standard closing morphological operator, but it will remove a lot of edges. So instead, we will apply a custom filter that removes small black regions that are surrounded completely by white pixels. This will remove a lot of noise while having little effect on actual edges.

We will scan the image for black pixels, and at each black pixel, we'll check the border of the 5 x 5 square around it to see if all the 5 x 5 border pixels are white. If they are all white, then we know we have a small island of black noise, so then we fill the whole block with white pixels to remove the black island. For simplicity in our 5 x 5 filter, we will ignore the two border pixels around the image and leave them as they are.

The following diagram shows the original image from an Android tablet on the left side, with a sketch mode in the center, showing small black dots of pepper noise and the result of our pepper noise removal shown on the right-hand side, where the skin looks cleaner:

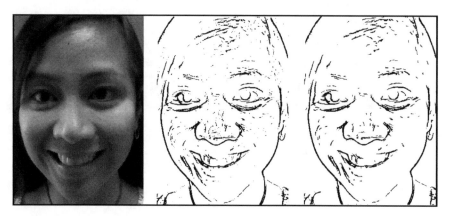

The following code can be named the `removePepperNoise()` function to edit the image in place for simplicity:

```
void removePepperNoise(Mat &mask)
{
    for (int y=2; y<mask.rows-2; y++) {
    // Get access to each of the 5 rows near this pixel.
    uchar *pUp2 = mask.ptr(y-2);
    uchar *pUp1 = mask.ptr(y-1);
    uchar *pThis = mask.ptr(y);
    uchar *pDown1 = mask.ptr(y+1);
    uchar *pDown2 = mask.ptr(y+2);

    // Skip the first (and last) 2 pixels on each row.
    pThis += 2;
    pUp1 += 2;
    pUp2 += 2;
    pDown1 += 2;
    pDown2 += 2;
    for (auto x=2; x<mask.cols-2; x++) {
        uchar value = *pThis; // Get pixel value (0 or 255).
        // Check if it's a black pixel surrounded bywhite
```

```
        // pixels (ie: whether it is an "island" of black).
        if (value == 0) {
            bool above, left, below, right, surroundings;
            above = *(pUp2 - 2) && *(pUp2 - 1) && *(pUp2) && *(pUp2 + 1)
                && *(pUp2 + 2);
            left = *(pUp1 - 2) && *(pThis - 2) && *(pDown1 - 2);
            below = *(pDown2 - 2) && *(pDown2 - 1) && (pDown2) &&
                (pDown2 + 1) && *(pDown2 + 2);
            right = *(pUp1 + 2) && *(pThis + 2) && *(pDown1 + 2);
            surroundings = above && left && below && right;
            if (surroundings == true) {
                // Fill the whole 5x5 block as white. Since we
                // knowthe 5x5 borders are already white, we just
                // need tofill the 3x3 inner region.
                *(pUp1 - 1) = 255;
                *(pUp1 + 0) = 255;
                *(pUp1 + 1) = 255;
                *(pThis - 1) = 255;
                *(pThis + 0) = 255;
                *(pThis + 1) = 255;
                *(pDown1 - 1) = 255;
                *(pDown1 + 0) = 255;
                *(pDown1 + 1) = 255;
                // Since we just covered the whole 5x5 block with
                // white, we know the next 2 pixels won't be
                // black,so skip the next 2 pixels on the right.
                pThis += 2;
                pUp1 += 2;
                pUp2 += 2;
                pDown1 += 2;
                pDown2 += 2;
            }
        }
        // Move to the next pixel on the right.
        pThis++;
        pUp1++;
        pUp2++;
        pDown1++;
        pDown2++;
        }
    }
}
```

That's all! Run the app in the different modes until you are ready to port it to the embedded device!

Porting from desktop to an embedded device

Now that the program works on the desktop, we can make an embedded system from it. The details given here are specific to Raspberry Pi, but similar steps apply when developing for other embedded Linux systems such as BeagleBone, ODROID, Olimex, Jetson, and so on.

There are several different options for running our code on an embedded system, each with some advantages and disadvantages in different scenarios.

There are two common methods for compiling the code for an embedded device:

- Copy the source code from the desktop onto the device and compile it directly on board the device. This is often referred to as **native compilation** since we are compiling our code natively on the same system that it will eventually run on.
- Compile all the code on the desktop but using special methods to generate code for the device, and then you copy the final executable program onto the device. This is often referred to as **cross-compilation** since you need a special compiler that knows how to generate code for other types of CPUs.

Cross-compilation is often significantly harder to configure than native compilation, especially if you are using many shared libraries, but since your desktop is usually a lot faster than your embedded device, cross-compilation is often much faster at compiling large projects. If you expect to be compiling your project hundreds of times, in order to work on it for months, and your device is quite slow compared to your desktops, such as the Raspberry Pi 1 or Raspberry Pi Zero, which are very slow compared to a desktop, then cross-compilation is a good idea. But in most cases, especially for small, simple projects, you should just stick with native compilation since it is easier.

Note that all the libraries used by your project will also need to be compiled for the device, so you will need to compile OpenCV for your device. Natively compiling OpenCV on a Raspberry Pi 1 can take hours, whereas cross-compiling OpenCV on a desktop might take just 15 minutes. But you usually only need to compile OpenCV once and then you'll have it for all your projects, so it is still worth sticking with native compilation of your project (including the native compilation of OpenCV) in most cases.

There are also several options for how to run the code on an embedded system:

- Use the same input and output methods you used on the desktop, such as the same video files, USB webcam, or keyboard as input, and display text or graphics on an HDMI monitor in the same way you were doing on the desktop.
- Use special devices for input and output. For example, instead of sitting at a desk using a USB webcam and keyboard as input and displaying the output on a desktop monitor, you could use the special Raspberry Pi Camera Module for video input, use custom GPIO push buttons or sensors for input, and use a 7-inch MIPI DSI screen or GPIO LED lights as the output, and then by powering it all with a common **portable USB charger**, you can be wearing the whole computer platform in your backpack or attaching it on your bicycle!
- Another option is to stream data in or out of the embedded device to other computers, or even use one device to stream out the camera data and one device to use that data. For example, you can use the GStreamer framework to configure the Raspberry Pi to stream H.264 compressed video from its camera module to the Ethernet network or through Wi-Fi, so that a powerful PC or server rack on the local network or the Amazon AWS cloud computing services can process the video stream somewhere else. This method allows a small and cheap camera device to be used in a complex project requiring large processing resources located somewhere else.

If you do wish to perform computer vision on board the device, be aware that some low-cost embedded devices such as Raspberry Pi 1, Raspberry Pi Zero, and BeagleBone Black have significantly less computing power than desktops or even cheap netbooks or smartphones, perhaps 10-50 times slower than your desktop, so depending on your application you might need a powerful embedded device or stream video to a separate computer, as mentioned previously. If you don't need much computing power (for example, you only need to process one frame every 2 seconds, or you only need to use 160 x 120 image resolution), then a Raspberry Pi Zero running some computer vision on board might be fast enough for your requirements. But many computer vision systems need far more computing power, and so if you want to perform computer vision on board the device, you will often want to use a much faster device with a CPU in the range of 2 GHz, such as a Raspberry Pi 3, ODROID-XU4, or Jetson TK1.

Equipment setup to develop code for an embedded device

Let's begin by keeping it as simple as possible, by using a USB keyboard and mouse and an HDMI monitor just like our desktop system, compiling the code natively on the device, and running our code on the device. Our first step will be to copy the code onto the device, install the build tools, and compile OpenCV and our source code on the embedded system.

Many embedded devices such as Raspberry Pi have an HDMI port and at least one USB port. Therefore, the easiest way to start using an embedded device is to plug in an HDMI monitor and USB keyboard and mouse for the device, to configure settings and see the output, while doing the code development and testing using your desktop machine. If you have a spare HDMI monitor, plug that into the device, but if you don't have a spare HDMI monitor, you might consider buying a small HDMI screen just for your embedded device.

Also, if you don't have a spare USB keyboard and mouse, you might consider buying a wireless keyboard and mouse that has a single USB wireless dongle, so you only use up a single USB port for both the keyboard and mouse. Many embedded devices use a 5V power supply, but they usually need more power (electrical current) than a desktop or laptop will provide in its USB port. So, you should obtain either a separate 5V USB charger (at least 1.5 amps, ideally 2.5 amps) or a portable USB battery charger that can provide at least 1.5 amps of output current. Your device might only use 0.5 amps most of the time, but there will be occasional times when it needs over 1 amp, so it's important to use a power supply that is rated for at least 1.5 amps or more, otherwise your device will occasionally reboot, or some hardware could behave strangely at important times, or the filesystem could become corrupt and you lose your files! A 1 amp supply might be good enough if you don't use cameras or accessories, but 2.0-2.5 amps is safer.

For example, the following photographs show a convenient setup containing a Raspberry Pi 3, a good quality 8 GB micro-SD card for $10 (http://ebay.to/2ayp6Bo), a 5-inch HDMI resistive touchscreen for $30-$45 (http://bit.ly/2aHQO2G), a wireless USB keyboard and mouse for $30 (http://ebay.to/2aN2oXi), a **5V 2.5 A** power supply for $5 (https://amzn.to/2UafanD), a USB webcam such as the very fast **PS3 Eye** for just $5 (http://ebay.to/2aVWCUS), a Raspberry Pi Camera Module v1 or v2 for $15-$30 (http://bit.ly/2aF9PxD), and an Ethernet cable for $2 (http://ebay.to/2aznnjd), connecting the Raspberry Pi to the same LAN network as your development PC or laptop. Notice that this HDMI screen is designed specifically for the Raspberry Pi, since the screen plugs directly into the Raspberry Pi below it, and has an HDMI male-to-male adapter (shown in the right-hand photo) for the Raspberry Pi so you don't need an HDMI cable, whereas other screens may require an HDMI cable (https://amzn.to/2Rvet6H), or MIPI DSI or SPI cable.

Also note that some screens and touch panels need configuration before they will work, whereas most HDMI screens should work without any configuration:

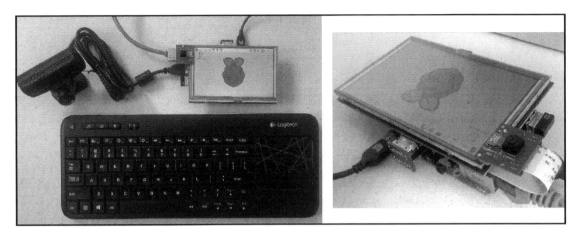

Notice the black USB webcam (on the far left of the LCD), the Raspberry Pi Camera Module (green and black board sitting on the top-left corner of the LCD), Raspberry Pi board (underneath the LCD), HDMI adapter (connecting the LCD to the Raspberry Pi underneath it), a blue Ethernet cable (plugged into a router), a small USB wireless keyboard and mouse dongle, and a micro-USB power cable (plugged into a **5V 2.5A** power supply).

Configuring a new Raspberry Pi

The following steps are specific to Raspberry Pi, so if you are using a different embedded device or you want a different type of setup, search the web about how to set up your board. To set up an Raspberry Pi 1, 2, or 3 (including their variants such as Raspberry Pi Zero, Raspberry Pi 2B, 3B, and so on, and Raspberry Pi 1A+ if you plug in a USB Ethernet dongle), follow these steps:

1. Get a fairly new, good quality micro-SD card of at least 8 GB. If you use a cheap micro-SD card or an old micro-SD card that you already used many times before and it has degraded in quality, it might not be reliable enough to boot the Raspberry Pi, so if you have trouble booting the Raspberry Pi, you should try a good quality Class 10 micro-SD card (such as SanDisk Ultra or better) that says it handles at least 45 Mbps or can handle 4K video.

2. Download and burn the latest **Raspbian IMG** (not NOOBS) to the micro-SD card. Note that burning an IMG is different to simply copying the file to SD. Visit `https://www.raspberrypi.org/documentation/installation/installing-images/` and follow the instructions for your desktop's OS to burn Raspbian to a micro-SD card. Be aware that you will lose any files that were previously on the card.

3. Plug a USB keyboard, mouse, and HDMI display into the Raspberry Pi, so you can easily run some commands and see the output.

4. Plug the Raspberry Pi into a 5V USB power supply with at least 1.5 A, ideally 2.5 A or higher. Computer USB ports aren't powerful enough.

5. You should see many pages of text scrolling while it is booting up Raspbian Linux, then it should be ready after 1 or 2 minutes.

6. If, after booting, it's just showing a black console screen with some text (such as if you downloaded **Raspbian Lite**), you are at the text-only login prompt. Log in by typing `pi` as the username and then hit *Enter*. Then, type `raspberry` as the password and hit *Enter* again.

7. Or if it booted to the graphical display, click on the black **Terminal** icon at the top to open a shell (Command Prompt).

8. Initialize some settings in your Raspberry Pi:

   - Type `sudo raspi-config` and hit *Enter* (see the following screenshot).
   - First, run **Expand Filesystem** and then finish and reboot your device, so the Raspberry Pi can use the whole micro-SD card.
   - If you use a normal (US) keyboard, not a British keyboard, in **Internationalization Options**, change to **Generic 104-key keyboard, Other, English (US)**, and then for the **AltGr** and similar questions, just hit *Enter* unless you are using a special keyboard.
   - In **Enable Camera**, enable the Raspberry Pi Camera Module.
   - In **Overclock Options**, set to Raspberry Pi 2 or similar to the device runs faster (but generates more heat).
   - In **Advanced Options**, enable the SSH server.
   - In **Advanced Options**, if you are using Raspberry Pi 2 or 3, change **Memory Split** to 256 MB so the GPU has plenty of RAM for video processing. For Raspberry Pi 1 or Zero, use 64 MB or the default.
   - Finish, then reboot the device.

9. (Optional): Delete Wolfram to save 600 MB of space on your SD card:

    ```
    sudo apt-get purge -y wolfram-engine
    ```

    It can be reinstalled using `sudo apt-get install wolfram-engine`.

    To see the remaining space on your SD card, run `df -h | head -2`:

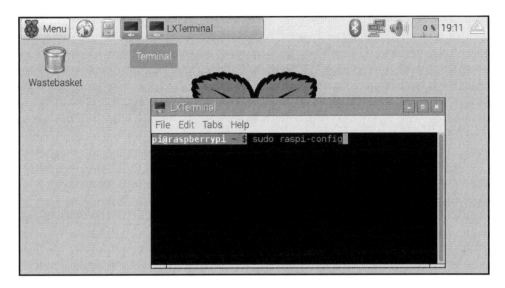

10. Assuming you plugged the Raspberry Pi into your internet router, it should already have internet access. So, update your Raspberry Pi to the latest Raspberry Pi firmware, software locations, OS, and software. **Warning**: many Raspberry Pi tutorials say you should run `sudo rpi-update`; however, in recent years, it's no longer a good idea to run `rpi-update` since it can give you an unstable system or firmware. The following instructions will update your Raspberry Pi to have stable software and firmware (note that these commands might take up to one hour):

    ```
    sudo apt-get -y update
    sudo apt-get -y upgrade
    sudo apt-get -y dist-upgrade
    sudo reboot
    ```

11. Find the IP address of the device:

    ```
    hostname -I
    ```

12. Try accessing the device from your desktop. For example, assume the device's IP address is `192.168.2.101`. Enter this on a Linux desktop:

```
ssh-X pi@192.168.2.101
```

Or, do this on a Windows desktop:
   1. Download, install, and run PuTTY
   2. Then in PuTTY, connect to the IP address (192.168.2.101), as the user `pi` with the password `raspberry`

13. Optionally, if you want your Command Prompt to be a different color than the commands and show the error value after each command, use this:

```
nano ~/.bashrc
```

14. Add this line to the bottom:

```
PS1="[e[0;44m]u@h: w ($?) $[e[0m] "
```

15. Save the file (hit *Ctrl + X*, then hit *Y*, and then hit *Enter*).
16. Start using the new settings:

```
source ~/.bashrc
```

17. To prevent the screensaver/screen blank power saving feature in Raspbian from turning off your screen on idle, use this:

```
sudo nano /etc/lightdm/lightdm.conf
```

18. And follow these steps:
   1. Look for the line that says `#xserver-command=X` (jump to line `87` by pressing *Alt + G* and then typing `87` and hitting *Enter*).
   2. Change it to `xserver-command=X -s 0 dpms`.
   3. Save the file (hit *Ctrl + X*, then hit *Y*, then hit *Enter*).

19. Finally, reboot the Raspberry Pi:

```
sudo reboot
```

You should be ready to start developing on the device now!

Installing OpenCV on an embedded device

There is a very easy way to install OpenCV and all its dependencies on a Debian-based embedded device such as Raspberry Pi:

```
sudo apt-get install libopencv-dev
```

However, that might install an old version of OpenCV from one or two years ago.

To install the latest version of OpenCV on an embedded device such as Raspberry Pi, we need to build OpenCV from the source code. First, we install a compiler and build system, then libraries for OpenCV to use, and finally OpenCV itself. Note that the steps for compiling OpenCV from source on Linux are the same whether you are compiling for desktop or for embedded systems. A Linux script, install_opencv_from_source.sh, is provided with this book; it is recommended you copy the file onto your Raspberry Pi (for example, with a USB flash stick) and run the script to download, build, and install OpenCV, including potential multi-core CPU and **ARM NEON SIMD** optimizations (depending on hardware support):

```
chmod +x install_opencv_from_source.sh
 ./install_opencv_from_source.sh
```

The script will stop if there is an error, for example, if you don't have internet access or a dependency package conflicts with something else you already installed. If the script stops with an error, try using info on the web to solve that error, then run the script again. The script will quickly check all the previous steps and then continue from where it finished last time. Note that it will take between 20 minutes and 12 hours depending on your hardware and software!

It's highly recommended to build and run a few OpenCV samples every time you install OpenCV, so when you have problems building your own code, at least you will know whether the problem is the OpenCV installation or a problem with your code.

Let's try to build the simple edge sample program. If we try the same Linux command to build it from OpenCV 2, we get a build error:

```
cd ~/opencv-4.*/samples/cpp
 g++ edge.cpp -lopencv_core -lopencv_imgproc -lopencv_highgui
 -o edge
 /usr/bin/ld: /tmp/ccDqLWSz.o: undefined reference to symbol
'_ZN2cv6imreadERKNS_6StringEi'
 /usr/local/lib/libopencv_imgcodecs.so.4..: error adding symbols: DSO
missing from command line
 collect2: error: ld returned 1 exit status
```

The second to last line of that error message tells us that a library was missing from the command line, so we simply need to add `-lopencv_imgcodecs` in our command next to the other OpenCV libraries we linked to. Now, you know how to fix the problem anytime you are compiling an OpenCV 3 program and you see that error message. So, let's do it correctly:

```
cd ~/opencv-4.*/samples/cpp
 g++ edge.cpp -lopencv_core -lopencv_imgproc -lopencv_highgui
 -lopencv_imgcodecs -o edge
```

It worked! So, now you can run the program:

```
./edge
```

Hit *Ctrl + C* on your keyboard to quit the program. Note that the edge program might crash if you try running the command in an SSH Terminal and you don't redirect the window to display on the device's LCD screen. So, if you are using SSH to remotely run the program, add `DISPLAY=:0` before your command:

```
DISPLAY=:0 ./edge
```

You should also plug a USB webcam into the device and test that it works:

```
g++ starter_video.cpp -lopencv_core -lopencv_imgproc
 -lopencv_highgui -lopencv_imgcodecs -lopencv_videoio \
 -o starter_video
 DISPLAY=:0 ./starter_video 0
```

Note: if you don't have a USB webcam, you can test using a video file:

```
DISPLAY=:0 ./starter_video ../data/768x576.avi
```

Now that OpenCV is successfully installed on your device, you can run the Cartoonifier applications we developed earlier. Copy the Cartoonifier folder onto the device (for example, by using a USB flash stick, or using scp to copy files over the network). Then, build the code just like you did for the desktop:

```
cd ~/Cartoonifier
 export OpenCV_DIR="~/opencv-3.1.0/build"
 mkdir build
 cd build
 cmake -D OpenCV_DIR=$OpenCV_DIR ..
 make
```

And run it:

```
DISPLAY=:0 ./Cartoonifier
```

And if all is fine, we will see a window with our application running as follows:

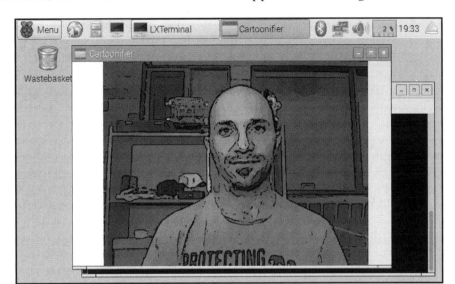

Using the Raspberry Pi Camera Module

While using a USB webcam on Raspberry Pi has the convenience of supporting identical behavior and code on the desktop as on an embedded device, you might consider using one of the official Raspberry Pi Camera Modules (referred to as the **Raspberry Pi Cams**). They have some advantages and disadvantages over USB webcams.

The Raspberry Pi Cams use the special MIPI CSI camera format, designed for smartphone cameras to use less power. They have a smaller physical size, faster bandwidth, higher resolutions, higher frame rates, and reduced latency compared to USB. Most USB 2.0 webcams can only deliver 640 x 480 or 1280 x 720 30 FPS video since USB 2.0 is too slow for anything higher (except for some expensive USB webcams that perform onboard video compression) and USB 3.0 is still too expensive. However, smartphone cameras (including the Raspberry Pi Cams) can often deliver 1920 x 1080 30 FPS or even Ultra HD/4K resolutions. The Raspberry Pi Cam v1 can, in fact, deliver upto 2592 x 1944 15 FPS or 1920 x 1080 30 FPS video even on a $5 Raspberry Pi Zero, thanks to the use of MIPI CSI for the camera and compatible video processing ISP and GPU hardware inside the Raspberry Pi. The Raspberry Pi Cams also support 640 x 480 in 90 FPS mode (such as for slow-motion capture), and this is quite useful for real-time computer vision so you can see very small movements in each frame, rather than large movements that are harder to analyze.

However, the Raspberry Pi Cam is a plain circuit board that is *highly sensitive* to electrical interference, static electricity, or physical damage (simply touching the small, flat orange cable with your finger can cause video interference or even permanently damage your camera!). The big flat white cable is far less sensitive but it is still very sensitive to electrical noise or physical damage. The Raspberry Pi Cam comes with a very short 15 cm cable. It's possible to buy third-party cables on eBay with lengths between 5 cm and 1 m, but cables 50 cm or longer are less reliable, whereas USB webcams can use 2 m to 5 m cables and can be plugged into USB hubs or active extension cables for longer distances.

There are currently several different Raspberry Pi Cam models, notably the NoIR version that doesn't have an internal infrared filter; therefore, a NoIR camera can easily see in the dark (if you have an invisible infrared light source), or see infrared lasers or signals far clearer than regular cameras that include an infrared filter inside them. There are also two different versions of Raspberry Pi Cam: Raspberry Pi Cam v1.3 and Raspberry Pi Cam v2.1, where v2.1 uses a wider angle lens with a Sony 8 megapixel sensor instead of a 5 megapixel **OmniVision** sensor, has better support for motion in low lighting conditions, and adds support for 3240 x 2464 video at 15 FPS and potentially up to 120 FPS video at 720p. However, USB webcams come in thousands of different shapes and versions, making it easy to find specialized webcams such as waterproof or industrial-grade webcams, rather than requiring you to create your own custom housing for a Raspberry Pi Cam.

IP cameras are also another option for a camera interface that can allow 1080p or higher resolution videos with Raspberry Pi, and IP cameras support not just very long cables, but potentially even work anywhere in the world using the internet. But IP cameras aren't quite as easy to interface with OpenCV as USB webcams or Raspberry Pi Cams.

In the past, Raspberry Pi Cams and the official drivers weren't directly compatible with OpenCV; you often used custom drivers and modified your code in order to grab frames from Raspberry Pi Cams, but it's now possible to access a Raspberry Pi Cam in OpenCV in the exact same way as a USB webcam! Thanks to recent improvements in the v4l2 drivers, once you load the v4l2 driver, the Raspberry Pi Cam will appear as a `/dev/video0` or `/dev/video1` file like a regular USB webcam. So, traditional OpenCV webcam code such as `cv::VideoCapture(0)` will be able to use it just like a webcam.

Installing the Raspberry Pi Camera Module driver

First, let's temporarily load the v4l2 driver for the Raspberry Pi Cam to make sure our camera is plugged in correctly:

```
sudo modprobe bcm2835-v4l2
```

If the command failed (if it printed an error message to the console, it froze, or the command returned a number besides 0), then perhaps your camera is not plugged in correctly. Shut down and then unplug power from your Raspberry Pi and try attaching the flat white cable again, looking at photos on the web to make sure it's plugged in the correct way around. If it is the correct way around, it's possible the cable wasn't fully inserted before you closed the locking tab on the Raspberry Pi. Also, check whether you forgot to click **Enable Camera** when configuring your Raspberry Pi earlier, using the `sudoraspi-config` command.

If the command worked (if the command returned 0 and no error was printed to the console), then we can make sure the v4l2 driver for the Raspberry Pi Cam is always loaded on bootup by adding it to the bottom of the `/etc/modules` file:

```
sudo nano /etc/modules
# Load the Raspberry Pi Camera Module v4l2 driver on bootup:
bcm2835-v4l2
```

After you save the file and reboot your Raspberry Pi, you should be able to run `ls /dev/video*` to see a list of cameras available on your Raspberry Pi. If the Raspberry Pi Cam is the only camera plugged into your board, you should see it as the default camera (`/dev/video0`), or if you also have a USB webcam plugged in, then it will be either `/dev/video0` or `/dev/video1`.

Let's test the Raspberry Pi Cam using the `starter_video` sample program we compiled earlier:

```
cd ~/opencv-4.*/samples/cpp
  DISPLAY=:0 ./starter_video 0
```

If it's showing the wrong camera, try `DISPLAY=:0 ./starter_video 1`.

Now that we know the Raspberry Pi Cam is working in OpenCV, let's try Cartoonifier:

```
cd ~/Cartoonifier
  DISPLAY=:0 ./Cartoonifier 0
```

Or, use `DISPLAY=:0 ./Cartoonifier 1` for the other camera.

Making Cartoonifier run in fullscreen

In embedded systems, you often want your application to be fullscreen and hide the Linux GUI and menu. OpenCV offers an easy method to set the fullscreen window property, but make sure you created the window using the NORMAL flag:

```
// Create a fullscreen GUI window for display on the screen.
namedWindow(windowName, WINDOW_NORMAL);
setWindowProperty(windowName, PROP_FULLSCREEN, CV_WINDOW_FULLSCREEN);
```

Hiding the mouse cursor

You might notice the mouse cursor is shown on top of your window even though you don't want to use a mouse in your embedded system. To hide the mouse cursor, you can use the xdotool command to move it to the bottom-right corner pixel, so it's not noticeable, but is still available if you want to occasionally plug in your mouse to debug the device. Install xdotool and create a short Linux script to run it with Cartoonifier:

```
sudo apt-get install -y xdotool
cd ~/Cartoonifier/build
```

After installing xdotool, now is the time to create the script, create a new file with your favorite editor with the name runCartoonifier.sh and the following content:

```
#!/bin/sh
# Move the mouse cursor to the screen's bottom-right pixel.
xdotoolmousemove 3000 3000
# Run Cartoonifier with any arguments given.
/home/pi/Cartoonifier/build/Cartoonifier "$@"
```

Finally, make your script executable:

```
chmod +x runCartoonifier.sh
```

Try running your script to make sure it works:

```
DISPLAY=:0 ./runCartoonifier.sh
```

Running Cartoonifier automatically after bootup

Often, when you build an embedded device, you want your application to be executed automatically after the device has booted up, rather than requiring the user to manually run your application. To automatically run our application after the device has fully booted up and logged in to the graphical desktop, create an `autostart` folder with a file in it with these contents, including the full path to your script or application:

```
mkdir ~/.config/autostart
 nano ~/.config/autostart/Cartoonifier.desktop
 [Desktop Entry]
 Type=Application
 Exec=/home/pi/Cartoonifier/build/runCartoonifier.sh
 X-GNOME-Autostart-enabled=true
```

Now, whenever you turn the device on or reboot it, Cartoonifier will begin running!

Speed comparison of Cartoonifier on desktop versus embedded

You will notice that the code runs much slower on Raspberry Pi than on your desktop! By far the two easiest ways to run it faster are to use a faster device or use a smaller camera resolution. The following table shows some frame rates, **frames per seconds (FPS)**, for both the *sketch* and *paint* modes of Cartoonifier on a desktop, Raspberry Pi 1, Raspberry Pi 2, Raspberry Pi 3, and Jetson TK1. Note that the speeds don't have any custom optimizations and only run on a single CPU core, and the timings include the time for rendering images to the screen. The USB webcam used is the fast PS3 Eye webcam running at 640 x 480 since it is the fastest low-cost webcam on the market.

It's worth mentioning that Cartoonifier is only using a single CPU core, but all the devices listed have four CPU cores except for Raspberry Pi 1, which has a single core, and many x86 computers have hyperthreading to give roughly eight CPU cores. So, if you wrote your code to efficiently make use of multiple CPU cores (or GPU), the speeds might be 1.5 to 3 times faster than the single-threaded figures shown:

Computer	Sketch mode	Paint mode
Intel Core i7 PC	20 FPS	2.7 FPS
Jetson TK1ARM CPU	16 FPS	2.3 FPS
Raspberry Pi 3	4.3 FPS	0.32 FPS (3 seconds/frame)
Raspberry Pi 2	3.2 FPS	0.28 FPS (4 seconds/frame)
Raspberry Pi Zero	2.5 FPS	0.21 FPS (5 seconds/frame)
Raspberry Pi 1	1.9 FPS	0.12 FPS (8 seconds/frame)

Notice that Raspberry Pi is extremely slow at running the code, especially the *paint* mode, so we will try simply changing the camera and the resolution of the camera.

Changing the camera and camera resolution

The following table shows how the speed of the *sketch* mode compares on Raspberry Pi 2 using different types of cameras and different camera resolutions:

Hardware	640 x 480 resolution	320 x 240 resolution
Raspberry Pi 2 with Raspberry Pi Cam	3.8 FPS	12.9 FPS
Raspberry Pi 2 with PS3 Eye webcam	3.2 FPS	11.7 FPS
Raspberry Pi 2 with unbranded webcam	1.8 FPS	7.4 FPS

As you can see, when using the Raspberry Pi Cam in 320 x 240, it seems we have a good enough solution to have some fun, even if it's not in the 20-30 FPS range that we would prefer.

Power draw of Cartoonifier running on desktop versus embedded system

We've seen that various embedded devices are slower than desktops, from the Raspberry Pi 1 being roughly 20 times slower than a desktop, up to Jetson TK1 being roughly 1.5 times slower than a desktop. But for some tasks, low speed is acceptable if it means there will also be significantly lower battery draw, allowing for small batteries or low year-round electricity costs for a server, or low heat generation.

Raspberry Pi has different models even for the same processor, such as Raspberry Pi 1B, Zero, and 1A+, which all run at similar speeds but have significantly different power draws. MIPI CSI cameras such as the Raspberry Pi Cam also use less electricity than webcams. The following table shows how much electrical power is used by different hardware running the same Cartoonifier code. Power measurements of Raspberry Pi were performed as shown in the following photo using a simple USB current monitor (for example, J7-T Safety Tester (http://bit.ly/2aSZa6H) for $5) and a DMM multimeter for the other devices:

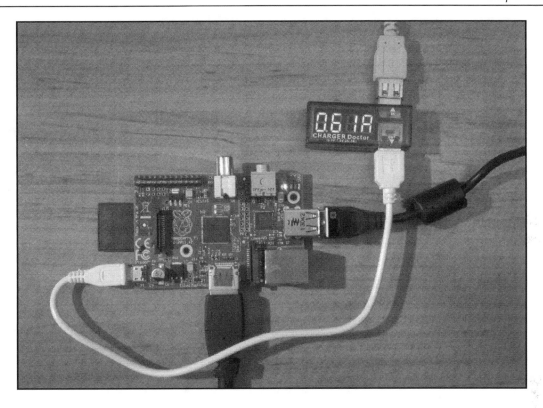

Idle power measures power when the computer is running but no major applications are being used, whereas **Cartoonifier power** measures power when Cartoonifier is running. **Efficiency** is Cartoonifier power/Cartoonifier speed in a 640 x 480 *sketch* mode:

Hardware	Idle power	Cartoonifier power	Efficiency
Raspberry Pi Zero with PS3 Eye	1.2 Watts	1.8 Watts	1.4 Frames per Watt
Raspberry Pi 1A+ with PS3 Eye	**1.1 Watts**	**1.5 Watts**	1.1 Frames per Watt
Raspberry Pi 1B with PS3 Eye	2.4 Watts	3.2 Watts	0.5 Frames per Watt
Raspberry Pi 2B with PS3 Eye	1.8 Watts	2.2 Watts	1.4 Frames per Watt
Raspberry Pi 3B with PS3 Eye	2.0 Watts	2.5 Watts	1.7 Frames per Watt
Jetson TK1 with PS3 Eye	2.8 Watts	4.3 Watts	**3.7 Frames per Watt**
Core i7 laptop with PS3 Eye	14.0 Watts	39.0 Watts	0.5 Frames per Watt

We can see that Raspberry Pi 1A+ uses the least power, but the most power efficient options are Jetson TK1 and Raspberry Pi 3B. Interestingly, the original Raspberry Pi (Raspberry Pi 1B) has roughly the same efficiency as an x86 laptop. All later Raspberry Pis are significantly more power efficient than the original (Raspberry Pi 1B).

Disclaimer: The author is a former employee of NVIDIA, which produced the Jetson TK1, but the results and conclusions are believed to be authentic.

Let's also look at the power draw of different cameras that work with Raspberry Pi:

Hardware	Idle power	Cartoonifier power	Efficiency
Raspberry Pi Zero with PS3 Eye	1.2 Watts	1.8 Watts	1.4 Frames per Watt
Raspberry Pi Zero with Raspberry Pi Cam v1.3	0.6 Watts	1.5 Watts	2.1 Frames per Watt
Raspberry Pi Zero with Raspberry Pi Cam v2.1	**0.55 Watts**	**1.3 Watts**	**2.4 Frames per Watt**

We see that Raspberry Pi Cam v2.1 is slightly more power efficient than Raspberry Pi Cam v1.3 and significantly more power efficient than a USB webcam.

Streaming video from Raspberry Pi to a powerful computer

Thanks to the hardware-accelerated video encoders in all modern ARM devices, including Raspberry Pi, a valid alternative to performing computer vision on board an embedded device is to use the device to just capture video and stream it across a network in real time to a PC or server rack. All Raspberry Pi models contain the same video encoder hardware, so an Raspberry Pi 1A+ or Raspberry Pi Zero with a Pi Cam is quite a good option for a low-cost, low-power portable video streaming server. Raspberry Pi 3 adds Wi-Fi for additional portable functionality.

There are numerous ways live camera video can be streamed from a Raspberry Pi, such as using the official Raspberry Pi V4L2 camera driver to allow the Raspberry Pi Cam to appear like a webcam, then using GStreamer, liveMedia, netcat, or VLC to stream the video across a network. However, these methods often introduce one or two seconds of latency and often require customizing the OpenCV client code or learning how to use GStreamer efficiently. So instead, the following section will show how to perform both the camera capture and network streaming using an alternative camera driver named **UV4L**:

1. Install UV4L on the Raspberry Pi by following the instructions at http://www.linux-projects.org/uv4l/installation/:

```
curl http://www.linux-projects.org/listing/uv4l_repo/lrkey.asc
sudo apt-key add -
sudo su
echo "# UV4L camera streaming repo:">> /etc/apt/sources.list
echo "deb http://www.linux-
projects.org/listing/uv4l_repo/raspbian/jessie main">>
/etc/apt/sources.list
exit
```

```
sudo apt-get update
sudo apt-get install uv4l uv4l-raspicam uv4l-server
```

2. Run the UV4L streaming server manually (on the Raspberry Pi) to check that it works:

```
sudo killall uv4l
sudo LD_PRELOAD=/usr/lib/uv4l/uv4lext/armv6l/libuv4lext.so
uv4l -v7 -f --sched-rr --mem-lock --auto-video_nr
--driverraspicam --encoding mjpeg
--width 640 --height 480 --framerate15
```

3. Test the camera's network stream from your desktop, following these steps to check all is working fine:
   - Install VLC Media Player.
   - Navigate to **Media | Open Network Stream** and enter `http://192.168.2.111:8080/stream/video.mjpeg`.
   - Adjust the URL to the IP address of your Raspberry Pi. Run `hostname -I` on Raspberry Pi to find its IP address.

4. Run the UV4L server automatically on bootup:

```
sudo apt-get install uv4l-raspicam-extras
```

5. Edit any UV4L server settings you want in `uv4l-raspicam.conf`, such as resolution and frame rate to customize the streaming:

```
sudo nano /etc/uv4l/uv4l-raspicam.conf
drop-bad-frames = yes
nopreview = yes
width = 640
height = 480
framerate = 24
```

You will need to reboot to make all changes take effect.

6. Tell OpenCV to use our network stream as if it was a webcam. As long as your installation of OpenCV can use FFMPEG internally, OpenCV will be able to grab frames from an MJPEG network stream just like a webcam:

```
./Cartoonifier http://192.168.2.101:8080/stream/video.mjpeg
```

Your Raspberry Pi is now using UV4L to stream the live 640 x 480 24 FPS video to a PC that is running Cartoonifier in *sketch* mode, achieving roughly 19 FPS (with 0.4 seconds of latency). Notice this is almost the same speed as using the PS3 Eye webcam directly on the PC (20 FPS)!

Note that when you are streaming the video to OpenCV, it won't be able to set the camera resolution; you need to adjust the UV4L server settings to change the camera resolution. Also note that instead of streaming MJPEG, we could have streamed H.264 video, which uses a lower bandwidth, but some computer vision algorithms don't handle video compression such as H.264 very well, so MJPEG will cause fewer algorithm problems than H.264.

 If you have both the official Raspberry Pi V4L2 driver and the UV4L driver installed, they will both be available as cameras 0 and 1 (devices /dev/video0 and /dev/video1), but you can only use one camera driver at a time.

Customizing your embedded system!

Now that you have created a whole embedded Cartoonifier system, and you know the basics of how it works and which parts do what, you should customize it! Make the video full screen, change the GUI, change the application behavior and workflow, change the Cartoonifier filter constants or the skin detector algorithm, replace the Cartoonifier code with your own project ideas, or stream the video to the cloud and process it there!

You can improve the skin detection algorithm in many ways, such as using a more complex skin detection algorithm (for example, using trained Gaussian models from many recent CVPR or ICCV conference papers at http://www.cvpapers.com), or add face detection (see the *Face detection* section of Chapter 17, *Face Detection and Recognition with the DNN Module*) to the skin detector, so it detects where the user's face is, rather than asking the user to put their face in the center of the screen. Be aware that face detection may take many seconds on some devices or high-resolution cameras, so they may be limited in their current real-time uses. But embedded system platforms are getting faster every year, so this may be less of a problem over time.

The most significant way to speed up embedded computer vision applications is to reduce the camera resolution absolutely as much as possible (for example, 0.5 megapixels instead of 5 megapixels), allocate and free images as rarely as possible, and perform image format conversions as rarely as possible. In some cases, there might be some optimized image processing or math libraries, or an optimized version of OpenCV from the CPU vendor of your device (for example, Broadcom, NVIDIA Tegra, Texas Instruments OMAP, or Samsung Exynos), or for your CPU family (for example, ARM Cortex-A9).

Summary

This chapter has shown several different types of image processing filters that can be used to generate various cartoon effects, from a plain sketch mode that looks like a pencil drawing, a paint mode that looks like a color painting, to a cartoon mode that overlays the *sketch* mode on top of the paint mode to appear like a cartoon. It also shows that other fun effects can be obtained, such as the evil mode, which greatly enhanced noisy edges and the alien mode, which changed the skin of a face to appear bright green.

There are many commercial smartphone apps that add similar fun effects on the user's face, such as cartoon filters and skin color changes. There are also professional tools using similar concepts, such as skin-smoothing video post-processing tools that attempt to beautify women's faces by smoothing their skin while keeping the edges and non-skin regions sharp, in order to make their faces appear younger.

This chapter shows how to port the application from a desktop to an embedded system by following the recommended guidelines of developing a working desktop version first, and then porting it to an embedded system and creating a user interface that is suitable for the embedded application. The image processing code is shared between the two projects so that the reader can modify the cartoon filters for the desktop application, and easily see those modifications in the embedded system as well.

Remember that this book includes an OpenCV installation script for Linux and full source code for all projects discussed.

In the next chapter, we are going to learn how to use **multiple view stereo** (**MVS**) and **structure from motion** (**SfM**) for 3D reconstruction, and how to export the final result in OpenMVG format.

14

Explore Structure from Motion with the SfM Module

Structure from motion (SfM) is the process of recovering both the positions of cameras looking at a scene, and the sparse geometry of the scene. The motion between the cameras imposes geometric constraints that can help us recover the *structure* of objects, hence why the process is called SfM. Since OpenCV v3.0+, a contributed (`"contrib"`) module called `sfm` was added, which assists in performing end-to-end SfM processing from multiple images. In this chapter, we will learn how to use the SfM module to reconstruct a scene to a sparse point cloud, including camera poses. Later, we will also *densify* the point cloud, adding many more points to it to make it dense by using an open **Multi-View Stereo (MVS)** package called OpenMVS. SfM is used for high-quality three-dimensional scanning, visual odometry for autonomous navigation, aerial photo mapping, and many more applications, making it one of the most fundamental pursuits within computer vision. Computer vision engineers are expected to be familiar with the core concepts of SfM, and the topic is regularly taught in computer vision courses.

The following topics will be covered in this chapter:

- Core concepts of SfM: **Multi-View Geometry (MVG)**, three-dimensional reconstruction, and **Multi-View Stereo (MVS)**
- Implementing a SfM pipeline using the OpenCV SfM modules
- Visualizing the reconstruction results
- Exporting the reconstruction to OpenMVG and densifying the sparse cloud into a full reconstruction

Technical requirements

These technologies and installations are required to build and run the code in this chapter:

- OpenCV 4 (compiled with the `sfm contrib` module)
- Eigen v3.3+ (required by the `sfm` module)
- Ceres solver v2+ (required by the `sfm` module)
- CMake 3.12+
- Boost v1.66+
- OpenMVS
- CGAL v4.12+ (required by OpenMVS)

The build instructions for the components listed, as well as the code to implement the concepts in this chapter, will be provided in the accompanying code repository. Using OpenMVS is optional, and we may stop after getting the sparse reconstruction. However, the full MVS reconstruction is much more impressive and useful; for instance, for 3D printing replicas.

Any set of photos with sufficient overlap may be sufficient for 3D reconstruction. For example, we may use a set of photos I took of the Crazy Horse memorial head in South Dakota that is bundled with this chapter code. The requirement is that the images should be taken with sufficient movement between them, but enough to have significant overlap to allow for a strong pair-wise match.

In the following example from the Crazy Horse memorial dataset, we can notice a slight change in view angle between the images, with a very strong overlap. Notice how we can also see a great variation below the statue where people are walking about; this will not interfere with the 3D reconstruction of the stone face:

The code files for chapter can be downloaded from `https://github.com/ PacktPublishing/Building-Computer-Vision-Projects-with-OpenCV4-and-CPlusPlus/ tree/master/Chapter14`.

Core concepts of SfM

Before we delve into the implementation of a SfM pipeline, let's revisit some key concepts that are an essential part of the process. The foremost class of theoretical topics in SfM is **epipolar geometry (EG)**, the geometry of multiple views or MVG, which builds upon knowledge of **image formation** and **camera calibration**; however, we will only brush over these basic subjects. After we cover a few basics in EG, we will shortly discuss **stereo reconstruction** and look over subjects such as **depth from disparity** and **triangulation**. Other crucial topics in SfM, such as **Robust Feature Matching**, are more mechanical than theoretical, and we will cover them as we advance in coding the system. We intentionally leave out some very interesting topics, such as **camera resectioning, PnP algorithms**, and **reconstruction factorization**, since these are handled by the underlying `sfm` module and we need not invoke them, although functions to perform them do exist in OpenCV.

All of these subjects were a source of an incredible amount of research and literature over the last four decades and serve as topics for thousands of academic papers, patents, and other publications. Hartley and Zisserman's *Multiple View Geometry* is by far the most prominent resource for SfM and MVG mathematics and algorithms, although an incredible secondary asset is Szeliski's *Computer Vision: Algorithms and Applications*, which explains SfM in great detail, focusing on Richard Szeliski's seminal contributions to the field. For a tertiary source of explanation, I recommend grabbing a copy of Prince's *Computer Vision: Models, Learning, and Inference*, which features beautiful figures, diagrams, and meticulous mathematical derivation.

Calibrated cameras and epipolar geometry

Our images begin with a projection. The 3D world they see through the lens is *flattened* down on the 2D sensor inside the camera, essentially losing all depth information. How can we then go back from 2D images to 3D structures? The answer, in many cases with standard intensity cameras, is MVG. Intuitively, if we can see (in 2D) an object from at least two views, we can estimate its distance from the cameras. We do that constantly as humans, with our two eyes. Our human depth perception comes from multiple (two) views, but not just that. In fact, human visual perception, as it pertains to sensing depth and 3D structure, is very complex and has to do with the muscles and sensors of the eyes, not just the *images* on our retinas and their processing in the brain. The human visual sense and its magical traits are well beyond the scope of this chapter; however, in more than one way, SfM (and all of computer vision!) is inspired by the human sense of vision.

Back to our cameras. In standard SfM, we utilize the **pinhole camera model**, which is a simplification of the entire optical, mechanical, electrical, and software process that goes on in real cameras. The pinhole model describes how real-world objects turn into pixels and involve some parameters that we call **intrinsic parameters**, since they describe the intrinsic features of the camera:

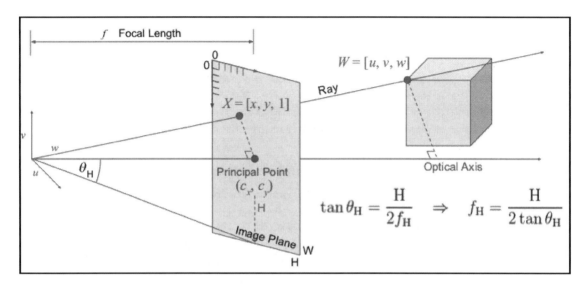

Using the pinhole model, we find the 2D positions of a 3D point on the image plane by applying a projection. Note how the 3D point w and the camera origin form a right-angled triangle, where the adjacent side equals w. The image point x shares the same angle with adjacent f, which is the distance from the origin to the image plane. This distance is called the **focal length**, but that name can be deceiving since the image plane is not actually the focal plane; we converge the two for simplicity. The elementary geometry of overlapping right-angled triangles will tell us that $x = u \cdot f/w$; however, since we deal with images, we must account for the **Principle Point** (c_x, c_y) and arrive at $x = u \cdot f/w + c_x$. If we do the same for the y axis, this follows:

$$
s \begin{bmatrix} x \\ y \\ 1 \end{bmatrix} = \begin{bmatrix} f_W & 0 & c_x \\ 0 & f_H & c_y \\ 0 & 0 & 1 \end{bmatrix} \begin{bmatrix} u \\ v \\ w \end{bmatrix}
$$

The 3 x 3 matrix is called the **intrinsic parameters matrix**, usually denoted as K; however, a number of things seem off about this equation and require explanation. First, we're missing the division by w, where did it go? Second, what is that mysterious s that came about on the LHS of the equation? The answer is **homogeneous coordinates**, meaning we add a 1 at the end of the vector. This useful notation allows us to linearize these operations and perform the division later. At the end of the matrix multiplication step, which we might do for thousands of points at once, we divide the result by the last entry in the vector, which happens to be exactly the w we're looking for. As for s, this is an unknown arbitrary scale factor we must keep in mind, which comes from a perspective in our projection. Imagine we had a toy car very close to the camera, and next to it a real-sized car 10 meters away from the camera; in the image, they would appear to be the same size. In other words, we could move the 3D point W anywhere along the ray going out from the camera and still get the same X coordinate in the image. That is the curse of perspective projection: we lose the depth information, which we mentioned at the beginning of this chapter.

One more thing we must consider is the pose of our camera in the world. Not all cameras are placed at the origin point $(0,0,0)$, especially if we have a system with many cameras. We conveniently place one camera at the origin, but the rest will have a rotation and translation (rigid transform) component with respect to themselves. We, therefore, add another matrix to the projection equation:

$$s \begin{bmatrix} x \\ y \\ 1 \end{bmatrix} = \begin{bmatrix} f_W & 0 & c_x \\ 0 & f_H & c_y \\ 0 & 0 & 1 \end{bmatrix} \begin{bmatrix} r_1 & r_2 & r_3 & t_x \\ r_4 & r_5 & r_6 & t_y \\ r_7 & r_8 & r_9 & t_z \end{bmatrix} \begin{bmatrix} u \\ v \\ w \\ 1 \end{bmatrix}$$

The new 3 x 4 matrix is usually called the **extrinsic parameters matrix** and carries 3 x 3 rotation and 3 x 1 translation components. Notice we use the same homogeneous coordinates trick to help incorporate the translation into the calculation by adding 1 at the end of $\vec{W}$. We will often see this entire equation written as $sX = K[R|t]W$ in the literature:

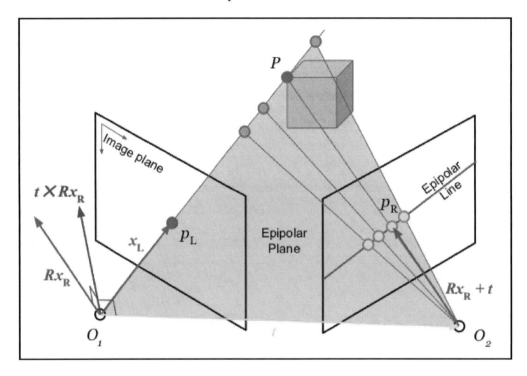

Consider two cameras looking at the same object point. As we just discussed, we can slide the *real* location of the 3D point along the axis from the camera and still observe the same 2D point, thus losing the depth information. Intuitively, two viewing angles should be enough to find the real 3D positions, as the rays from both viewpoints converge at it. Indeed, as we slide the point on the ray, in the other camera looking from a different angle, this position changes. In fact, any point in camera **L** (left) will correspond to a *line* in camera **R** (right), called the **epipolar line** (sometimes known as **epiline**), which lies on the **epipolar plane** constructed by the two cameras' optical centers and the 3D point. This can be used as a geometric constraint between the two views that can help us find a relationship.

We already know that between the two cameras, there's a rigid transform $[R|t]$. If we want to represent x_R, a point in camera **R**, in the coordinate frame of camera **L**, we can $Rx_R + t$ write . If we take the cross product $t \times Rx_R$, we will receive a vector *perpendicular* to the epipolar plane. Therefore, it follows that $x_L \cdot t \times Rx_R = 0$ since x_L lies *on* the epipolar plane and a dot product would yield 0. We take the skew symmetric form for the cross product and we can write $x_L^T [t]_\times Rx_R = 0$, then combine this into a single matrix $x_L^T E x_R = 0$. We call E the **essential matrix**. The essential matrix gives us an **epipolar constraint** over all pairs of points between camera L and camera R that converge at a real 3D point. If a pair of points (from **L** and **R**) fails to satisfy this constraint, it is most likely not a valid pairing. We can also estimate the essential matrix using a number of point pairings since they simply construct a homogeneous system of linear equations. The solution can be easily obtained with an eigenvalue or **singular value decomposition (SVD)**.

So far in our geometry, we assumed our cameras were normalized, essentially meaning $K = I$, the identity matrix. However, in real-life images with particular pixel sizes and focal lengths, we must account for the real intrinsic. To that end, we can apply the inverse K of on both sides: $(K^{-1}x_L)^T E K^{-1} x_R = x_L^T K^{-T} E K^{-1} x_R = x_L^T F x_R = 0$. This new matrix we end up with is called the **fundamental matrix**, which can be estimated right from enough pairings of pixel coordinate points. We can then get the essential matrix if we know K; however, the fundamental matrix may serve as a good epipolar constraint all on its own.

Stereo reconstruction and SfM

In SfM, we would like to recover both the poses of cameras and the position of 3D feature points. We have just seen how simple 2D pair matches of points can help us estimate the essential matrix and thus encode the rigid geometric relationship between views: $[R|t]$. The essential matrix can be decomposed into R and t by way of SVD, and having found R and t , we proceed with finding the 3D points and fulfilling the SfM task for the two images.

We have seen the geometric relationship between two 2D views and the 3D world; however, we are yet to see how to recover 3D shape from the 2D views. One insight we had is that given two views of the same point, we can cross the two rays from the optic center of the cameras and the 2D points on the image plane, and they will converge on the 3D point. This is the basic idea of **triangulation.** One simple way to go about solving for the 3D point is to write the projection equation and equate, since the 3D point (W) is common, $x_\mathrm{L} = P_\mathrm{L} W, x_\mathrm{R} = P_\mathrm{R} W$, where the P matrices are the $K[R|t]$ projection matrices. The equations can be worked into a homogeneous system of linear equations and can be solved, for example, by SVD. This is known as the **direct linear method** for triangulation; however, it is severely sub-optimal since it makes no direct minimization of a meaningful error functor. Several other methods have been suggested, including looking at the closest point between the rays, which generally do not directly intersect, known as the **mid-point method**.

After getting a baseline 3D reconstruction from two views, we can proceed with adding more views. This is usually done in a different method, employing a match between existing 3D and incoming 2D points. The class of algorithms is called **Point-n-Perspective (PnP)**, which we will not discuss here. Another method is to perform pairwise stereo reconstruction, as we've seen already, and calculate the scaling factor, since each image pair reconstructed may result in a different scale, as discussed earlier.

Another interesting method for recovering depth information is to further utilize the epipolar lines. We know that a point in image **L** will lie on a line in image **R**, and we can also calculate the line precisely using E. The task is, therefore, to find the right point on the epipolar line in image **R** that best matches the point in image L. This line matching method may be called **stereo depth reconstruction**, and since we can recover the depth information for almost every pixel in the image, it is most times a **dense** reconstruction. In practice, the epipolar lines are first **rectified** to be completely horizontal, mimicking a **pure horizontal translation** between the images. This reduces the problem of matching only on the x axis:

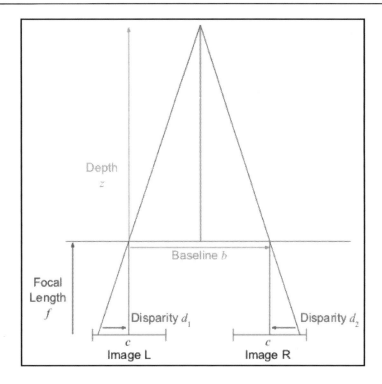

The major appeal of horizontal translation is **disparity**, which describes the distance an interest point travels horizontally between the two images. In the preceding diagram, we can notice that due to right overlapping triangles: $\frac{B}{z} = \frac{d}{f}$, which leads to $d = \frac{B \cdot f}{z}$. The baseline B (horizontal motion), and the focal length f are constant with respect to the particular 3D point and its distance from the camera. Therefore, the insight is that the **disparity is inversely proportional to depth**. The smaller the disparity, the farther the point is from the camera. When we look at the horizon from a moving train's window, the faraway mountains move very slowly, while the close by trees move very fast. This effect is also known as **parallax**. Using disparity for 3D reconstruction is at the base of all stereo algorithms.

Another topic of wide research is MVS, which utilizes the epipolar constraint to find matching points from multiple views at once. Scanning the epilines in multiple images all at once can impose further constraints on the matching features. Only when a match that satisfies all the constraints is found is it considered. When we recover multiple camera positions, we could employ MVS to get a dense reconstruction, which is what we will do later in this chapter.

Implementing SfM in OpenCV

OpenCV has an abundance of tools to implement a full-fledged SfM pipeline from first principles. However, such a task is very demanding and beyond the scope of this chapter. The former edition of this book presented just a small taste of what building such a system will entail, but luckily now we have at our disposal a tried and tested technique integrated right into OpenCV's API. Although the sfm module allows us to get away with simply providing a non-parametric function with a list of images to crunch and receive a fully reconstructed scene with a sparse point cloud and camera poses, we will not take that route. Instead, we will see in this section some useful methods that will allow us to have much more control over the reconstruction and exemplify some of the topics we discussed in the last section, as well as be more robust to noise.

This section will begin with the very basics of SfM: **matching images** using key points and feature descriptors. We will then advance to finding **tracks**, and multiple views of similar features through the image set, using a match graph. We proceed with **3D reconstruction**, **3D visualization**, and finally MVS with OpenMVS.

Image feature matching

SfM, as presented in the last section, relies on the understanding of the geometric relationship between images as it pertains to the visible objects in them. We saw that we can calculate the exact motion between two images with sufficient information on how the objects in the images move. The essential or fundamental matrices, which can be estimated linearly from image features, can be decomposed to the rotation and translation elements that define a **3D rigid transform**. Thereafter, this transform can help us triangulate the 3D position of the objects, from the 3D-2D projection equations or from a dense stereo matching over the rectified epilines. It all begins with image feature matching, so we will see how to obtain robust and noise-free matching.

OpenCV has an extensive offering of 2D feature **detectors** (also called **extractors**) and **descriptors**. Features are designed to be invariant to image deformations so they can be matched through translation, rotation, scaling, and other more complicated transformations (affine, projective) of the objects in the scene. One of the latest additions to OpenCV's APIs is the AKAZE feature extractor and detector, which presents a very good compromise between speed of calculation and robustness to transformation. AKAZE was shown to outperform other prominent features, such as **ORB** (short for **Oriented BRIEF**) and **SURF** (short for **Speeded Up Robust Features**).

The following snippet will extract an AKAZE key point, calculate AKAZE features for each of the images we collect in imagesFilenames, and save them in the keypoints and descriptors arrays respectively:

```
auto detector = AKAZE::create();
auto extractor = AKAZE::create();

for (const auto& i : imagesFilenames) {
    Mat grayscale;
    cvtColor(images[i], grayscale, COLOR_BGR2GRAY);
    detector->detect(grayscale, keypoints[i]);
    extractor->compute(grayscale, keypoints[i], descriptors[i]);

    CV_LOG_INFO(TAG, "Found " + to_string(keypoints[i].size()) + "
    keypoints in " + i);
}
```

Note we also convert the images to grayscale; however, this step may be omitted and the results will not suffer.

Here's a visualization of the detected features in two adjacent images. Notice how many of them repeat; this is known as feature **repeatability**, which is one of the most desired functions in a good feature extractor:

Next up is matching the features between every pair of images. OpenCV provides an excellent feature matching suite. AKAZE feature descriptors are *binary*, meaning they cannot be regarded as binary-encoded numbers when matched; they must be compared on the bit level with bit-wise operators. OpenCV offers a **Hamming distance** metric for binary feature matchers, which essentially count the number of incorrect matches between the two-bit sequences:

```
vector<DMatch> matchWithRatioTest(const DescriptorMatcher& matcher,
                                  const Mat& desc1,
                                  const Mat& desc2)
{
    // Raw match
    vector< vector<DMatch> > nnMatch;
```

```
        matcher.knnMatch(desc1, desc2, nnMatch, 2);

        // Ratio test filter
        vector<DMatch> ratioMatched;
        for (size_t i = 0; i < nnMatch.size(); i++) {
            const DMatch first = nnMatch[i][0];
            const float dist1 = nnMatch[i][0].distance;
            const float dist2 = nnMatch[i][1].distance;

            if (dist1 < MATCH_RATIO_THRESHOLD * dist2) {
                ratioMatched.push_back(first);
            }
        }

        return ratioMatched;
    }
```

The preceding function not only invokes our matcher (for example, a
`BFMatcher(NORM_HAMMING)`) regularly, it also performs the **ratio test**. This simple test is a
very fundamental concept in many computer vision algorithms that rely on feature
matching (such as SfM, panorama stitching, sparse tracking, and more). Instead of looking
for a single match for a feature from image *A* in image *B*, we look for two matches in image
B and make sure there is *no confusion*. Confusion in matching may arise if two potential
matching-feature descriptors are too similar (in terms of their distance metric) and we
cannot tell which of them is the correct match for the query, so we discard them both to
prevent confusion.

Next, we implement a **reciprocity filter**. This filter only allows feature matches that match
(with a ratio test) in *A* to *B*, as well as *B* to *A*. Essentially, this is making sure there's a one-
to-one match between features in image *A* and those in image *B*: a symmetric match. The
reciprocity filter removes even more ambiguity and contributes to a cleaner, more robust
match:

```
    // Match with ratio test filter
    vector<DMatch> match = matchWithRatioTest(matcher, descriptors[imgi],
    descriptors[imgj]);

    // Reciprocity test filter
    vector<DMatch> matchRcp = matchWithRatioTest(matcher, descriptors[imgj],
    descriptors[imgi]);
    vector<DMatch> merged;
    for (const DMatch& dmrecip : matchRcp) {
        bool found = false;
        for (const DMatch& dm : match) {
            // Only accept match if 1 matches 2 AND 2 matches 1.
            if (dmrecip.queryIdx == dm.trainIdx and dmrecip.trainIdx ==
```

```
                dm.queryIdx) {
                    merged.push_back(dm);
                    found = true;
                    break;
                }
            }
            if (found) {
                continue;
            }
        }
```

Lastly, we apply the **epipolar constraint**. Every two images that have a valid rigid transformation between them would comply with the epipolar constraint over their feature points, $x_L^T F x_R = 0$, and those who don't pass this test (with sufficient success) are likely not a good match and may contribute to noise. We achieve this by calculating the fundamental matrix with a voting algorithm (RANSAC) and checking for the ratio of inliers to outliers. We apply a threshold to discard matches with a low survival rate with respect to the original match:

```
// Fundamental matrix filter
vector<uint8_t> inliersMask(merged.size());
vector<Point2f> imgiPoints, imgjPoints;
for (const DMatch& m : merged) {
    imgiPoints.push_back(keypoints[imgi][m.queryIdx].pt);
    imgjPoints.push_back(keypoints[imgj][m.trainIdx].pt);
}
findFundamentalMat(imgiPoints, imgjPoints, inliersMask);

vector<DMatch> final;
for (size_t m = 0; m < merged.size(); m++) {
    if (inliersMask[m]) {
        final.push_back(merged[m]);
    }
}

if ((float)final.size() / (float)match.size() < PAIR_MATCH_SURVIVAL_RATE) {
    CV_LOG_INFO(TAG, "Final match '" + imgi + "'->'" + imgj + "' has less
than "+to_string(PAIR_MATCH_SURVIVAL_RATE)+" inliers from orignal. Skip");
    continue;
}
```

We can see the effect of each of the filtering steps, raw match, ratio, reciprocity, and epipolar, in the following figure:

Finding feature tracks

The concept of **feature tracks** was introduced in SfM literature as early as 1992 in Tomasi and Kanade's work (*Shape and Motion from Image Streams*, 1992) and made famous in Snavely and Szeliski's seminal photo tourism work from 2007 for large-scale unconstrained reconstructions. Tracks are simply the 2D positions of a single scene feature, an interesting point, over a number of views. Tracks are important since they maintain consistency across frames than can be composed into a global optimization problem, as Snavely suggested. Tracks are specifically important to us since OpenCV's `sfm` module allows to reconstruct a scene by providing just the 2D tracks across all the views:

Having already found a pair-wise match between all views, we have the required information to find tracks within those matched features. If we follow feature *i* in the first image to the second image through the match, then from the second image to the third image through their own match, and so on, we would end up with its track. This sort of bookkeeping can easily become too hard to implement in a straightforward fashion with standard data structures. However, it can be simply done if we represent all the matches in a **match graph**. Each node in the graph would be a feature detected in a single image, and edges would be the matches we recovered. From the feature nodes of the first image, we would have many edges to the feature nodes of the second image, third image, fourth image, and so on (for matches not discarded by our filters). Since our matches are reciprocal (symmetric), the graph can be undirected. Moreover, the reciprocity test ensures that for feature *i* in the first image, there is **only one** matching feature *j* in the second image, and vice versa: feature *j* will only match back to feature *i*.

The following is a visual example of such a match graph. The node colors represent the image from which the feature point (node) has originated. Edges represent a match between image features. We can notice the very strong pattern of a feature matching chain from the first image to the last:

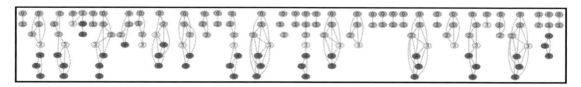

To code the match graph, we can use the **Boost Graph Library** (**BGL**), which has an extensive API for graph processing and algorithms. Constructing the graph is straightforward; we simply augment the nodes with the image ID and feature ID, so later we can trace back the origin:

```
using namespace boost;

struct ImageFeature {
    string image;
    size_t featureID;
};
typedef adjacency_list < listS, vecS, undirectedS, ImageFeature > Graph;
typedef graph_traits < Graph >::vertex_descriptor Vertex;
map<pair<string, int>, Vertex> vertexByImageFeature;

Graph g;

// Add vertices - image features
for (const auto& imgi : keypoints) {
    for (size_t i = 0; i < imgi.second.size(); i++) {
        Vertex v = add_vertex(g);
        g[v].image = imgi.first;
        g[v].featureID = i;
        vertexByImageFeature[make_pair(imgi.first, i)] = v;
    }
}

// Add edges - feature matches
for (const auto& match : matches) {
    for (const DMatch& dm : match.second) {
        Vertex& vI = vertexByImageFeature[make_pair(match.first.first,
dm.queryIdx)];
        Vertex& vJ = vertexByImageFeature[make_pair(match.first.second,
dm.trainIdx)];
        add_edge(vI, vJ, g);
```

```
        }
    }
```

Looking at a visualization of the resulting graph (using `boost::write_graphviz()`), we can see many cases where our matching is erroneous. A bad match chain will involve more than one feature from the same image in the chain. We marked a few such instances in the following figure; notice some chains have two or more nodes with the same color:

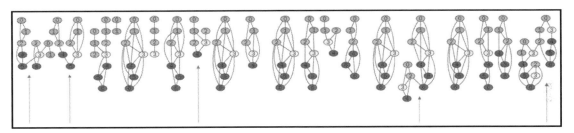

We can notice the chains are essentially connected components in the graph. Extracting the components is simple using `boost::connected_components()`:

```
// Get connected components
std::vector<int> component(num_vertices(gFiltered), -1);
int num = connected_components(gFiltered, &component[0]);
map<int, vector<Vertex> > components;
for (size_t i = 0; i != component.size(); ++i) {
    if (component[i] >= 0) {
        components[component[i]].push_back(i);
    }
}
```

We can filter out the bad components (with more than one feature from any one image) to get a clean match graph.

3D reconstruction and visualization

Having obtained the tracks in principle, we need to align them in a data structure that OpenCV's SfM module expects. Unfortunately, the `sfm` module is not very well documented, so this part we have to figure out on our own from the source code. We will be invoking the following function under the `cv::sfm::` namespace, which can be found in `opencv_contrib/modules/sfm/include/opencv2/sfm/reconstruct.hpp`:

```
void reconstruct(InputArrayOfArrays points2d, OutputArray Ps, OutputArray
points3d, InputOutputArray K, bool is_projective = false);
```

The opencv_contrib/modules/sfm/src/simple_pipeline.cpp file has a major hint as to what that function expects as input:

```
static void
parser_2D_tracks( const std::vector<Mat> &points2d, libmv::Tracks &tracks )
{
  const int nframes = static_cast<int>(points2d.size());
  for (int frame = 0; frame < nframes; ++frame) {
    const int ntracks = points2d[frame].cols;
    for (int track = 0; track < ntracks; ++track) {
      const Vec2d track_pt = points2d[frame].col(track);
      if ( track_pt[0] > 0 && track_pt[1] > 0 )
        tracks.Insert(frame, track, track_pt[0], track_pt[1]);
    }
  }
}
```

In general, the sfm module uses a reduced version of libmv (https://developer.blender.org/tag/libmv/), which is a well-established SfM package used for 3D reconstruction for cinema production with the Blender 3D (https://www.blender.org/) graphics software.

We can tell the tracks need to be placed in a vector of multiple individual cv::Mat, where each contains an aligned list of cv::Vec2d as columns, meaning it has two rows of double. We can also deduce that missing (unmatched) feature points in a track will have a negative coordinate. The following snippet will extract tracks in the desired data structure from the match graph:

```
vector<Mat> tracks(nViews); // Initialize to number of views

// Each component is a track
const size_t nViews = imagesFilenames.size();
tracks.resize(nViews);
for (int i = 0; i < nViews; i++) {
    tracks[i].create(2, components.size(), CV_64FC1);
    tracks[i].setTo(-1.0); // default is (-1, -1) - no match
}
int i = 0;
for (auto c = components.begin(); c != components.end(); ++c, ++i) {
    for (const int v : c->second) {
        const int imageID = imageIDs[g[v].image];
        const size_t featureID = g[v].featureID;
        const Point2f p = keypoints[g[v].image][featureID].pt;
        tracks[imageID].at<double>(0, i) = p.x;
        tracks[imageID].at<double>(1, i) = p.y;
    }
}
```

We follow up with running the reconstruction function, collecting the sparse 3D point cloud and the color for each 3D point, and afterward, visualize the results (using functions from `cv::viz::`):

```
cv::sfm::reconstruct(tracks, Rs, Ts, K, points3d, true);
```

This will produce a sparse reconstruction with a point cloud and camera positions, visualized in the following image:

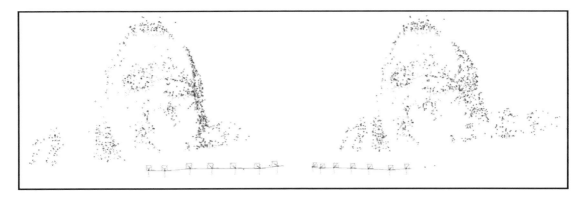

Re-projecting the 3D points back on the 2D images we can validate a correct reconstruction:

See the entire code for reconstruction and visualization in the accompanying source repository.

Notice the reconstruction is very sparse; we only see 3D points where features have matched. This doesn't make for a very appealing effect when getting the geometry of objects in the scene. In many cases, SfM pipelines do not conclude with a sparse reconstruction, which is not useful for many applications, such as 3D scanning. Next, we will see how to get a **dense** reconstruction.

MVS for dense reconstruction

With the sparse 3D point cloud and the positions of the cameras, we can proceed with dense reconstruction using MVS. We already learned the basic concept of MVS in the first section; however, we do not need to implement this from scratch, but rather we can use the **OpenMVS** project. To use OpenMVS for cloud densifying, we must save our project in a specialized format. OpenMVS provides a class for saving and loading `.mvs` projects, the `MVS::Interface` class, defined in `MVS/Interface.h`.

Let's start with the camera:

```
MVS::Interface interface;
MVS::Interface::Platform p;

// Add camera
MVS::Interface::Platform::Camera c;
c.K = Matx33d(K_); // The intrinsic matrix as refined by the bundle
adjustment
c.R = Matx33d::eye(); // Camera doesn't have any inherent rotation
c.C = Point3d(0,0,0); // or translation
c.name = "Camera1";
const Size imgS = images[imagesFilenames[0]].size();
c.width = imgS.width; // Size of the image, to normalize the intrinsics
c.height = imgS.height;
p.cameras.push_back(c);
```

When adding the camera poses (views), we must take care. OpenMVS expects to get the rotation and **center** of the camera, and not the camera pose matrix for point projection $[R|t]$. We therefore must translate the translation vector to represent the center of the camera by applying the inverse rotation $-R^t t$:

```
// Add views
p.poses.resize(Rs.size());
for (size_t i = 0; i < Rs.size(); ++i) {
    Mat t = -Rs[i].t() * Ts[i]; // Camera *center*
    p.poses[i].C.x = t.at<double>(0);
    p.poses[i].C.y = t.at<double>(1);
    p.poses[i].C.z = t.at<double>(2);
    Rs[i].convertTo(p.poses[i].R, CV_64FC1);

    // Add corresponding image (make sure index aligns)
    MVS::Interface::Image image;
    image.cameraID = 0;
    image.poseID = i;
    image.name = imagesFilenames[i];
    image.platformID = 0;
```

```
        interface.images.push_back(image);
    }
    p.name = "Platform1";
    interface.platforms.push_back(p);
```

After adding the point cloud to the `Interface` as well, we can proceed with the cloud densifying in the command line:

```
$ ${openMVS}/build/bin/DensifyPointCloud -i crazyhorse.mvs
18:48:32 [App ] Command line: -i crazyhorse.mvs
18:48:32 [App ] Camera model loaded: platform 0; camera 0; f 0.896x0.896;
poses 7
18:48:32 [App ] Image loaded 0: P1000965.JPG
18:48:32 [App ] Image loaded 1: P1000966.JPG
18:48:32 [App ] Image loaded 2: P1000967.JPG
18:48:32 [App ] Image loaded 3: P1000968.JPG
18:48:32 [App ] Image loaded 4: P1000969.JPG
18:48:32 [App ] Image loaded 5: P1000970.JPG
18:48:32 [App ] Image loaded 6: P1000971.JPG
18:48:32 [App ] Scene loaded from interface format (11ms):
7 images (7 calibrated) with a total of 5.25 MPixels (0.75 MPixels/image)
1557 points, 0 vertices, 0 faces
18:48:32 [App ] Preparing images for dense reconstruction completed: 7
images (125ms)
18:48:32 [App ] Selecting images for dense reconstruction completed: 7
images (5ms)
Estimated depth-maps 7 (100%, 1m44s705ms)
Filtered depth-maps 7 (100%, 1s671ms)
Fused depth-maps 7 (100%, 421ms)
18:50:20 [App ] Depth-maps fused and filtered: 7 depth-maps, 1653963
depths, 263027 points (16%%) (1s684ms)
18:50:20 [App ] Densifying point-cloud completed: 263027 points
(1m48s263ms)
18:50:21 [App ] Scene saved (489ms):
7 images (7 calibrated)
263027 points, 0 vertices, 0 faces
18:50:21 [App ] Point-cloud saved: 263027 points (46ms)
```

This process might take a few minutes to complete. However, once it's done, the results are very impressive. The dense point cloud has a whopping **263,027 3D points**, compared to just 1,557 in the sparse cloud. We can visualize the dense OpenMVS project using the `Viewer` app bundled in OpenMVS:

OpenMVS has several more functions to complete the reconstruction, such as extracting a triangular mesh from the dense point cloud.

Summary

This chapter focused on SfM and its implementation with OpenCV's `sfm` contributed module and OpenMVS. We explored some theoretical concepts in multiple view geometry, and several practical matters: extracting key feature points, matching them, creating and analyzing the match graph, running the reconstruction, and finally performing MVS to densify the sparse 3D point cloud.

In the next chapter, we will see how to use OpenCV's `face contrib` module to detect facial landmarks in photos, as well as detecting the direction a face is pointing with the `solvePnP` function.

Face Landmark and Pose with the Face Module

15

Face landmark detection is the process of finding points of interest in an image of a human face. It recently saw a spur of interest in the computer vision community, as it has many compelling applications; for example, detecting emotion through facial gestures, estimating gaze direction, changing facial appearance (**face swap**), augmenting faces with graphics, and puppeteering of virtual characters. We can see many of these applications in today's smartphones and PC web-camera programs. To achieve these applications, the landmark detector must find dozens of points on the face, such as corners of the mouth, corners of eyes, the silhouette of the jaws, and many more. To that end, many algorithms were developed, and a few were implemented in OpenCV. In this chapter, we will discuss the process of face landmark (also known as **facemark**) detection using the `cv::face` module, which provides an API for inference, as well as training of a facemark detector. We will see how to apply the facemark detector to locating the direction of the face in 3D.

The following topics will be covered in this chapter:

- Introducing face landmark detection history and theory, and an explanation of the algorithms implemented in OpenCV
- Utilizing OpenCV's `face` module for face landmark detection
- Estimating the approximate direction of the face by leveraging 2D–3D information

Technical requirements

The following technologies and installations are required to build the code in this chapter:

- OpenCV v4 (compiled with the `face contrib` module)
- Boost v1.66+

Build instructions for the preceding components listed, as well as the code to implement the concepts presented in this chapter, will be provided in the accompanying code repository.

To run the facemark detector, a pre-trained model is required. Although training the detector model is certainly possible with the APIs provided in OpenCV, some pre-trained models are offered for download. One such model can be obtained from `https://raw.githubusercontent.com/kurnianggoro/GSOC2017/master/data/lbfmodel.yaml`, supplied by the contributor of the algorithm implementation to OpenCV (during the 2017 **Google Summer of Code (GSoC)**).

The facemark detector can work with any image; however, we can use a prescribed dataset of facial photos and videos that are used to benchmark facemark algorithms. Such a dataset is **300-VW**, available through **Intelligent Behaviour Understanding Group (iBUG)**, a computer vision group at Imperial College London: `https://ibug.doc.ic.ac.uk/resources/300-VW/`. It contains hundreds of videos of facial appearances in media, carefully annotated with 68 facial landmark points. This dataset can be used for training the facemark detector, as well as to understand the performance level of the pre-trained model we use. The following is an excerpt from one of the 300-VW videos with ground truth annotation:

Image reproduced under Creative Commons license

The code files for this chapter can be downloaded from `https://github.com/PacktPublishing/Building-Computer-Vision-Projects-with-OpenCV4-and-CPlusPlus/tree/master/Chapter15`.

Theory and context

Facial landmark detection algorithms automatically find the locations of key landmark points on facial images. Those key points are usually prominent points locating a facial component, such as eye corner or mouth corner, to achieve a higher-level understanding of the face shape. To detect a decent range of facial expressions, for example, points around the jawline, mouth, eyes, and eyebrows are needed. Finding facial landmarks proves to be a difficult task for a variety of reasons: great variation between subjects, illumination conditions, and occlusions. To that end, computer vision researchers proposed dozens of landmark detection algorithms over the past three decades.

A recent survey of facial landmark detection (Wu and Ji, 2018) suggests separating landmark detectors into three groups: holistic methods, **constrained local model** (CLM) methods, and regression methods:

- Wu and Ji pose the **holistic methods** as ones that model the complete appearance of the face's pixel intensities
- **CLM methods** examine *local* patches around each landmark in combination with a global model
- **Regression methods** iteratively try to predict landmark locations using a cascade of small updates learned by regressors

Active appearance models and constrained local models

A canonical example of a holistic method is the **active appearance model** (AAM) from the late '90s, usually attributed to the work of T.F. Cootes (1998). In AAM, the goal is to iteratively match a known face rendering (from the training data) to the target input image, which upon convergence gives the shape, and thus, landmarks. The AAM method and its derivatives were extremely popular, and still take up a fair share of attention. However AAM's successor, CLM methods, have shown far better performance under illumination changes and occlusions, and rapidly took the lead. Mostly attributed to the work of Cristinacce and Cootes (2006) and Saragih et al. (2011), CLM methods model the pixel intensity appearance of each landmark locally (patch), as well as incorporating a global shape beforehand to cope with occlusions and false local detections.

CLMs can be generally described as looking to minimize, where p is a facial shape *pose* that can be decomposed to its D landmark $x_d(p)$ points, as follows:

$$\hat{p} = \arg\min_{p} Q(p) + \sum_{d=1}^{D} \text{Distance}(x_d(p), I)$$

Facial poses are primarily obtained by way of **principal component analysis (PCA)**, and the landmarks are the result of the inverse PCA operation. Using PCA is useful, since most facial shape poses are strongly correlated, and the full landmark position space is highly redundant. A distance function (denoted Distance) is used to determine how close a given landmark model point is to the image observation I. In many cases, the distance function is a patch-to-patch similarity measure (template matching), or usage of edge-based features, such as the **histogram of gradients (HOG)**. The term $Q(p)$ is used for regularization over improbable or extreme face shape poses.

Regression methods

In contrast, *regression methods* employ a more simplistic, but powerful approach. These methods use machine learning, by way of regression, an *update step* to an initial positioning of the landmarks and iterate until the positions converge, where $\hat{S}^{(t)}$ is the shape at time t, and $r_t(I, \hat{S}^{(t)})$ is the result of running the regressor r on the image I and the current shape, demonstrated as follows:

$$\hat{S}^{(t+1)} = \hat{S}^{(t)} + r_t(I, \hat{S}^{(t)})$$

By cascading these update operations, the final landmark positions are obtained.

This approach allows consuming enormous amounts of training data and letting go of the handcrafted models for the local similarity and global constraints that are the center of CLM methods. The prevailing regression method is **gradient boosting trees (GBT)**, which offer very fast inference, simple implementations, and are parallelizable as a forest.

There are yet newer approaches to facial landmark detection, utilizing deep learning. These new methods either directly regress the position of the facial landmarks from the image by employing **convolutional neural networks (CNN)**, or use a hybrid approach of CNNs with a 3D model and cascaded-regression methods.

OpenCV's `face` module (first introduced in OpenCV v3.0) that contains implementations for AAM, Ren et al. (2014) and Kazemi et al. (2014) regression type methods. In this chapter, we will employ Ren et al.'s (2014) method, since it presents the best results given the pre-trained model provided by the contributors. Ren et al.'s method learns the best **local binary features** (**LBF**), a very short binary code that describes the visual appearance around a point for each landmark, as well as to learn the shape update step by regression.

Facial landmark detection in OpenCV

Landmark detection starts with **face detection**, finding faces in the image and their extents (bounding boxes). Facial detection has long been considered a solved problem, and OpenCV contains one of the first robust face detectors freely available to the public. In fact, OpenCV, in its early days, was majorly known and used for its fast face detection feature, implementing the canonical Viola-Jones boosted cascade classifier algorithm (Viola et al. 2001, 2004), and providing a pre-trained model. While face detection has grown much since those early days, the fastest and easiest method for detecting faces in OpenCV is still to use the bundled cascade classifiers, by means of the `cv::CascadeClassifier` class provided in the `core` module.

We implement a simple helper function to detect faces with the cascade classifier, shown as follows:

```
void faceDetector(const Mat& image,
                  std::vector<Rect> &faces,
                  CascadeClassifier &face_cascade) {
    Mat gray;

    // The cascade classifier works best on grayscale images
    if (image.channels() > 1) {
        cvtColor(image, gray, COLOR_BGR2GRAY);
    } else {
        gray = image.clone();
    }

    // Histogram equalization generally aids in face detection
    equalizeHist(gray, gray);

    faces.clear();

    // Run the cascade classifier
    face_cascade.detectMultiScale(
        gray,
        faces,
```

```
        1.4, // pyramid scale factor
        3,   // lower thershold for neighbors count
        // here we hint the classifier to only look for one face
        CASCADE_SCALE_IMAGE + CASCADE_FIND_BIGGEST_OBJECT);
}
```

We may want to tweak the two parameters that govern the face detection: pyramid scale factor and number of neighbors. The pyramid scale factor is used to create a pyramid of images within which the detector will try to find faces. This is how multi-scale detection is achieved, since the bare detector has a fixed aperture. In each step of the image pyramid, the image is downscaled by this factor, so a small factor (closer to 1.0) will result in many images, longer runtime, but more accurate results. We also have control of the lower threshold for a number of neighbors. This comes into play when the cascade classifier has multiple positive face classifications in close proximity. Here, we instruct the overall classification to only return a face bound if it has at least three neighboring positive face classifications. A lower number (an integer, close to 1) will return more detections, but will also introduce false positives.

We must initialize the cascade classifier from the OpenCV-provided models (XML files of the serialized models are provided in the $OPENCV_ROOT/data/haarcascades directory). We use the standard trained classifier on frontal faces, demonstrated as follows:

```
const string cascade_name =
"$OPENCV_ROOT/data/haarcascades/haarcascade_frontalface_default.xml";

CascadeClassifier face_cascade;
if (not face_cascade.load(cascade_name)) {
    cerr << "Cannot load cascade classifier from file: " << cascade_name <<
endl;
    return -1;
}

// ... obtain an image in img

vector<Rect> faces;
faceDetector(img, faces, face_cascade);

// Check if any faces were detected or not
if (faces.size() == 0) {
    cerr << "Cannot detect any faces in the image." << endl;
    return -1;
}
```

A visualization of the results of the face detector is shown in the following screenshot:

The facemark detector will work around the detected faces, beginning at the bounding boxes. However, first we must initialize the `cv::face::Facemark` object, demonstrated as follows:

```
#include <opencv2/face.hpp>

using namespace cv::face;

// ...

const string facemark_filename = "data/lbfmodel.yaml";
Ptr<Facemark> facemark = createFacemarkLBF();
facemark->loadModel(facemark_filename);
cout << "Loaded facemark LBF model" << endl;
```

The `cv::face::Facemark` abstract API is used for all the landmark detector flavors, and offers base functionality for implementation for inference and training according to the specific algorithm. Once loaded, the `facemark` object can be used with its `fit` function to find the face shape, shown as follows:

```
vector<Rect> faces;
faceDetector(img, faces, face_cascade);

// Check if faces detected or not
if (faces.size() != 0) {
    // We assume a single face so we look at the first only
    cv::rectangle(img, faces[0], Scalar(255, 0, 0), 2);

    vector<vector<Point2f> > shapes;

    if (facemark->fit(img, faces, shapes)) {
        // Draw the detected landmarks
        drawFacemarks(img, shapes[0], cv::Scalar(0, 0, 255));
    }
} else {
    cout << "Faces not detected." << endl;
}
```

A visualization of the results of the landmark detector (using `cv::face::drawFacemarks`) is shown in the following screenshot:

Measuring error

Visually, the results seem very good. However, since we have the ground truth data, we may elect to analytically compare it to the detection and get an error estimate. We can use a standard mean Euclidean distance metric ($\frac{1}{n} \sum_i^n \|X_i - \hat{y}_i\|_{L_2}$) to tell how close each predicted landmark is to the ground truth on average:

```
float MeanEuclideanDistance(const vector<Point2f>& A, const
vector<Point2f>& B) {
    float med = 0.0f;
    for (int i = 0; i < A.size(); ++i) {
        med += cv::norm(A[i] - B[i]);
    }
    return med / (float)A.size();
}
```

A visualization of the results with the prediction (red) and ground truth (green) overlaid, shown in the following screenshot:

We can see the average error over all landmarks is roughly only one pixel for these particular video frames.

Estimating face direction from landmarks

Having obtained the facial landmarks, we can attempt to find the direction of the face. The 2D face landmark points essentially conform to the shape of the head. So, given a 3D model of a generic human head, we can find approximate corresponding 3D points for a number of facial landmarks, as shown in the following photo:

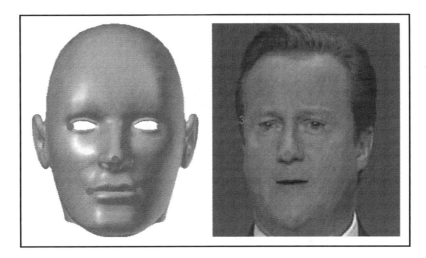

Estimated pose calculation

From these 2D–3D correspondences, we can calculate 3D pose (rotation and translation) of the head, with respect to the camera, by way of the **Point-n-Perspective (PnP)** algorithm. The details of the algorithm and object pose detection are beyond the scope of this chapter; however, we can quickly rationalize why just a handful of 2D–3D point correspondences are suffice to achieve this. The camera that took the preceding picture has a **rigid** transformation, meaning it has moved a certain distance from the object, as well as rotated somewhat, with respect to it. In very broad terms, we can then write the relationship between points on the image (near the camera) and the object as follows:

$$
\begin{pmatrix} x \\ y \\ 1 \end{pmatrix} = s \begin{pmatrix} f_x & 0 & c_x \\ 0 & f_y & c_y \\ 0 & 0 & 1 \end{pmatrix} \begin{pmatrix} r_1 & r_2 & r_3 & t_1 \\ r_4 & r_5 & r_6 & t_2 \\ r_7 & r_8 & r_9 & t_3 \end{pmatrix} \begin{pmatrix} U \\ V \\ W \\ 1 \end{pmatrix}
$$

This is an equation where U, V, W are the object's 3D position, and x, y are points in the image. This equation also includes a projection, governed by the camera intrinsic parameters (focal length f and center point c), that transforms the 3D points to 2D image points, up to scale s. Say we are given the intrinsic parameters by calibrating the camera, or we approximate them, we are left to find 12 coefficients for the rotation and translation. If we had enough 2D and 3D corresponding points, we can write a system of linear equations, where each point can contribute two equations, to solve for all of these coefficients. In fact, it was shown that we don't need six points, since the rotation has less than nine degrees of freedom, we can make do with just four points. OpenCV provides an implementation to find the rotation and translation with its `cv::solvePnP` functions of the `calib3d` module.

We line up the 3D and 2D points and employ `cv::solvePnP`:

```
vector<Point3f> objectPoints {
        {8.27412, 1.33849, 10.63490},      //left eye corner
        {-8.27412, 1.33849, 10.63490},     //right eye corner
        {0, -4.47894, 17.73010},           //nose tip
        {-4.61960, -10.14360, 12.27940},   //right mouth corner
        {4.61960, -10.14360, 12.27940},    //left mouth corner
};
vector<int> landmarksIDsFor3DPoints {45, 36, 30, 48, 54}; // 0-index

// ...
vector<Point2f> points2d;
for (int pId : landmarksIDsFor3DPoints) {
    points2d.push_back(shapes[0][pId] / scaleFactor);
}

solvePnP(objectPoints, points2d, K, Mat(), rvec, tvec, true);
```

The K matrix for the camera intrinsics we estimate from size the preceding image.

Projecting the pose on the image

After obtaining the rotation and translation, we project four points from the object coordinate space to the preceding image: tip of the nose, x axis direction, y axis direction, and z axis direction, and draw the arrows in the preceding image:

```
vector<Point3f> objectPointsForReprojection {
        objectPoints[2],                    // tip of nose
        objectPoints[2] + Point3f(0,0,15),  // nose and Z-axis
        objectPoints[2] + Point3f(0,15,0),  // nose and Y-axis
        objectPoints[2] + Point3f(15,0,0)   // nose and X-axis
};
```

```
//...

vector<Point2f> projectionOutput(objectPointsForReprojection.size());
projectPoints(objectPointsForReprojection, rvec, tvec, K, Mat(),
projectionOutput);
arrowedLine(out, projectionOutput[0], projectionOutput[1],
Scalar(255,255,0));
arrowedLine(out, projectionOutput[0], projectionOutput[2],
Scalar(0,255,255));
arrowedLine(out, projectionOutput[0], projectionOutput[3],
Scalar(255,0,255));
```

This results in a visualization of the direction the face is pointing, as shown in the following screenshots:

Summary

In this chapter, we learned how to use OpenCV's `face contrib` module and the `cv::Facemark` API to detect facial landmarks in the image, and then use the landmarks with `cv::solvePnP()` to find the approximate direction of the face. The APIs are simple and straightforward, but pack a powerful punch. With knowledge of landmark detection, many exciting applications can be implemented, such as augmented reality, face swap, identification, and puppeteering.

16
Number Plate Recognition with Deep Convolutional Networks

This chapter introduces us to the steps needed to create an application for **Automatic Number Plate Recognition (ANPR)**. There are different approaches and techniques based on different situations; for example, an infrared camera, fixed car position, and light conditions. We can proceed to construct an ANPR application to detect automobile license plates in a photograph taken between two and three meters from a car, in ambiguous light conditions, and with a non-parallel ground with minor perspective distortions in the automobile's plate.

The main purpose of this chapter is to introduce us to image segmentation and feature extraction, pattern recognition basics, and two important pattern recognition algorithms, the **Support Vector Machine (SVM)** and **deep neural network (DNN)**, using **convolutional networks**. In this chapter, we will cover the following topics:

- ANPR
- Plate detection
- Plate recognition

Introduction to ANPR

ANPR, sometimes known by other terms, such as **Automatic License Plate Recognition (ALPR)**, **Automatic Vehicle Identification (AVI)**, or **car plate recognition (CPR)**, is a surveillance method that uses **optical character recognition (OCR)** and other methods such as segmentation and detection to read vehicle registration plates.

The best results in an ANPR system can be obtained with an **infrared (IR)** camera, because the segmentation steps for detection and OCR segmentation are easy and clean, and they minimize errors. This is due to the laws of light, the basic one being that the angle of incidence equals **Angle reflection**. We can see this basic reflection when we see a smooth surface, such as a plane mirror. Reflection off rough surfaces such as paper leads to a type of reflection known as **scatter or diffuse reflection**. However, the majority of the country plates have a special characteristic named **Retroreflection**: the surface of the plate is made with a material that is covered with thousands of tiny hemispheres that cause light to be reflected back to the source, as we can see in the following diagram:

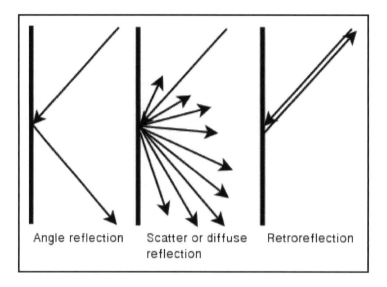

Angle reflection   Scatter or diffuse reflection   Retroreflection

If we use a camera with a filter-coupled, structured infrared light projector, we can retrieve just the infrared light, and then we have a very high-quality image to segment, with which we can subsequently detect and recognize the plate number independent of any lighting environment, as shown in the following image:

We will not use IR photographs in this chapter; we will use regular photographs so that we do not obtain the best results, and we get a higher level of detection errors and higher false recognition rate than if we used an IR camera. However, the steps for both are the same.

Each country has different license plate sizes and specifications. It is useful to know these specifications in order to get the best results and reduce errors. Algorithms used in this chapter are designed for explaining the basics of ANPR and designed for license plates used in Spain, but we can extend it to any country or specification.

In this chapter, we will work with license plates from Spain. In Spain, there are three different sizes and shapes of license plates, but we will only use the most common (large) license plate, which has a width of 520 mm and a height of 110 mm. Two groups of characters are separated by a 41 mm space, and a 14 mm space separates each individual character. The first group of characters is four numeric digits, and the second group three letters excluding the vowels *A*, *E*, *I*, *O* or *U*, or the letters *N* or *Q*. All characters have dimensions of 45 mm by 77 mm.

This data is important for character segmentation, since we can check both the character and blank spaces to verify that we get a character and no other image segment:

ANPR algorithm

Before explaining the ANPR code, we need to define the main steps and tasks in the ANPR algorithm. ANPR is divided into two main steps, plate detection and plate recognition:

- Plate detection has the purpose of detecting the location of the plate in the whole camera frame.
- When a plate is detected in an image, the plate segment is passed to the second step (plate recognition), which uses an OCR algorithm to determine the alphanumeric characters on the plate.

In the following diagram, we can see the two main algorithm steps, plate detection and plate recognition. After these steps, the program paints in the camera image the plate's characters that have been detected. The algorithms can return bad results, or may not return any result:

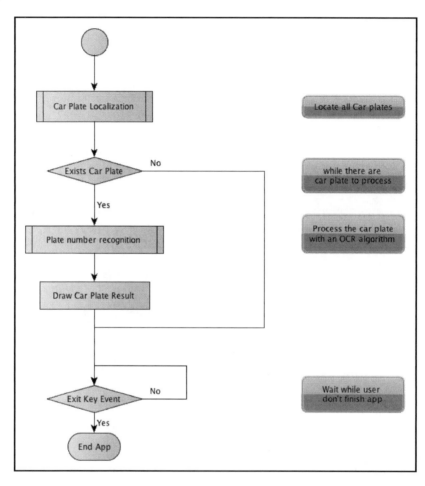

In each step shown in the previous diagram, we will define three additional steps that are commonly used in pattern recognition algorithms. These steps are as follows:

1. **Segmentation**: This step detects and removes each patch/region of interest in the image.
2. **Feature extraction**: This step extracts from each patch a set of characteristics.
3. **Classification**: This step extracts each character from the plate recognition step, or classifies each image patch into a *plate* or *no plate* in the plate detection step.

In the following diagram, we can see these pattern recognition steps in the application as a whole:

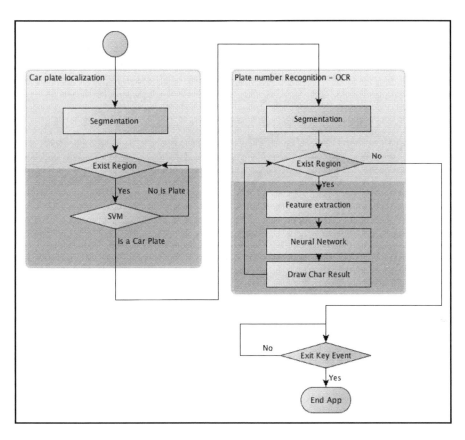

Aside from the main application, whose purpose is to detect and recognize a car plate number, we will briefly explain two more tasks that are usually not explained:

- How to train a pattern recognition system
- How to evaluate it

These tasks, however, can be more important than the main application, because if we do not train the pattern recognition system correctly, our system can fail and not work correctly; different patterns need different training and evaluation processes. We need to evaluate our system with different environments, conditions, and features to get the best results. These two tasks are sometimes done together, since different features can produce different results, which we can see in the evaluation section.

Plate detection

In this step, we have to detect all the plates in a current camera frame. To do this task, we divide it in to two main steps: segmentation and segment classification. The feature step is not explained because we use the image patch as a vector feature.

In the first step (segmentation), we will apply different filters, morphological operations, contour algorithms, and validations to retrieve parts of the image that could contain a plate.

In the second step (classification), we will apply an SVM classifier to each image patch, our feature. Before creating our main application, we will train with two different classes: *plate* and *non-plate*. We will work with parallel frontal view color images with 800 pixels of width and that are taken between two and four meters from a car. These requirements are important for correct segmentation. We can perform detection if we create a multi-scale image algorithm.

In the following image, we will shown each process involved in plate detection:

The processes involved are as follows:

- Sobel filter
- Threshold operation
- Close morphological operation
- Mask of one of filled area
- In red, possible detected plates (feature images)
- Plates detected by SVM classifier

Segmentation

Segmentation is the process of dividing an image into multiple segments. This process is to simplify the image for analysis and make feature extraction easier.

One important feature of plate segmentation is the high number of vertical edges in a license plate, assuming that the image was taken frontally and the plate is not rotated and without perspective distortion. This feature can be exploited during the first segmentation step to eliminate regions that don't have any vertical edges.

Before finding vertical edges, we need to convert the color image to a grayscale image (because color can't help us in this task) and remove possible noise generated from the camera or other ambient noise. We will apply a 5x5 gaussian blur and remove noise. If we don't apply a noise removal method, we can get a lot of vertical edges that produce fail detection:

```
//convert image to gray
Mat img_gray;
cvtColor(input, img_gray, CV_BGR2GRAY);
blur(img_gray, img_gray, Size(5,5));
```

To find the vertical edges, we will use a `Sobel` filter and find the first horizontal derivate. The derivate is a mathematical function that allows us to find vertical edges on an image. The definition of the `Sobel` function in OpenCV is as follows:

```
void Sobel(InputArray src, OutputArray dst, int ddepth, int xorder, int
yorder, int ksize=3, double scale=1, double delta=0, int
borderType=BORDER_DEFAULT )
```

Here, `ddepth` is the destination image depth; `xorder` is the order of the derivate by x; `yorder` is the order of the derivate by y; `ksize` is the kernel size of one, three, five, or seven; `scale` is an optional factor for computed derivative values; `delta` is an optional value added to the result; and `borderType` is the pixel interpolation method.

Then, for our case, we can use `xorder=1`, `yorder=0`, and `ksize=3`:

```
//Find vertical lines. Car plates have high density of vertical
lines
Mat img_sobel;
Sobel(img_gray, img_sobel, CV_8U, 1, 0, 3, 1, 0);
```

After applying a `Sobel` filter, we will apply a threshold filter to obtain a binary image with a threshold value obtained through Otsu's method. Otsu's algorithm needs an 8-bit input image, and Otsu's method automatically determines the optimal threshold value:

```
//threshold image
Mat img_threshold;
threshold(img_sobel, img_threshold, 0, 255,
CV_THRESH_OTSU+CV_THRESH_BINARY);
```

To define Otsu's method in the threshold function, we will combine the type parameter with the `CV_THRESH_OTSU` value, and the threshold value parameter is ignored.

When the `CV_THRESH_OTSU` value is defined, the threshold function returns the optimal threshold value obtained by Otsu's algorithm.

By applying a close morphological operation, we can remove blank spaces between each vertical edge line and connect all regions that have a high number of edges. In this step, we have possible regions that can contain plates.

First, we will define our structural element to use in our morphological operation. We will use the `getStructuringElement` function to define a structural rectangular element with a 17 by 3 dimension size in our case; this may be different in other image sizes:

```
Mat element = getStructuringElement(MORPH_RECT, Size(17, 3));
```

Then, we will use this structural element in a close morphological operation using the `morphologyEx` function:

```
morphologyEx(img_threshold, img_threshold, CV_MOP_CLOSE, element);
```

After applying these functions, we have regions in the image that could contain a plate; however, most of the regions do not contain license plates. These regions can be split by means of connected component analysis, or by using the `findContours` function. This last function retrieves the contours of a binary image with different methods and results. We only need to get the external contours with any hierarchical relationship and any polygonal approximation results:

```
//Find contours of possibles plates
  vector< vector< Point>> contours;
  findContours(img_threshold,
    contours, // a vector of contours
    CV_RETR_EXTERNAL, // retrieve the external contours
    CV_CHAIN_APPROX_NONE); // all pixels of each contours
```

For each contour detected, extract the bounding rectangle of minimal area. OpenCV brings up the `minAreaRect` function for this task. This function returns a rotated `RotatedRect` rectangle class. Then, using a vector iterator over each contour, we can get the rotated rectangle and make some preliminary validations before we classify each region:

```
//Start to iterate to each contour founded
 vector<vector<Point>>::iterator itc= contours.begin();
 vector<RotatedRect> rects;

 //Remove patch that has no inside limits of aspect ratio and
 area.
 while (itc!=contours.end()) {
     //Create bounding rect of object
     RotatedRect mr= minAreaRect(Mat(*itc));
     if(!verifySizes(mr)){
         itc= contours.erase(itc);
     }else{
         ++itc;
         rects.push_back(mr);
     }
 }
```

We make basic validations for the regions detected based on their area and aspect ratio. We will consider that a region can be a plate if the aspect ratio is approximately *520/110 = 4.727272* (plate width divided by plate height), with an error margin of 40% and an area based on a minimum of 15 pixels and a maximum of 125 pixels for the height of the plate. These values are calculated depending on the image size and camera position:

```
bool DetectRegions::verifySizes(RotatedRect candidate ){
    float error=0.4;
    //Spain car plate size: 52x11 aspect 4,7272
    const float aspect=4.7272;
    //Set a min and max area. All other patchs are discarded
    int min= 15*aspect*15; // minimum area
    int max= 125*aspect*125; // maximum area
    //Get only patches that match to a respect ratio.
    float rmin= aspect-aspect*error;
    float rmax= aspect+aspect*error;

    int area= candidate.size.height * candidate.size.width;
    float r= (float)candidate.size.width
    /(float)candidate.size.height;
    if(r<1)
        r= 1/r;

    if(( area < min || area > max ) || ( r < rmin || r > rmax )){
```

```
            return false;
        }else{
            return true;
        }
    }
```

We can make even more improvements using the license plate's white background property. All plates have the same background color, and we can use a flood fill algorithm to retrieve the rotated rectangle for precise cropping.

The first step to crop the license plate is to get several seeds near the last rotated rectangle center. Then, we will get the minimum size of the plate between the width and height, and use it to generate random seeds near the patch center.

We want to select the white region, and we need several seeds to touch at least one white pixel. Then, for each seed, we use a `floodFill` function to draw a new mask image to store the new closest cropping region:

```
for(int i=0; i< rects.size(); i++){
  //For better rect cropping for each possible box
  //Make floodFill algorithm because the plate has white background
  //And then we can retrieve more clearly the contour box
  circle(result, rects[i].center, 3, Scalar(0,255,0), -1);
  //get the min size between width and height
  float minSize=(rects[i].size.width < rects[i].size.height)?
  rects[i].size.width:rects[i].size.height;
  minSize=minSize-minSize*0.5;
  //initialize rand and get 5 points around center for floodFill algorithm
  srand ( time(NULL) );
  //Initialize floodFill parameters and variables
  Mat mask;
  mask.create(input.rows + 2, input.cols + 2, CV_8UC1);
  mask= Scalar::all(0);
  int loDiff = 30;
  int upDiff = 30;
  int connectivity = 4;
  int newMaskVal = 255;
  int NumSeeds = 10;
  Rect ccomp;
  int flags = connectivity + (newMaskVal << 8 ) + CV_FLOODFILL_FIXED_RANGE +
CV_FLOODFILL_MASK_ONLY;
  for(int j=0; j<NumSeeds; j++){
      Point seed;
      seed.x=rects[i].center.x+rand()%(int)minSize-(minSize/2);
      seed.y=rects[i].center.y+rand()%(int)minSize-(minSize/2);
      circle(result, seed, 1, Scalar(0,255,255), -1);
      int area = floodFill(input, mask, seed, Scalar(255,0,0), &ccomp,
```

```
Scalar(loDiff, loDiff, loDiff), Scalar(upDiff, upDiff, upDiff), flags);
```

The `floodFill` function fills a connected component with a color into a mask image starting from a point seed, and sets the maximum lower and upper brightness/color difference between the pixel to fill and the pixel's neighbors or pixel seed:

```
int floodFill(InputOutputArray image, InputOutputArray mask, Point seed,
Scalar newVal, Rect* rect=0, Scalar loDiff=Scalar(), Scalar
upDiff=Scalar(), int flags=4 )
```

The `newval` parameter is the new color we want to incorporate into the image when filling. The `loDiff` and `upDiff` parameters are the maximum lower and maximum upper brightness/color difference between the pixel to fill and the pixel neighbors or pixel seed.

The parameter flag is a combination of the following bits:

- **Lower bits**: These bits contain the connectivity values, four (by default) or eight, used within the function. Connectivity determines which neighbors of a pixel are considered.
- **Upper bits**: These can be 0 or a combination of the following values: CV_FLOODFILL_FIXED_RANGE and CV_FLOODFILL_MASK_ONLY.

CV_FLOODFILL_FIXED_RANGE sets the difference between the current pixel and the seed pixel. CV_FLOODFILL_MASK_ONLY will only fill the image mask and not change the image itself.

Once we have a crop mask, we will get a minimal area rectangle from the image mask points and check the validity size again. For each mask, a white pixel gets the position and uses the `minAreaRect` function to retrieve the closest crop region:

```
//Check new floodFill mask match for a correct patch.
//Get all points detected for get Minimal rotated Rect
vector<Point> pointsInterest;
Mat_<uchar>::iterator itMask= mask.begin<uchar>();
Mat_<uchar>::iterator end= mask.end<uchar>();
for( ; itMask!=end; ++itMask)
    if(*itMask==255)
        pointsInterest.push_back(itMask.pos());
    RotatedRect minRect = minAreaRect(pointsInterest);
    if(verifySizes(minRect)){
```

The segmentation process is finished, and we have valid regions. Now, we can crop each detected region, remove possible rotation, crop the image region, resize the image, and equalize the light of the cropped image regions.

First, we need to generate the transform matrix with `getRotationMatrix2D` to remove possible rotations in the detected region. We need to pay attention to height, because `RotatedRect` can be returned and rotated at 90 degrees. So, we have to check the rectangle aspect and, if it is less than 1, we need to rotate it by 90 degrees:

```
//Get rotation matrix
float r= (float)minRect.size.width / (float)minRect.size.height;
float angle=minRect.angle;
if(r<1)
    angle=90+angle;
Mat rotmat= getRotationMatrix2D(minRect.center, angle,1);
```

With the transform matrix, we now can rotate the input image by an affine transformation (an affine transformation preserves parallel lines) with the `warpAffine` function, where we set the input and destination images, the transform matrix, the output size (same as the input in our case), and the interpolation method to use. We can define the border method and border value if required:

```
//Create and rotate image
Mat img_rotated;
warpAffine(input, img_rotated, rotmat, input.size(),
CV_INTER_CUBIC);
```

After we rotate the image, we will crop the image with `getRectSubPix`, which crops and copies an image portion of width and height centered on a point. If the image is rotated, we need to change the width and height sizes with the C++ `swap` function:

```
//Crop image
Size rect_size=minRect.size;
if(r < 1)
    swap(rect_size.width, rect_size.height);
Mat img_crop;
getRectSubPix(img_rotated, rect_size, minRect.center, img_crop);
```

Cropped images are not good for use in training and classification since they do not have the same size. Also, each image contains different light conditions, accentuating the differences between them. To resolve this, we resize all the images to the same width and height, and apply a light histogram equalization:

```
Mat resultResized;
resultResized.create(33,144, CV_8UC3);
resize(img_crop, resultResized, resultResized.size(), 0, 0, INTER_CUBIC);
//Equalize croped image
Mat grayResult;
cvtColor(resultResized, grayResult, CV_BGR2GRAY);
blur(grayResult, grayResult, Size(3,3));
```

```
equalizeHist(grayResult, grayResult);
```

For each detected region, we store the cropped image and its position in a vector:

```
output.push_back(Plate(grayResult,minRect.boundingRect()));
```

Now that we have possible detected regions, we have to classify whether each possible region is a plate or not. In the next section, we are going to learn how to create a classification based on SVM.

Classification

After we preprocess and segment all possible parts of an image, we now need to decide whether each segment is (or is not) a license plate. To do this, we will use an SVM algorithm.

An SVM is a pattern recognition algorithm included in a family of supervised learning algorithms that was originally created for binary classification. Supervised learning is the machine learning algorithm technique that is trained with labeled data. We need to train the algorithm with an amount of data that is labeled; each dataset needs to have a class.

The SVM creates one or more hyperplanes, which are used to discriminate each class of data.

A classic example is a 2D point set that defines two classes; the SVM searches the optimal line that differentiates each class:

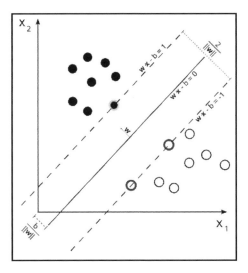

The first task before any classification is to train our classifier; this is a job to be undertaken prior to the main application and is referred to as "offline training." This is not an easy job because it requires a sufficient amount of data to train the system, but a bigger dataset does not always imply the best results. In our case, we do not have enough data due to the fact that there are no public license plate databases. Because of this, we need to take hundreds of car photos, and then preprocess and segment all of them.

We trained our system with 75 license plate images and 35 images without license plates, containing a 144 x 33 pixel resolution. We can see a sample of this data in the following image. This is not a large dataset, but sufficient to obtain decent results for our chapter. In a real application, we would need to train with more data:

To easily understand how machine learning works, we will proceed to use the image pixel features of the classifier algorithm (keep in mind that there are better methods and features to train an SVM, such as **principal components analysis (PCA)**, Fourier transform, and texture analysis).

We need to create the images to train our system using the `DetectRegions` class and set the `savingRegions` variable to `true` in order to save the images. We can use the `segmentAllFiles.sh` bash script to repeat the process on all image files in a folder. This can be taken from the source code of the book.

To make this easier, we will store all image training data that is processed and prepared into an XML file for use directly with the SVM function. The `trainSVM.cpp` application creates this file using the folders and number of image files.

Training data for a machine learning OpenCV algorithm is stored in an *NxM* matrix, with *N* samples and *M* features. Each dataset is saved as a row in the training matrix.

The classes are stored in another matrix with nx1 size, where each class is identified by a `float` number.

OpenCV has an easy way to manage a data file in the XML or YAML formats with the `FileStorage` class. This class lets us store and read OpenCV variables and structures, or our custom variables. With this function, we can read the training data matrix and training classes and save them in SVM_TrainingData and SVM_Classes:

```
FileStorage fs;
fs.open("SVM.xml", FileStorage::READ);
Mat SVM_TrainingData;
Mat SVM_Classes;
fs["TrainingData"] >>SVM_TrainingData;
fs["classes"] >>SVM_Classes;
```

Now, we have the training data in the SVM_TrainingData variable and labels in SVM_Classes. Then, we only have to create the training data object that connects data and labels to be used in our machine learning algorithm. To do this, we will use the TrainData class as an OpenCV pointer Ptr class as follows:

```
Ptr<TrainData> trainData = TrainData::create(SVM_TrainingData, ROW_SAMPLE,
SVM_Classes);
```

We will create the classifier object using the SVM class using the Ptr or with OpenCV 4 using the std::shared_ptr OpenCV class:

```
Ptr<SVM> svmClassifier = SVM::create()
```

Now, we need to set the SVM parameters, which define the basic parameters to use in an SVM algorithm. To do this, we only have to change some object variables. After different experiments, we will choose the next parameter's setup:

```
svmClassifier->setTermCriteria(TermCriteria(TermCriteria::MAX_ITER, 1000,
0.01));
svmClassifier->setC(0.1);
svmClassifier->setKernel(SVM::LINEAR);
```

We chose `1000` iterations for training, a `C` param variable optimization of `0.1`, and finally a kernel function.

We only need to train our classifier with the `train` function and the training data:

```
svmClassifier->train(trainData);
```

Our classifier is ready to predict a possible cropped image using the predict function of our SVM class; this function returns the class identifier `i`. In our case, we will label the *plate* class with one and the *no plate* class with zero. Then, for each detected region that can be a plate, we will use SVM to classify it as *plate* or *no plate*, and save only the correct responses. The following code is a part of a main application called online processing:

```
vector<Plate> plates;
for(int i=0; i< posible_regions.size(); i++)
{
    Mat img=posible_regions[i].plateImg;
    Mat p= img.reshape(1, 1);//convert img to 1 row m features
    p.convertTo(p, CV_32FC1);
    int response = (int)svmClassifier.predict( p );
    if(response==1)
        plates.push_back(posible_regions[i]);
}
```

Plate recognition

The second step in license plate recognition aims to retrieve the characters of the license plate with OCR. For each detected plate, we proceed to segment the plate for each character and use an **artificial neural network** machine learning algorithm to recognize the character. Also, in this section, you will learn how to evaluate a classification algorithm.

OCR segmentation

First, we will obtain a plate image patch as an input to the OCR segmentation function with an equalized histogram. We then need to apply only a threshold filter and use this threshold image as the input of a **Find contours** algorithm. We can observe this process in the following image:

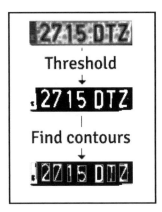

This segmentation process is coded as follows:

```
Mat img_threshold;
threshold(input, img_threshold, 60, 255, CV_THRESH_BINARY_INV);
if(DEBUG)
    imshow("Threshold plate", img_threshold);
    Mat img_contours;
    img_threshold.copyTo(img_contours);
    //Find contours of possibles characters
    vector< vector< Point>> contours;
    findContours(img_contours, contours, // a vector of contours
        CV_RETR_EXTERNAL, // retrieve the external contours
        CV_CHAIN_APPROX_NONE); // all pixels of each contours
```

We used the CV_THRESH_BINARY_INV parameter to invert the threshold output by turning the white input values black and the black input values white. This is needed to get the contours of each character, because the contours algorithm searches for white pixels.

For each detected contour, we can make a size verification and remove all regions where the size is smaller or the aspect is not correct. In our case, the characters have a 45/77 aspect, and we can accept a 35% error of aspect for rotated or distorted characters. If an area is higher than 80%, we will consider that region to be a black block and not a character. For counting the area, we can use the countNonZero function, which counts the number of pixels with a value higher than zero:

```
bool OCR::verifySizes(Mat r){
    //Char sizes 45x77
    float aspect=45.0f/77.0f;
    float charAspect= (float)r.cols/(float)r.rows;
    float error=0.35;
    float minHeight=15;
    float maxHeight=28;
```

```
//We have a different aspect ratio for number 1, and it can be ~0.2
float minAspect=0.2;
float maxAspect=aspect+aspect*error;
//area of pixels
float area=countNonZero(r);
//bb area
float bbArea=r.cols*r.rows;
//% of pixel in area
float percPixels=area/bbArea;
if(percPixels < 0.8 && charAspect > minAspect && charAspect <
maxAspect && r.rows >= minHeight && r.rows < maxHeight)
    return true;
else
    return false;
}
```

If a segmented character is verified, we have to preprocess it to set the same size and position for all characters, and save it in a vector with the auxiliary `CharSegment` class. This class saves the segmented character image and the position that we need to order the characters, because the find contour algorithm does not return the contours in the correct order required.

Character classification using a convolutional neural network

Before we start to work with a convolutional neural network and deep learning, we are going to introduce these topics and the tools to create our DNN.

Deep learning is part of the machine learning family and can be supervised, semi-supervised, or unsupervised. DNNs are not a new concept in the scientific community. The term was introduced into the machine learning community in 1986 by Rina Dechter, and into artificial neural networks by Igor Aizenberg in the year 2000. But research in this area was started in the early 1980, where studies such as neocognitron were the inspiration for convolutional neural networks.

But it wasn't before 2009 that deep learning started its revolution. In 2009, as well as new research algorithms, advances in hardware renewed interest in deep learning using NVidia GPUs to speed up training algorithms that previously could take days or months, and are now 100x faster.

A convolutional neural network, ConvNet, or CNN, is a class of Deep Learning algorithm based on a feed-forward network and applied mainly to computer vision. CNNs use a variation of the multilayer perceptron, allowing us to extract shift invariant features automatically. CNNs use relatively little preprocessing compared to a hand classical machine learning engineered. Feature extraction is a major advantage over other machine learning algorithms.

Convolutional neural networks consist of an input and output layer with multiple hidden layers, like a classical artificial neural network, with the difference that the input normally is the raw pixels of the image and the hidden layers consist of convolutional layers and pooling layers, fully connected or normalized.

Now, we are going to briefly explain the most frequently used layers in a convolutional neural network:

- **Convolutional:** This layer applies a convolution operation filter to the input, passing the result to the next layers. This layer works like a typical computer vision filter (sobel, canny, and so on), but the kernel filters are learned in the training phase. The main benefit of using this layer is to reduce the common fully connected feedforward neural networks, for example, a 100 x 100 image has 10,000 weights, but, using CNN, the problem is reduced to the kernel size; for example, applying a kernel of 5 x 5 and 32 different filters, there are only $5*5*32=800$. At the same time, the filters explode all the possibilities of feature extraction.
- **Pooling:** This layer combines the outputs of a group of neurons into a single one. The most common is max pooling, which returns the maximum value of the group of input neurons. Another frequently used approach in deep learning is average pooling. This layer brings to the CNN the possibility of extracting higher-level features in layers following.
- **Flatten:** Flatten is not a DNN layer, but is a common operation to convert a matrix to a simple vector; this step is required to apply other layers and, finally, get the classification.
- **Fully connected:** This is the same as the traditional multi-layer perceptron, where every neuron in the previous layer is connected to the next layer with an activation function.
- **Dropout:** This layer is a regularization for reducing overfitting; it's a frequently used layer for performing accuracy on the model.
- **Loss layer:** This is normally the last layer in a DNN, and specifies how to train and calculate errors to perform the predictions. A very common loss layer is Softmax for classification.

OpenCV deep learning is not designed to train deep learning models, and it's not supported because there are very stable and powerful open source projects focused only on deep learning, such as TensorFlow, Caffe, and Torch. Then, OpenCV has an interface to import and read the most important models.

Then, we are going to develop our CNN for OCR classification in TensorFlow, which is one of the most frequently used and popular software libraries for deep learning, originally developed by Google researchers and engineers.

Creating and training a convolutional neural network with TensorFlow

This section will explore how to train a new TensorFlow model, but before we start to create our model, we have to check our image dataset and generate the resources that we need to train our models.

Preparing the data

We have 30 characters and numbers, distributed along 702 images in our dataset with the following distribution. We can check that there are more than 30 images for numbers, but some letters such as **K**, **M**, and **P**, have fewer images samples:

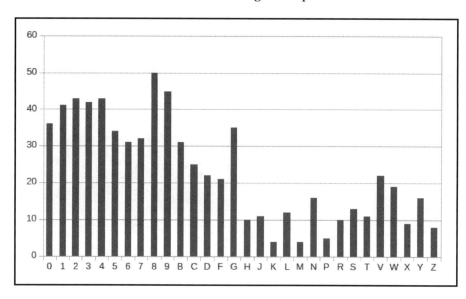

In the following image, we can see a small sample of images from our dataset:

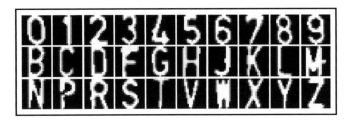

This dataset is very small for deep learning. Deep learning requires a huge amount of samples and is a common technique. In some cases, use a dataset augmentation over the original dataset. Dataset augmentation is a way of creating new samples by applying different transformations, such as rotations, flipping the image, perspective distortions, and adding noise.

There are multiple ways to augment a dataset: we can create our own script or use open source libraries for this task. We are going to use Augmentor (`https://github.com/ mdbloice/Augmentor`). Augmentor is a Python library that allows us to create the number of samples we require by applying the transformations we think are more convenient for our problem.

To install Augmentor through `pip`, we have to execute the following command:

```
pip install Augmentor
```

After installing the library, we create a small Python script to generate and increase the number of samples changing variable `number_samples` and apply the following: random distortion; a shear; and skew and rotation distortion, as we can see in the next Python script:

```
import Augmentor
number_samples = 20000
p = Augmentor.Pipeline("./chars_seg/chars/")
p.random_distortion(probability=0.4, grid_width=4, grid_height=4,
magnitude=1)
p.shear(probability=0.5, max_shear_left=5, max_shear_right=5)
p.skew_tilt(probability=0.8, magnitude=0.1)
p.rotate(probability=0.7, max_left_rotation=5, max_right_rotation=5)
p.sample(number_samples)
```

This script will generate an output folder where all the images will be stored, maintaining the same paths as the original path. We need to generate two datasets, one for training, and another to test our algorithm. Then, we are going to generate one of 20,000 images for training and 2,000 for test by changing the `number_samples`.

Now that we have sufficient images, we have to feed them into the TensorFlow algorithm. TensorFlow allows multiple input data formats, such as a CSV file with images and labels, Numpy data files, and the recommended TFRecordDataset.

 Visit `http://blog.damiles.com/2018/06/18/tensorflow-tfrecodataset.html` for more info about why it is better to use TFRecordDataset instead of CSV files with image references.

Before generating TFRecordDataset, we need to have installed the TensorFlow software. We can install it using `pip` with the following command for the CPU:

```
pip install tensorflow
```

Or, if you have an NVIDIA card with Cuda support, you can use the GPU distribution:

```
pip install tensorflow-gpu
```

Now, we can create the dataset file to train our model using the script provided, `create_tfrecords_from_dir.py`, passing two parameters, the input folder where the images are located, and the output file. We have to call this script twice, once for training and another for testing, to generate both files separately. We can see an example of the call in the next snippet:

```
python ./create_tfrecords_from_dir.py -i ../data/chars_seg/DNN_data/test -o
../data/chars_seg/DNN_data/test.tfrecords
python ./create_tfrecords_from_dir.py -i ../data/chars_seg/DNN_data/train -
o ../data/chars_seg/DNN_data/train.tfrecords
```

The script generates `test.tfrecords` and `train.tfrecords` files, where the labels are numbers assigned automatically and ordered by folder name. The `train` folder must have the following structure:

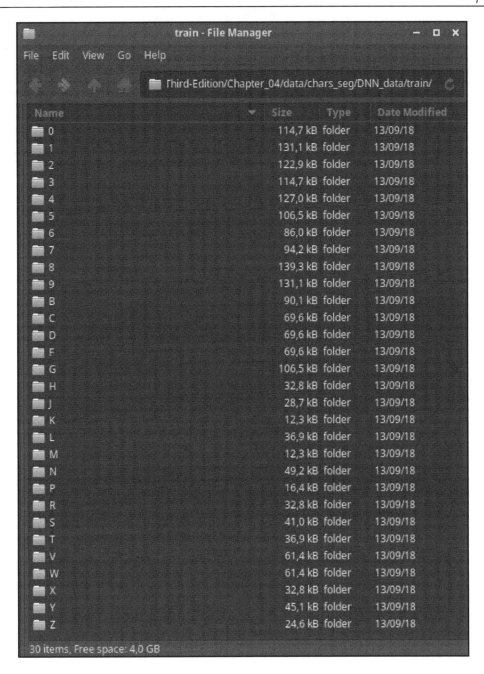

Now, we have the datasets and we are ready to create our model and start to train and evaluate.

Creating a TensorFlow model

TensorFlow is an open source software library that focuses on high-performance numerical computation and deep learning with access and support to CPUs, GPUs, and TPUs (Tensor Process Units, new Google hardware specialized for deep learning purposes). This library is not an easy library and has a high learning curve, but the introduction of Keras (a library on top of TensorFlow) as a part of TensorFlow makes the learning curve easier, but still requires a huge learning curve itself.

In this chapter, we cannot explain how to use TensorFlow because we will require a separate book for this topic alone, but we are going to explain the structure of the CNN we are going to use. We will show how to use an online visual tool called TensorEditor to generate, in a few minutes, TensorFlow code that we can download and train locally on our computer, or use the same online tool to train our model if we don't have enough computer processing power. If you want to read about and learn TensorFlow, we suggest you read any of the relevant Packt Publishing books or the TensorFlow tutorials.

The CNN layer structure that we are going to create is a simple convolutional network:

- **Convolutional Layer 1:** 32 filters of 5 x 5 with ReLU activation function
- **Pooling Layer 2:** Max pooling with 2 x 2 filters and a stride of 2
- **Convolutional Layer 3:** 64 filters of 5 x 5 with ReLU activation function
- **Pooling Layer 4:** Max pooling with 2 x 2 filter and a stride of 2
- **Dense Layer 5:** 1,024 neurons
- **Dropout Layer 6:** Dropout regularization with a rate of 0.4
- **Dense Layer 7:** 30 neurons, one for each number and character
- **SoftMax Layer 8:** Softmax layer loss function with gradient descent optimizer with a learning rate of 0.001 and 20,000 training steps.

We can see a basic graph of the model we have to generate in the following diagram:

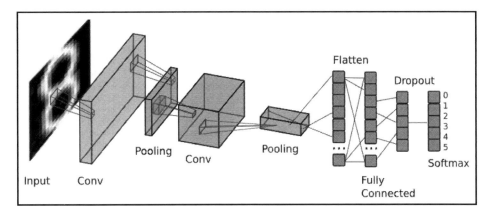

TensorEditor is an online tool that allows us to create models for TensorFlow and train on the cloud, or download the Python 2.7 code and execute it locally. After registering for the online free tool, we can generate the model, as shown in the following diagram:

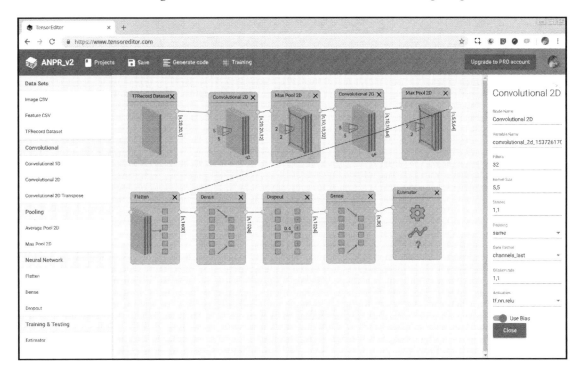

To add a layer, we choose it by clicking on the left-hand menu and it will appear on the editor. We can drag and drop to change its position and double-click to change its parameters. Clicking on the small dots of each node, allows us to link each node/layer. This editor shows us the parameters we choose visually and the output size of each layer; we can see in the following image that the convolutional layer has a kernel of 5 x 5 x 32 and an output of **n x 20 x 20 x 32**; the n variable means that we can compute one or multiple images at the same time for each training epoch:

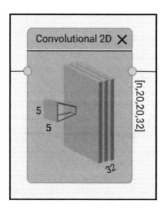

After creating the CNN layer structure in TensorEditor, we can now download the TensorFlow code by clicking on **Generate code** and downloading the Python code, as shown in the following screenshot:

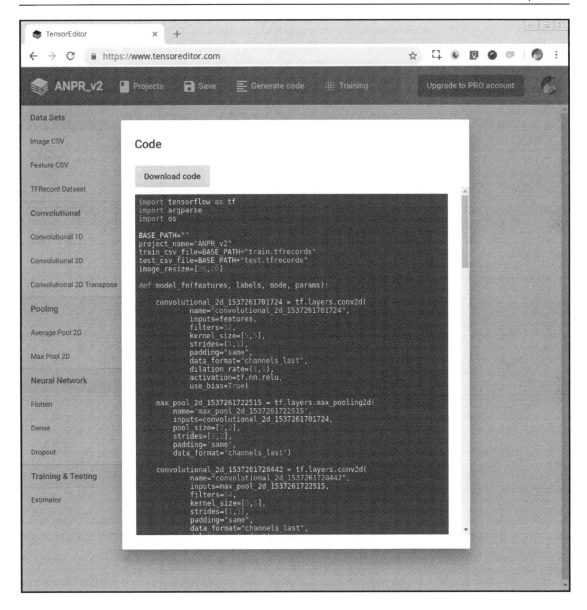

Now, we can start training our algorithm using TensorFlow with the following command:

```
python code.py --job-dir=./model_output
```

Here, the `--job-dir` parameter defines the output folder in which we store the output model trained. In the terminal, we can see the output of each iteration, together with the loss result and accuracy. We can see an example in the following screenshot:

Output of the algorithm training command

We can use TensorBoard, a TensorFlow tool, which gives us information about the training and graphs. To activate TensorBoard, we have to use this command:

```
tensorboard --logdir ./model_output
```

Here, the `--logdir` parameter, where we save our model and checkpoints, must be identified. After launching TensorBoard, we can access it with this URL: `http://localhost:6006`. This awesome tool shows us the graph generated by TensorFlow, where we can explore every operation and variable, clicking on each node, as we can see in the next screenshot:

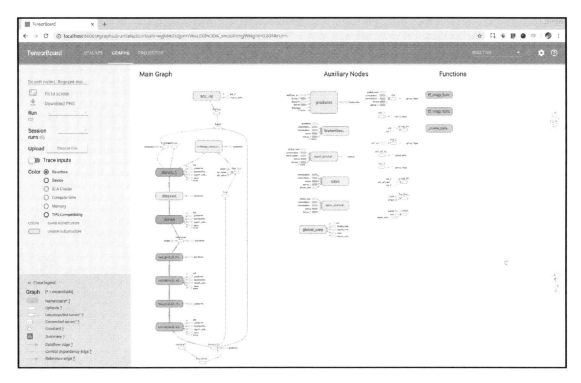

TensorBoard GRAPHS

Or, we can explore the results obtained, such as for loss values in each epoch step or accuracy metrics. The results obtained with the training model per epoch are shown in the following screenshot:

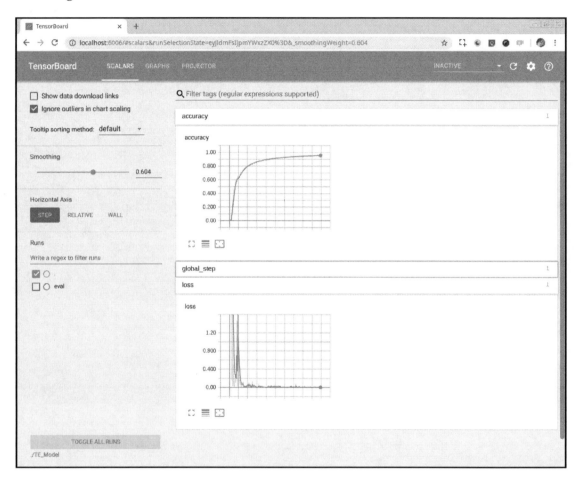

Training on an i7 6700HQ CPU with 8 GB RAM takes a long time, around 50 hours; a bit more than two days of training. If you use a basic NVIDIA GPU, this task can be reduced to around 2-3 hours.

If you want to train in TensorEditor, it can take 10-15 minutes and will download the model after training the models, with the possibility of downloading the full output model or a frozen and optimized model. The concept of freezing will be described in the following section, *Preparing a model for OpenCV*. We can see the result of training in TensorEditor in the next screenshot:

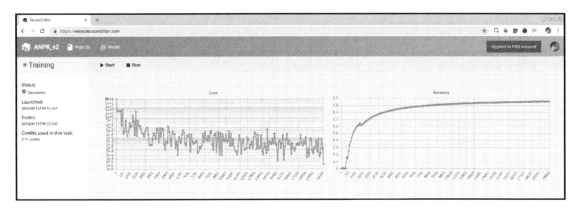

Training in TensorEditor

Analyzing the results obtained, we attain an accuracy level of around 96%, much better than the old algorithm explained in the second edition of this book, where we attained an accuracy level of only 92% using feature extraction and a simple artificial neural network.

After we finish training, all models and variables are stored in the job folder defined when we launched the TensorFlow script. Now, we have to prepare the finished result to integrate and import it into OpenCV.

Preparing a model for OpenCV

TensorFlow generates multiple files when we train a new model, generating files for events that store accuracy and loss, and other metrics obtained in each step; also, some files will store the variable results obtained for each step or checkpoint. These variables are the weights that networks learn in training. But it's not convenient to share all these files in production, as OpenCV would not be able to manage them. At the same time, there are nodes that are used only for training and not for inference. We have to remove these nodes from the model, nodes such as dropouts layers or training input iterators.

To put our model into production, we need to do the following:

- Freeze our graph
- Remove nodes/layers that are not required
- Optimize for inference

Freezing takes the graph definition and a set of checkpoints and merges them together into a single file, converting the variables into constants. To freeze our model, we have to move into the saved model folder and execute the following script provided by TensorFlow:

```
freeze_graph --input_graph=graph.pbtxt --input_checkpoint=model.ckpt-20000
--output_graph frozen_graph.pb --output_node_names=softmax_tensor
```

Now, we generate a new file called *frozen_graph.pb,* which is the merged and frozen graph. Then, we have to remove the input layers used for training purposes. If we review the graph using TensorBoard, we can see that our input to the first convolutional neural network is the `IteratorGetNext` node, which we have to cut and set as a single layer input of a 20 x 20 pixel image of one channel. Then, we can use the TensorFlow *transform_graph* application, which allows us to change the graph, cutting or modifying the TensorFlow model graph. To remove the layer connected to the ConvNet, we execute the following code:

```
transform_graph --in_graph="frozen_graph.pb" --
out_graph="frozen_cut_graph.pb" --inputs="IteratorGetNext" --
outputs="softmax_tensor" --transforms='strip_unused_nodes(type=half,
shape="1,20,20,1") fold_constants(ignore_errors=true) fold_batch_norms
fold_old_batch_norms sort_by_execution_order'
```

It's very important to add the `sort_by_execution_order` parameter to ensure that the layers are stored in order in the model graph, to allow OpenCV to correctly import the model. OpenCV sequentially imports the layers from the graph model, checking that all previous layers, operations, or variables are imported; if not, we will receive an import error. TensorEditor doesn't take care of the execution order in the graph to construct and execute it.

After executing `transform_graph`, we have a new model saved as `frozen_cut_graph.pb`. The final step requires us to optimize the graph, removing all training operations and layers such as dropout. We are going to use the following command to optimize our model for production/inference; this application is provided by TensorFlow:

```
optimize_for_inference.py --input frozen_cut_graph.pb --output
frozen_cut_graph_opt.pb --frozen_graph True --input_names IteratorGetNext -
-output_names softmax_tensor
```

The output of this is a file called `frozen_cut_graph_opt.pb`. This file is our final model, which we can import and use in our OpenCV code.

Import and use model in OpenCV C++ code

Importing a deep learning model into OpenCV is very easy; we can import models from TensorFlow, Caffe, Torch, and Darknet. All imports are very similar, but, in this chapter, we are going to learn how to import a TensorFlow model.

To import a TensorFlow model, we can use the `readNetFromTensorflow` method, which accepts two parameters: the first parameter is the model in protobuf format, and the second is the text graph definition in protobuf format, too. The second parameter is not required, but in our case, we have to prepare our model for inference, and we have to optimize it to import to OpenCV too. Then, we can import the model with the following code:

```
dnn::Net dnn_net= readNetFromTensorflow("frozen_cut_graph_opt.pb");
```

To classify each detected segment of our plate, we have to put each image segment into our `dnn_net` and obtain the probabilities. This is the full code to classify each segment:

```
for(auto& segment : segments){
    //Preprocess each char for all images have same sizes
    Mat ch=preprocessChar(segment.img);
    // DNN classify
    Mat inputBlob;
    blobFromImage(ch, inputBlob, 1.0f, Size(20, 20), Scalar(), true,
false);
    dnn_net.setInput(inputBlob);

    Mat outs;
    dnn_net.forward(outs);
    cout << outs << endl;
    double max;
    Point pos;
    minMaxLoc( outs, NULL, &max, NULL, &pos);
    cout << "---->" << pos << " prob: " << max << " " <<
strCharacters[pos.x] << endl;
    input->chars.push_back(strCharacters[pos.x]);
    input->charsPos.push_back(segment.pos);
}
```

We are going to explain this code a bit more. First, we have to preprocess each segment to get the same-sized image with 20 x 20 pixels. This preprocessed image must be converted as a blob saved in a `Mat` structure. To convert it to a blob, we are going to use the `blobFromImage` function, which creates four-dimensional data with optional resize, scale, crop, or swap channel blue and red. The function has the following parameters:

```
void cv::dnn::blobFromImage (
```

```
         InputArray image,
         OutputArray blob,
         double scalefactor = 1.0,
         const Size & size = Size(),
         const Scalar & mean = Scalar(),
         bool swapRB = false,
         bool crop = false,
         int ddepth = CV_32F
)
```

The definitions of each one are as follows:

- `image`: Input image (with one, three, or four channels).
- `blob`: Output blob mat.
- `size`: Spatial size for the output image.
- `mean`: Scalar with mean values, which are subtracted from channels. Values are intended to be in (mean-R, mean-G, mean-B) order if the image has BGR ordering and `swapRB` is `true`.
- `scalefactor`: Multiplier for image values.
- `swapRB`: A flag that indicates the need to swap the first and last channels in a three-channel image.
- `crop`: A flag that indicates whether the image will be cropped after resizing
- `ddepth`: Depth of output `blob`. Choose `CV_32F` or `CV_8U`.

This generated blob can be added as an input to our DNN using `dnn_net.setInput(inputBlob)`.

Once the input blob is set up for our network, we only need to pass the input forward to obtain our results. This is the purpose of the `dnn_net.forward(outs)` function, which returns a `Mat` with the softmax prediction results. The result obtained is a row of `Mat` where each column is the label; then, to get the label with the highest probability, we only need to get the max position of this `Mat`. We can use the `minMaxLoc` function to retrieve the label value, and if we so desire, the probability value too.

Finally, to close the ANPR application, we only have to save, in the input plate data, the new segment position and the label obtained.

If we execute the application, we will obtain a result like this:

Summary

In this chapter, you learned how an Automatic Number Plate Recognition program works and its two important steps: plate localization and plate recognition.

In the first step, you learned how to segment an image by looking for patches where we may have a plate, and using simple heuristics and the SVM algorithm to make a binary classification for patches with *plates* and *no plates*.

In the second step, you learned how to segment using the find contours algorithm, create a deep learning model with TensorFlow, and train and import it into OpenCV. You also learned how to increase the number of samples in your dataset using augmentation techniques.

In the next chapter, you will learn how to create a face recognition application using eigenfaces and deep learning.

17
Face Detection and Recognition with the DNN Module

In this chapter, we are going to learn the main techniques of face detection and recognition. Face detection is the process whereby faces are located in a whole image. In this chapter, we are going to cover different techniques to detect faces in images, from classic algorithms using cascade classifiers with Haar features to newer techniques using deep learning. Face recognition is the process of identifying a person that appears in an image. We are going to cover the following topics in this chapter:

- Face detection with different methods
- Face preprocessing
- Training a machine learning algorithm from collected faces
- Face recognition
- Finishing touches

Introduction to face detection and face recognition

Face recognition is the process of putting a label to a known face. Just like humans learn to recognize their family, friends, and celebrities just by seeing their face, there are many techniques for recognize a face in computer vision.

These generally involve four main steps, defined as follows:

1. **Face detection**: This is the process of locating a face region in an image (the large rectangle near the center of the following screenshot). This step does not care who the person is, just that it is a human face.
2. **Face preprocessing**: This is the process of adjusting the face image to look clearer and similar to other faces (a small grayscale face in the top center of the following screenshot).
3. **Collecting and learning faces**: This is a process of saving many preprocessed faces (for each person that should be recognized), and then learning how to recognize them.
4. **Face recognition**: This is the process that checks which of the collected people are most similar to the face in the camera (a small rectangle in the top right of the following screenshot).

 Note that the phrase **face recognition** is often used by the general public to refer to finding the positions of faces (that is, face detection, as described in *step 1*), but this book will use the formal definition of face recognition referring to *step 4*, and face detection referring to *Step 1*.

The following screenshot shows the final `WebcamFaceRec` project, including a small rectangle at the top-right corner highlighting the recognized person. Also, notice the confidence bar that is next to the preprocessed face (a small face at the top center of the rectangle marking the face), which in this case shows roughly 70 percent confidence that it has recognized the correct person:

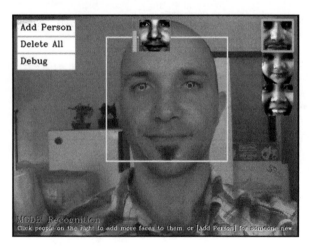

Current face detection techniques are quite reliable in real-world conditions, whereas current face recognition techniques are much less reliable when used in real-world conditions. For example, it is easy to find research papers showing face recognition accuracy rates above 95 percent, but when testing those same algorithms yourself, you may often find that accuracy is lower than 50 percent. This comes from the fact that current face recognition techniques are very sensitive to exact conditions in images, such as the type of lighting, direction of lighting and shadows, exact orientation of the face, expression of the face, and the current mood of the person. If they are all kept constant when training (collecting images), as well as when testing (from the camera image), then face recognition should work well, but if the person was standing to the left-hand side of the lights in a room when training, and then stood to the right-hand side while testing with the camera, it may give quite bad results. So, the dataset used for training is very important.

Face preprocessing aims to reduce these problems by making sure the face always appears to have similar brightness and contrast, and perhaps making sure the features of the face will always be in the same position (such as aligning the eyes and/or nose to certain positions). A good face preprocessing stage will help improve the reliability of the whole face recognition system, so this chapter will place some emphasis on face preprocessing methods.

Despite the big claims about using face recognition for security in the media, it is unlikely that the current face recognition methods alone are reliable enough for any true security system. However, they can be used for purposes that don't need high reliability, such as playing personalized music for different people entering a room, or a robot that says your name when it sees you. There are also various practical extensions to face recognition, such as gender recognition, age recognition, and emotion recognition.

Face detection

Until the year 2000, there were many different techniques used for finding faces, but all of them were either very slow, very unreliable, or both. A major change came in 2001 when Viola and Jones invented the Haar-based cascade classifier for object detection, and in 2002 when it was improved by Lienhart and Maydt. The result is an object detector that is both fast (it can detect faces in real time on a typical desktop with a VGA webcam) and reliable (it detects approximately 95 percent of frontal faces correctly). This object detector revolutionized the field of face recognition (as well as that of robotics and computer vision in general), as it finally allowed real-time face detection and face recognition, especially as Lienhart himself wrote the object detector that comes free with OpenCV! It works not only for frontal faces but also side-view faces (referred to as profile faces), eyes, mouths, noses, company logos, and many other objects.

This object detector was extended in OpenCV v2.0 to also use LBP features for detection based on the work done by Ahonen, Hadid, and Pietikäinen in 2006, as LBP-based detectors are potentially several times faster than Haar-based detectors, and don't have the licensing issues that many Haar detectors have.

OpenCV has implemented deep learning from v3.4 and it's more stable in v4.0. In this chapter, we will show how to use **Single Shot Multibox Detector** (**SSD**) algorithm for face detection.

The basic idea of the Haar-based face detector is that if you look at most frontal faces, the region with the eyes should be darker than the forehead and cheeks, the region with the mouth should be darker than the cheeks, and so on. It typically performs about 20 stages of comparisons like this to decide whether it is a face or not, but it must do this at each possible position in the image, and for each possible size of the face, so in fact, it often does thousands of checks per image. The basic idea of the LBP-based face detector is similar to the Haar-based one, but it uses histograms of pixel intensity comparisons, such as edges, corners, and flat regions.

Rather than have a person decide which comparisons would best define a face, both Haar and LBP-based face detectors can be automatically trained to find faces from a large set of images, with the information stored as XML files to be used later. These cascade classifier detectors are typically trained using at least 1,000 unique face images and 10,000 non-face images (for example, photos of trees, cars, and text), and the training process can take a long time even on a multi-core desktop (typically a few hours for LBP, but one week for Haar!). Luckily, OpenCV comes with some pretrained Haar and LBP detectors for you to use! In fact, you can detect frontal faces, profile (side-view) faces, eyes, or noses just by loading different cascade classifier XML files into the object detector and choosing between the Haar and LBP detector, based on which XML file you choose.

Implementing face detection using OpenCV cascade classifiers

As mentioned previously, OpenCV v2.4 comes with various pretrained XML detectors that you can use for different purposes. The following table lists some of the most popular XML files:

Type of cascade classifier	XML filename
Face detector (default)	`haarcascade_frontalface_default.xml`
Face detector (fast Haar)	`haarcascade_frontalface_alt2.xml`
Face detector (fast LBP)	`lbpcascade_frontalface.xml`

Profile (side-looking) face detector	`haarcascade_profileface.xml`
Eye detector (separate for left and right)	`haarcascade_lefteye_2splits.xml`
Mouth detector	`haarcascade_mcs_mouth.xml`
Nose detector	`haarcascade_mcs_nose.xml`
Whole person detector	`haarcascade_fullbody.xml`

Haar-based detectors are stored in the `data/haarcascades` folder and LBP-based detectors are stored in the `datal/bpcascades` folder of the OpenCV root folder, such as `C:\\opencv\\data\\lbpcascades`.

For our face recognition project, we want to detect frontal faces, so let's use the LBP face detector because it is the fastest and doesn't have patent licensing issues. Note that the pretrained LBP face detector that comes with OpenCV v2.x is not tuned as well as the pretrained Haar face detectors, so if you want more reliable face detection then you may want to train your own LBP face detector or use a Haar face detector.

Loading a Haar or LBP detector for object or face detection

To perform object or face detection, first you must load the pretrained XML file using OpenCV's `CascadeClassifier` class as follows:

```
CascadeClassifier faceDetector;
faceDetector.load(faceCascadeFilename);
```

This can load Haar or LBP detectors just by giving a different filename. A very common mistake when using this is to provide the wrong folder or filename, but depending on your build environment, the `load()` method will either return `false` or generate a C++ exception (and exit your program with an assert error). So it is best to surround the `load()` method with a `try... catch` block, and display an error message to the user if something went wrong. Many beginners skip checking for errors, but it is crucial to show a help message to the user when something did not load correctly; otherwise, you may spend a very long time debugging other parts of your code before eventually realizing something did not load. A simple error message can be displayed as follows:

```
CascadeClassifier faceDetector;
try {
  faceDetector.load(faceCascadeFilename);
} catch (cv::Exception e) {}
if ( faceDetector.empty() ) {
  cerr << "ERROR: Couldn't load Face Detector (";
  cerr << faceCascadeFilename << ")!" << endl;
  exit(1);
}
```

Accessing the webcam

To grab frames from a computer's webcam, or even from a video file, you can simply call the `VideoCapture::open()` function with the camera number or video filename, then grab the frames using the C++ stream operator, as mentioned in the, *Accessing the webcam* section in `Chapter 13`, *Cartoonifier and Skin Color Analysis on the Raspberry Pi.*

Detecting an object using the Haar or LBP classifier

Now that we have loaded the classifier (just once during initialization), we can use it to detect faces in each new camera frame. But first, we should do some initial processing of the camera image just for face detection by performing the following steps:

1. **Grayscale color conversion**: Face detection only works on grayscale images. So we should convert the color camera frame to grayscale.
2. **Shrinking the camera image**: The speed of face detection depends on the size of the input image (it is very slow for large images but fast for small images), and yet detection is still fairly reliable, even at low resolutions. So we should shrink the camera image to a more reasonable size (or use a large value for `minFeatureSize` in the detector, as explained in the following sections).
3. **Histogram equalization**: Face detection is not as reliable in low light conditions. So we should perform histogram equalization to improve the contrast and brightness.

Grayscale color conversion

We can easily convert an RGB color image to grayscale using the `cvtColor()` function. But we should only do this if we know we have a color image (that is, it is not a grayscale camera), and we must specify the format of our input image (usually three-channel BGR on desktop or four-channel BGRA on mobile). So, we should allow three different input color formats, as shown in the following code:

```
Mat gray;
if (img.channels() == 3) {
  cvtColor(img, gray, COLOR_BGR2GRAY);
}
else if (img.channels() == 4) {
  cvtColor(img, gray, COLOR_BGRA2GRAY);
}
else {
  // Access the grayscale input image directly.
  gray = img;
}
```

Shrinking the camera image

We can use the `resize()` function to shrink an image to a certain size or scale factor. Face detection usually works quite well for any image whose size is greater than 240 x 240 pixels (unless you need to detect faces that are far away from the camera), because it will look for any faces larger than the `minFeatureSize` (typically 20 x 20 pixels). So let's shrink the camera image to be 320 pixels wide; it doesn't matter if the input is a VGA webcam or a five megapixel HD camera. It is also important to remember and enlarge the detection results, because if you detect faces in a shrunken image, then the results will also be shrunken. Note that instead of shrinking the input image, you could use a large value for the `minFeatureSize` variable in the detector instead. We must also ensure the image does not become fatter or thinner. For example, a widescreen 800 x 400 image when shrunk to 300 x 200 would make a person look thin. So, we must keep the aspect ratio (the ratio of width to height) of the output the same as the input. Let's calculate how much to shrink the image width by, then apply the same scale factor to the height as well, as follows:

```
const int DETECTION_WIDTH = 320;
// Possibly shrink the image, to run much faster.
Mat smallImg;
float scale = img.cols / (float) DETECTION_WIDTH;
if (img.cols > DETECTION_WIDTH) {
  // Shrink the image while keeping the same aspect ratio.
  int scaledHeight = cvRound(img.rows / scale);
  resize(img, smallImg, Size(DETECTION_WIDTH, scaledHeight));
}
else {
  // Access the input directly since it is already small.
  smallImg = img;
}
```

Histogram equalization

We can easily perform histogram equalization to improve the contrast and brightness of an image, using the `equalizeHist()` function. Sometimes this will make the image look strange, but in general it should improve the brightness and contrast, and help face detection. The `equalizeHist()` function is used as follows:

```
// Standardize the brightness & contrast, such as
// to improve dark images.
Mat equalizedImg;
equalizeHist(inputImg, equalizedImg);
```

Detecting the face

Now that we have converted the image to grayscale, shrunk the image, and equalized the histogram, we are ready to detect the faces using the `CascadeClassifier::detectMultiScale()` function! There are many parameters, listed as follows, that we pass to this function:

- `minFeatureSize`: This parameter determines the minimum face size that we care about, typically 20 x 20 or 30 x 30 pixels, but this depends on your use case and image size. If you are performing face detection on a webcam or smartphone where the face will always be very close to the camera, you could enlarge this to 80 x 80 to have much faster detection, or if you want to detect far away faces, such as on a beach with friends, then leave this as 20 x 20.

- `searchScaleFactor`: This parameter determines how many different sizes of faces to look for; typically it would be `1.1` for good detection, or `1.2` for faster detection, which does not find the face as often.

- `minNeighbors`: This parameter determines how sure the detector should be that it has detected a face; its typically a value of `3`, but you can set it higher if you want more reliable faces, even if many faces are not detected.

- `flags`: This parameter allows you to specify whether to look for all faces (default), or only look for the largest face (`CASCADE_FIND_BIGGEST_OBJECT`). If you only look for the largest face, it should run faster. There are several other parameters you can add to make the detection about 1% or 2% faster, such as `CASCADE_DO_ROUGH_SEARCH` or `CASCADE_SCALE_IMAGE`.

The output of the `detectMultiScale()` function will be a `std::vector` of the `cv::Rect` type object. For example, if it detects two faces, then it will store an array of two rectangles in the output. The `detectMultiScale()` function is used as follows:

```
int flags = CASCADE_SCALE_IMAGE; // Search for many faces.
Size minFeatureSize(20, 20);     // Smallest face size.
float searchScaleFactor = 1.1f;  // How many sizes to search.
int minNeighbors = 4;            // Reliability vs many faces.

// Detect objects in the small grayscale image.
std::vector<Rect> faces;
faceDetector.detectMultiScale(img, faces, searchScaleFactor,
            minNeighbors, flags, minFeatureSize);
```

We can see whether any faces were detected by looking at the number of elements stored in our vector of rectangles, that is, by using the `objects.size()` function.

As mentioned earlier, if we gave a shrunken image to the face detector, the results will also be shrunken, so we need to enlarge them if we want to see the face regions for the original image. We also need to make sure faces on the border of the image stay completely within the image, as OpenCV will now raise an exception if this happens, as shown by the following code:

```
// Enlarge the results if the image was temporarily shrunk.
if (img.cols > scaledWidth) {
  for (auto& object:objects ) {
    object.x = cvRound(object.x * scale);
    object.y = cvRound(object.y * scale);
    object.width = cvRound(object.width * scale);
    object.height = cvRound(object.height * scale);
  }
}
// If the object is on a border, keep it in the image.
for (auto& object:objects) {
  if (object.x < 0)
    object.x = 0;
  if (object.y < 0)
    object.y = 0;
  if (object.x + object.width > img.cols)
    object.x = img.cols - object.width;
  if (object.y + object.height > img.rows)
    object.y = img.rows - object.height;
}
```

Note that the preceding code will look for all faces in the image, but if you only care about one face, then you could change the `flags` variable as follows:

```
int flags = CASCADE_FIND_BIGGEST_OBJECT |
            CASCADE_DO_ROUGH_SEARCH;
```

The `WebcamFaceRec` project includes a wrapper around OpenCV's Haar or LBP detector, to make it easier to find a face or eye within an image, for example:

```
Rect faceRect;     // Stores the result of the detection, or -1.
int scaledWidth = 320;    // Shrink the image before detection.
detectLargestObject(cameraImg, faceDetector, faceRect, scaledWidth);
if (faceRect.width > 0)
cout << "We detected a face!" << endl;
```

Now that we have a face rectangle, we can use it in many ways, such as to extract or crop the face from the original image. The following code allows us to access the face:

```
// Access just the face within the camera image.
Mat faceImg = cameraImg(faceRect);
```

The following photo shows the typical rectangular region given by the face detector:

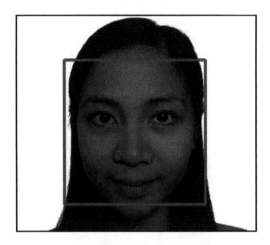

Implementing face detection using the OpenCV deep learning module

From OpenCV 3.4, the deep learning module was available as a contrib source (`https://github.com/opencv/opencv_contrib`), but from version 4.0, deep learning is part of OpenCV core. This means that OpenCV deep learning is stable and in good maintenance.

We can use a pretrained Caffe model based on the SSD deep learning algorithm for faces. This algorithm allows us to detect multiple objects in an image in a single deep learning network, returning a class and bounding box per object detected.

To load the pretrained Caffe, model we need to load two files:

- Proto file or configuration model; in our case, the file is saved in `data/deploy.prototxt`
- Binary trained model, which has the weights of each variable; in our case, the file is saved in `data/res10_300x300_ssd_iter_140000_fp16.caffemodel`

The following code allows us to load the model into OpenCV:

```
dnn::Net net = readNetFromCaffe("data/deploy.prototxt",
"data/res10_300x300_ssd_iter_14000_fp16.caffemodel");
```

After loading the deep learning network, per each frame that we capture with the webcam, we have to convert as a blob image that deep learning network can understand. We have to use the `blobFromImage` function as follows:

```
Mat inputBlob = blobFromImage(frame, 1.0, Size(300, 300), meanVal, false,
false);
```

Where the first parameter is the input image, the second is a scaled factor for each pixel value, the third is the output spatial size, the fourth is a `Scalar` value to be subtracted from each channel, the fifth is a flag to swap the *B* and *R* channels, and the last parameter, and if we set the last parameter to true, it crops the image after resized.

Now, we have prepared the input image for the deep neural network; to set it to the net, we have to call the following function:

```
net.setInput(inputBlob);
```

Finally, we can call to network to predict as follows:

```
Mat detection = net.forward();
```

Face preprocessing

As mentioned earlier, face recognition is extremely vulnerable to changes in lighting conditions, face orientation, face expression, and so on, so it is very important to reduce these differences as much as possible. Otherwise, the face recognition algorithm will often think there is more similarity between the faces of two different people in the same conditions, than between two images of the same person.

The easiest form of face preprocessing is just to apply histogram equalization using the `equalizeHist()` function, like we just did for face detection. This may be sufficient for some projects where the lighting and positional conditions won't change by much. But for reliability in real-world conditions, we need many sophisticated techniques, including facial feature detection (for example, detecting eyes, nose, mouth, and eyebrows). For simplicity, this chapter will just use eye detection and ignore other facial features such as the mouth and nose, which are less useful.

The following photo shows an enlarged view of a typical preprocessed face, using the techniques that will be covered in this section:

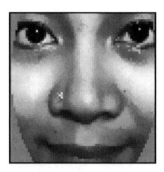

Eye detection

Eye detection can be very useful for face preprocessing, because for frontal faces, you can always assume a person's eyes should be horizontal and on opposite sides of the face, and should have a fairly standard position and size within a face, despite changes in facial expressions, lighting conditions, camera properties, distance to camera, and so on.

It is also useful to discard false positives, when the face detector says it has detected a face and it is actually something else. It is rare that the face detector and two eye detectors will all be fooled at the same time, so if you only process images with a detected face and two detected eyes, then it will not have many false positives (but will also give fewer faces for processing, as the eye detector will not work as often as the face detector).

Some of the pretrained eye detectors that come with OpenCV v2.4 can detect an eye whether it is open or closed, whereas some of them can only detect open eyes.

Eye detectors that detect open or closed eyes are as follows:

- `haarcascade_mcs_lefteye.xml` (and `haarcascade_mcs_righteye.xml`)
- `haarcascade_lefteye_2splits.xml` (and `haarcascade_righteye_2splits.xml`)

Eye detectors that detect open eyes only are as follows:

- `haarcascade_eye.xml`
- `haarcascade_eye_tree_eyeglasses.xml`

As the open or closed eye detectors specify which eye they are trained on, you need to use a different detector for the left and the right eye, whereas the detectors for just open eyes can use the same detector for left or right eyes.

 The `haarcascade_eye_tree_eyeglasses.xml` detector can detect the eyes if the person is wearing glasses, but is not reliable if they don't wear glasses.

If the XML filename says *left eye*, it means the actual left eye of the person, so in the camera image it would normally appear on the right-hand side of the face, not on the left-hand side!

The list of four eye detectors mentioned is ranked in approximate order from most reliable to least reliable, so if you know you don't need to find people with glasses, then the first detector is probably the best choice.

Eye search regions

For eye detection, it is important to crop the input image to just show the approximate eye region, just like doing face detection and then cropping to just a small rectangle where the left eye should be (if you are using the left eye detector), and the same for the right rectangle for the right eye detector.

If you just do eye detection on a whole face or whole photo, then it will be much slower and less reliable. Different eye detectors are better suited to different regions of the face; for example, the `haarcascade_eye.xml` detector works best if it only searches in a very tight region around the actual eye, whereas the `haarcascade_mcs_lefteye.xml` and `haarcascade_lefteye_2splits.xml` detect work best when there is a large region around the eye.

The following table lists some good search regions of the face for different eye detectors (when using the LBP face detector), using relative coordinates within the detected face rectangle (`EYE_SX` is the eye search x position, `EYE_SY` is the eye search y position, `EYE_SW` is the eye search width, and `EYE_SH` is the eye search height):

Cascade classifier	EYE_SX	EYE_SY	EYE_SW	EYE_SH
haarcascade_eye.xml	0.16	0.26	0.30	0.28
haarcascade_mcs_lefteye.xml	0.10	0.19	0.40	0.36
haarcascade_lefteye_2splits.xml	0.12	0.17	0.37	0.36

Here is the source code to extract the left eye and right eye regions from a detected face:

```
int leftX = cvRound(face.cols * EYE_SX);
int topY = cvRound(face.rows * EYE_SY);
int widthX = cvRound(face.cols * EYE_SW);
int heightY = cvRound(face.rows * EYE_SH);
int rightX = cvRound(face.cols * (1.0-EYE_SX-EYE_SW));

Mat topLeftOfFace = faceImg(Rect(leftX, topY, widthX, heightY));
Mat topRightOfFace = faceImg(Rect(rightX, topY, widthX, heightY));
```

The following photo shows the ideal search regions for the different eye detectors, where the `haarcascade_eye.xml` and `haarcascade_eye_tree_eyeglasses.xml` files are best with the small search region, and
the `haarcascade_mcs_*eye.xml` and `haarcascade_*eye_2splits.xml` files are best with larger search regions. Note that the detected face rectangle is also shown, to give an idea of how large the eye search regions are compared to the detected face rectangle:

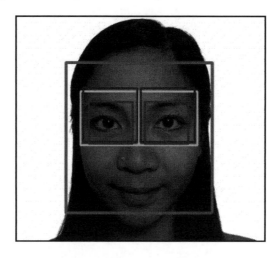

The approximate detection properties of the different eye detectors while using the eye search regions are given in the following table:

Cascade classifier	Reliability*	Speed**	Eyes found	Glasses
haarcascade_mcs_lefteye.xml	80%	18 msec	Open or closed	no
haarcascade_lefteye_2splits.xml	60%	7 msec	Open or closed	no
haarcascade_eye.xml	40%	5 msec	Open only	no
haarcascade_eye_tree_eyeglasses.xml	15%	10 msec	Open only	yes

Reliability values show how often both eyes will be detected after LBP frontal face detection, when no eyeglasses are worn and both eyes are open. If the eyes are closed, then the reliability may drop, and if eyeglasses are worn, then both reliability and speed will drop.

Speed values are in milliseconds for images scaled to the size of 320 x 240 pixels on an Intel Core i7 2.2 GHz (averaged across 1,000 photos). Speed is typically much faster when eyes are found than when eyes are not found, as it must scan the entire image, but `haarcascade_mcs_lefteye.xml` is still much slower than the other eye detectors.

For example, if you shrink a photo to 320 x 240 pixels, perform a histogram equalization on it, use the LBP frontal face detector to get a face, then extract the *left eye region* and *right eye region* from the face using the `haarcascade_mcs_lefteye.xml` values, then perform a histogram equalization on each eye region. Then, if you use the `haarcascade_mcs_lefteye.xml` detector on the left eye (which is actually in the top-right of your image) and use the `haarcascade_mcs_righteye.xml` detector on the right eye (the top-left part of your image), each eye detector should work in roughly 90 percent of photos with LBP-detected frontal faces. So if you want both eyes detected, then it should work in roughly 80 percent of photos with LBP-detected frontal faces.

Note that while it is recommended to shrink the camera image before detecting faces, you should detect eyes at the full camera resolution, because eyes will obviously be much smaller than faces, so you need as much resolution as you can get.

Based on the table, it seems that when choosing an eye detector to use, you should decide whether you want to detect closed eyes or only open eyes. And remember that you can even use one eye detector, and if it does not detect an eye, then you can try with another one.

For many tasks, it is useful to detect eyes whether they are open or closed, so if speed is not crucial, it is best to search with the `mcs_*eye` detector first, and if it fails, then search with the `eye_2splits` detector.

But for face recognition, a person will appear quite different if their eyes are closed, so it is best to search with the plain `haarcascade_eye` detector first, and if it fails, then search with the `haarcascade_eye_tree_eyeglasses` detector.

We can use the same `detectLargestObject()` function we used for face detection to search for eyes, but instead of asking to shrink the images before eye detection, we specify the full eye region width to get better eye detection. It is easy to search for the left eye using one detector, and if it fails, then try another detector (the same for the right eye). The eye detection is done as follows:

```
CascadeClassifier eyeDetector1("haarcascade_eye.xml");
CascadeClassifier eyeDetector2("haarcascade_eye_tree_eyeglasses.xml");
...
Rect leftEyeRect;     // Stores the detected eye.
// Search the left region using the 1st eye detector.
detectLargestObject(topLeftOfFace, eyeDetector1, leftEyeRect,
topLeftOfFace.cols);
// If it failed, search the left region using the 2nd eye
// detector.
if (leftEyeRect.width <= 0)
  detectLargestObject(topLeftOfFace, eyeDetector2,
          leftEyeRect, topLeftOfFace.cols);
// Get the left eye center if one of the eye detectors worked.
Point leftEye = Point(-1,-1);
if (leftEyeRect.width <= 0) {
  leftEye.x = leftEyeRect.x + leftEyeRect.width/2 + leftX;
  leftEye.y = leftEyeRect.y + leftEyeRect.height/2 + topY;
}

// Do the same for the right eye
...

// Check if both eyes were detected.
if (leftEye.x >= 0 && rightEye.x >= 0) {
  ...
}
```

With the face and both eyes detected, we'll perform face preprocessing by combining the following steps:

1. **Geometrical transformation and cropping**: This process includes scaling, rotating, and translating the images so that the eyes are aligned, followed by the removal of the forehead, chin, ears, and background from the face image.
2. **Separate histogram equalization for left and right sides**: This process standardizes the brightness and contrast on both the left- and right-hand sides of the face independently.
3. **Smoothing**: This process reduces the image noise using a bilateral filter.
4. **Elliptical mask**: The elliptical mask removes some remaining hair and background from the face image.

The following photos shows the face preprocessing *Step 1* to *Step 4* applied to a detected face. Notice how the final photo has good brightness and contrast on both sides of the face, whereas the original does not:

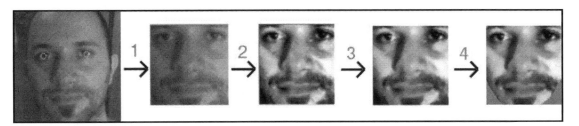

Geometrical transformation

It is important that the faces are all aligned together, otherwise the face recognition algorithm might be comparing part of a nose with part of an eye, and so on. The output of the face detection we've just seen will give aligned faces to some extent, but it is not very accurate (that is, the face rectangle will not always be starting from the same point on the forehead).

To have better alignment, we will use eye detection to align the face, so the positions of the two detected eyes line up perfectly in the desired positions. We will do the geometrical transformation using the `warpAffine()` function, which is a single operation that will do the following four things:

- Rotate the face so that the two eyes are horizontal
- Scale the face so that the distance between the two eyes is always the same
- Translate the face so that the eyes are always centered horizontally, and at the desired height
- Crop the outer parts of the face, since we want to crop away the image background, hair, forehead, ears, and chin

Affine warping takes an affine matrix that transforms the two detected eye locations into the two desired eye locations, and then crops to a desired size and position. To generate this affine matrix, we will get the center between the eyes, calculate the angle at which the two detected eyes appear, and look at their distance apart, as follows:

```
// Get the center between the 2 eyes.
Point2f eyesCenter;
eyesCenter.x = (leftEye.x + rightEye.x) * 0.5f;
eyesCenter.y = (leftEye.y + rightEye.y) * 0.5f;
```

```
// Get the angle between the 2 eyes.
double dy = (rightEye.y - leftEye.y);
double dx = (rightEye.x - leftEye.x);
double len = sqrt(dx*dx + dy*dy);

// Convert Radians to Degrees.
double angle = atan2(dy, dx) * 180.0/CV_PI;

// Hand measurements shown that the left eye center should
// ideally be roughly at (0.16, 0.14) of a scaled face image.
const double DESIRED_LEFT_EYE_X = 0.16;
const double DESIRED_RIGHT_EYE_X = (1.0f - 0.16);

// Get the amount we need to scale the image to be the desired
// fixed size we want.
const int DESIRED_FACE_WIDTH = 70;
const int DESIRED_FACE_HEIGHT = 70;
double desiredLen = (DESIRED_RIGHT_EYE_X - 0.16);
double scale = desiredLen * DESIRED_FACE_WIDTH / len;
```

Now, we can transform the face (rotate, scale, and translate) to get the two detected eyes to be in the desired eye positions in an ideal face, as follows:

```
// Get the transformation matrix for the desired angle & size.
Mat rot_mat = getRotationMatrix2D(eyesCenter, angle, scale);
// Shift the center of the eyes to be the desired center.
double ex = DESIRED_FACE_WIDTH * 0.5f - eyesCenter.x;
double ey = DESIRED_FACE_HEIGHT * DESIRED_LEFT_EYE_Y -
  eyesCenter.y;
rot_mat.at<double>(0, 2) += ex;
rot_mat.at<double>(1, 2) += ey;
// Transform the face image to the desired angle & size &
// position! Also clear the transformed image background to a
// default grey.
Mat warped = Mat(DESIRED_FACE_HEIGHT, DESIRED_FACE_WIDTH,
  CV_8U, Scalar(128));
warpAffine(gray, warped, rot_mat, warped.size());
```

Separate histogram equalization for left and right sides

In real-world conditions, it is common to have strong lighting on one half of the face and weak lighting on the other. This has an enormous effect on the face recognition algorithm, as the left- and right-hand sides of the same face will seem like very different people. So, we will perform histogram equalization separately on the left and right halves of the face, to have a standardized brightness and contrast on each side of the face.

If we simply applied histogram equalization on the left half and then again on the right half, we would see a very distinct edge in the middle because the average brightness is likely to be different on the left and the right side. So to remove this edge, we will apply the two histogram equalizations gradually from the left or right-hand side toward the center, and mix it with a whole face histogram equalization.

Then, the far left-hand side will use the left histogram equalization, the far right-hand side will use the right histogram equalization, and the center will use a smooth mix of the left and right values and the whole face equalized value.

The following screenshot shows how the left-equalized, whole-equalized, and right-equalized images are blended together:

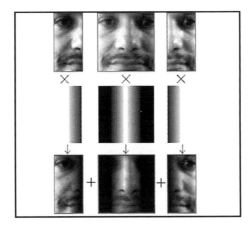

To perform this, we need copies of the whole face equalized, as well as the left half equalized and the right half equalized, which is done as follows:

```
int w = faceImg.cols;
int h = faceImg.rows;
Mat wholeFace;
equalizeHist(faceImg, wholeFace);
int midX = w/2;
Mat leftSide = faceImg(Rect(0,0, midX,h));
Mat rightSide = faceImg(Rect(midX,0, w-midX,h));
equalizeHist(leftSide, leftSide);
equalizeHist(rightSide, rightSide);
```

Now, we combine the three images together. As the images are small, we can easily access the pixels directly using the `image.at<uchar>(y,x)` function, even if it is slow; so let's merge the three images by directly accessing pixels in the three input images and output images, as follows:

```
for (int y=0; y<h; y++) {
  for (int x=0; x<w; x++) {
    int v;
    if (x < w/4) {
      // Left 25%: just use the left face.
      v = leftSide.at<uchar>(y,x);
    }
    else if (x < w*2/4) {
      // Mid-left 25%: blend the left face & whole face.
      int lv = leftSide.at<uchar>(y,x);
      int wv = wholeFace.at<uchar>(y,x);
      // Blend more of the whole face as it moves
      // further right along the face.
      float f = (x - w*1/4) / (float)(w/4);
      v = cvRound((1.0f - f) * lv + (f) * wv);
    }
    else if (x < w*3/4) {
      // Mid-right 25%: blend right face & whole face.
      int rv = rightSide.at<uchar>(y,x-midX);
      int wv = wholeFace.at<uchar>(y,x);
      // Blend more of the right-side face as it moves
      // further right along the face.
      float f = (x - w*2/4) / (float)(w/4);
      v = cvRound((1.0f - f) * wv + (f) * rv);
    }
    else {
      // Right 25%: just use the right face.
      v = rightSide.at<uchar>(y,x-midX);
    }
    faceImg.at<uchar>(y,x) = v;
  } // end x loop
} //end y loop
```

This separated histogram equalization should significantly help reduce the effect of different lighting on the left- and right-hand sides of the face, but we must understand that it won't completely remove the effect of one-sided lighting, since the face is a complex 3D shape with many shadows.

Smoothing

To reduce the effect of pixel noise, we will use a bilateral filter on the face, as a bilateral filter is very good at smoothing most of an image while keeping edges sharp. Histogram equalization can significantly increase the pixel noise, so we will make the filter strength `20.0` to cover heavy pixel noise, and use a neighborhood of just two pixels as we want to heavily smooth the tiny pixel noise, but not the large image regions, as follows:

```
Mat filtered = Mat(warped.size(), CV_8U);
bilateralFilter(warped, filtered, 0, 20.0, 2.0);
```

Elliptical mask

Although we have already removed most of the image background, forehead, and hair when we did the geometrical transformation, we can apply an elliptical mask to remove some of the corner regions, such as the neck, which might be in shadow from the face, particularly if the face is not looking perfectly straight toward the camera. To create the mask, we will draw a black-filled ellipse onto a white image. One ellipse to perform this has a horizontal radius of 0.5 (that is, it covers the face width perfectly), a vertical radius of 0.8 (as faces are usually taller than they are wide), and centered at the coordinates 0.5, 0.4, as shown in the following screenshot, where the elliptical mask has removed some unwanted corners from the face:

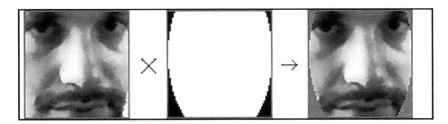

We can apply the mask when calling the `cv::setTo()` function, which would normally set a whole image to a certain pixel value, but as we will give a mask image, it will only set some parts to the given pixel value. We will fill the image in with gray so that it should have less contrast to the rest of the face, as follows:

```
// Draw a black-filled ellipse in the middle of the image.
// First we initialize the mask image to white (255).
Mat mask = Mat(warped.size(), CV_8UC1, Scalar(255));
double dw = DESIRED_FACE_WIDTH;
double dh = DESIRED_FACE_HEIGHT;
Point faceCenter = Point( cvRound(dw * 0.5),
  cvRound(dh * 0.4) );
Size size = Size( cvRound(dw * 0.5), cvRound(dh * 0.8) );
```

```
ellipse(mask, faceCenter, size, 0, 0, 360, Scalar(0),
    CV_FILLED);

// Apply the elliptical mask on the face, to remove corners.
// Sets corners to gray, without touching the inner face.
filtered.setTo(Scalar(128), mask);
```

The following enlarged screenshot shows a sample result from all the face preprocessing stages. Notice it is much more consistent for face recognition at different brightness, face rotations, angles from camera, backgrounds, positions of lights, and so on. This preprocessed face will be used as input to the face recognition stages, both when collecting faces for training and when trying to recognize input faces:

Collecting faces and learning from them

Collecting faces can be just as simple as putting each newly preprocessed face into an array of preprocessed faces from the camera, as well as putting a label into an array (to specify which person the face was taken from). For example, you could use 10 preprocessed faces of the first person and 10 preprocessed faces of a second person, so the input to the face recognition algorithm will be an array of 20 preprocessed faces, and an array of 20 integers (where the first 10 numbers are 0 and the next 10 numbers are 1).

The face recognition algorithm will then learn how to distinguish between the faces of the different people. This is referred to as the training phase, and the collected faces are referred to as the training set. After the face recognition algorithm has finished training, you can then save the generated knowledge to a file or memory and later use it to recognize which person is seen in front of the camera. This is referred to as the testing phase. If you used it directly from a camera input, then the preprocessed face would be referred to as the test image, and if you tested with many images (such as from a folder of image files), it would be referred to as the testing set.

It is important that you provide a good training set that covers the types of variations you expect to occur in your testing set. For example, if you will only test with faces that are looking perfectly straight ahead (such as ID photos), then you only need to provide training images with faces that are looking perfectly straight ahead. But if the person might be looking to the left, or up, then you should make sure the training set also includes faces of that person doing this, otherwise the face recognition algorithm will have trouble recognizing them, as their face will appear quite different. This also applies to other factors, such as facial expression (for example, if the person is always smiling in the training set, but not smiling in the testing set) or lighting direction (for example, a strong light is to the left-hand side in the training set but to the right-hand side in the testing set), then the face recognition algorithm will have difficulty recognizing them. The face preprocessing steps that we just saw will help reduce these issues, but it certainly won't remove these factors, particularly the direction that the face is looking, as it has a large effect on the position of all elements in the face.

One way to obtain a good training set that will cover many different real-world conditions is for each person to rotate their head from looking left, to up, to right, to down, then looking directly straight. Then, the person tilts their head sideways and then up and down, while also changing their facial expression, such as alternating between smiling, looking angry, and having a neutral face. If each person follows a routine such as this while collecting faces, then there is a much better chance of recognizing everyone in real-world conditions.

For even better results, it should be performed again with one or two more locations or directions, such as by turning the camera around 180 degrees, walking in the opposite direction, and then repeating the whole routine, so that the training set would include many different lighting conditions.

So, in general, having 100 training faces for each person is likely to give better results than having just 10 training faces for each person, but if all 100 faces look almost identical, then it will still perform badly, because it is more important that the training set has enough variety to cover the testing set, rather than to just have a large number of faces. So, to make sure the faces in the training set are not all too similar, we should add a noticeable delay between each collected face. For example, if the camera is running at 30 frames per second, then it might collect 100 faces in just several seconds when the person has not had time to move around, so it is better to collect just one face per second while the person moves their face around. Another simple method to improve the variation in the training set is to only collect a face if it is noticeably different from the previously collected face.

Collecting preprocessed faces for training

To make sure there is at least a one-second gap between collecting new faces, we need to measure how much time has passed. This is done as follows:

```
// Check how long since the previous face was added.
double current_time = (double)getTickCount();
double timeDiff_seconds = (current_time -
  old_time) / getTickFrequency();
```

To compare the similarity of two images, pixel by pixel, you can find the relative L2 error, which just involves subtracting one image from the other, summing the squared value of it, and then getting the square root of it. So if the person had not moved at all, subtracting the current face from the previous face should give a very low number at each pixel, but if they had just moved slightly in any direction, subtracting the pixels would give a large number and so the L2 error will be high. As the result is summed over all pixels, the value will depend on the image resolution. So to get the mean error, we should divide this value by the total number of pixels in the image. Let's put this in a handy function, getSimilarity(), as follows:

```
double getSimilarity(const Mat A, const Mat B) {
  // Calculate the L2 relative error between the 2 images.
  double errorL2 = norm(A, B, CV_L2);
  // Scale the value since L2 is summed across all pixels.
  double similarity = errorL2 / (double)(A.rows * A.cols);
  return similarity;
}

...

// Check if this face looks different from the previous face.
double imageDiff = MAX_DBL;
if (old_prepreprocessedFacepreprocessedFace.data) {
  imageDiff = getSimilarity(preprocessedFace,
    old_prepreprocessedFace);
}
```

This similarity will often be less than 0.2 if the image did not move much, and higher than 0.4 if the image did move, so let's use 0.3 as our threshold for collecting a new face.

There are many tricks we can perform to obtain more training data, such as using mirrored faces, adding random noise, shifting the face by a few pixels, scaling the face by a percentage, or rotating the face by a few degrees (even though we specifically tried to remove these effects when preprocessing the face!). Let's add mirrored faces to the training set, so that we have both a larger training set and a reduction in the problems of asymmetrical faces, or if a user is always oriented slightly to the left or right during training but not testing. This is done as follows:

```
// Only process the face if it's noticeably different from the
// previous frame and there has been a noticeable time gap.
if ((imageDiff > 0.3) && (timeDiff_seconds > 1.0)) {
  // Also add the mirror image to the training set.
  Mat mirroredFace;
  flip(preprocessedFace, mirroredFace, 1);

  // Add the face & mirrored face to the detected face lists.
  preprocessedFaces.push_back(preprocessedFace);
  preprocessedFaces.push_back(mirroredFace);
  faceLabels.push_back(m_selectedPerson);
  faceLabels.push_back(m_selectedPerson);

  // Keep a copy of the processed face,
  // to compare on next iteration.
  old_prepreprocessedFace = preprocessedFace;
  old_time = current_time;
}
```

This will collect the `std::vector` arrays, `preprocessedFaces`, and `faceLabels` for a preprocessed face, as well as the label or ID number of that person (assuming it is in the integer `m_selectedPerson` variable).

To make it more obvious to the user that we have added their current face to the collection, you could provide a visual notification by either displaying a large white rectangle over the whole image, or just displaying their face for just a fraction of a second so they realize a photo was taken. With OpenCV's C++ interface, you can use the + overloaded `cv::Mat` operator to add a value to every pixel in the image and have it clipped to 255 (using `saturate_cast`, so it doesn't overflow from white back to black!). Assuming `displayedFrame` will be a copy of the color camera frame that should be shown, insert this after the preceding code for face collection:

```
// Get access to the face region-of-interest.
Mat displayedFaceRegion = displayedFrame(faceRect);
// Add some brightness to each pixel of the face region.
displayedFaceRegion += CV_RGB(90,90,90);
```

Training the face recognition system from collected faces

After you have collected enough faces for each person to recognize, you must train the system to learn the data using a machine learning algorithm suited for face recognition. There are many different face recognition algorithms in the literature, the simplest of which are Eigenfaces and artificial neural networks. Eigenfaces tends to work better than ANNs, and despite its simplicity, it tends to work almost as well as many more complex face recognition algorithms, so it has become very popular as the basic face recognition algorithm for beginners, as well as for new algorithms to be compared to.

Any reader who wishes to work further on face recognition is recommended to read the theory behind the following:

- Eigenfaces (also referred to as **principal component analysis (PCA)**
- Fisherfaces (also referred to as **linear discriminant analysis (LDA)**
- Other classic face recognition algorithms (many are available at http://www.facerec.org/algorithms/)
- Newer face recognition algorithms in recent computer vision research papers (such as CVPR and ICCV at http://www.cvpapers.com/), as there are hundreds of face recognition papers published each year

However, you don't need to understand the theory of these algorithms in order to use them as shown in this book. Thanks to the OpenCV team and Philipp Wagner's libfacerec contribution, OpenCV v2.4.1 provided cv::Algorithm as a simple and generic method to perform face recognition using one of several different algorithms (even selectable at runtime) without necessarily understanding how they are implemented. You can find the available algorithms in your version of OpenCV by using the Algorithm::getList() function, such as with the following code:

```
vector<string> algorithms;
Algorithm::getList(algorithms);
cout << "Algorithms: " << algorithms.size() << endl;
for (auto& algorithm:algorithms) {
  cout << algorithm << endl;
}
```

Here are the three face recognition algorithms available in OpenCV v2.4.1:

- `FaceRecognizer.Eigenfaces`: Eigenfaces, also referred to as PCA, first used by Turk and Pentland in 1991
- `FaceRecognizer.Fisherfaces`: Fisherfaces, also referred to as LDA, invented by Belhumeur, Hespanha, and Kriegman in 1997
- `FaceRecognizer.LBPH`: Local Binary Pattern Histograms, invented by Ahonen, Hadid, and Pietikäinen in 2004

> More information on these face recognition algorithm implementations can be found with documentation, samples, and Python equivalents for each of them on Philipp Wagner's websites (`http://bytefish.de/blog` and `http://bytefish.de/dev/libfacerec/`).

These face recognition-algorithms are available through the `FaceRecognizer` class in OpenCV's `contrib` module. Due to dynamic linking, it is possible that your program is linked to the `contrib` module, but it is not actually loaded at runtime (if it was deemed as not required). So it is recommended to call the `cv::initModule_contrib()` function before trying to access the `FaceRecognizer` algorithms. This function is only available from OpenCV v2.4.1, so it also ensures that the face recognition algorithms are at least available to you at compile time:

```
// Load the "contrib" module is dynamically at runtime.
bool haveContribModule = initModule_contrib();
if (!haveContribModule) {
  cerr << "ERROR: The 'contrib' module is needed for ";
  cerr << "FaceRecognizer but hasn't been loaded to OpenCV!";
  cerr << endl;
  exit(1);
}
```

To use one of the face recognition algorithms, we must create a `FaceRecognizer` object using the `cv::Algorithm::create<FaceRecognizer>()` function. We pass the name of the face recognition algorithm we want to use as a string to this `create` function. This will give us access to that algorithm, if it is available in the OpenCV version. So, it may be used as a runtime error check to ensure the user has OpenCV v2.4.1 or newer. An example of this is shown as follows:

```
string facerecAlgorithm = "FaceRecognizer.Fisherfaces";
Ptr<FaceRecognizer> model;
// Use OpenCV's new FaceRecognizer in the "contrib" module:
model = Algorithm::create<FaceRecognizer>(facerecAlgorithm);
if (model.empty()) {
  cerr << "ERROR: The FaceRecognizer [" << facerecAlgorithm;
```

```
        cerr << "] is not available in your version of OpenCV. ";
        cerr << "Please update to OpenCV v2.4.1 or newer." << endl;
        exit(1);
    }
```

Once we have loaded the `FaceRecognizer` algorithm, we simply call the `FaceRecognizer::train()` function with our collected face data, as follows:

```
    // Do the actual training from the collected faces.
    model->train(preprocessedFaces, faceLabels);
```

This one line of code will run the whole face recognition training algorithm that you selected (for example, Eigenfaces, Fisherfaces, or potentially other algorithms). If you have just a few people with less than 20 faces, then this training should return very quickly, but if you have many people with many faces, it is possible that the `train()` function will take several seconds, or even minutes, to process all the data.

Viewing the learned knowledge

While it is not necessary, it is quite useful to view the internal data structures that the face recognition algorithm generated when learning your training data, particularly if you understand the theory behind the algorithm you selected and want to verify it worked, or find out why it is not working as you hoped. The internal data structures can be different for different algorithms, but luckily they are the same for Eigenfaces and Fisherfaces, so let's just look at those two. They are both based on 1D eigenvector matrices that appear somewhat like faces when viewed as 2D images; therefore, it is common to refer to eigenvectors as Eigenfaces when using the **Eigenface** algorithm or as Fisherfaces when using the **Fisherface** algorithm.

In simple terms, the basic principle of Eigenfaces is that it will calculate a set of special images (Eigenfaces), and blending ratios (Eigenvalues), which when combined in different ways, can generate each of the images in the training set, but can also be used to differentiate the many face images in the training set from each other. For example, if some of the faces in the training set had a moustache and some did not, then there would be at least one eigenface that shows a moustache, and so the training faces with a moustache would have a high blending ratio for that eigenface to show that they contained a moustache, and the faces without a moustache would have a low blending ratio for that eigenvector.

If the training set has five people with twenty faces for each person, then there would be 100 Eigenfaces and Eigenvalues to differentiate the 100 total faces in the training set, and in fact these would be sorted, so the first few Eigenfaces and Eigenvalues would be the most critical differentiators, and the last few Eigenfaces and Eigenvalues would just be random pixel noises that don't actually help to differentiate the data. So it is common practice to discard some of the last Eigenfaces, and just keep the first 50 or so Eigenfaces.

In comparison, the basic principle of Fisherfaces is that instead of calculating a special eigenvector and eigenvalue for each image in the training set, it only calculates one special eigenvector and eigenvalue for each person. So, in the preceding example that has five people with twenty faces for each person, the Eigenfaces algorithm would use 100 Eigenfaces and Eigenvalues, whereas the Fisherfaces algorithm would use just five Fisherfaces and Eigenvalues.

To access the internal data structures of the Eigenfaces and Fisherfaces algorithms, we must use the `cv::Algorithm::get()` function to obtain them at runtime, as there is no access to them at compile time. The data structures are used internally as part of mathematical calculations, rather than for image processing, so they are usually stored as floating-point numbers typically ranging between 0.0 and 1.0, rather than 8-bit `uchar` pixels ranging from 0 to 255, similar to pixels in regular images. Also, they are often either a 1D row or column matrix, or they make up one of the many 1D rows or columns of a larger matrix. So, before you can display many of these internal data structures, you must reshape them to be the correct rectangular shape, and convert them to 8-bit `uchar` pixels between 0 and 255. As the matrix data might range from 0.0 to 1.0, or -1.0 to 1.0, or anything else, you can use the `cv::normalize()` function with the `cv::NORM_MINMAX` option to make sure it outputs data ranging between 0 and 255, no matter what the input range may be. Let's create a function to perform this reshaping to a rectangle and conversion to 8-bit pixels for us, as follows:

```
// Convert the matrix row or column (float matrix) to a
// rectangular 8-bit image that can be displayed or saved.
// Scales the values to be between 0 to 255.
Mat getImageFrom1DFloatMat(const Mat matrixRow, int height)
{
  // Make a rectangular shaped image instead of a single row.
  Mat rectangularMat = matrixRow.reshape(1, height);
  // Scale the values to be between 0 to 255 and store them
  // as a regular 8-bit uchar image.
  Mat dst;
  normalize(rectangularMat, dst, 0, 255, NORM_MINMAX,
    CV_8UC1);
  return dst;
}
```

To make it easier to debug OpenCV code and even more so, when internally debugging the `cv::Algorithm` data structure, we can use the `ImageUtils.cpp` and `ImageUtils.h` files to display information about a `cv::Mat` structure easily, as follows:

```
Mat img = ...;
printMatInfo(img, "My Image");
```

You will see something similar to the following printed on your console:

My Image: 640w480h 3ch 8bpp, range[79,253][20,58][18,87]

This tells you that it is 640 elements wide and 480 high (that is, a 640 x 480 image or a 480 x 640 matrix, depending on how you view it), with three channels per pixel that are 8-bits each (that is, a regular BGR image), and it shows the minimum and maximum values in the image for each of the color channels.

> It is also possible to print the actual contents of an image or matrix by using the `printMat()` function instead of the `printMatInfo()` function. This is quite handy for viewing matrices and multichannel-float matrices, as these can be quite tricky to view for beginners.
> The `ImageUtils` code is mostly for OpenCV's C interface, but is gradually including more of the C++ interface over time. The most recent version can be found at http://shervinemami.info/openCV.html.

Average face

Both the Eigenfaces and Fisherfaces algorithms first calculate the average face that is the mathematical average of all the training images, so they can subtract the average image from each facial image to have better face recognition results. So, let's view the average face from our training set. The average face is named mean in the Eigenfaces and Fisherfaces implementations, shown as follows:

```
Mat averageFace = model->get<Mat>("mean");
printMatInfo(averageFace, "averageFace (row)");
// Convert a 1D float row matrix to a regular 8-bit image.
averageFace = getImageFrom1DFloatMat(averageFace, faceHeight);
printMatInfo(averageFace, "averageFace");
imshow("averageFace", averageFace);
```

You should now see an average face image on your screen similar to the following (enlarged) photo, which is a combination of a man, a woman, and a baby. You should also see similar text to this shown on your console:

```
averageFace (row): 4900w1h 1ch 64bpp, range[5.21,251.47]
averageFace: 70w70h 1ch 8bpp, range[0,255]
```

The image will appear as shown in the following screenshot:

Notice that `averageFace (row)` was a single-row matrix of 64-bit floats, whereas `averageFace` is a rectangular image with 8-bit pixels, covering the full range from 0 to 255.

Eigenvalues, Eigenfaces, and Fisherfaces

Let's view the actual component values in the Eigenvalues (as text), shown as follows:

```
Mat eigenvalues = model->get<Mat>("eigenvalues");
printMat(eigenvalues, "eigenvalues");
```

For Eigenfaces, there is one Eigenvalue for each face, so if we have three people with four faces each, we get a column vector with 12 Eigenvalues sorted from best to worst as follows:

```
eigenvalues: 1w18h 1ch 64bpp, range[4.52e+04,2.02836e+06]
2.03e+06
1.09e+06
5.23e+05
4.04e+05
2.66e+05
2.31e+05
1.85e+05
1.23e+05
9.18e+04
7.61e+04
6.91e+04
4.52e+04
```

For Fisherfaces, there is just one eigenvalue for each extra person, so if there are three people with four faces each, we just get a row vector with two Eigenvalues as follows:

```
eigenvalues: 2w1h 1ch 64bpp, range[152.4,316.6]
317, 152
```

To view the eigenvectors (as Eigenface or Fisherface images), we must extract them as columns from the big eigenvector matrix. As data in OpenCV and C/C++ is normally stored in matrices using row-major order, it means that to extract a column, we should use the Mat::clone() function to ensure the data will be continuous, otherwise we can't reshape the data into a rectangle. Once we have a continuous column, Mat, we can display the eigenvectors using the getImageFrom1DFloatMat() function just like we did for the average face:

```
// Get the eigenvectors
Mat eigenvectors = model->get<Mat>("eigenvectors");
printMatInfo(eigenvectors, "eigenvectors");

// Show the best 20 Eigenfaces
for (int i = 0; i < min(20, eigenvectors.cols); i++) {
  // Create a continuous column vector from eigenvector #i.
  Mat eigenvector = eigenvectors.col(i).clone();

  Mat eigenface = getImageFrom1DFloatMat(eigenvector,
    faceHeight);
  imshow(format("Eigenface%d", i), eigenface);
}
```

The following screenshot displays eigenvectors as images. You can see that for three people with four faces, there are 12 Eigenfaces (left-hand side of the screenshot), or two Fisherfaces (right-hand side of the screenshot):

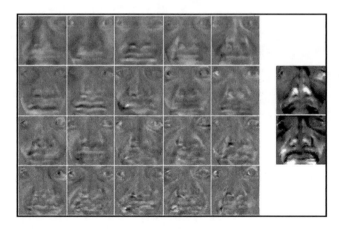

Notice that both Eigenfaces and Fisherfaces seem to have a resemblance to some facial features, but they don't really look like faces. This is simply because the average face was subtracted from them, so they just show the differences for each Eigenface from the average face. The numbering shows which Eigenface it is, because they are always ordered from the most significant Eigenface to the least significant Eigenface, and if you have 50 or more Eigenfaces, then the later Eigenfaces will often just show random image noise and therefore should be discarded.

Face recognition

Now that we have trained the Eigenfaces or Fisherfaces machine learning algorithm with our set of training images and face labels, we are finally ready to figure out who a person is, just from a facial image! This last step is referred to as face recognition or face identification.

Face identification – recognizing people from their faces

Thanks to OpenCV's `FaceRecognizer` class, we can identify the person in a photo simply by calling the `FaceRecognizer::predict()` function on a facial image as follows:

```
int identity = model->predict(preprocessedFace);
```

This `identity` value will be the label number that we originally used when collecting faces for training, for example, zero for the first person, one for the second person, and so on.

The problem with this identification is that it will always predict one of the given people, even if the input photo is of an unknown person, or of a car. It would still tell you which person is the most likely person in that photo, so it can be difficult to trust the result! The solution is to obtain a confidence metric so we can judge how reliable the result is, and if it seems that the confidence is too low, then we assume it is an unknown person.

Face verification—validating that it is the claimed person

To confirm whether the result of the prediction is reliable or it should be taken as an unknown person, we perform **face verification** (also referred to as **face authentication**) to obtain a confidence metric showing whether the single face image is similar to the claimed person (as opposed to face identification, which we just performed, comparing the single face image with many people).

OpenCV's `FaceRecognizer` class can return a confidence metric when you call the `predict()` function, but unfortunately the confidence metric is simply based on the distance in eigen-subspace, so it is not very reliable. The method we will use is to reconstruct the facial image using the *eigenvectors* and Eigenvalues, and compare this reconstructed image with the input image. If the person had many of their faces included in the training set, then the reconstruction should work quite well from the learned eigenvectors and Eigenvalues, but if the person did not have any faces in the training set (or did not have any that have similar lighting and facial expressions to the test image), then the reconstructed face will look very different from the input face, signaling that it is probably an unknown face.

Remember we said earlier that the Eigenfaces and Fisherfaces algorithms are based on the notion that an image can be roughly represented as a set of eigenvectors (special face images) and Eigenvalues (blending ratios). So if we combine all the eigenvectors with the Eigenvalues from one of the faces in the training set, then we should obtain a fairly close replica of that original training image. The same applies with other images that are similar to the training set; if we combine the trained eigenvectors with the Eigenvalues from a similar test image, we should be able to reconstruct an image that is somewhat a replica of the test image.

Once again, OpenCV's `FaceRecognizer` class makes it quite easy to generate a reconstructed face from any input image, by using the `subspaceProject()` function to project onto the eigenspace and the `subspaceReconstruct()` function to go back from the eigenspace to the image space. The trick is that we need to convert it from a floating-point row matrix to a rectangular 8-bit image (like we did when displaying the average face and Eigenfaces), but we don't want to normalize the data, as it is already in the ideal scale to compare with the original image. If we normalized the data, it would have a different brightness and contrast from the input image, and it would become difficult to compare the image similarity just by using the L2 relative error. This is done as follows:

```
// Get some required data from the FaceRecognizer model.
Mat eigenvectors = model->get<Mat>("eigenvectors");
Mat averageFaceRow = model->get<Mat>("mean");
```

```
// Project the input image onto the eigenspace.
Mat projection = subspaceProject(eigenvectors, averageFaceRow,
   preprocessedFace.reshape(1,1));

// Generate the reconstructed face back from the eigenspace.
Mat reconstructionRow = subspaceReconstruct(eigenvectors,
   averageFaceRow, projection);

// Make it a rectangular shaped image instead of a single row.
Mat reconstructionMat = reconstructionRow.reshape(1,
   faceHeight);

// Convert the floating-point pixels to regular 8-bit uchar.
Mat reconstructedFace = Mat(reconstructionMat.size(), CV_8U);
reconstructionMat.convertTo(reconstructedFace, CV_8U, 1, 0);
```

The following screenshot shows two typical reconstructed faces. The face on the left-hand side was reconstructed well because it was from a known person, whereas the face on the right-hand side was reconstructed badly because it was from an unknown person, or a known person but with unknown lighting conditions/facial expression/face direction:

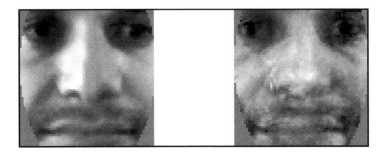

We can now calculate how similar this reconstructed face is to the input face by using the getSimilarity() function we created previously for comparing two images, where a value less than 0.3 implies that the two images are very similar. For Eigenfaces, there is one eigenvector for each face, so reconstruction tends to work well, and therefore we can typically use a threshold of 0.5, but Fisherfaces has just one eigenvector for each person, so reconstruction will not work as well, and therefore it needs a higher threshold, say 0.7. This is done as follows:

```
similarity = getSimilarity(preprocessedFace, reconstructedFace);
if (similarity > UNKNOWN_PERSON_THRESHOLD) {
   identity = -1;     // Unknown person.
}
```

Now, you can just print the identity to the console, or use it wherever your imagination takes you! Remember that this face recognition method and this face verification method are only reliable in the conditions that you train them for. So to obtain good recognition accuracy, you will need to ensure that the training set of each person covers the full range of lighting conditions, facial expressions, and angles that you expect to test with. The face preprocessing stage helped reduce some differences with lighting conditions and in-plane rotation (if the person tilts their head toward their left or right shoulder), but for other differences, such as out-of-plane rotation (if the person turns their head toward the left-hand side or right-hand side), it will only work if it is covered well in your training set.

Finishing touches—saving and loading files

You could potentially add a command-line-based method that processes input files and saves them to disk, or even perform face detection, face preprocessing, and/or face recognition as a web service. For these types of projects, it is quite easy to add the desired functionality by using the `save` and `load` functions of the `FaceRecognizer` class. You may also want to save the trained data, and then load it on program startup.

Saving the trained model to an XML or YML file is very easy, and is shown as follows:

```
model->save("trainedModel.yml");
```

You may also want to save the array of preprocessed faces and labels, if you want to add more data to the training set later.

For example, here is some sample code for loading the trained model from a file. Note that you must specify the face recognition algorithm (for example, `FaceRecognizer.Eigenfaces` or `FaceRecognizer.Fisherfaces`) that was originally used to create the trained model:

```
string facerecAlgorithm = "FaceRecognizer.Fisherfaces";
model = Algorithm::create<FaceRecognizer>(facerecAlgorithm);
Mat labels;
try {
  model->load("trainedModel.yml");
  labels = model->get<Mat>("labels");
} catch (cv::Exception &e) {}
if (labels.rows <= 0) {
  cerr << "ERROR: Couldn't load trained data from "
          "[trainedModel.yml]!" << endl;
  exit(1);
}
```

Finishing touches—making a nice and interactive GUI

While the code given so far in this chapter is sufficient for a whole face recognition system, there still needs to be a way to put the data into the system and a way to use it. Many face recognition systems for research will choose the ideal input to be text files, listing where the static image files are stored on the computer, as well as other important data, such as the true name or identity of the person, and perhaps true pixel coordinates of regions of the face (such as the ground truth of where the face and eye centers actually are). This would either be collected manually or by another face recognition system.

The ideal output would then be a text file comparing the recognition results with the ground truth, so that statistics may be obtained for comparing the face recognition system with other face recognition systems.

However, as the face recognition system in this chapter is designed for learning as well as practical fun purposes, rather than competing with the latest research methods, it is useful to have an easy-to-use GUI that allows face collection, training, and testing interactively from the webcam in real time. So this section will show you an interactive GUI that provides these features. The reader is expected to either use the GUI that comes with this book, or modify it for their own purposes, or ignore this GUI and design their own to perform the face recognition techniques discussed so far.

As we need the GUI to perform multiple tasks, let's create a set of modes or states that the GUI will have, with buttons or mouse clicks for the user to change modes:

- **Startup**: This state loads and initializes the data and webcam.
- **Detection**: This state detects faces and shows them with preprocessing, until the user clicks on the **Add Person** button.
- **Collection**: This state collects faces for the current person, until the user clicks anywhere in the window. This also shows the most recent face of each person. The user clicks either one of the existing people or the **Add Person** button to collect faces for different people.
- **Training**: In this state, the system is trained with the help of all the collected faces of all the collected people.
- **Recognition**: This consists of highlighting the recognized person and showing a confidence meter. The user clicks either one of the people or the **Add Person** button to return to mode 2 (*Collection*).

To quit, the user can hit the *Esc* key in the window at any time. Let's also add a **Delete All** mode that restarts a new face recognition system, and a **Debug** button that toggles the display of extra debug information. We can create an enumerated mode variable to show the current mode.

Drawing the GUI elements

To display the current mode on the screen, let's create a function to draw text easily. OpenCV comes with a cv::putText() function with several fonts and anti-aliasing, but it can be tricky to place the text in the location that you want. Luckily, there is also a cv::getTextSize() function to calculate the bounding box around the text, so we can create a wrapper function to make it easier to place text.

We want to be able to place text along any edge of the window, make sure it is completely visible, and also to allow placing multiple lines or words of text next to each other without overwriting. So here is a wrapper function to allow you to specify either left-justified or right-justified, as well as to specify top-justified or bottom-justified, and return the bounding box so we can easily draw multiple lines of text on any corner or edge of the window:

```
// Draw text into an image. Defaults to top-left-justified
// text, so give negative x coords for right-justified text,
// and/or negative y coords for bottom-justified text.
// Returns the bounding rect around the drawn text.
Rect drawString(Mat img, string text, Point coord, Scalar
  color, float fontScale = 0.6f, int thickness = 1,
  int fontFace = FONT_HERSHEY_COMPLEX);
```

Now to display the current mode on the GUI, as the background of the window will be the camera feed, it is quite possible that if we simply draw text over the camera feed, it might be the same color as the camera background! So, let's just draw a black shadow of text that is just one pixel apart from the foreground text we want to draw. Let's also draw a line of helpful text below it, so the user knows the steps to follow. Here is an example of how to draw some text using the drawString() function:

```
string msg = "Click [Add Person] when ready to collect faces.";
// Draw it as black shadow & again as white text.
float txtSize = 0.4;
int BORDER = 10;
drawString (displayedFrame, msg, Point(BORDER, -BORDER-2),
  CV_RGB(0,0,0), txtSize);
Rect rcHelp = drawString(displayedFrame, msg, Point(BORDER+1,
  -BORDER-1), CV_RGB(255,255,255), txtSize);
```

The following partial screenshot shows the mode and information at the bottom of the GUI window, overlaid on top of the camera image:

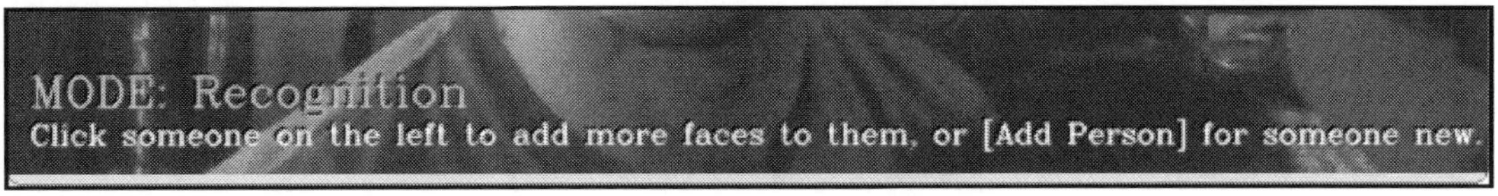

We mentioned that we want a few GUI buttons, so let's create a function to draw a GUI button easily, as follows:

```
// Draw a GUI button into the image, using drawString().
// Can give a minWidth to have several buttons of same width.
// Returns the bounding rect around the drawn button.
Rect drawButton(Mat img, string text, Point coord,
  int minWidth = 0)
{
  const int B = 10;
  Point textCoord = Point(coord.x + B, coord.y + B);
  // Get the bounding box around the text.
  Rect rcText = drawString(img, text, textCoord,
    CV_RGB(0,0,0));
  // Draw a filled rectangle around the text.
  Rect rcButton = Rect(rcText.x - B, rcText.y - B,
    rcText.width + 2*B, rcText.height + 2*B);
  // Set a minimum button width.
  if (rcButton.width < minWidth)
    rcButton.width = minWidth;
  // Make a semi-transparent white rectangle.
  Mat matButton = img(rcButton);
  matButton += CV_RGB(90, 90, 90);
  // Draw a non-transparent white border.
  rectangle(img, rcButton, CV_RGB(200,200,200), 1, LINE_AA);

  // Draw the actual text that will be displayed.
  drawString(img, text, textCoord, CV_RGB(10,55,20));

  return rcButton;
}
```

Now, we create several clickable GUI buttons using the `drawButton()` function, which will always be shown at the top-left of the GUI, as shown in the following partial screenshot:

As we mentioned, the GUI program has some modes that it switches between (as a finite state machine), beginning with the Startup mode. We will store the current mode as the `m_mode` variable.

Startup mode

In the Startup mode, we just need to load the XML detector files to detect the face and eyes and initialize the webcam, which we've already covered. Let's also create a main GUI window with a mouse callback function that OpenCV will call whenever the user moves or clicks their mouse in our window. It may also be desirable to set the camera resolution to something reasonable; for example, 640 x 480, if the camera supports it. This is done as follows:

```
// Create a GUI window for display on the screen.
namedWindow(windowName);

// Call "onMouse()" when the user clicks in the window.
setMouseCallback(windowName, onMouse, 0);

// Set the camera resolution. Only works for some systems.
videoCapture.set(CAP_PROP_FRAME_WIDTH, 640);
videoCapture.set(CAP_PROP_FRAME_HEIGHT, 480);

// We're already initialized, so let's start in Detection mode.
m_mode = MODE_DETECTION;
```

Detection mode

In the Detection mode, we want to continuously detect faces and eyes, draw rectangles or circles around them to show the detection result, and show the current preprocessed face. In fact, we will want these to be displayed no matter which mode we are in. The only thing special about the Detection mode is that it will change to the next mode (*Collection*) when the user clicks the **Add Person** button.

If you remember from the detection step, in this chapter, the output of our detection stage will be as follows:

- `Mat preprocessedFace`: The preprocessed face (if face and eyes were detected)
- `Rect faceRect`: The detected face region coordinates
- `Point leftEye, rightEye`: The detected left and right eye center coordinates

So, we should check whether a preprocessed face was returned, and draw a rectangle and circles around the face and eyes if they were detected, as follows:

```
bool gotFaceAndEyes = false;
if (preprocessedFace.data)
  gotFaceAndEyes = true;

if (faceRect.width > 0) {
  // Draw an anti-aliased rectangle around the detected face.
  rectangle(displayedFrame, faceRect, CV_RGB(255, 255, 0), 2,
    CV_AA);

  // Draw light-blue anti-aliased circles for the 2 eyes.
  Scalar eyeColor = CV_RGB(0,255,255);
  if (leftEye.x >= 0) {    // Check if the eye was detected
    circle(displayedFrame, Point(faceRect.x + leftEye.x,
      faceRect.y + leftEye.y), 6, eyeColor, 1, LINE_AA);
  }
  if (rightEye.x >= 0) {    // Check if the eye was detected
    circle(displayedFrame, Point(faceRect.x + rightEye.x,
      faceRect.y + rightEye.y), 6, eyeColor, 1, LINE_AA);
  }
}
```

We will overlay the current preprocessed face at the top center of the window as follows:

```
int cx = (displayedFrame.cols - faceWidth) / 2;
if (preprocessedFace.data) {
  // Get a BGR version of the face, since the output is BGR.
  Mat srcBGR = Mat(preprocessedFace.size(), CV_8UC3);
  cvtColor(preprocessedFace, srcBGR, COLOR_GRAY2BGR);

  // Get the destination ROI.
  Rect dstRC = Rect(cx, BORDER, faceWidth, faceHeight);
  Mat dstROI = displayedFrame(dstRC);

  // Copy the pixels from src to dst.
  srcBGR.copyTo(dstROI);
}
```

```
// Draw an anti-aliased border around the face.
rectangle(displayedFrame, Rect(cx-1, BORDER-1, faceWidth+2,
    faceHeight+2), CV_RGB(200,200,200), 1, LINE_AA);
```

The following screenshot shows the displayed GUI when in the Detection mode. The preprocessed face is shown at the top center, and the detected face and eyes are marked:

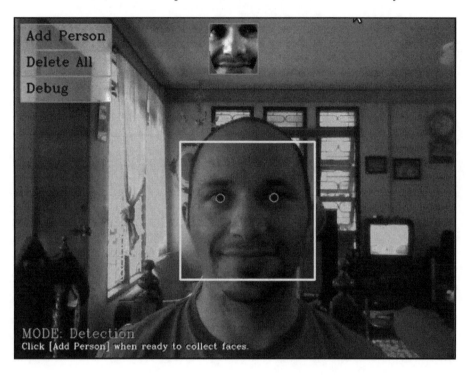

Collection mode

We enter the Collection mode when the user clicks on the **Add Person** button to signal that they want to begin collecting faces for a new person. As mentioned previously, we have limited the face collection to one face per second, and then only if it has changed noticeably from the previously collected face. And remember, we decided to collect not only the preprocessed face, but also the mirror image of the preprocessed face.

In the Collection mode, we want to show the most recent face of each known person and let the user click on one of those people to add more faces to them, or click the **Add Person** button to add a new person to the collection. The user must click somewhere in the middle of the window to continue to the next mode (*Training mode*).

So, first we need to keep a reference to the latest face that was collected for each person. We'll do this by updating the `m_latestFaces` array of integers, which just stores the array index of each person from the big `preprocessedFaces` array (that is, the collection of all faces of the all the people). As we also store the mirrored face in that array, we want to reference the second-last face, not the last face. This code should be appended to the code that adds a new face (and mirrored face) to the `preprocessedFaces` array:

```
// Keep a reference to the latest face of each person.
m_latestFaces[m_selectedPerson] = preprocessedFaces.size() - 2;
```

We just have to remember to always grow or shrink the `m_latestFaces` array whenever a new person is added or deleted (for example, due to the user clicking on the **Add Person** button). Now, let's display the most recent face for each of the collected people on the right-hand side of the window (both in the Collection mode and Recognition mode later) as follows:

```
m_gui_faces_left = displayedFrame.cols - BORDER - faceWidth;
m_gui_faces_top = BORDER;
for (int i=0; i<m_numPersons; i++) {
  int index = m_latestFaces[i];
  if (index >= 0 && index < (int)preprocessedFaces.size()) {
    Mat srcGray = preprocessedFaces[index];
    if (srcGray.data) {
      // Get a BGR face, since the output is BGR.
      Mat srcBGR = Mat(srcGray.size(), CV_8UC3);
      cvtColor(srcGray, srcBGR, COLOR_GRAY2BGR);

      // Get the destination ROI
      int y = min(m_gui_faces_top + i * faceHeight,
      displayedFrame.rows - faceHeight);
      Rect dstRC = Rect(m_gui_faces_left, y, faceWidth,
      faceHeight);
      Mat dstROI = displayedFrame(dstRC);

      // Copy the pixels from src to dst.
      srcBGR.copyTo(dstROI);
    }
  }
}
```

We also want to highlight the current person being collected, using a thick red border around their face. This is done as follows:

```
if (m_mode == MODE_COLLECT_FACES) {
  if (m_selectedPerson >= 0 &&
    m_selectedPerson < m_numPersons) {
    int y = min(m_gui_faces_top + m_selectedPerson *
    faceHeight, displayedFrame.rows - faceHeight);
    Rect rc = Rect(m_gui_faces_left, y, faceWidth, faceHeight);
    rectangle(displayedFrame, rc, CV_RGB(255,0,0), 3, LINE_AA);
  }
}
```

The following partial screenshot shows the typical display when faces for several people have been collected. The user can click on any of the people at the top right to collect more faces for that person:

Training mode

When the user finally clicks in the middle of the window, the face recognition algorithm will begin training on all the collected faces. But it is important to make sure there have been enough faces or people collected, otherwise the program may crash. In general, this just requires making sure there is at least one face in the training set (which implies there is at least one person). But the Fisherfaces algorithm looks for comparisons between people, so if there are less than two people in the training set, it will also crash. So, we must check whether the selected face recognition algorithm is Fisherfaces. If it is, then we require at least two people with faces, otherwise we require at least one person with a face. If there isn't enough data, then the program goes back to the Collection mode so the user can add more faces before training.

To check there are at least two people with collected faces, we can make sure that when a user clicks on the **Add Person** button, a new person is only added if there isn't any empty person (that is, a person that was added but does not have any collected faces yet). If there are just two people, and we are using the Fisherfaces algorithm, then we must make sure an m_latestFaces reference was set for the last person during the Collection mode. Then, m_latestFaces[i] is initialized to −1 when there still haven't been any faces added to that person, and it becomes 0 or higher once faces for that person have been added. This is done as follows:

```
// Check if there is enough data to train from.
bool haveEnoughData = true;
if (!strcmp(facerecAlgorithm, "FaceRecognizer.Fisherfaces")) {
  if ((m_numPersons < 2) ||
  (m_numPersons == 2 && m_latestFaces[1] < 0) ) {
    cout << "Fisherfaces needs >= 2 people!" << endl;
    haveEnoughData = false;
  }
}
if (m_numPersons < 1 || preprocessedFaces.size() <= 0 ||
  preprocessedFaces.size() != faceLabels.size()) {
  cout << "Need data before it can be learnt!" << endl;
  haveEnoughData = false;
}

if (haveEnoughData) {
  // Train collected faces using Eigenfaces or Fisherfaces.
  model = learnCollectedFaces(preprocessedFaces, faceLabels,
        facerecAlgorithm);

  // Now that training is over, we can start recognizing!
  m_mode = MODE_RECOGNITION;
}
else {
  // Not enough training data, go back to Collection mode!
  m_mode = MODE_COLLECT_FACES;
}
```

The training may take a fraction of a second, or it may take several seconds or even minutes, depending on how much data is collected. Once the training of collected faces is complete, the face recognition system will automatically enter the *Recognition mode*.

Recognition mode

In the Recognition mode, a confidence meter is shown next to the preprocessed face, so the user knows how reliable the recognition is. If the confidence level is higher than the unknown threshold, it will draw a green rectangle around the recognized person to show the result easily. The user can add more faces for further training if they click on the **Add Person** button or one of the existing people, which causes the program to return to the Collection mode.

Now, we have obtained the recognized identity and the similarity with the reconstructed face, as mentioned earlier. To display the confidence meter, we know that the L2 similarity value is generally between 0 and 0.5 for high confidence, and between 0.5 and 1.0 for low confidence, so we can just subtract it from 1.0 to get the confidence level between 0.0 to 1.0.

Then, we just draw a filled rectangle using the confidence level as the ratio, shown as follows:

```
int cx = (displayedFrame.cols - faceWidth) / 2;
Point ptBottomRight = Point(cx - 5, BORDER + faceHeight);
Point ptTopLeft = Point(cx - 15, BORDER);

// Draw a gray line showing the threshold for "unknown" people.
Point ptThreshold = Point(ptTopLeft.x, ptBottomRight.y -
  (1.0 - UNKNOWN_PERSON_THRESHOLD) * faceHeight);
rectangle(displayedFrame, ptThreshold, Point(ptBottomRight.x,
ptThreshold.y), CV_RGB(200,200,200), 1, CV_AA);

// Crop the confidence rating between 0 to 1 to fit in the bar.
double confidenceRatio = 1.0 - min(max(similarity, 0.0), 1.0);
Point ptConfidence = Point(ptTopLeft.x, ptBottomRight.y -
  confidenceRatio * faceHeight);

// Show the light-blue confidence bar.
rectangle(displayedFrame, ptConfidence, ptBottomRight,
  CV_RGB(0,255,255), CV_FILLED, CV_AA);

// Show the gray border of the bar.
rectangle(displayedFrame, ptTopLeft, ptBottomRight,
  CV_RGB(200,200,200), 1, CV_AA);
```

To highlight the recognized person, we draw a green rectangle around their face as follows:

```
if (identity >= 0 && identity < 1000) {
  int y = min(m_gui_faces_top + identity * faceHeight,
    displayedFrame.rows - faceHeight);
  Rect rc = Rect(m_gui_faces_left, y, faceWidth, faceHeight);
  rectangle(displayedFrame, rc, CV_RGB(0,255,0), 3, CV_AA);
}
```

The following partial screenshot shows a typical display when running in Recognition mode, showing the confidence meter next to the preprocessed face at the top center, and highlighting the recognized person in the top right corner:

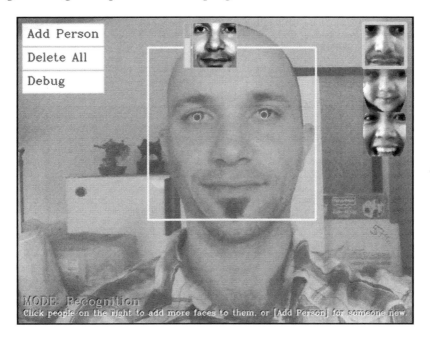

Checking and handling mouse clicks

Now that we have all our GUI elements drawn, we need to process mouse events. When we initialized the display window, we told OpenCV that we want a mouse event callback to our `onMouse` function.

We don't care about mouse movement, only the mouse clicks, so first we skip the mouse events that aren't for the left mouse button click as follows:

```
void onMouse(int event, int x, int y, int, void*)
{
  if (event != CV_EVENT_LBUTTONDOWN)
    return;

  Point pt = Point(x,y);

  ... (handle mouse clicks)
  ...
}
```

As we obtained the drawn rectangle bounds of the buttons when drawing them, we just check whether the mouse click location is in any of our button regions by calling OpenCV's `inside()` function. Now, we can check for each button we have created.

When the user clicks on the **Add Person** button, we add one to the `m_numPersons` variable, allocate more space in the `m_latestFaces` variable, select the new person for the collection, and begin the Collection mode (no matter which mode we were previously in).

But there is one complication: to ensure that we have at least one face for each person when training, we will only allocate space for a new person if there isn't already a person with zero faces. This will ensure that we can always check the value of `m_latestFaces[m_numPersons-1]` to see if a face has been collected for every person. This is done as follows:

```
if (pt.inside(m_btnAddPerson)) {
  // Ensure there isn't a person without collected faces.
  if ((m_numPersons==0) ||
      (m_latestFaces[m_numPersons-1] >= 0)) {
    // Add a new person.
    m_numPersons++;
    m_latestFaces.push_back(-1);
  }
  m_selectedPerson = m_numPersons - 1;
  m_mode = MODE_COLLECT_FACES;
}
```

This method can be used to test for other button clicks, such as toggling the debug flag as follows:

```
else if (pt.inside(m_btnDebug)) {
  m_debug = !m_debug;
}
```

To handle the **Delete All** button, we need to empty various data structures that are local to our main loop (that is, not accessible from the mouse event callback function), so we change to the **Delete All** mode and then we can delete everything from inside the main loop. We must also deal with the user clicking the main window (that is, not a button). If they clicked on one of the people on the right-hand side, then we want to select that person and change to the Collection mode. Or, if they clicked in the main window while in the Collection mode, then we want to change to the Training mode. This is done as follows:

```
else {
  // Check if the user clicked on a face from the list.
  int clickedPerson = -1;
  for (int i=0; i<m_numPersons; i++) {
    if (m_gui_faces_top >= 0) {
      Rect rcFace = Rect(m_gui_faces_left,
      m_gui_faces_top + i * faceHeight, faceWidth, faceHeight);
      if (pt.inside(rcFace)) {
        clickedPerson = i;
        break;
      }
    }
  }
  // Change the selected person, if the user clicked a face.
  if (clickedPerson >= 0) {
    // Change the current person & collect more photos.
    m_selectedPerson = clickedPerson;
    m_mode = MODE_COLLECT_FACES;
  }
  // Otherwise they clicked in the center.
  else {
    // Change to training mode if it was collecting faces.
    if (m_mode == MODE_COLLECT_FACES) {
      m_mode = MODE_TRAINING;
    }
  }
}
```

Summary

This chapter has shown you all the steps required to create a real-time face recognition application, with enough preprocessing to allow some differences between the training set conditions and the testing set conditions, just using basic algorithms. We used face detection to find the location of a face within the camera image, followed by several forms of face preprocessing to reduce the effects of different lighting conditions, camera and face orientations, and facial expressions.

We then trained an Eigenfaces or Fisherfaces machine learning system with the preprocessed faces we collected, and finally we performed face recognition to see who the person is with face verification, providing a confidence metric in case it is an unknown person.

Rather than providing a command-line tool that processes image files in an offline manner, we combined all the preceding steps into a self-contained real-time GUI program to allow immediate use of the face recognition system. You should be able to modify the behavior of the system for your own purposes, such as to allow automatic login on your computer, or if you are interested in improving recognition reliability, then you can read conference papers about recent advances in face recognition to potentially improve each step of the program until it is reliable enough for your specific needs. For example, you could improve the face preprocessing stages, or use a more advanced machine learning algorithm, or an even better face verification algorithm, based on methods at `http://www.facerec.org/algorithms/` and `http://www.cvpapers.com`.

References

- *Rapid Object Detection Using a Boosted Cascade of Simple Features, P. Viola and M.J. Jones, Proceedings of the IEEE Transactions on CVPR 2001, Vol. 1, pp. 511-518*
- *An Extended Set of Haar-like Features for Rapid Object Detection, R. Lienhart and J. Maydt, Proceedings of the IEEE Transactions on ICIP 2002, Vol. 1, pp. 900-903*
- *Face Description with Local Binary Patterns: Application to Face Recognition, T. Ahonen, A. Hadid and M. Pietikäinen, Proceedings of the IEEE Transactions on PAMI 2006, Vol. 28, Issue 12, pp. 2037-2041*
- *Learning OpenCV: Computer Vision with the OpenCV Library, G. Bradski and A. Kaehler, pp. 186-190, O'Reilly Media.*
- *Eigenfaces for recognition, M. Turk and A. Pentland, Journal of Cognitive Neuroscience 3, pp. 71-86*
- *Eigenfaces vs. Fisherfaces: Recognition using class specific linear projection, P.N. Belhumeur, J. Hespanha and D. Kriegman, Proceedings of the IEEE Transactions on PAMI 1997, Vol. 19, Issue 7, pp. 711-720*
- *Face Recognition with Local Binary Patterns, T. Ahonen, A. Hadid and M. Pietikäinen, Computer Vision - ECCV 2004, pp. 469-48*

18
Android Camera Calibration and AR Using the ArUco Module

Mobile devices running Google's Android outnumber all other mobile OSes and, in recent years, they have featured incredible computing power alongside high-quality cameras, which allows them to perform computer vision at the highest levels. One of the most sought after applications for mobile computer vision is **augmented reality (AR)**. Blending real and virtual worlds has applications in entertainment and gaming, medicinel and healthcare, industry and defense, and many more. The world of mobile AR is advancing quickly, with new compelling demos popping up daily, and it is undeniably an engine for mobile hardware and software development. In this chapter, we will learn how to implement an AR application from scratch in the Android ecosystem, by using OpenCV's ArUco `contrib` module, **Android's Camera2 APIs**, as well as the **jMonkeyEngine 3D game engine**. However, first we will begin with simply calibrating our Android device's camera using ArUco's ChArUco calibration board, which provides a more robust alternative to OpenCV's `calib3d` chessboards.

The following topics will be covered in this chapter:

- Introduction to light theory of camera intrinsic parameters and calibration process
- Implementing camera calibration in Android using Camera2 APIs and ArUco
- Implementing a *see-through* AR world with jMonkeyEngine and ArUco markers

Technical requirements

The technologies and softwares used in this chapter are the following:

- OpenCV v3 or v4 Android SDK compiled with the ArUco contrib module: `https://github.com/Mainvooid/opencv-android-sdk-with-contrib`
- Android Studio v3.2+
- Android device running Android OS v6.0+

Build instructions for these components, as well as the code to implement the concepts presented in this chapter, will be provided in the accompanying code repository.

To run the examples, a printed calibration board is required. The board image can be generated programmatically with the ArUco `cv::aruco::CharucoBoard::draw` function, and can then be printed using a home printer. The board works best if it is glued to a hard surface, such as a cardboard or plastic sheet. After printing the board, precise measurements of the board marker's size should be taken (with a ruler or caliper), to make the calibration results more accurate and true to the real world.

The code for this chapter can be accessed through GitHub: `https://github.com/PacktPublishing/Building-Computer-Vision-Projects-with-OpenCV4-and-CPlusPlus/tree/master/Chapter18`.

Augmented reality and pose estimation

Augmented reality (AR) is a concept coined in the early 1990s by Tom Caudell. He proposed AR as a mix between real-world rendering from a camera and computer generated graphics that smoothly blend together to create the illusion of virtual objects existing in the real world. In the past few decades, AR has made great strides, from an eccentric technology with very few real applications, to a multi-billion industry in many verticals: defense, manufacturing, healthcare, entertainment, and more. However, the core concept remains the same (in camera-based AR): register graphics on top of 3D geometry in the scene. Thus, AR has ultimately been about 3D geometry reconstruction from images, tracking this geometry, and 3D graphics rendering registered to the geometry. Other types of augmented reality use different sensors than the camera. One of the most well known examples is AR performed with the gyroscope and compass on a mobile phone, such as in the Pokemon Go app.

In the past, AR was mostly based on using **fiducial markers**, clearly contrasting (mostly black and white), usually rectangular printed markers (see examples of such markers in the following section). The reason for using them was that they can be found easily in the image, for they are high contrast, and they have four (or more) clear corners by which we can calculate the plane of the marker with respect to the camera. This has been the practice since the very first AR applications of the 90s, and it is still a highly used method today in many AR technology prototypes. This type of AR detection will be used in this chapter, but, nowadays AR technology has shifted toward other 3D geometry reconstruction methods, such as **natural markers** (non-rectangular, mostly unstructured), **structure-from-motion (SfM)**, and **mapping-and-tracking** (also known as **simultaneous localization and mapping (SLAM)**).

One other reason for the meteoric rise of AR in recent years is the advent of mobile computing. While in the past, rendering 3D graphics and running complex computer vision algorithms required a powerful PC, today even low-end mobile devices can tackle both tasks with ease. Today's mobile GPUs and CPUs are powerful enough to process much more demanding tasks than fiducial-based AR. Major mobile OS developers, such as Google and Apple, already offer AR toolkits based on SfM and SLAM, with inertial sensors fusion that operate at speeds greater than real-time. AR is also being incorporated into other mobile devices, such as head-worn displays, cars, and even flying drones equipped with cameras.

Camera calibration

In our vision task at hand, recovering geometry in the scene, we will employ the **pinhole camera model**, which is a big simplification of the way images are acquired in our advanced digital cameras. The pinhole model essentially describes the transformation of world objects to pixels in the camera images. The following diagram illustrates this process:

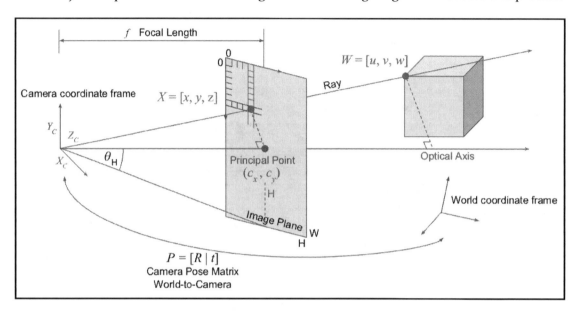

Camera images have a local 2D coordinate frame (in pixels), while the location of 3D objects in the world are described in arbitrary units of length, such as millimeters, meters, or inches. To reconcile these two coordinate frames, the pinhole camera model offers two transforms: **perspective projection** and **camera pose**. The camera pose transform (denoted P in the preceding diagram) aligns the coordinates of the objects with the local coordinate frame of the camera, for example, if an object is right in front of the camera's optical axis at 10 meters away, its coordinates become 0, 0, 10 at meters scale. The pose (a rigid transform) is composed of a rotation R and translation t components, and results in a new 3D position aligned with the camera's local coordinate frame as follows:

$$X = \begin{pmatrix} x \\ y \\ z \end{pmatrix} = R \begin{pmatrix} u \\ v \\ w \end{pmatrix} + t = \begin{pmatrix} r_1 & r_2 & r_3 & t_x \\ r_4 & r_5 & r_6 & t_y \\ r_7 & r_8 & r_9 & t_y \end{pmatrix} \begin{pmatrix} u \\ v \\ w \\ 1 \end{pmatrix} = PW'$$

Where W' are the **homogenous coordinates** of the 3D point W, obtained by adding a one to the end of the vector.

The next step is to project the aligned 3D points onto the image plane. Intuitively, in the preceding diagram we can see the aligned 3D point and the 2D pixel point exist on a ray from the camera center, which imposes an overlapping right triangles (90-degree) constraint. It therefore means if we know the z coordinate and the f coefficient, we can calculate the point on the image plane (x_I, y_I) by dividing by z; this is called the **perspective divide**. First, we divide by z to bring the point to normalized coordinates (distance one from the camera projection center), then we multiply it by a factor that correlates the real camera's focal length and the size of pixels on the image plane. Finally, we add the offset from the camera's center of projection (**principal point**) to end up at the pixel position:

$$x' = x/z$$
$$y' = y/z$$
$$x_I = f_x \cdot x' + c_x$$
$$y_I = f_y \cdot y' + c_y$$

In reality, there are more factors for determining the positions of objects in the image than simply the focal length, such as distortion from the lens (**radial, barrel distortion**), that involve non-linear calculations. This projection transformation is often expressed in a single matrix, known as the **camera intrinsic parameters matrix** and usually denoted by K:

$$s \begin{pmatrix} x_I \\ y_I \\ 1 \end{pmatrix} = KPW' = \begin{pmatrix} f_x & 0 & c_x \\ 0 & f_y & c_y \\ 0 & 0 & 1 \end{pmatrix} \begin{pmatrix} r_1 & r_2 & r_3 & t_x \\ r_4 & r_5 & r_6 & t_y \\ r_7 & r_8 & r_9 & t_y \end{pmatrix} \begin{pmatrix} u \\ v \\ w \\ 1 \end{pmatrix}$$

The process of **camera calibration** is the process of finding the coefficients of K (and the **distortion parameters**), which is a fundamental step for any precise work in computer vision. It is usually done by way of an optimization problem given measurements of correlated 3D and 2D points. Given enough corresponding image points (x_I, y_I) and 3D points (u, v, w), one can construct a **re-projection** cost functor such as the following:

$$L = \sum_i \left\| p_i^I - \hat{K}PW_i' \right\|_{L_2}$$

The re-projection cost function here looks to minimize the Euclidean distance between the original 2D image point p_i and the 3D image as re-projected on the scene using the projection and pose matrices: KPW_i.

Starting from approximate values for the K matrix (the principal point can be, for example, the exact center of the image), we can estimate the values of P in a direct linear fashion by setting up an over-constrained linear system, or an algorithm, such as **Point-n-Perspective (PnP)**. Then, we can proceed iteratively using the gradient over L with regards to to the parameters of K to slowly improve them until convergence, using a gradient descent algorithm such as **Levenberg-Marquardt**. The details of these algorithms are beyond the scope of this chapter; however, they are implemented in OpenCV for the purpose of camera calibration.

Augmented reality markers for planar reconstruction

AR fiducial markers are used for their convenience in finding the plane they lie on with regards to the camera. An AR marker usually has strong corners or other geometric features (for example, circles) that are clearly and quickly detectable. The 2D landmarks are arranged in a way that is pre-known to the detector, so we can easily establish 2D-3D point correspondence. The following are examples of AR fiducial markers:

In this example, there are several types of 2D landmarks. In the rectangular markers, these are the corners of the rectangles and the inner rectangles, while in the QR code (middle), these are the three big boxed rectangles. The non-rectangular markers are using the center of the circles as the 2D positions.

Given our 2D points on the marker and their paired 3D coordinates (in millimeters), we can write the following equation for each pair, using the principles we saw in the last section:

$$
\begin{pmatrix} x_i \\ y_i \\ 1 \end{pmatrix} = \underbrace{[\,R_{3\times3} \quad t\,]}_{P} W_i' = \begin{pmatrix} r_1 & r_2 & r_3 & t_x \\ r_4 & r_5 & r_6 & t_y \\ r_7 & r_8 & r_9 & t_y \end{pmatrix} \begin{pmatrix} u_i \\ v_i \\ 0 \\ 1 \end{pmatrix} = \begin{pmatrix} r_1 & r_2 & t_x \\ r_4 & r_5 & t_y \\ r_7 & r_8 & t_z \end{pmatrix} \begin{pmatrix} u_i \\ v_i \\ 1 \end{pmatrix}
$$

Notice that since the marker is flat and, without loss of generality, it exists on the ground plane, its z-coordinate is zero, and we can therefore omit the third column of the P matrix. We are left with a 3 x 3 matrix to find. Note we can still recover the entire rotation matrix; since it is orthonormal, we can use the first two columns to find the third by a cross product: $R^3 = R^1 \times R^2$. The remaining 3 x 3 matrix is a **homography**; it transforms between one plane (image plane) and another (marker plane). We can estimate the values of the matrix by constructing a system of homogeneous linear equations, as follows:

$$
\begin{pmatrix} x_i \\ y_i \\ 1 \end{pmatrix} - \begin{pmatrix} r_1 & r_2 & t_x \\ r_4 & r_5 & t_y \\ r_7 & r_8 & t_z \end{pmatrix} \begin{pmatrix} u_i \\ v_i \\ 1 \end{pmatrix} = \begin{pmatrix} 0 \\ 0 \\ 0 \end{pmatrix}
$$

Which can be worked into the following homogenous system of equations:

$$
\begin{pmatrix}
x_1 & -u_1 & -v_1 & -1 & 0 & 0 & 0 & 0 & 0 & 0 & 0 & 0 \\
0 & 0 & 0 & 0 & y_1 & -u_1 & -v_1 & -1 & 0 & 0 & 0 & 0 \\
0 & 0 & 0 & 0 & 0 & 0 & 0 & 0 & 1 & -u_1 & -v_1 & -1 \\
\vdots & \vdots & \vdots & \vdots & \vdots & \vdots & \vdots & \vdots & \vdots & \vdots & \vdots & \vdots \\
x_n & -u_n & -v_n & -1 & 0 & 0 & 0 & 0 & 0 & 0 & 0 & 0 \\
0 & 0 & 0 & 0 & y_n & -u_n & -v_n & -1 & 0 & 0 & 0 & 0 \\
0 & 0 & 0 & 0 & 0 & 0 & 0 & 0 & 1 & -u_n & -v_n & -1
\end{pmatrix}
\begin{pmatrix} 1 \\ r_1 \\ r_2 \\ t_x \\ 1 \\ r_4 \\ r_5 \\ t_y \\ 1 \\ r_8 \\ r_9 \\ t_z \end{pmatrix}
=
\begin{pmatrix} 0 \\ 0 \\ 0 \\ \vdots \\ 0 \\ 0 \\ 0 \end{pmatrix}
$$

We can solve this problem by taking the **singular value decomposition** of the A matrix, $A = U\Sigma V^t$, and the last column of V as the solution, and we can find P. This will only work with a planar marker, because of our flatness assumption from before. For calibration with 3D objects, more instrumentation of the linear system is needed in order to recover a valid orthonormal rotation. Other algorithms also exist, such as the **Perspective-n-Point (PnP)** algorithm we mentioned earlier. This concludes the theoretical underpinning we will need for creating an augmented reality effect. In the next chapter, we will begin constructing an application in Android to implement these ideas.

Camera access in Android OS

Most, if not all, mobile phone devices running Android are equipped with a video-capable camera, and the Android OS provides APIs to access the raw data stream from it. Up until Android version 5 (API level 21), Google recommended using the older Camera API; however, in recent versions, the API was deprecated in favor of the new Camera2 API, which we will use. A good example guide for using the Camera2 API is provided for Android developers by Google: `https://github.com/googlesamples/android-Camera2Basic`. In this section, we will only recount a few important elements, and the complete code can be viewed in the accompanying repository.

First, using the camera requires user permissions. In the `AndroidManifest.xml` file, we flag the following:

```
<uses-permission android:name="android.permission.CAMERA" />
<uses-permission
android:name="android.permission.WRITE_EXTERNAL_STORAGE" />
<uses-permission
android:name="android.permission.READ_EXTERNAL_STORAGE"/>
```

We also request file storage access for saving intermediate data or debugging images. The next step is to request permissions from the user, if not already granted earlier, with an on-screen dialog as soon as the application starts:

```
if (context.checkSelfPermission(Manifest.permission.CAMERA) !=
PackageManager.PERMISSION_GRANTED) {
    context.requestPermissions(new String[] { Manifest.permission.CAMERA },
REQUEST_PERMISSION_CODE);
    return; // break until next time, after user approves
}
```

Note that some further instrumentation is needed to handle the return from the permissions request.

Finding and opening the camera

Next, we try to find a suitable back-facing camera by scanning the list of available cameras on the device. A characteristics flag is given to the camera if it's back-facing, as follows:

```
CameraManager manager = (CameraManager)
context.getSystemService(Context.CAMERA_SERVICE);
try {
    String camList[] = manager.getCameraIdList();
    mCameraID = camList[0]; // save as a class member - mCameraID
    for (String cameraID : camList) {
        CameraCharacteristics characteristics =
manager.getCameraCharacteristics(cameraID);
        if(characteristics.get(CameraCharacteristics.LENS_FACING) ==
CameraCharacteristics.LENS_FACING_BACK) {
            mCameraID = cameraID;
            break;
        }
    }
    Log.i(LOGTAG, "Opening camera: " + mCameraID);
    CameraCharacteristics characteristics =
manager.getCameraCharacteristics(mCameraID);
    manager.openCamera(mCameraID, mStateCallback, mBackgroundHandler);
} catch (...) {
    /* ... */
}
```

When the camera is opened, we look through the list of available image resolutions and pick a good size. A good size will be something not too big, so calculation won't be lengthy, and a resolution that corresponds with the screen resolution, so it covers the entire screen:

```
final int width = 1280; // 1280x720 is a good wide-format size, but we can
query the
final int height = 720; // screen to see precisely what resolution it is.

CameraCharacteristics characteristics =
manager.getCameraCharacteristics(mCameraID);
StreamConfigurationMap map =
characteristics.get(CameraCharacteristics.SCALER_STREAM_CONFIGURATION_MAP);
int bestWidth = 0, bestHeight = 0;
final float aspect = (float)width / height;
for (Size psize : map.getOutputSizes(ImageFormat.YUV_420_888)) {
    final int w = psize.getWidth(), h = psize.getHeight();
    // accept the size if it's close to our target and has similar aspect
ratio
    if ( width >= w && height >= h &&
        bestWidth <= w && bestHeight <= h &&
```

```
        Math.abs(aspect - (float)w/h) < 0.2 )
    {
        bestWidth = w;
        bestHeight = h;
    }
}
```

We're now ready to request access to the video feed. We will be requesting access to the raw data coming from the camera. Almost all Android devices will provide a YUV 420 stream, so it's good practice to target that format; however, we will need a conversion step to get RGB data, as follows:

```
mImageReader = ImageReader.newInstance(mPreviewSize.getWidth(),
mPreviewSize.getHeight(), ImageFormat.YUV_420_888, 2);
// The ImageAvailableListener will get a function call with each frame
mImageReader.setOnImageAvailableListener(mHandler, mBackgroundHandler);

mPreviewRequestBuilder =
mCameraDevice.createCaptureRequest(CameraDevice.TEMPLATE_PREVIEW);
mPreviewRequestBuilder.addTarget(mImageReader.getSurface());

mCameraDevice.createCaptureSession(Arrays.asList(mImageReader.getSurface())
,
        new CameraCaptureSession.StateCallback() {
            @Override
            public void onConfigured( CameraCaptureSession
cameraCaptureSession) {
                mCaptureSession = cameraCaptureSession;
                // ... setup auto-focus here
                mHandler.onCameraSetup(mPreviewSize); // notify interested
parties
            }

            @Override
            public void onConfigureFailed(CameraCaptureSession
cameraCaptureSession) {
                Log.e(LOGTAG, "createCameraPreviewSession failed");
            }
        }, mBackgroundHandler);
```

From this point on, our class that
implements `ImageReader.OnImageAvailableListener` will be called with each frame
and we can access the pixels:

```
@Override
public void onImageAvailable(ImageReader imageReader) {
    android.media.Image image = imageReader.acquireLatestImage();
    //such as getting a grayscale image by taking just the Y component
(from YUV)
    mPreviewByteBufferGray.rewind();
    ByteBuffer buffer = image.getPlanes()[0].getBuffer();
    buffer.rewind();
    buffer.get(mPreviewByteBufferGray.array());
    image.close(); // release the image - Important!
}
```

At this point, we can send the byte buffer for processing in OpenCV. Next up, we will
develop the camera calibration process with the `aruco` module.

Camera calibration with ArUco

To perform camera calibration as we discussed earlier, we must obtain corresponding
2D-3D point pairings. With ArUco marker detection, this task is made simple. ArUco
provides a tool to create a **calibration board**, a grid of squares and AR markers, in which all
the parameters are known: number, size, and position of markers. We can print such a
board with our home or office printer, with the image for printing supplied by the ArUco
API:

```
Ptr<aruco::Dictionary> dict =
aruco::Dictionary::get(aruco::DICT_ARUCO_ORIGINAL);
Ptr<aruco::GridBoard> board = aruco::GridBoard::create(
    10      /* N markers x */,
    7       /* M markers y */,
    14.0f   /* marker width (mm) */,
    9.2f    /* marker separation (mm) */,
    dict);
Mat boardImage;
board->draw({1000, 700}, boardImage, 25); // an image of 1000x700 pixels
cv::imwrite("ArucoBoard.png", boardImage);
```

Here is an example of such a board image, a result of the preceding code:

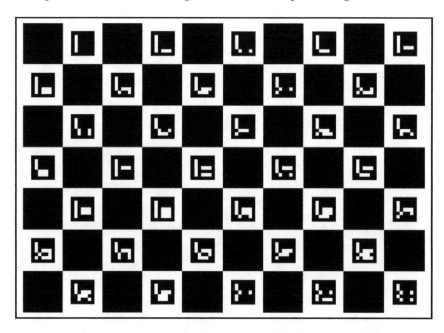

We need to obtain multiple views of the board by moving either the camera or the board. It is handy to paste the board on a piece of rigid cardboard or plastic to keep the paper flat while moving the board, or keep it flat on a table while moving the camera around it. We can implement a very simple Android UI for capturing the images with just three buttons, **CAPTURE**, **CALIBRATE**, and **DONE**:

The **CAPTURE** button simply grabs the grayscale image buffer, as we saw earlier, and calls a native C++ function to detect the ArUco markers and save them to memory:

```
extern "C"
JNIEXPORT jint JNICALL
Java_com_packt_masteringopencv4_opencvarucoar_CalibrationActivity_addCalibr
ation8UImage(
```

```
    JNIEnv *env,
    jclass type,
    jbyteArray data_, // java: byte[] , a 8 uchar grayscale image buffer
    jint w,
    jint h)
{
    jbyte *data = env->GetByteArrayElements(data_, NULL);
    Mat grayImage(h, w, CV_8UC1, data);

    vector< int > ids;
    vector< vector< Point2f > > corners, rejected;

    // detect markers
    aruco::detectMarkers(grayImage, dict, corners, ids, params, rejected);
    __android_log_print(ANDROID_LOG_DEBUG, LOGTAG, "found %d markers",
ids.size());

    allCorners.push_back(corners);
    allIds.push_back(ids);
    allImgs.push_back(grayImage.clone());
    imgSize = grayImage.size();

    __android_log_print(ANDROID_LOG_DEBUG, LOGTAG, "%d captures",
allImgs.size());

    env->ReleaseByteArrayElements(data_, data, 0);

    return allImgs.size(); // return the number of captured images so far
}
```

Here is an example of ArUco marker boards detected using the previous function. A visualization of the detected markers can be achieved with `cv::aruco::drawDetectedMarkers`. Points from the markers that were detected properly will be used for calibration:

After obtaining enough images (around 10 images from various viewpoints is usually sufficient), the **CALIBRATE** button calls another native function that runs the `aruco::calibrateCameraAruco` function, with the saved arrays of point correspondences as follows:

```
extern "C"
JNIEXPORT void JNICALL
Java_com_packt_masteringopencv4_opencvarucoar_CalibrationActivity_doCalibra
tion(
    JNIEnv *env,
    jclass type)
{

    vector< Mat > rvecs, tvecs;

    cameraMatrix = Mat::eye(3, 3, CV_64F);
    cameraMatrix.at< double >(0, 0) = 1.0;

    // prepare data for calibration: put all marker points in a single
array
    vector< vector< Point2f > > allCornersConcatenated;
    vector< int > allIdsConcatenated;
    vector< int > markerCounterPerFrame;
    markerCounterPerFrame.reserve(allCorners.size());
    for (unsigned int i = 0; i < allCorners.size(); i++) {
        markerCounterPerFrame.push_back((int)allCorners[i].size());
        for (unsigned int j = 0; j < allCorners[i].size(); j++) {
            allCornersConcatenated.push_back(allCorners[i][j]);
            allIdsConcatenated.push_back(allIds[i][j]);
        }
    }

    // calibrate camera using aruco markers
    double arucoRepErr;
    arucoRepErr = aruco::calibrateCameraAruco(allCornersConcatenated,
                                              allIdsConcatenated,
                                              markerCounterPerFrame,
                                              board, imgSize, cameraMatrix,
                                              distCoeffs, rvecs, tvecs,
CALIB_FIX_ASPECT_RATIO);

    __android_log_print(ANDROID_LOG_DEBUG, LOGTAG, "reprojection err:
%.3f", arucoRepErr);
    stringstream ss;
    ss << cameraMatrix << endl << distCoeffs;
    __android_log_print(ANDROID_LOG_DEBUG, LOGTAG, "calibration: %s",
ss.str().c_str());
```

```
    // save the calibration to file
    cv::FileStorage fs("/sdcard/calibration.yml", FileStorage::WRITE);
    fs.write("cameraMatrix", cameraMatrix);
    fs.write("distCoeffs", distCoeffs);
    fs.release();
}
```

The **DONE** button will advance the application to AR mode, where the calibration values are used for pose estimation.

Augmented reality with jMonkeyEngine

Having calibrated the camera, we can proceed with implementing our AR application. We will make a very simple application that only shows a plain 3D box on top of the marker, using the **jMonkeyEngine (JME)** 3D rendering suite. JME is very feature-rich, and full-blown games are implemented using it (such as Rising World); we could extend our AR application into a real AR game with additional work. When looking over this chapter, the code needed to create a JME application is much more extensive than what we will see here, and the full code is available in the book's code repository.

To start, we need to provision JME to show the view from the camera behind the overlaid 3D graphics. We will create a texture to store the RGB image pixels, and a quad to show the texture. The quad will be rendered by an **orthographic** camera (without perspective), since it's a simple 2D image without depth.

The following code will create a `Quad`, a simple, flat, four-vertex 3D object that will hold the camera view texture and stretch it to cover the whole screen. Then, a `Texture2D` object will be attached to the `Quad`, so we can replace it with new images as they arrive. Lastly, we will create a `Camera` with orthographic projection and attach the textured `Quad` to it:

```
// A quad to show the background texture
Quad videoBGQuad = new Quad(1, 1, true);
mBGQuad = new Geometry("quad", videoBGQuad);
final float newWidth = (float)screenWidth / (float)screenHeight;
final float sizeFactor = 0.825f;

// Center the Quad in the middle of the screen.
mBGQuad.setLocalTranslation(-sizeFactor / 2.0f * newWidth, -sizeFactor /
2.0f, 0.f);

// Scale (stretch) the width of the Quad to cover the wide screen.
mBGQuad.setLocalScale(sizeFactor * newWidth, sizeFactor, 1);

// Create a new texture which will hold the Android camera preview frame
```

```
pixels.
Material BGMat = new Material(assetManager,
"Common/MatDefs/Misc/Unshaded.j3md");
mCameraTexture = new Texture2D();
BGMat.setTexture("ColorMap", mCameraTexture);
mBGQuad.setMaterial(BGMat);

// Create a custom virtual camera with orthographic projection
Camera videoBGCam = cam.clone();
videoBGCam.setParallelProjection(true);
// Create a custom viewport and attach the quad
ViewPort videoBGVP = renderManager.createMainView("VideoBGView",
videoBGCam);
videoBGVP.attachScene(mBGQuad);
```

Next, we set up a virtual **perspective** Camera to show the graphic augmentation. It's important to use the calibration parameters we obtained earlier so that the virtual and real cameras align. We use the **focal length** parameter from the calibration to set the **frustum** (view trapezoid) of the new Camera object, by converting it to the **field-of-view (FOV)** angle in degrees:

```
Camera fgCam = new Camera(settings.getWidth(), settings.getHeight());
fgCam.setLocation(new Vector3f(0f, 0f, 0f));
fgCam.lookAtDirection(Vector3f.UNIT_Z.negateLocal(), Vector3f.UNIT_Y);

// intrinsic parameters
final float f = getCalibrationFocalLength();

// set up a perspective camera using the calibration parameter
final float fovy = (float)Math.toDegrees(2.0f *
(float)Math.atan2(mHeightPx, 2.0f * f));
final float aspect = (float) mWidthPx / (float) mHeightPx;
fgCam.setFrustumPerspective(fovy, aspect, fgCamNear, fgCamFar);
```

The camera is situated at the origin, facing the -z direction, and pointing up the *y*-axis, to match the coordinate frame from OpenCV's pose estimation algorithms.

Finally, the running demo shows the virtual cube over the background image, covering the AR marker preciesly:

Summary

This chapter introduced two key topics in computer vision: camera calibration and camera/object pose estimation. We saw the theoretical background for achieving these concepts in practice, as well as their implementation in OpenCV using the `aruco` contrib module. Finally, we built an Android application that runs the ArUco code in native functions to calibrate the camera and then detect the AR marker. We used the jMonkeyEngine 3D rendering engine to create a very simple augmented reality application using ArUco calibration and detection.

In the next chapter, we will see how to use OpenCV in an iOS app environment to build a panorama stitching application. Using OpenCV in a mobile environment is a very popular feature of OpenCV, as the library provides pre-built binaries and releases for both Android and iOS.

19
iOS Panoramas with the Stitching Module

Panoramic imaging has existed since the early days of photography. In those ancient times, roughly 150 years ago, it was called the art of **panography**, carefully putting together individual images using tape or glue to recreate a panoramic view. With the advancement of computer vision, panorama stitching became a handy tool in almost all digital cameras and mobile devices. Nowadays, creating panoramas is as simple as swiping the device or camera across the view, the stitching calculations happen immediately, and the final expanded scene is available for viewing. In this chapter, we will implement a modest panoramic image stitching application on the iPhone using OpenCV's precompiled library for iOS. We will first examine a little of the math and theory behind image stitching, choose the relevant OpenCV functions to implement it, and finally integrate it into an iOS app with a basic UI.

The following topics will be covered in this chapter:

- Introduction to the concept of image stitching and panorama building
- OpenCV's image stitching module and its functions
- Building a Swift iOS application UI for panorama capturing
- Integrating OpenCV component written in Objective C++ with the Swift application

Technical requirements

The following technologies and installations are required to recreate the contents of this chapter:

- macOSX machine (for example, MacBook, iMac) running macOS High Sierra v10.13+

- iPhone 6+ running iOS v11+
- Xcode v9+
- CocoaPods v1.5+: `https://cocoapods.org/`
- OpenCV v4.0 installed via CocoaPods

Build instructions for the preceding components, as well as the code to implement the concepts presented in this chapter, will be provided in the accompanying code repository.

The code for this chapter can be accessed via GitHub: `https://github.com/ PacktPublishing/Building-Computer-Vision-Projects-with-OpenCV4-and-CPlusPlus/ tree/master/Chapter19.`

Panoramic image stitching methods

Panoramas are essentially multiple images fused together into a single image. The process of panorama creation from multiple images involves many steps; some are common to other computer vision tasks, such as the following:

- Extracting 2D features
- Matching pairs of images based on their features
- Transforming or warping images to a communal frame
- Using (blending) the seams between the images for the pleasing continuous effect of a larger image

Some of these basic operations are also commonplace in **Structure-from-Motion (SfM)**, **3D reconstruction**, **visual odometry**, and **simultaneous localization and mapping (SLAM)**. We've already discussed some of these in Chapter 14, *Explore Structure from Motion with the SfM Module* and Chapter 18, *Android Camera Calibration and AR Using the ArUco Module*. The following is a rough image of the panorama creation process:

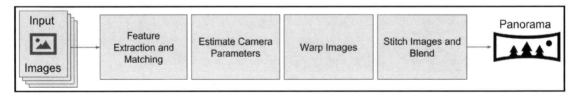

In this section, we will briefly review feature matching, camera pose estimation, and image warping. In reality, panorama stitching has multiple pathways and classes, depending on the type of input and required output. For example, if the camera has a fisheye lens (with an extremely high degree view angle) a special process is needed.

Feature extraction and robust matching for panoramas

We create panoramas from overlapping images. In the overlapping region, we look for common visual features that **register** (align) the two images together. In SfM or SLAM, we do this on a frame-by-frame basis, looking for matching features in a real-time video sequence where the overlap between frames is extremely high. However, in panoramas we get frames with a big motion component between them, where the overlap might be as low as just 10%-20% of the image. At first, we extract image features, such as the **scale invariant feature transform (SIFT), speeded up robust features** (SURF), **oriented BRIEF (ORB)**, or another kind of feature, and then match them between the images in the panorama. Note the SIFT and SURF features are protected by patents and cannot be used for commercial purposes. ORB is a considered a free alternative, but not as robust.

The following image shows extracted features and their matching:

Affine constraint

For a robust and meaningful pairwise matching, we often apply a geometric constraint. One such constraint can be an **affine transform**, a transform that allows only for scale, rotation, and translation. In 2D, an affine transform can be modeled in a 2 x 3 matrix:

$$\hat{X} = \begin{pmatrix} \hat{x} \\ \hat{y} \end{pmatrix} = \begin{pmatrix} r_1 & r_2 & t_x \\ r_3 & r_4 & t_y \end{pmatrix} \begin{pmatrix} x \\ y \\ 1 \end{pmatrix} = MX$$

$$\hat{M} = \underset{M}{\operatorname{argmin}} \sum_i \left\| X_i^{\mathrm{L}} - M X_i^{\mathrm{R}} \right\|_{\mathrm{L}_2}$$

To impose the constraint, we look for an affine transform $\hat{M}$ that minimizes the distance (error) between matching points from the left X_i^{L} and right X_i^{R} images.

Random sample consensus (RANSAC)

In the preceding image, we illustrate the fact that not all points conform to the affine constraint, and most of the matched pairs are discarded as incorrect. Therefore, in most cases we employ a voting-based estimation method, such as **random sample consensus (RANSAC)**, where a group of points is chosen at random to solve for a hypothesis of M directly (via a homogeneous linear system) and then a voting is cast between all points to support or reject this hypothesis.

The following is a pseudo-algorithm for RANSAC:

1. Find matches between points in image i and image j.
2. Initialize the hypothesis for the transform between image i and j, with minimal support.
3. While not converged:
    1. Pick a small random set of point-pairs. For an affine transform, three pairs will suffice.
    2. Calculate the affine transform T directly based on the pairs set, for instance with a linear equation set
    3. Calculate the support. For each point p in the entire i, j matching:
        - If the distance (the **error**) between the transformed point in image j and the matched point in image i is within a small threshold t: $\|p_i - Tp_j\| < t$,add 1 to the support counter.
    4. If the support count is bigger than the current hypothesis' support, take T as the new hypothesis.
    5. Optional: if the support is large enough (or a different breaking policy is true), break; otherwise, keep iterating.
4. Return the latest and best supported hypothesis transform.
5. Also, return the **support mask**: a binary variable stating whether a point in the matching was supporting the final hypothesis.

The output of the algorithm will provide the transform that has the highest support, and the support mask can be used to discard points that are not supportive. We can also reason about the number of supporting points, for example, if we observe less than 50% supporting points, we can deem this match as bad and not try to match the two images at all.

There are alternatives to RANSAC, such as the **least median squares (LMedS)** algorithm, which is not too different from RANSAC: instead of counting supporting points, it calculates the median of the square error for each transform hypothesis, and finally return the hypothesis with the least median square error.

Homography constraint

While affine transforms are useful for stitching scanned documents (for example, from a flatbed scanner), they cannot be used for stitching photo panoramas. For stitching photos, we can employ the same process to find a **homography**, a transform between one plane and another, instead of an affine transform, which has eight degrees of freedom, and is represented in a 3 x 3 matrix as follows:

$$\hat{X} = s \begin{pmatrix} \hat{x} \\ \hat{y} \\ 1 \end{pmatrix} = \begin{pmatrix} h_1 & h_2 & h_3 \\ h_4 & h_5 & h_6 \\ h_7 & h_8 & 1 \end{pmatrix} \begin{pmatrix} x \\ y \\ 1 \end{pmatrix} = HX$$

Once a proper matching has been found, we can find an ordering of the images to sequence them for the panorama, essentially to understand how the images relate to one another. In most cases, in panoramas the assumption is that the photographer (camera) is standing still and only rotating on its axis, sweeping from left to right, for example. Therefore, the goal is to recover the rotation component between the camera poses. Homographies can be decomposed to recover rotation, if we regard the input as purely rotational:
$\hat{X} = HX = KRK^{-1}X$. If we assume the homography was originally composed from the camera intrinsic (calibration), matrix K, and a 3 x 3 rotation matrix R, we can recover R if we know K. The intrinsic matrix can be calculated by camera calibration ahead of time, or can be estimated during the panorama creation process.

Bundle Adjustment

When a transformation has been achieved *locally* between all photo *pairs*, we can further optimize our solution in a *global* step. This is called the process of **bundle adjustment**, and is widely constructed as a global optimization of all the reconstruction parameters (camera or image transforms). Global bundle adjustment is best performed if all the matched points between images are put in the same coordinate frame, for example, a 3D space, and there are constraints that span more than two images. For example, if a feature point appears in more than two images in the panorama, it can be useful for *global* optimization, since it involves registering three or more views.

The goal in most bundle adjustment methods is to minimize the **reconstruction error**. This means, looking to bring the approximate parameters of the views, for example, camera or image transforms, to values such that the re-projected 2D points back on the original views will align with minimal error. This can be expressed mathematically like so:

$$\{\hat{T}\}_{j=1}^{n_{\text{images}}} = \underset{\{T\}_{j=1}^{n_{\text{images}}}}{\arg\min} \sum_{i=1}^{n_{\text{points}}} v_{ij} \|X_i - \text{Proj}(T_j, X_i)\|^2$$

Where we look for the best camera or image transforms T, such that the distance between original point X_i and reprojected point $Proj(T_j, X_i)$ is minimal. The binary variable v_{ij} marks whether point i can be seen in image j, and can contribute to the error. These kinds of optimization problems can be solved with **iterative non-linear least squares** solvers, such as **Levenberg-Marquardt**, since the previous *Proj* function is usually non-linear.

Warping images for panorama creation

Given that we know the homographies between images, we can apply their inverse to project all the images on the same plane. However, a direct warping using the homography ends up with a stretched-out look if, for example, all the images are projected on the plane of the first image. In the following image, we can see a stitching of 4 images using *concatenated* homography (perspective) warping, meaning all the images are registered to the plane of the first image, which illustrates the ungainly stretching:

To cope with this problem, we think of the panorama as looking at the images from inside a cylinder, where the images are projected on the wall of the cylinder, and we rotate the camera at the center. To achieve this effect, we first need to warp the images to **cylindrical coordinates**, as if the round wall of the cylinder was undone and flattened to a rectangle. The following diagram explains the process of cylindrical warping:

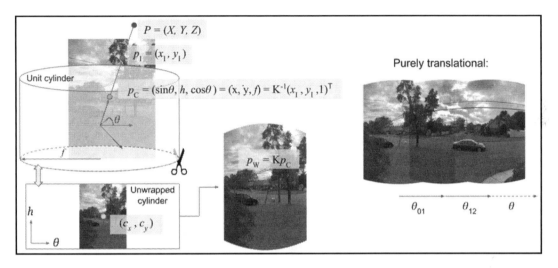

To wrap the image in cylindrical coordinates, we first apply the inverse of the intrinsic matrix to get the pixel in normalized coordinates. We now assume the pixel is a point on the surface of the cylinder, which is parameterized by the height h and the angle θ. Height h essentially corresponds to the y coordinate, while the x and z (which are perpendicular to one another with regards to y) exist on a unit circle and therefore correspond to $\sin\theta$ and $\cos\theta$, respectively. To get the warped image in the same pixel size as the original image, we can apply the intrinsic matrix K again; however, we can change the focal length parameter f, for example, to affect the output resolution of our panorama.

In the cylindrical warping model, the relationship between the images becomes purely translational, and in fact governed by a single parameter: θ. To stitch the images in the same plane, we simply need to find the θs, just a single degree of freedom, which is simple compared to finding eight parameters for the homography between every two consecutive images. One major drawback of the cylindrical method is that we assume the camera's rotational axis motion is perfectly aligned with its up axis, as well as static in its place, which is almost never the case with handheld cameras. Still, cylindrical panoramas produce highly pleasing results. Another option for warping is **spherical coordinates**, which allow for more options in stitching the images in both x and y axes.

Project overview

This project will include two major parts as follows:

- iOS application to support capturing the panorama
- OpenCV Objective-C++ code for creating the panorama from the images and integrating into the application

The iOS code will mostly be concerned with building the UI, accessing the camera, and capturing images. Then, we will focus on getting the images to OpenCV data structures and running the image stitching functions from the `stitch` module.

Setting up an iOS OpenCV project with CocoaPods

To start using OpenCV in iOS, we must import the library compiled for iOS devices. This is easily done with CocoaPods, which is a vast repository of external packages for iOS and macOS with a convenient command-line package manager utility called `pod`.

We begin by creating an empty Xcode project for iOS, with the "*Single View App*" template. Make sure to select a Swift project, and not an Objective-C one. The Objective-C++ code we will see will be added later.

After the project in initialized in a certain directory, we execute the `pod init` command in the terminal within that directory. This will create a new file called `Podfile` in the directory. We need to edit the file to look like the following:

```
# Uncomment the next line to define a global platform for your project
# platform :ios, '9.0'

target 'OpenCV Stitcher' do
  use_frameworks!
  # Pods for OpenCV Stitcher
  pod 'OpenCV2', '4.0.0.beta'
end
```

Essentially, just adding `pod 'OpenCV2', '4.0.0'` to the `target` tells CocoaPods to download and unpack the OpenCV framework in our project. Afterwards, we run `pod install` in the Terminal in the same directory, which will set up our project and Workspace to include all the Pods (just OpenCV v4 in our case). To start working on the project, we open the `$(PROJECT_NAME).xcworkspace` file, rather than the `.xcodeproject` file as usual with Xcode projects.

iOS UI for panorama capture

Before we delve into the OpenCV code for turning an image collection into a panorama, we will first build a UI to support the easy capture of a sequence of overlapping images. First, we must make sure we have access to the camera as well as saved images. Open the `Info.plist` file and add the following three rows:

Key		Type	Value
▼ Information Property List		Dictionary	(17 items)
Privacy - Photo Library Additions...	⌄	String	This app uses the photo library for saving images
Privacy - Photo Library Usage Des...	⌄	String	This app uses the photo library for saving images
Privacy - Camera Usage Description	⌄	String	This app uses the camera for creating panoramas
Localization native development re...	⌄	String	$(DEVELOPMENT_LANGUAGE)
Executable file	⌄	String	$(EXECUTABLE_NAME)
Bundle identifier	⌄	String	$(PRODUCT_BUNDLE_IDENTIFIER)
InfoDictionary version	⌄	String	6.0
Bundle name	⌄	String	$(PRODUCT_NAME)
Bundle OS Type code	⌄	String	APPL
Bundle versions string, short	⌄	String	1.0
Bundle version	⌄	String	1
Application requires iPhone enviro...	⌄	Boolean	YES
Launch screen interface file base...	⌄	String	LaunchScreen
Main storyboard file base name	⌄	String	Main
▼ Required device capabilities	⌄	Array	(1 item)
Item 0		String	armv7
▶ Supported interface orientations	⌄	Array	(3 items)
▶ Supported interface orientations (i...	⌄	Array	(4 items)

To start building the UI, we create a view with a `View` object for the camera preview on the right, and an overlapping `ImageView` on the left. `ImageView` should cover some area of the camera preview View, to help guide the user in capturing an image with enough overlap from the last. We can also add a few `ImageView` instances on top to show the previously captured images, and on the bottom a **Capture** button and a **Stitch** button to control the application flow:

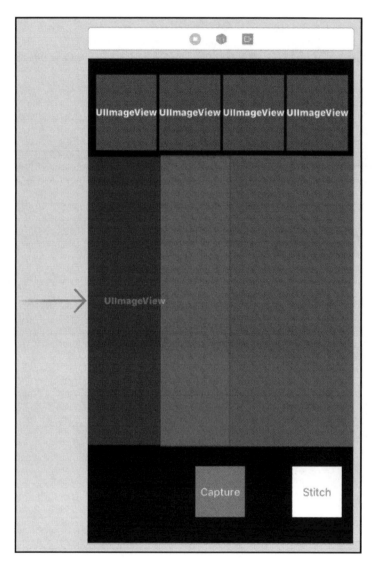

To connect the camera preview to the preview View, we must do the following:

1. Start a capture session (`AVCaptureSession`)
2. Select a device (`AVCaptureDevice`)
3. Set up the capture session with input from the device (`AVCaptureDeviceInput`)
4. Add an output for capturing photos (`AVCapturePhotoOutput`)

Most of these can be set up immediately when they are initialized as members of the ViewController class. The following code shows setting up the capture session, device, and output on the fly:

```
class ViewController: UIViewController, AVCapturePhotoCaptureDelegate {

    private lazy var captureSession: AVCaptureSession = {
        let s = AVCaptureSession()
        s.sessionPreset = .photo
        return s
    }()
    private let backCamera: AVCaptureDevice? =
AVCaptureDevice.default(.builtInWideAngleCamera, for: .video, position:
.back)

    private lazy var photoOutput: AVCapturePhotoOutput = {
        let o = AVCapturePhotoOutput()
        o.setPreparedPhotoSettingsArray([AVCapturePhotoSettings(format:
[AVVideoCodecKey: AVVideoCodecType.jpeg])], completionHandler: nil)
        return o
    }()
    var capturePreviewLayer: AVCaptureVideoPreviewLayer?
```

The rest of the initialization can be done from the `viewDidLoad` function, for example, adding the capture input to the session and creating a preview layer for showing the camera feed onscreen. The following code shows the rest of the initialization process, adding the input and output to the capture session, and setting up the preview layer.

```
    override func viewDidLoad() {
        super.viewDidLoad()

        let captureDeviceInput = try AVCaptureDeviceInput(device:
backCamera!)
        captureSession.addInput(captureDeviceInput)
        captureSession.addOutput(photoOutput)

        capturePreviewLayer = AVCaptureVideoPreviewLayer(session:
captureSession)
        capturePreviewLayer?.videoGravity =
```

```
AVLayerVideoGravity.resizeAspect
        capturePreviewLayer?.connection?.videoOrientation =
AVCaptureVideoOrientation.portrait
        // add the preview layer to the view we designated for preview
        let previewViewLayer = self.view.viewWithTag(1)!.layer
        capturePreviewLayer?.frame = previewViewLayer.bounds
        previewViewLayer.insertSublayer(capturePreviewLayer!, at: 0)
        previewViewLayer.masksToBounds = true
        captureSession.startRunning()
    }
```

With the preview set up, all that is left is to handle the photo capture on a click. The following code shows how a button click (TouchUpInside) will trigger the photoOutput function via delegate, and then simply add the new image to a list as well as save it to memory in the photo gallery.

```
@IBAction func captureButton_TouchUpInside(_ sender: UIButton) {
    photoOutput.capturePhoto(with: AVCapturePhotoSettings(), delegate:
self)
}

var capturedImages = [UIImage]()

func photoOutput(_ output: AVCapturePhotoOutput, didFinishProcessingPhoto
photo: AVCapturePhoto, error: Error?) {
    let cgImage = photo.cgImageRepresentation()!.takeRetainedValue()
    let image = UIImage(cgImage: cgImage)
    prevImageView.image = image // save the last photo, for the overlapping
ImageView
    capturedImages += [image] // add to array of captured photos
    // save to photo gallery on phone as well
    PHPhotoLibrary.shared().performChanges({
            PHAssetChangeRequest.creationRequestForAsset(from: image)
    }, completionHandler: nil)
}
```

This will allow us to capture multiple images in succession while helping the user align one image with the next. Here is an example of the UI running on the phone:

Next, we will see how to take the images to an Objective-C++ context, where we can work with the OpenCV C++ API for panorama stitching.

OpenCV stitching in an Objective-C++ wrapper

For working in iOS, OpenCV provides its usual C++ interface that can be invoked from Objective-C++. In recent years, however, Apple has encouraged iOS application developers to use the more versatile Swift language for building applications and forgo Objective-C. Luckily, a bridge between Swift and Objective-C (and Objective-C++) can be easily created, allowing us to invoke Objective-C functions from Swift. Xcode automates much of the process, and creates the necessary glue code.

To start, we create a new file (Command-N) in Xcode and select **Cocoa Touch Class**, as shown in the following screenshot:

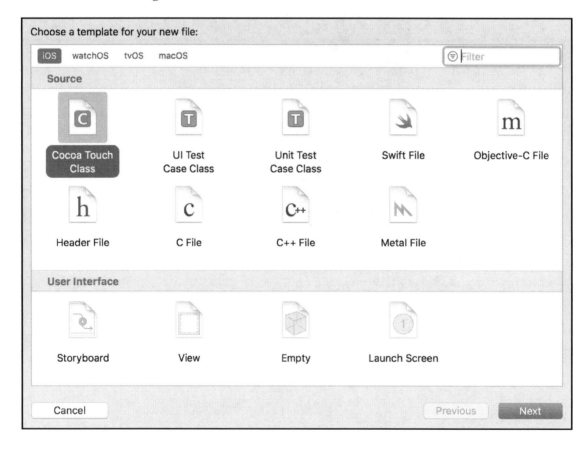

Choose a meaningful name for the file (for example, StitchingWrapper) and make sure to select **Objective-C** as the language, as shown in the following screenshot:

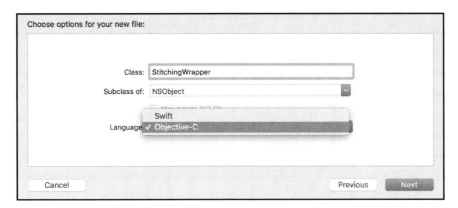

Next, as shown in the following screenshot, confirm that Xcode should create a **bridging header** for your Objective-C code:

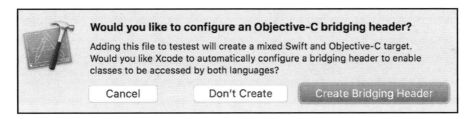

This process will result in three files: StitchingWrapper.h, StitchingWrapper.m, and OpenCV Stitcher-Bridging-Header.h. We should manually rename StitchingWrapper.m to StitchingWrapper.mm, to enable Objective-C++ over plain Objective-C. At this point, we are prepared to start using OpenCV in our Objective-C++ code.

In StitchingWrapper.h, we will define a new function that will accept an NSMutableArray* as the list of images captured by our earlier UI Swift code:

```
@interface StitchingWrapper : NSObject

+ (UIImage* _Nullable)stitch:(NSMutableArray*) images;

@end
```

And, in the Swift code for our ViewController, we can implement a function to handle a click on the **Stitch** button, where we create the `NSMutableArray` from the `capturedImages` Swift array of `UIImage`s:

```
@IBAction func stitch_TouchUpInside(_ sender: Any) {
    let image = StitchingWrapper.stitch(NSMutableArray(array:
capturedImages, copyItems: true))
    if image != nil {
        PHPhotoLibrary.shared().performChanges({ // save stitching result
to gallery
                PHAssetChangeRequest.creationRequestForAsset(from: image!)
        }, completionHandler: nil)
    }
}
```

Back on the Objective-C++ side, firstly we need to get the OpenCV `cv::Mat` objects from the `UIImage*`s input, like so:

```
+ (UIImage* _Nullable)stitch:(NSMutableArray*) images {
    using namespace cv;
    std::vector<Mat> imgs;
    for (UIImage* img in images) {
        Mat mat;
        UIImageToMat(img, mat);
        if ([img imageOrientation] == UIImageOrientationRight) {
            rotate(mat, mat, cv::ROTATE_90_CLOCKWISE);
        }
        cvtColor(mat, mat, cv::COLOR_BGRA2BGR);
        imgs.push_back(mat);
    }
```

Finally, we're ready to call the `stitching` function on the array of images, like so:

```
Mat pano;
Stitcher::Mode mode = Stitcher::PANORAMA;
Ptr<Stitcher> stitcher = Stitcher::create(mode, false);
try {
    Stitcher::Status status = stitcher->stitch(imgs, pano);
    if (status != Stitcher::OK) {
        NSLog(@"Can't stitch images, error code = %d", status);
        return NULL;
    }
} catch (const cv::Exception& e) {
    NSLog(@"Error %s", e.what());
    return NULL;
}
```

An example of an output panorama created with this code (note the use of cylindrical warping) is shown as follows:

You may notice some changes in illumination between the four images, while the edges have been blended. Dealing with varying illumination can be addressed in the OpenCV image stitching API using the `cv::detail::ExposureCompensator` base API.

Summary

In this chapter, we've learned about panorama creation. We've seen some of the underlying theory and practice in panorama creation, implemented in OpenCV's `stitching` module. We then turned our focus to creating an iOS application that helps a user to capture images for panorama stitching with overlapping views. Lastly, we saw how to invoke OpenCV code from a Swift application to run the `stitching` functions on the captures images, resulting in a finished panorama.

The next chapter will focus on selection strategies for OpenCV algorithms given a problem at hand. We will see how to reason about a computer vision problem and its solution offering in OpenCV, as well as how to compare competing algorithms in order to make informed selections.

Further reading

Rick Szeliski's book on computer vision: http://szeliski.org/Book/

OpenCV's tutorial on image stitching: https://docs.opencv.org/trunk/d8/d19/tutorial_stitcher.html

OpenCV's tutorial on homography warping: https://docs.opencv.org/3.4.1/d9/dab/tutorial_homography.html#tutorial_homography_Demo5

20
Finding the Best OpenCV Algorithm for the Job

Any computer vision problem can be solved in different ways. Each way has its pros and cons and relative measures of success, depending on the data, resources, or goals. Working with OpenCV, a computer vision engineer has many algorithmic options on hand to solve a given task. Making the right choice in an informed way is extremely important since it can have a tremendous impact on the success of the entire solution, and prevent you from being boxed into a rigid implementation. This chapter will discuss some methods to follow when considering options in OpenCV. We will discuss the areas in computer vision that OpenCV covers, ways to select between competing algorithms if more than one exists, how to measure the success of an algorithm, and finally how to measure success in a robust way with a pipeline.

The following topics will be covered in this chapter:

- Is it covered in OpenCV? Computer vision topics with algorithms available in OpenCV.
- Which algorithm to pick? Topics with multiple available solutions in OpenCV.
- How to know which algorithm is best? Establishing metrics for measuring algorithm success.
- Using a pipeline to test different algorithms on the same data.

Technical requirements

The technologies and installations used in this chapter are the following:

- OpenCV v3 or v4 with Python bindings
- Jupyter Notebook server

Build instructions for the components listed above, as well as the code to implement the concepts presented in this chapter, will be provided in the accompanying code repository.

The code for this chapter can be accessed through GitHub: `https://github.com/PacktPublishing/Building-Computer-Vision-Projects-with-OpenCV4-and-CPlusPlus/tree/master/Chapter20`.

Is it covered in OpenCV?

When first tackling a computer vision problem, any engineer should first asks: should I implement a solution from scratch, from a paper or known method, or use an existing solution and fit it to my needs?

This question goes hand-in-hand with the offering of implementations in OpenCV. Luckily, OpenCV has very wide and extensive coverage of both canonical and specific computer vision tasks. On the other hand, not all OpenCV implementations are easily applied to a given problem. For example, while OpenCV offers some object recognition and classification capabilities, it is by far inferior to the state-of-the-art computer vision one would see in conferences and the literature. Over the last few years, and certainly in OpenCV v4.0, there's an effort to easily integrate deep convolutional neural networks with OpenCV APIs (through the core `dnn` module) so engineers can enjoy all the latest and greatest work.

We made an effort to list the current offering of algorithms in OpenCV v4.0, along with a subjective estimation of the coverage they give of the grand computer vision subject. We also note whether OpenCV provides GPU implementation coverage, and whether the topic is covered in the core modules or in the contrib modules. Contrib modules vary; some modules are very mature and offer documentation and tutorials (for example, `tracking`), while others are a black box implementation with very poor documentation (for example, `xobjectdetect`). Having core module implementation is a good sign there is going to be adequate documentation, examples, and robustness.

The following is a list of topics in computer vision with their level of offering in OpenCV:

Topic	Coverage	OpenCV offering	Core?	GPU?
Image processing	Very good	Linear and non-linear filtering, transformations, colorspaces, histograms, shape analysis, edge detection	Yes	Good
Feature detection	Very good	Corner detection, key-point extraction, descriptor calculation	Yes + contrib	Poor

Segmentation	Mediocre	Watershed, contour and connected component analysis, binarization and thresholding, GrabCut, foreground-background segmentation, superpixels	Yes + contrib	Poor
Image alignment, stitching, Stabilization	Good	Panoramic stitching pipeline, Video stabilization pipeline, template matching, transform estimation, warping, seamless stitching	Yes + contrib	Poor
Structure from motion	Poor	Camera pose estimation, essential and fundamental matrix estimation, integration with external SfM library	Yes + contrib	None
Motion estimation, optical flow, tracking	Good	Optical flow algorithms, Kalman filter, object tracking framework, multi-target tracking	Mostly contrib	Poor
Stereo and 3D reconstruction	Good	Stereo matching framework, triangulation, structured light scanning	Yes + contrib	Good
Camera calibration	Very good	Calibration from several patterns, stereo rig calibration	Yes + contrib	None
Object detection	Mediocre	Cascade classifiers, QR code detector, face landmark detector, 3D object recognition, text detection	Yes + contrib	Poor
Object recognition, classification	Poor	Eigen and Fisher face recognition, bag-of-words	Mostly contrib	None
Computational photography	Mediocre	Denoising, HDR, superresolution	Yes + contrib	None

While OpenCV does a tremendous job with traditional computer vision algorithms, such as image processing, camera calibration, feature extraction, and other topics, it also has poor coverage of important topics such as SfM and object classification. In other topics, such as segmentation, it has a decent offering, but again falls short of state of the art, although that has moved almost exclusively to convolutional networks and can essentially be implemented with the `dnn` module.

In some topics, such as feature detection, extraction, and matching, as well as camera calibration, OpenCV is considered to be the most comprehensive, free, and usable library today, used in probably many thousands of applications. However, in the course of a computer vision project, engineers may consider decoupling from OpenCV after the prototyping phase since the library is heavy and adds significantly to the overhead in building and deploying (an acute problem for mobile applications). In those cases, OpenCV is a good crutch for prototyping, because of its wide offering, usefulness for testing, and choosing between different algorithms for the same task, for example, for calculating a 2D feature. Beyond prototyping, numerous other considerations become more important, such as the execution environment, stability and maintainability of the code, permissions and licensing, and more. At that stage, using OpenCV should satisfy the requirements of the product, including the considerations mentioned.

Algorithm options in OpenCV

OpenCV has many algorithms covering the same subject. When implementing a new processing pipeline, sometimes there is more than one choice for a step in the pipeline. For example, in Chapter 14, *Explore Structure from Motion with the SfM Module*, we made an arbitrary decision to use AKAZE features for finding landmarks between the images to estimate camera motion, and sparse 3D structure, however; there are many more kinds of 2D features available in OpenCV's features2D module. A more sensible mode of operation should have been to select the type of feature algorithm to use based on its performance, with respect to our needs. At the very least, we need to be aware of the different options.

Again, we looked to create a convenient way to see whether there are multiple options for the same task. We created a table where we list specific computer vision tasks that have multiple algorithm implementations in OpenCV. We also strived to mark whether algorithms have a common abstract API, and thus, easily and completely interchangeable within the code. While OpenCV offers the cv::Algorithm base class abstraction for most if not all of its algorithms, the abstraction is at a very high level and gives very little power to polymorphism and interchangeability. From our review, we exclude the machine learning algorithms (the ml module and the cv::StatsModel common API) since they are not proper computer vision algorithms, as well as low-level image processing algorithms, which do in fact have overlapping implementations (for example, the Hough detector family). We also exclude the GPU CUDA implementations that shadow several core topics such as object detection, background segmentation, 2D features, and more, since they are mostly replicas of the CPU implementations.

The following are topics with multiple implementations in OpenCV:

Topic	Implementations	Base API?
Optical flow	`video` **module:** `SparsePyrLKOpticalFlow`, `FarnebackOpticalFlow`, `DISOpticalFlow`, `VariationalRefinement` `optflow` **contrib module:** `DualTVL1OpticalFlow`, `OpticalFlowPCAFlow`	Yes
Object tracking	`track` **contrib module:** `TrackerBoosting`, `TrackerCSRT`, `TrackerGOTURN`, `TrackerKCF`, `TrackerMedianFlow`, `TrackerMIL`, `TrackerMOSSE`, `TrackerTLD` **External:** `DetectionBasedTracker`	Yes[1]

Object detection	`objdetect` **module:** `CascadeClassifier`, `HOGDescriptor`, `QRCodeDetector`,
	`linemod` **contrib module:** `Detector`
	`aruco` **contrib module:** `aruco::detectMarkers`
		No[2]

2D features	OpenCV's most established common API.
	`features2D` **module:** `AgastFeatureDetector`, `AKAZE`, `BRISK`, `FastFeatureDetector`, `GFTTDetector`, `KAZE`, `MSER`, `ORB`, `SimpleBlobDetector`
	`xfeatures2D` **contrib module:** `BoostDesc`, `BriefDescriptorExtractor`, `DAISY`, `FREAK`, `HarrisLaplaceFeatureDetector`, `LATCH`, `LUCID`, `MSDDetector`, `SIFT`, `StarDetector`, `SURF`, `VGG`
		Yes

Feature matching	`BFMatcher`, `FlannBasedMatcher`	Yes
Background subtraction	`video` **module:** `BackgroundSubtractorKNN`, `BackgroundSubtractorMOG2` `bgsegm` **contrib module:** `BackgroundSubtractorCNT`, `BackgroundSubtractorGMG`, `BackgroundSubtractorGSOC`, `BackgroundSubtractorLSBP`, `BackgroundSubtractorMOG`	Yes

Camera calibration	`calib3d` **module:** `calibrateCamera`, `calibrateCameraRO`, `stereoCalibrate`
	`aruco` **contrib module:** `calibrateCameraArcuo`, `calibrateCameraCharuco`
	`ccalib` **contrib module:** `omnidir::calibrate`, `omnidir::stereoCalibrate`
		No

Stereo reconstruction	calib3d **module:** StereoBM, StereoSGBM stereo **contrib module:** StereoBinaryBM, StereoBinarySGBM ccalib **contrib module:** omnidir::stereoReconstruct	Partial[3]
Pose estimation	solveP3P, solvePnP, solvePnPRansac	No

[1] Only for the classes in the track contrib module.

[2] Some classes share functions with the same name, but no inherited abstract class.

[3] Each module has a base within itself, but not shared across modules.

When approaching a problem with a few algorithmic options, it's important not to commit too early to one execution path. We may use the preceding table above to see options exist, and then explore them. Next, we will discuss how to select from a pool of options.

Which algorithm is best?

Computer vision is a world of knowledge and a decades-long research pursuit. Unlike many other disciplines, computer vision is not strongly hierarchical or vertical, which means new solutions for given problems are not always better and may not be based on preceding work. Being an applied field, computer vision algorithms are created with attention to the following aspects, which may explain the non-vertical development:

- **Computation resources**: CPU, GPU, embedded system, memory footprint, network connectivity.
- **Data**: Size of images, number of images, number of image stream (cameras), data type, sequentiality, lighting conditions, types of scenes, and so on.
- **Performance requirements**: Real-time output or another timing constraint (for example, human perception), accuracy and precision.
- **Meta-algorithmic**: Algorithm simplicity (cross-reference Occam's Razor theorem), implementation system and external tools, availability of formal proof.

With every algorithm created in order to cater for perhaps a certain one of these considerations, one can never know for sure that it will outperform all others without properly testing some or all of them. Granted, testing all algorithms for a given problem is *unrealistic*, even if the implementations are indeed available, and OpenCV certainly has many implementations available, as we've seen in the last section. On the other hand, computer vision engineers will be remiss if they do not consider the possibility that their implementations are not optimal because of their algorithm choices. This in essence flows from the *no free lunch* theorem, which states, in broad strokes, that no single algorithm is the best one over the entire space of possible datasets.

It is, therefore, a very welcome practice to test a set of different algorithmic options before committing to the best one out of that set. But how do we find the *best one*? The word *best* implies that each one will be *better* (or *worse*) than the others, which in turn suggests there is an objective scale or measurement in which they are all scored and ranked in order. Obviously, there is not a single measure (**metric**) for all algorithms in all problems each problem will have its own. In many cases, the metric for success will form a measurement of **error**, deviation from a known **ground truth** value that was sourced from humans or other algorithms we can trust. In optimization, this is known as a **loss function** or cost function, a function that we wish to minimize (sometimes maximize) in order to find the best option that has the lowest score. Another prominent class of metrics cares less about the output performance (for example, error) and more about runtime timing, memory footprint, capacity and throughput, and so on.

The following is a partial list of metrics we may see in select computer vision problems:

Task	Example metrics
Reconstruction, registration, feature matching	**Mean absolute error (MAE), mean squared error (MSE), root mean squared error (RMSE), sum of squared distances (SSD)**
Object classification, recognition	Accuracy, precision, recall, f1-score, **false-positive rate (FPR)**
Segmentation, object detection	**Intersection-over-Union (IoU)**
Feature detection	**Repeatability, precision recall**

The why to find the best algorithm for a given task is either to set all the options at our disposal in a test scenario and measure their performance on the metrics of choice, or obtain someone else's measurements on a standard experiment or dataset. The highest ranking option should be picked, where the ranking is derived from a combination of the metrics (in the case of just a single metric, it's an easy task). Next, we will try our hand at such a task, and make an *informed* choice on the best algorithm.

Example comparative performance test of algorithms

As an example, we will set up a scenario where we are required to align overlapping images, like what is done in panorama or aerial photo stitching. One important feature that we need to measure performance is to have a **ground truth**, a precise measurement of the true condition that we are trying to recover with our approximation method. Ground truth data can be obtained from datasets made available for researchers to test and compare their algorithms; indeed, many of these datasets exist and computer vision researchers use them all the time. One good resource for finding computer vision datasets is **Yet Another Computer Vision Index To Datasets (YACVID)**, `https://riemenschneider.hayko.at/ vision/dataset/`, which has been actively maintained for the past eight years and contains hundreds of links to datasets. The following is also a good resource for data: `https:// github.com/jbhuang0604/awesome-computer-vision#datasets`.

We, however, will pick a different way to get ground truth, which is well practiced in computer vision literature. We will create a contrived situation within our parametric control, and create a benchmark that we can vary to test different aspects of our algorithms. For our example, we will take a single image and split it into two overlapping images, and apply some transformations to one of them. The fusing of the images with our algorithm will try to recreate the original fused image, but it will likely not do a perfect job. Choices we make in selecting the pieces in our system (for example, the type of 2D feature, the feature matching algorithm, and the transform recovery algorithm) will affect the final result, which we will measure and compare. Working with artificial ground truth data gives us a lot of control over the conditions and level in our trials.

Consider the following image and its two-way overlapping split:

Image: https://pixabay.com/en/forest-forests-tucholski-poland-1973952/

The left image we keep untouched, while we perform artificial transformations on the right image to see how well our algorithm will be able to undo them. To keep things simple, we will only rotate the right image at several brackets, like so:

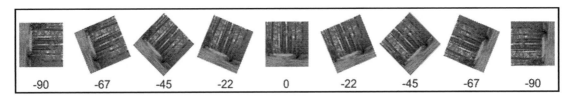

We add a middle bracket for the *no rotation* case, in which the right image is only translated somewhat. This makes up our ground truth data, where we know exactly what transformation occurred and what the original input was.

Our goal is to measure the success of different 2D feature descriptor types in aligning images. One measure for our success can be the **Mean Squared Error (MSE)** over the pixels of the final re-stitched image. If the transformation recovery wasn't very well done, the pixels will not align perfectly, and thus we expect to see a high MSE. As the MSE approaches zero, we know the stitching was done well. We may also wish to know, for practical reasons, which feature is the most efficient, so we can also take a measurement of execution time. To this end, our algorithm can be very simple:

1. Split original image *left image* and *right image*.
2. For each of the feature types (SURF, SIFT, ORB, AKAZE, BRISK), do the following:
    1. Find keypoints and features in the left image.
    2. For each rotation angle [-90, -67, ..., 67, 90] do the following:
        1. Rotate the right image by the rotation angle.
        2. Find keypoints and features in the rotated right image.
        3. Match keypoints between the rotated right image and the left image.
        4. Estimate a rigid 2D transform.
        5. Transform according to the estimation.
        6. Measure the **MSE** of the final result with the original unsplit image.
        7. Measure the overall **time** it takes to extract, compute, and match features, and perform the alignment.

As a quick optimization, we can cache the rotated images, and not calculate them for each feature type. The rest of the algorithm remains untouched. Additionally, to keep things fair in terms of timing, we should take care to have a similar number of keypoints extracted for each feature type (for example, 2,500 keypoints), which can be done by setting the threshold for the keypoint extraction functions.

Note the alignment execution pipeline is oblivious of the feature type, and works exactly the same given the matched keypoints. This is a very important feature for testing many options. With OpenCV's `cv::Feature2D` and `cv::DescriptorMatcher` common base API, it is possible to achieve this, since all features and matchers implement them. However, if we take a look at the table in the *Is it covered in OpenCV?* section, we can see that this may not be possible for all vision problem in OpenCV, so we may need to add our own instrumentation code to make this comparison possible.

In the accompanying code, we can find the Python implementation of this routine, which provides the following results. To test rotation invariance, we vary the angle and measure the reconstruction MSE:

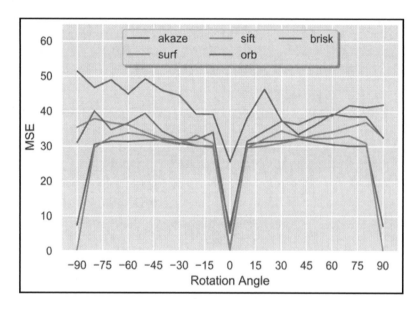

With the same experiments, we record the mean MSE across all experiments for a feature type, and also the mean execution time, shown as follows:

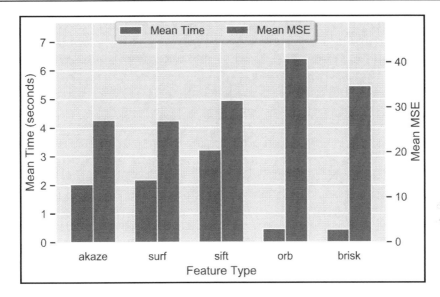

Results analysis, we can clearly see some features performing better than others in terms of MSE, with respect to both the different rotation angles and overall, and we can also see a big variance in the timing. It seems AKAZE and SURF are the highest performers in terms of alignment success across the rotation angle domain, with an advantage for AKAZE in higher rotations (~60°). However, at very small angular variation (rotation angle close to 0°), SIFT achieves practically perfect reconstruction with MSE around zero, and it also does as well as if not better then, the others with rotations below 30°. ORB does very badly throughout the domain, and BRISK, while not as bad, rarely was able to beat any of the forerunners.

Considering timing, ORB and BRISK (which are essentially the same algorithm) are the clear winners, but they both are far behind the others in terms of reconstruction accuracy. AKAZE and SURF are the leaders with neck-and-neck timing performance.

Now, it is up to us as the application developers to rank the features according to the requirements of the project. With the data from this test we performed, it should be easy to make a decision. If we are looking for speed, we would choose BRISK, since it's the fastest and performs better than ORB. If we are looking for accuracy, we would choose AKAZE, since it's the best performer and is faster than SURF. Using SURF in itself is a problem, since the algorithm is not free and it is protected by patent, so we are lucky to find AKAZE as a free and adequate alternative.

This was a very rudimentary test, only looking at two simple measures (MSE and time) and only one varied parameter (rotation). In a real situation, we may wish to insert more complexity into the transformations, according to the requirements of our system. For example, we may use full perspective transformation, rather than just rigid rotation. Additionally, we may want to do a deeper statistical analysis of the results. In this test, we only ran the alignment process once for each rotation condition, which is not good for capturing a good measure of timing, since some of the algorithms may benefit from executing in succession (for example, loading static data to memory). If we have multiple executions, we can reason about the variance in the executions, and calculate the standard deviation or error to give our decision making process more information. Lastly, given enough data, we can perform statistical inference processes and hypothesis testing, such as a **t-test** or **analysis of variance (ANOVA)**, to determine whether the minute differences between the conditions (for example, AKAZE and SURF) have **statistical significance** or are too noisy to tell apart.

Summary

Choosing the best computer vision algorithm for the job is an illusive process, which is the reason many engineers do not perform it. While published survey work on different choices provides benchmark performance, in many situations it doesn't model the particular system requirements an engineer might encounter, and new tests must be implemented. The major problem in testing algorithmic options is instrumentation code, which is an added work for engineers, and not always simple. OpenCV provides base APIs for algorithms in several vision problem domains, but the cover age is not complete. On the other hand, OpenCV has very extensive coverage of problems in computer vision, and is one of the premier frameworks to perform such tests.

Making an informed decision when picking an algorithm is a very important aspect of vision engineering, with many elements to optimize for, for example, speed, accuracy, simplicity, memory footprint, and even availability. Each vision system project has particular requirements that affect the weight each of these elements receives, and thus the final decision. With relatively simple OpenCV code, we saw how to gather data, chart it, and make an informed decision about a toy problem.

In the next chapter we discuss the history of the OpenCV open source project, as well as some common pitfalls when using OpenCV with suggested solutions for them.

21
Avoiding Common Pitfalls in OpenCV

OpenCV has been around for more than 15 years now. It contains many implementations that are outdated or unoptimized and are relics of the past. An advanced OpenCV engineer should know how to avoid basic mistakes in navigating the OpenCV APIs, and see their project to algorithmic success.

In this chapter, we will review the historic development of OpenCV, and the gradual increase in the framework and algorithmic offering, alongside the development of computer vision at large. We will use this knowledge to see how to figure out whether a newer alternative exists within OpenCV for our algorithm of choice. Lastly, we will discuss how to identify and avoid common problems or sub-optimal choices while creating computer vision systems with OpenCV.

The following topics will be covered in this chapter:

- A historic review of OpenCV and the latest wave of computer vision research
- Checking the date at which an algorithm became available in OpenCV, and whether it's a sign that it is outdated
- Addressing pitfalls in building computer vision systems in OpenCV

History of OpenCV from v1 to v4

OpenCV started as the brainchild of **Gray Bradsky**, once a computer vision engineer at **Intel**, around the early 2000s. Bradsky and a team of engineers, mostly from Russia, developed the first versions of OpenCV internally at Intel before making v0.9 of it **open source software** (**OSS**) in 2002. Bradsky then transitioned to **Willow Garage**, with the former founding members of OpenCV. Among them were Viktor Eurkhimov, Sergey Molinov, Alexander Shishkov, and Vadim Pisarevsky (who eventually started the company **ItSeez**, which was acquired in 2016 by Intel), who began supporting the young library as an open source project.

Version 0.9 had a predominantly C API and already sported image data manipulation functions and pixel access, image processing, filtering, colorspace transformations, geometric and shape analysis (for example, morphologic functions, Hough transforms, contour finding), motion analysis, basic machine learning (K-means, HMM), camera pose estimation, basic linear algebra (SVD, Eigen decomposition), and more. Many of these functions lasted through the ages, even into today's versions of OpenCV. Version 1.0 was released in 2006, and it marked the beginning of the library as the dominant force in OSS computer vision. In late 2008, Bradsky and **Adrian Kaehler** published the best-selling *Learning OpenCV* book based on OpenCV v1.1pre1, which was a smashing worldwide success, and served for years to come as the definitive guide to OpenCV's C API.

For its completeness, OpenCV v1 became a very popular framework for vision work in both academic and industrial applications, especially in the robotics domain, although it was just a small departure from v0.9 in terms of feature offering. After the release of v1.0 (late 2006), the OpenCV project went into years of hibernation, as the founding team was occupied with other projects and the open source community wasn't as established as it became years later. The project released v1.1pre1 in late 2008 with minor additions; however, the foundation of OpenCV as the most well-known vision library came with version 2.x, which introduced the very successful **C++ API**. Versions 2.x lasted *6 years* (2009-2015) as the stable branch of OpenCV, and the branch was maintained even until very recently, in early 2018 (the last version, 2.4.13.6, was released in February 2018), almost *10 years* later. Version 2.4, released in mid-2012, had a very stable and successful API, lasted for three years, and also introduced a very wide offering of features.

Versions 2.x introduced the **CMake** build system, which was also used at the time by the **MySQL** project, to align with its goal to be completely **cross-platform**. Apart from the new C++ API, v2.x also brought the concept of **modules** (in v2.2, circa 2011), which can be built, included, and linked separately, based on the project assembly necessity, forsaking v1.x's cv, cvaux, ml, and so on. The 2D feature suit was extended, as well as the machine learning capabilities, built-in face recognition cascade models, 3D reconstruction functionality, and most importantly the coverage of **Python** bindings. Early investment in Python made OpenCV the best tool for vision prototyping available at that time, and probably still today. Version 2.4, released in mid-2012, continued development until 2018, with v2.5 never released due to fears of breaking API changes and simply rebranded as v3.0 (ca. mid-2013). Version 2.4.x continued to bring more important features such as **Android** and **iOS** support, **CUDA** and **OpenCL** implementations, CPU optimizations (for example, SSE and other SIMD architectures), and an incredible amount of new algorithms.

Version 3.0, first released out of beta in late 2015, was first received with lukewarm adoption from the community. They were looking for a stable API, since some APIs had breaking changes and a drop-in replacement was impossible. The header structure also changed (from opencv2/<module>/<module>.hpp to opencv2/<module>.hpp), making the transition even harder. Version 2.4.11+ (February 2015) had instrumentation to bridge the API gap between the versions, and documentation was installed to help developers transition to v3.0 (https://docs.opencv.org/3.4/db/dfa/tutorial_transition_guide.html). Version 2.x maintained a very strong hold, with many package management systems (for example, Ubuntu's apt) still serving it as the stable version of OpenCV, while version 3.x was advancing at a very fast pace.

After years of cohabitation and planning, version 2.4.x gave way to version 3.x, which boasted a revamped API (many abstractions and base classes introduced) and improved GPU support via the new **Transparent API (T-API)**, which allowed the use of GPU code interchangeably with regular CPU code. A separate repository for community-contributed code was established, opencv-contrib, removing it from the main code as a module in v2.4.x, with improved build stability and timing. Another big change was the machine learning support in OpenCV, which was greatly improved and revised from v2.4. Version 3.x was also pushed for better Android support and optimizations for CPU architectures beyond Intel x86 (for example, ARM, NEON) via the OpenCV **HAL (Hardware Acceleration Layer)**, which later merged into the core modules. The first emergence of deep neural networks in OpenCV was recorded in v3.1 (December 2015) as a contrib module, and almost two years later in v3.3 (August 2017) was upgraded to a core module, opencv-dnn. The 3.x versions brought tremendous improvements to optimization and compatibility with GPU and CPU architectures, with support from Intel, Nvidia, AMD, and Google, and became OpenCV's hallmark as the optimized computer vision library.

Version 4.0 marks the mature state of OpenCV as the major open source project it is today. The old C API (of which many functions date back to v0.9) was let go and instead **C++11** was made *mandatory*, which also rid the library of its `cv::String` and `cv::Ptr` hybrids. Version 4.0 keeps track of further optimization for CPUs and GPUs; however, the most interesting addition is the **Graph API (G-API) module**. G-API brings the spirit of the times to OpenCV, with support for building compute graphs for computer vision, with heterogeneous execution on CPU and GPU, following the very big success of Google's **TensorFlow** deep learning library and Facebook's **PyTorch**. With long-standing investment in deep learning and machine learning, Python and other languages, execution graphs, cross-compatibility, and a wide offering of optimized algorithms, OpenCV is established as a forward-looking project with very strong community support, which makes it fifteen years later the leading open computer vision library in existence.

The history of this book series, *Mastering OpenCV*, is intertwined with the development history of OpenCV as the major library for open source computer vision. The first edition, released in 2012, was based on the everlasting v2.4.x branch. This dominated the OpenCV scene in 2009-2016. The second edition, released in 2017, hailed the dominance of OpenCV v3.1+ in the community (started in mid-2016). The third edition, the one you are reading now, welcomes OpenCV v4.0.0 into the fold, released in late October 2018.

OpenCV and the data revolution in computer vision

OpenCV existed before the data revolution in computer vision. In the late 1990s, access to big amounts of data was not a simple task for computer vision researchers. Fast access to the internet was not common, and even universities and big research institutes were not strongly networked. The limited storage capacities of personal and bigger institutional computers did not allow researchers and students to work with big amounts of data, let alone having the computational power (memory and CPU) required to do so. Thus, the research on large-scale computer vision problems was restricted to a selected list of laboratories worldwide, among them MIT's **Computer Science and Artificial Intelligence Lab (CSAIL)**, the University of Oxford Robotics Research Group, **Carnegie Mellon (CMU)** Robotics Institute, and the **California Institute of Technology (CalTech)** Computational Vision Group. These laboratories also had the resources to curate big amounts of data on their own to serve the work of local scientists, and their compute clusters were powerful enough to work with that scale of data.

However, the beginning of the 2000s brought a change to this landscape. Fast internet connections enabled it to become a hub for research and data exchange, and in parallel, compute and storage power exponentially increased year over year. This democratization of large-scale computer vision work has brought the creation of seminal big datasets for computer vision work, such as **MNIST** (1998), **CMU PIE** (2000), **CalTech 101** (2003), and **MIT's LabelMe** (2005). The release of these datasets also spurred algorithm research around large-scale image classification, detection, and recognition. Some of the most seminal work in computer vision was enabled directly or indirectly by these datasets, for example, **LeCun's** handwriting recognition (circa 1990), **Viola and Jones'** cascaded boosting face detector (2001), **Lowe's** SIFT (1999, 2004), **Dalal's** HoG people classifier (2005), and many more.

The second half of the 2000s saw a sharp increase in data offerings, with many big datasets released, such as **CalTech 256** (2006), **ImageNet** (2009), **CIFAR-10** (2009), and **PASCAL VOC** (2010), all of which still play a vital role in today's research. With the advent of deep neural networks around 2010-2012, and the momentous winning of the ImageNet large-scale visual recognition (ILSVRC) competition by **Krizhevsky and Hinton's AlexNet** (2012), large datasets became the fashion, and the computer vision world had changed. ImageNet itself has grown to monstrous proportions (more than 14 million photos), and other big datasets did too, such as **Microsoft's COCO** (2015, with 2.5 million photos), **OpenImages V4** (2017, with less than nine million photos), and **MIT's ADE20K** (2017, with nearly 500,000 object segmentation instances). This recent trend pushed researchers to think on a larger scale, and today's machine learning that tackles such data will often have tens and hundreds of millions of parameters (in a deep neural network), compared to dozens of parameters ten years ago.

OpenCV's early claim to fame was its built-in implementation of the Viola and Jones face detection method, based on a cascade of boosted classifiers, which was a reason for many to select OpenCV in their research or practice. However, OpenCV did not target data-driven computer vision at first. In v1.0, the only machine learning algorithms were the cascaded boosting, hidden Markov model, and some unsupervised methods (such as K-means clustering and expectation maximization). Much of the focus was on image processing, geometric shape and morphological analysis, and so on. Versions 2.x and 3.x added a great deal of standard machine learning capabilities to OpenCV; among them were decision trees, randomized forests and gradient boosting trees, **support vector machines** (**SVM**), logistic regression, Naive Bayes classification, and more. As it stands, OpenCV is not a data-driven machine learning library, and in recent versions this becomes more obvious. The `opencv_dnn` core module lets developers use models learned with external tools (for example, TensorFlow) to run in an OpenCV environment, where OpenCV provides the image preprocessing and post-processing. Nevertheless, OpenCV plays a crucial role in data-driven pipelines, and plays a meaningful role in the scene.

Historic algorithms in OpenCV

When starting to work on an OpenCV project, one should be aware of its historical past. OpenCV has existed for more than 15 years as an open source project, and despite its very dedicated management team that aims to better the library and keep it relevant, some implementations are more outdated than others. Some APIs are left for backward compatibility with previous versions, and others are targeted at specific algorithmic circumstances, all while newer algorithms are added.

Any engineer looking to choose the best performing algorithm for his work should have the tools to inquire about a specific algorithm to see *when* it was added and what are its *origins* (for example, a research paper). That is not to suggest that anything *new* is necessarily *better*, as some basic and older algorithms are excellent performers, and in most cases there's a clear trade-off between various metrics. For example, a data-driven deep neural network to perform image binarization (turning a color, or grayscale image to black-and-white) will likely reach the highest *accuracy*. However, the **Otsu method** (1979) for adaptive binary thresholding is incredibly *fast* and performs quite well in many situations. The key is therefore to know the requirements, as well as the details of the algorithm.

How to check when an algorithm was added to OpenCV

One of the simplest things to do in order to learn more about an OpenCV algorithm is to see when it was added to the source tree. Luckily, OpenCV as an open source project has retained most of its code's history, and changes were logged in various released versions. There are several useful resources to access this information, as follows:

- The OpenCV source repository: `https://github.com/opencv/opencv`
- The OpenCV change logs: `https://github.com/opencv/opencv/wiki/ChangeLog`
- The OpenCV attic: `https://github.com/opencv/opencv_attic`
- The OpenCV documentation: `https://docs.opencv.org/master/index.html`

Let's examine, for example, the algorithm in the `cv::solvePnP(...)` function, which is one of the most useful functions for object (or camera) pose estimation. This function is heavily used in 3D reconstruction pipelines. We can locate `solvePnP` in the `opencv/modules/calib3d/src/solvepnp.cpp` file. Using the search feature in GitHub, we can trace `solvepnp.cpp` back to its initial commit (`https://github.com/opencv/opencv/commit/04461a53f1a484499ce81bcd4e25a714488cf600`) on April 4, 2011.

There, we can see the original `solvePnP` function originally resided in `calibrate3d.cpp`, so we can trace that function back as well. However, we soon discover that there is not much history for that file, as it originated from the initial commit to the new OpenCV repository in May 2010. A search in the attic repository doesn't reveal anything beyond what exists in the original repository. The oldest version of `solvePnP` we have is from May 11, 2010 (https://github.com/opencv/opencv_attic/blob/ 8173f5ababf09218cc4838e5ac7a70328696a48d/opencv/modules/calib3d/src/ calibration.cpp) and it looks like this:

```
void cv::solvePnP( const Mat& opoints, const Mat& ipoints,
                   const Mat& cameraMatrix, const Mat& distCoeffs,
                   Mat& rvec, Mat& tvec, bool useExtrinsicGuess )
{
    CV_Assert(opoints.isContinuous() && opoints.depth() == CV_32F &&
             ((opoints.rows == 1 && opoints.channels() == 3) ||
              opoints.cols*opoints.channels() == 3) &&
             ipoints.isContinuous() && ipoints.depth() == CV_32F &&
             ((ipoints.rows == 1 && ipoints.channels() == 2) ||
              ipoints.cols*ipoints.channels() == 2));
    rvec.create(3, 1, CV_64F);
    tvec.create(3, 1, CV_64F);
    CvMat _objectPoints = opoints, _imagePoints = ipoints;
    CvMat _cameraMatrix = cameraMatrix, _distCoeffs = distCoeffs;
    CvMat _rvec = rvec, _tvec = tvec;
    cvFindExtrinsicCameraParams2(&_objectPoints, &_imagePoints,
&_cameraMatrix,
                                  &_distCoeffs, &_rvec, &_tvec,
useExtrinsicGuess );
}
```

We can clearly see it is a simple wrapper around the old C API's `cvFindExtrinsicCameraParams2`. The code for this C API function exists in `calibration.cpp` (https://github.com/opencv/opencv/blob/ 8f15a609afc3c08ea0a5561ca26f1cf182414ca2/modules/calib3d/src/calibration. cpp#L1043), and we can verify it as it has not changed since May 2010. The newer version of `solvePnP` (latest commit in November 2018) adds much more functionality, adding another function (allowing the use of **RANdom SAmple Consensus (RANSAC)**) and several specialty PnP algorithms such as EPnP, P3P, AP3P, DLS, UPnP, and also retaining the old C API (`cvFindExtrinsicCameraParams2`) method when supplying the `SOLVEPNP_ITERATIVE` flag to the function. The old C function, upon inspection, seems to solve the pose estimation problem by either finding a **homography**, in the case of planar objects, or using the **DLT method**, and then performing an iterative refinement.

As per usual, it'd be a mistake to directly assume the old C method is inferior to the other methods. However, the newer methods are indeed methods suggested decades after the DLT method (which dates back to the 1970s). For example, the UPnP method was proposed in just *2013* by Penate-Sanchez et al. (2013). Again, without careful examination of the particular data at hand and a comparative study, we cannot conclude which algorithm performs best with respect to the requirements (speed, accuracy, memory, and so on), although we can conclude that computer vision research has certainly advanced in *40 years* from the 1970s to the 2010s. Penate-Sanchez et al. actually show in their paper that UPnP performs much better than DLT, in terms of both speed and accuracy, based on empirical studies they carried out with real and simulated data. Please refer to `Chapter 20`, *Finding the Best OpenCV Algorithm for the Job*, for tips on how to compare algorithm options.

In-depth inspection of the OpenCV code should be a routine job for serious computer vision engineers. It not only reveals potential optimizations and guides choices by focusing on newer methods, but it also may teach much about the algorithms themselves.

Common pitfalls and suggested solutions

OpenCV is very feature rich and provides multiple solutions and paths to resolve a visual-understanding problem. With this great power also comes hard work, choosing and crafting the best processing pipeline for the project requirements. Having multiple options means that probably finding the exact best performing solution is next to impossible, as many pieces are interchangeable and testing *all* the possible options is out of our reach. This problem's exponential complexity is compounded by the input data; more unknown variance in the incoming data will make our algorithm choices even more unstable. In other words, working with OpenCV, or any other computer vision library, is still a matter of experience and art. A priori intuition as to the success of one or another route to a solution is something computer vision engineers develop with years of experience, and for the most part there are no shortcuts.

There is, however, the option of learning from someone else's experience. If you've purchased this book, it likely means you are looking to do just so. In this section, we have prepared a partial list of problems that we encountered in our years of work as computer vision engineers. We also look to propose solutions for these problems, like we used in our own work. The list focuses on problems arising from computer vision engineering; however, any engineer should also be aware of common problems in *general purpose software and system engineering*, which we do not enumerate here. In practice, no system implementation is without some problems, bugs, or under-optimizations, and even after following our list, one will probably find there is much more left to do.

The primary common pitfall in any engineering field is **making assumptions instead of assertions**. For any engineer, if there's an option to measure something, it should be measured, even by approximation, establishment of lower and upper bounds, or measuring a different highly correlated phenomenon. For some examples on which metrics can be used for measurement in OpenCV, refer to Chapter 20, *Finding the Best OpenCV Algorithm for the Job*. The best made decisions are the informed ones, based on hard data and visibility; however, that is often not the privilege of an engineer. Some projects require a fast and cold start that forces an engineer to rapidly build up a solution from scratch, without much data or intuition. In such cases, the following advice can save a lot of grief:

- **Not comparing algorithm options**: One pitfall engineers often make is choosing algorithms categorically based on what they encounter first, something they've done in the past and seemed to work, or something that has a nice tutorial (someone else's experience). This is called the **anchoring** or **focalism cognitive bias**, a well-known problem in decision making theory. Reiterating the words from the last chapter, the choice of algorithm can have tremendous impact on the results of the entire pipeline and project, in terms of accuracy, speed, resources, and otherwise. Making uninformed decisions when selecting algorithms is not a good idea.
    - **Solution**: OpenCV has many ways to assist in testing different options seamlessly, through common base APIs (such as Feature2D, DescriptorMatcher, SparseOpticalFlow, and more) or common function signatures (such as solvePnP and solvePnPRansac). High-level programming languages, such as Python, have even more flexibility in interchanging algorithms; however, this is also possible in C++ beyond polymorphism, with some instrumentation code. After establishing a pipeline, see how you can interchange some of the algorithms (for example, feature type or matcher type, thresholding technique) or their parameters (for example, threshold values, algorithm flags) and measure the effect on the final result. Strictly changing parameters is often called **hyperparameter tuning**, which is standard practice in machine learning.

- **Not unit testing homegrown solutions or algorithms**: It is often a programmer's fallacy to believe their work is bug-free, and that they've covered all edge cases. It is far better to err on the side of caution when it comes to computer vision algorithms, since in many cases the input space is vastly unknown, as it is incredibly highly dimensional. Unit tests are excellent tools to make sure functionality doesn't break on unexpected input, invalid data, or edge cases (for example, an empty image) and has a graceful degradation.

  - **Solution**: Establish unit tests for any meaningful function in your code, and make sure to cover the important parts. For example, any function that either reads or writes image data is a good candidate for a unit test. The unit test is a simple piece of code that usually invokes the function a number of times with different arguments, testing the function's ability (or inability) to handle the input. Working in C++, there are many options for a test framework; one such framework is part of the Boost C++ package, **Boost.Test** (https://www.boost.org/doc/libs/1_66_0/libs/test/doc/html/index.html). Here is an example:

    ```
    #define BOOST_TEST_MODULE binarization test
    #include <boost/test/unit_test.hpp>

    BOOST_AUTO_TEST_CASE ( binarization_test )
    {
        // On empty input should return empty output
    BOOST_TEST(binarization_function(cv::Mat()).empty())
        // On 3-channel color input should return 1-
    channel output
        cv::Mat input = cv::imread("test_image.png");
        BOOST_TEST(binarization_function(input).channels()
    == 1)
    }
    ```

    After compiling this file, it creates an executable that will perform the tests and exit with a status of 0 if all tests passed or 1 if any of them failed. It is common to mix this approach with **CMake's CTest** (https://cmake.org/cmake/help/latest/manual/ctest.1.html) feature (via ADD_TEST in the CMakeLists.txt files), which facilitates building tests for many parts of the code and running them all upon command.

- **Not checking data ranges**: A common problem in computer vision programming is to assume a range for the data, for example a range of [0, 1] for floating-point pixels (`float`, `CV_32F`) or [0, 255] for byte pixels (`unsigned char`, `CV_8U`). There really are no guarantees that these assumptions hold in any situation, since the memory block can hold any value. The problems that arise from these errors are mostly value saturation, when trying to write a value bigger than the representation; for example, writing 325 into a byte that can hold [0, 255] will saturate to 255, losing a great deal of precision. Other potential problems are differences between expected and actual data, for example, expecting a depth image in the range of [0, 2048] (for example, two meters in millimeters) only to see the actual range is [0, 1], meaning it was normalized somehow. This can lead to underperformance in the algorithm, or a complete breakdown (imagine dividing the [0, 1] range by 2048 again).
  - **Solution**: Check the input data range and make sure it is what you expect. If the range is not within acceptable bounds, you may throw an `out_of_range` exception (a standard library class, visit `https://en.cppreference.com/w/cpp/error/out_of_range` for more details). You can also consider using `CV_ASSERT` to check the range, which will trigger a `cv::error` exception on failure.

- **Data types, channels, conversion, and rounding errors**: One of the most vexing problems in OpenCV's `cv::Mat` data structure is that it doesn't carry data type information on its variable type. A `cv::Mat` can hold any type of data (`float`, `uchar`, `int`, `short`, and so on) in any size, and a receiving function cannot know what data is inside the array without inspection or convention. The problem is also compounded by the number of channels, as an array can hold any number of them arbitrarily (for example, a `cv::Mat` can hold `CV_8UC1` or `CV_8UC3`). Failing to have a known data type can lead to runtime exceptions from OpenCV functions that don't expect such data, and therefore to potential crashing of the entire application. Problems with handling multiple data types on the same input `cv::Mat` may lead to other issues of conversion. For example, if we know an incoming array holds `CV_32F` (by checking `input.type() == CV_32F`), we may `input.convertTo(out, CV_8U)` to "normalize" it to a `uchar` character; however, if the `float` data is in the [0, 1] range, the output conversion will have all 0s and 1s in a [0, 255] image, which may be a problem.

- **Solution**: Prefer `cv::Mat_<>` types (for example, `cv::Mat_<float>`) over `cv::Mat` to also carry the data type, establish very clear conventions on variable naming (for example `cv::Mat image_8uc1`), test to make sure the types you expect are the types you get, or create a "normalization" scheme to turn any unexpected input type to the type you would like into work with in your function. Using `try .. catch` blocks is also a good practice when data type uncertainty is feared.

- **Colorspace-originating problems: RGB versus perceptual (HSV, L*a*b*) versus technical (YUV)**: Colorspaces are a way to encode color information in numeric values in a pixel array (image). However, there are a number of problems with this encoding. The foremost problem is that any colorspace eventually becomes a series of numbers stored in the array, and OpenCV does not keep track of colorspace information in `cv::Mat` (for example, an array may hold 3-byte RGB or 3-byte HSV, and the variable user cannot tell the difference). This is not a good thing, because we tend to think we can do any kind of numeric manipulation on numeric data and it will make sense. However, in some colorspaces, certain manipulations need to be cognizant of the colorspace. For example, in the very useful **HSV (Hue, Saturation, Value)** colorspace, one must remember the **H (Hue)** is in fact a measure of *degrees* [0,360] that usually is compressed to [0,180] to fit in a `uchar` character. There is, therefore, no sense in putting a value of 200 in the H channel, as it violates the colorspace definition and leads to unexpected problems. Same goes for linear operations. If for example, we wish to dim an image by 50%, in RGB we simply divide all channels by two; however, in HSV (or L*a*b*, Luv, and so on) one must only perform the division on the **V (Value)** or **L (Luminance)** channels.

  The problem becomes much worse when working with non-byte images, such as YUV420 or RGB555 (16-bit colorspaces). These images store pixel values on the *bit* level, not the byte level, compounding data for more than one pixel or one channel in the same byte. For example, an RGB555 pixel is stored in two bytes (16 bits): one bit unused, then five bits for red, five bits for green, and five bits for blue. All kinds of numeric operations (for example, arithmetics) in that case fail, and may cause irreparable corruption to the data.

- **Solution**: Always know the colorspace of the data you process. When reading images from files using cv::imread, you may assume they are read in **BGR** order (standard OpenCV pixel data storage). When no colorspace information is available, you may rely on heuristics or test the input. In general, you should be wary of images with only two channels, as they are more than likely a bit-packed colorspace. Images with four channels are usually **ARGB** or **RGBA**, adding an **alpha channel**, and again introduce some uncertainty. Testing for perceptual colorspaces can be done visually, by displaying the channels to the screen. The worst of the bit-packing problem comes from working with image files, memory blocks from external libraries, or sources. Within OpenCV, most of the work is done on single-channel grayscale or BGR data, but when it comes to saving to the file, or preparing an image memory block for use in a different library, then it is important to keep track of colorspace conversions. Remember cv::imwrite expects *BGR* data, and not any other format.

- **Accuracy versus speed versus resources (CPU, memory) trade-offs and optimization**: Most of the problems in computer vision have trade-offs between their computation and resource efficiency. Some algorithms are fast because they cache in memory crucial data with a fast lookup efficiency; others may be fast because of a rough approximation they make on the input or output that reduces accuracy. In most cases, one fetching trait comes at the expense of another. Not paying attention to these trade-offs, or paying too much attention to them, can become a problem. A common pitfall for engineers is around matters of **optimization**. There is under-or **over-optimization**, **premature optimization**, unnecessary optimization, and more. When looking to optimize an algorithm, there's a tendency to treat all optimizations as equals, when in fact there is usually just one culprit (code line or method) causing most of the inefficiency. Dealing with algorithmic tradeoff or optimization is mostly a problem of research and development *time*, rather than *result*. Engineers may spend too much or not enough time in optimization, or optimize at the wrong time.

- **Solution**: Know the algorithms before or while employing them. If you choose an algorithm, make sure you have an understanding of its the complexity (runtime and resource) by testing it, or at least by looking at the OpenCV documentation pages. For example, when matching image features, one should know the brute-force matcher `BFMatcher` is often a few orders of magnitude slower than the approximate FLANN-based matcher `FlannBasedMatcher`, especially if preloading and caching the features is possible.

Summary

OpenCV is becoming a mature computer vision library, more than 15 years in the making. During that time, it saw many revolutions happen, both in the computer vision world and in the OpenCV community.

In this chapter, we reviewed OpenCV's past through a practical lens of understanding how to work with it better. We focused on one particular good practice, inspecting the historical OpenCV code to find the origins of an algorithm, in order to make better choices. To cope with the abundance of functionality and features, we also proposed solutions to some common pitfalls in developing computer vision applications with OpenCV.

Further reading

Refer to the following links for more information:

- **OpenCV Change Logs**: https://github.com/opencv/opencv/wiki/ChangeLog
- **OpenCV Meeting notes**: https://github.com/opencv/opencv/wiki/Meeting_notes
- **OpenCV Releases**: https://github.com/opencv/opencv/releases
- **OpenCV Attic Releases**: https://github.com/opencv/opencv_attic/releases
- **Interview with Gary Bradsky, 2011**: https://www.youtube.com/watch?v=bbnftjY-_lE

Other Books You May Enjoy

If you enjoyed this book, you may be interested in these other books by Packt:

Computer Vision with OpenCV 3 and Qt5
Amin Ahmadi Tazehkandi

ISBN: 9781788472395

- Get an introduction to Qt IDE and SDK
- Be introduced to OpenCV and see how to communicate between OpenCV and Qt
- Understand how to create UI using Qt Widgets
- Know to develop cross-platform applications using OpenCV 3 and Qt 5
- Explore the multithreaded application development features of Qt5
- Improve OpenCV 3 application development using Qt5
- Build, test, and deploy Qt and OpenCV apps, either dynamically or statically
- See Computer Vision technologies such as filtering and transformation of images, detecting and matching objects, template matching, object tracking, video and motion analysis, and much more
- Be introduced to QML and Qt Quick for iOS and Android application development

OpenCV 3.x with Python By Example - Second Edition
Gabriel Garrido

ISBN: 9781788396905

- Detect shapes and edges from images and videos
- How to apply filters on images and videos
- Use different techniques to manipulate and improve images
- Extract and manipulate particular parts of images and videos
- Track objects or colors from videos
- Recognize specific object or faces from images and videos
- How to create Augmented Reality applications
- Apply artificial neural networks and machine learning to improve object recognition

Leave a review - let other readers know what you think

Please share your thoughts on this book with others by leaving a review on the site that you bought it from. If you purchased the book from Amazon, please leave us an honest review on this book's Amazon page. This is vital so that other potential readers can see and use your unbiased opinion to make purchasing decisions, we can understand what our customers think about our products, and our authors can see your feedback on the title that they have worked with Packt to create. It will only take a few minutes of your time but is valuable to other potential customers, our authors, and Packt. Thank you!

Index